DATE DUE

MCSA 70-742 Cert Guide: Identity with Windows Server 2016

Benjamin Finkel

800 East 96th Street
Indianapolis, Indiana 46240 USA

MCSA 70-742 Cert Guide

Copyright © 2017 by Pearson Education, Inc.

ISBN-10: 0-7897-5703-6
ISBN-13: 978-0-7897-5703-6

Library of Congress Control Number: 2017935716

Printed in the United States of America

1   17

Trademark Acknowledgments

All terms mentioned in this book that are known to be trademarks or service marks have been appropriately capitalized. Pearson IT Certification cannot attest to the accuracy of this information. Use of a term in this book should not be regarded as affecting the validity of any trademark or service mark.

Windows is a registered trademark of Microsoft Corporation.

Warning and Disclaimer

This book is designed to provide information about the Microsoft MCSA 70-742 Identity with Windows Server 2016 exam. Every effort has been made to make this book as complete and accurate as possible, but no warranty or fitness is implied. The information provided is on an "as is" basis. The author and the publisher shall have neither liability nor responsibility to any person or entity with respect to any loss or damages arising from the information contained in this book or from the use of the supplemental online content or programs accompanying it.

Special Sales

For information about buying this title in bulk quantities, or for special sales opportunities (which may include electronic versions; custom cover designs; and content particular to your business, training goals, marketing focus, or branding interests), please contact our corporate sales department at corpsales@pearsoned.com or (800) 382-3419.

For government sales inquiries, please contact governmentsales@pearsoned.com.

For questions about sales outside the U.S., please contact intlcs@pearsoned.com.

Editor-in-Chief
Mark Taub

Product Line Manager
Brett Bartow

Acquisitions Editor
Michelle Newcomb

Managing Editor
Sandra Schroeder

Development Editor
Christopher Cleveland

Project Editor
Lori Lyons

Copy Editor
Geneil Breeze

Technical Editor
Chris Crayton

Publishing Coordinator
Vanessa Evans

Cover Designer
Chuti Prasertsith

Composition
Bronkella Publishing

Indexer
Kenneth D. Johnson

Proofreader
Gill Editorial Services

Contents at a Glance

Part VI: Appendices

Elements Available on the Book Website

Table of Contents

About the Author

Benjamin Finkel has had his hands on a keyboard since his father brought home the original Compaq portable when he was just four years old. He began professional consulting in 1997 directly out of high school. Ben spent the next 17 years developing and supporting systems in a wide variety of industries, from health care to finance to medical research, before becoming a full-time trainer with CBT Nuggets. Today he lives near Niagara Falls, New York, with his wife and two children. When he's not busy learning about the next big thing in IT, he enjoys snowboarding, reading, and dissuading his wife from adopting yet another cat.

About the Technical Reviewer

Chris Crayton (MCSE) is an author, technical consultant, and trainer. He has worked as a computer technology and networking instructor, information security director, network administrator, network engineer, and PC specialist. Chris has authored several print and online books on PC repair, CompTIA A+, CompTIA Security+, and Microsoft Windows. He has also served as technical editor and content contributor on numerous technical titles for several leading publishing companies. He holds numerous industry certifications, has been recognized with many professional teaching awards, and has served as a state-level SkillsUSA competition judge.

Dedication

This book is dedicated to my parents, Sidney and Anna Finkel. They're the reason I found a passion in IT in the first place and throughout my entire life have always supported, encouraged, and believed in me. Thanks guys!

Acknowledgments

I want to thank the small army of individuals at Pearson who helped to make this book possible, especially Michelle Newcomb for her introduction to and guidance through the process, Chris Cleveland for his patience with me and thoroughness in review, and Chris Crayton for his invaluable and detailed feedback. Thank you as well to all the additional people at Pearson whose hard work is reflected in these pages. This book is a collaborative effort and only exists by virtue of all their input. I would also like to thank Anthony Sequeira for getting me into this mess in the first place.

We Want to Hear from You!

As the reader of this book, *you* are our most important critic and commentator. We value your opinion and want to know what we're doing right, what we could do better, what areas you'd like to see us publish in, and any other words of wisdom you're willing to pass our way.

We welcome your comments. You can email or write to let us know what you did or didn't like about this book—as well as what we can do to make our books better.

Please note that we cannot help you with technical problems related to the topic of this book.

When you write, please be sure to include this book's title and author as well as your name and email address. We will carefully review your comments and share them with the author and editors who worked on the book.

Email: feedback@pearsonitcertification.com

Mail: Pearson IT Certification
        ATTN: Reader Feedback
        800 East 96th Street
        Indianapolis, IN 46240 USA

Reader Services

Register your copy of *MCSA 70-742 Cert Guide* at www.pearsonitcertification.com for convenient access to downloads, updates, and corrections as they become available. To start the registration process, go to www.pearsonitcertification.com/register and log in or create an account*. Enter the product ISBN 9780789757036 and click Submit. When the process is complete, you will find any available bonus content under Registered Products.

*Be sure to check the box that you would like to hear from us to receive exclusive discounts on future editions of this product.

Introduction

MCSA 70-742 Cert Guide: Identity with Windows Server 2016 is designed to prepare you to implement and administer the identity management tools contained within Windows Server 2016. It is structured around the objectives and topics published by Microsoft for exam 70-742. With this book you get a direct and hands-on approach to identity management with technologies such as Active Directory, Group Policy, and Federation Services. Not only will this book help to prepare you for the certification exam, it will ensure you have a fundamental understanding of the way in which you can leverage these powerful tools regardless of the size or complexity of your organization.

With the release of Windows Server 2016, Microsoft has once again restructured the layout of the certification exams needed to obtain your MCSA on Windows Server. In previous iterations, each exam focused on a wide array of products and features across the Windows Server platform. With this release, the exams have been retooled to each focus on a single area of the technology. Exam 70-742 is centered on the Active Directory product suite and its ancillary services. It is the third of three exams required to complete your MCSA certification. The exam relies heavily on use-case scenarios and real-world situations. These questions test your knowledge of the proper way to deploy and configure Active Directory when faced with challenges that are common when operating Windows Server in the real world.

This book covers all the topics listed in Microsoft's exam objectives, and each chapter includes key topics and preparation tasks to assist you in mastering this information. Reviewing tables and practicing test questions will help you practice your knowledge on all subject areas.

About the 70-742 Identity with Windows Server 2016 Exam

The 70-742 Identity with Windows Server 2016 exam is the third of three exams required to complete your MCSA certification. It has been designed for individuals who already have experience administering Active Directory in an enterprise environment and want to transition their responsibilities to the next career level. The 70-742 exam tests candidates' understanding of the role Active Directory and its ancillary services, with a particular focus on best-practice solutions to real-world challenges. It assumes a high degree of familiarity with the material covered in earlier exams, including Windows Server administration and network design and implementation.

The 70-742 Identity with Windows Server 2016 exam is a computer-based test that has 40 to 60 questions and a 120 minute time limit. All exam information is managed by Microsoft and always subject to change, so candidates should monitor the Microsoft certificate site for any exam updates at https://www.microsoft.com/en-us/learning/exam-70-742.aspx.

You can take the exam at Pearson VUE testing centers. You can register with VUE at www.vue.com/microsoft.

70-742 Exam Topics

Table I-1 lists the topics of the 70-742 exam and indicates the chapter in the book where they are covered.

Table I-1   70-742 Exam Topics

Exam Topic	Chapter
Install and configure Active Directory Domain Services (AD DS)	
Install and configure domain controllers	
Install a new forest	Chapter 2
Add or remove a domain controller from a domain	Chapter 2
Upgrade a domain controller	Chapter 2
Install AD DS on a Server Core installation	Chapter 2
Install a domain controller from Install from Media (IFM)	Chapter 2
Resolve DNS SRV record registration issues	Chapter 2
Configure a global catalog server	Chapter 2
Transfer and seize operations master roles	Chapter 2
Install and configure a read-only domain controller (RDOC)	Chapter 2
Configure domain controller cloning	Chapter 2
Create and manage Active Directory users and computers	
Automate the creation of Active Directory accounts	Chapter 3
Create, copy, configure, and delete users and computers	Chapter 3
Configure templates	Chapter 3
Perform bulk Active Directory operations	Chapter 3
Configure user rights	Chapter 3
Implement offline domain join	Chapter 3

Exam Topic	Chapter
Manage inactive and disabled accounts	Chapter 3
Automate unlocking of disabled accounts using Windows PowerShell	Chapter 3
Automate password resets using Windows PowerShell	Chapter 3
Create and manage Active Directory groups and organizational units (OUs)	
Configure group nesting	Chapter 4
Convert groups, including security, distribution, universal, domain local, and domain global	Chapter 4
Manage group membership using Group Policy	Chapter 4
Enumerate group membership	Chapter 4
Automate group membership management using Windows PowerShell	Chapter 4
Delegate the creation and management of Active Directory groups and OUs	Chapter 4
Manage default Active Directory containers	Chapter 4
Create, copy, configure, and delete groups and OUs	Chapter 4
Manage and maintain AD DS	
Configure service authentication and account policies	
Create and configure Service Accounts	Chapter 5
Create and configure Group Managed Service Accounts (gMSAs)	Chapter 5
Configure Kerberos Constrained Delegation (KCD)	Chapter 5
Manage Service Principal Names (SPNs)	Chapter 5
Configure virtual accounts	Chapter 5
Configure domain and local user password policy settings	Chapter 5
Configure and apply Password Settings Objects (PSOs)	Chapter 5
Delegate password settings management	Chapter 5
Configure account lockout policy settings	Chapter 5
Configure Kerberos policy settings within Group Policy	Chapter 5
Maintain Active Directory	
Back up Active Directory and SYSVOL	Chapter 6
Manage Active Directory offline	Chapter 6
Perform offline defragmentation of an Active Directory database	Chapter 6
Clean up metadata	Chapter 6
Configure Active Directory snapshots	Chapter 6

Exam Topic	Chapter
Perform object- and container-level recovery	Chapter 6
Perform Active Directory restore	Chapter 6
Configure and restore objects by using the Active Directory Recycle Bin	Chapter 6
Configure replication to Read-Only Domain Controllers (RODCs)	Chapter 6
Configure Password Replication Policy (PRP) for RODC	Chapter 6
Monitor and manage replication	Chapter 6
Upgrade SYSVOL replication to Distributed File System Replication (DFSR)	Chapter 6
Configure Active Directory in a complex enterprise environment	
Configure a multi-domain and multi-forest Active Directory infrastructure	Chapter 7
Deploy Windows Server 2016 domain controllers within a pre-existing Active Directory environment	Chapter 7
Upgrade existing domains and forests	Chapter 7
Configure domain and forest functional levels	Chapter 7
Configure multiple user principal name (UPN) suffixes	Chapter 7
Configure external, forest, shortcut, and realm trusts	Chapter 7
Configure trust authentication	Chapter 7
Configure SID filtering	Chapter 7
Configure name suffix routing	Chapter 7
Configure sites and subnets	Chapter 7
Create and configure site links	Chapter 7
Manage site coverage	Chapter 7
Manage registration of SRV records	Chapter 7
Move domain controllers between sites	Chapter 7
Create and manage Group Policy	
Create and manage Group Policy Objects (GPOs)	
Configure a central store	Chapter 8
Manage starter GPOs	Chapter 8
Configure GPO links	Chapter 8
Configure multiple local Group Policies	Chapter 8
Back up, import, copy, and restore GPOs	Chapter 8
Create and configure a migration table	Chapter 8

Exam Topic	Chapter
Reset default GPOs	Chapter 8
Delegate Group Policy management	Chapter 8
Detect health issues using the Group Policy Infrastructure Status dashboard	Chapter 8
Configure Group Policy processing	
Configure processing order and precedence	Chapter 9
Configure blocking of inheritance	Chapter 9
Configure enforced policies	Chapter 9
Configure security filtering and Windows Management Instrumentation (WMI) filtering	Chapter 9
Configure loopback processing	Chapter 9
Configure and manage slow-link processing and Group Policy caching	Chapter 9
Configure client-side extension (CSE) behaviour	Chapter 9
Force a Group Policy update	Chapter 9
Configure Group Policy settings	
Configure software installation	Chapter 10
Configure folder redirection	Chapter 10
Configure scripts	Chapter 10
Configure administrative templates	Chapter 10
Import security templates	Chapter 10
Import a custom administrative template file	Chapter 10
Configure property filters for administrative templates	Chapter 10
Configure Group Policy preferences	
Configure printer preferences	Chapter 11
Define network drive mappings	Chapter 11
Configure power options	Chapter 11
Configure custom registry settings	Chapter 11
Configure Control Panel settings	Chapter 11
Configure Internet Explorer settings	Chapter 11
Configure file and folder deployment	Chapter 11
Configure shortcut deployment	Chapter 11
Configure item-level targeting	Chapter 11

Exam Topic	Chapter
Implement Active Directory Certificate Services (AD CS)	
Install and configure AD CS	
Install Active Directory Integrated Enterprise Certificate Authority (CA)	Chapter 12
Install offline root and subordinate CAs	Chapter 12
Install standalone CAs	Chapter 12
Configure Certificate Revocation List (CRL) distribution points	Chapter 12
Install and configure Online Responder	Chapter 12
Implement administrative role separation	Chapter 12
Configure CA backup and recovery	Chapter 12
Manage certificates	
Manage certificate templates	Chapter 13
Implement and manage certificate deployment, validation, and revocation	Chapter 13
Manage certificate renewal	Chapter 13
Manage certificate enrollment and renewal for computers and users using Group Policies	Chapter 13
Configure and manage key archival and recovery	Chapter 13
Implement identity federation and access solutions	
Install and configure Active Directory Federation Services (AD FS)	
Upgrade and migrate previous AD FS workloads to Windows Server 2016	Chapter 14
Implement claims-based authentication, including Relying Party Trusts	Chapter 14
Configure authentication policies	Chapter 14
Configure multi-factor authentication	Chapter 14
Implement and configure device registration	Chapter 14
Integrate AD FS with Microsoft Passport	Chapter 14
Configure for use with Microsoft Azure and Office 365	Chapter 14
Configure AD FS to enable authentication of users stored in LDAP directories	Chapter 14
Implement Web Application Proxy (WAP)	
Install and configure WAP	Chapter 15
Implement WAP in pass-through mode	Chapter 15
Implement WAP as AD FS proxy	Chapter 15
Integrate WAP with AD FS	Chapter 15

Exam Topic	Chapter
Configure AD FS requirements	Chapter 15
Publish web apps via WAP	Chapter 15
Publish Remote Desktop Gateway applications	Chapter 15
Configure HTTP to HTTPS redirects	Chapter 15
Configure internal and external Fully Qualified Domain Names (FQDNs)	Chapter 15
Install and configure Active Directory Rights Management Services (AD RMS)	
Install a licensor certificate AD RMS server	Chapter 16
Manage AD RMS Service Connection Point (SCP)	Chapter 16
Manage AD RMS templates	Chapter 16
Configure Exclusion Policies	Chapter 16
Back up and restore AD RMS	Chapter 16

About the MCSA 70-742 Cert Guide

This book maps to the topic areas of the 70-742 exam and uses a number of features to help you understand the topics and prepare for the exam.

Objectives and Methods

This book uses several key methodologies to help you discover the exam topics on which you need more review, to help you fully understand and remember those details, and to help you prove to yourself that you have retained your knowledge of those topics. This book does not try to help you pass the exams only by memorization but by truly learning and understanding the topics. This book is designed to help you pass the 70-742 exam by using the following methods:

- Helping you discover which exam topics you have not mastered

- Providing explanations and information to fill in your knowledge gaps

- Supplying exercises that enhance your ability to recall and deduce the answers to test questions

- Providing practice exercises on the topics and the testing process via test questions on the companion website

Book Features

To help you customize your study time using this book, the core chapters have several features that help you make the best use of your time:

- **"Do I Know This Already?" quiz**: Each chapter begins with a quiz that helps you determine how much time you need to spend studying that chapter.

- **Foundation Topics**: These are the core sections of each chapter. They explain the concepts for the topics in that chapter.

- **Exam Preparation Tasks**: After the "Foundation Topics" section of each chapter, the "Exam Preparation Tasks" section lists a series of study activities that you should do at the end of the chapter. Each chapter includes the activities that make the most sense for studying the topics in that chapter:

  - **Review All the Key Topics**: The Key Topics icon appears next to the most important items in the "Foundation Topics" section of the chapter. The "Review All Key Topics" section lists the key topics from the chapter, along with their page numbers. Although the contents of the entire chapter could be on the exam, you should definitely know the information listed in each key topic, so you should review these.

  - **Complete the Tables and Lists from Memory**: To help you memorize some lists of facts, many of the more important lists and tables from the chapter are included in a document on the companion website. This document lists only partial information, allowing you to complete the table or list.

  - **Define Key Terms**: Although the exam may be unlikely to ask a question such as "Define this term," the Microsoft MCSA exams do require that you learn and know a lot of Windows Server administration terminology. This section lists the most important terms from the chapter, asking you to write a short definition and compare your answer to the glossary at the end of the book.

  - **End-of-Chapter Review Questions**: Confirm that you understand the content that you just covered by answering review questions.

- **Web-based practice exam**: The companion website includes the Pearson Test Prep practice test software that allows you to take practice exam questions. Use these to prepare with a sample exam and to pinpoint topics where you need more study.

How This Book Is Organized

This book contains 16 core chapters—Chapters 1 through 16. Chapter 17 includes some preparation tips and suggestions for how to approach the exam. Each core chapter covers a subset of the topics on the 70-742 exam. The core chapters are organized into parts. They cover the following topics:

Part I: Installing and Configuring Active Directory Domain Services (AD DS)

- **Chapter 1, "Introducing Active Directory 2016,"** covers the fundamentals of the Microsoft Active Directory product suite including Active Directory Domain Services, Group Policy, Active Directory Certificate Services, and Active Directory Federation Services.

- **Chapter 2, "Installing and Configuring Domain Controllers,"** covers the fundamentals of promoting member servers on to the role of domain controller. This includes installing primary domain controllers, read-only domain controllers, and domain controllers on the Windows Server Core environment. This chapter also covers advanced topics such as Install from Media (IFM) and transferring flexible single master operator (FSMO) roles.

- **Chapter 3, "Creating and Managing Active Directory Users and Computers,"** covers the operations for creating and maintaining user and computer objects in Active Directory. This includes configuring template accounts, performing bulk operations, and working with disabled accounts and password resets.

- **Chapter 4, "Creating and Managing Active Directory Groups and Organizational Units,"** covers the operations and purpose behind security and distribution groups and organizational units. It covers how to add and remove users from groups and OUs, automate those tasks with Windows PowerShell, and delegate permission to manage groups and OUs to other users on the domain.

Part II: Managing and Maintaining Active Directory Domain Services

- **Chapter 5, "Configuring Service Authentication and Account Policies,"** covers the operations for creating and managing service accounts and Group Managed Service Accounts (gMSAs) as well as Kerberos Constrained Delegation (KCD). It also covers how to configure and apply password settings to various entities in the domain and manage account lockout policies.

- **Chapter 6, "Maintaining Active Directory,"** covers directory maintenance including proper backup and restore procedures for disaster recovery and business continuity. It also covers newer features such as the Active Directory Recycle Bin, which allows recovery in some instances without a full restore.

Finally, this chapter makes sure you can troubleshoot and monitor automated directory tasks such as database and SYSVOL replication.

- **Chapter 7, "Configuring Active Directory in a Complex Enterprise Environment,"** covers the special considerations required when deploying Active Directory into an existing infrastructure with varying levels and versions of Windows Server. It also discusses basic tasks for dealing with multi-domain and multi-forest deployments such as User Principal Name (UPN) suffixes and cross forest trusts.

Part III: Creating and Managing Group Policy

- **Chapter 8, "Creating and Managing Group Policy Objects (GPOs),"** covers the basic tasks for working with Group Policy such as creating and linking GPOs to domains and OUs. It also covers how to manage those GPOs, create copies, and work with local Group Policies.

- **Chapter 9, "Configuring Group Policy Processing,"** covers the management of Group Policy processing and ensuring appropriate GPOs apply when desired. This includes blocking inheritance, enforcing policies, filtering policies, and forcing Group Policy updates.

- **Chapter 10, "Configuring Group Policy Settings,"** covers various Group Policy features such as forcing software installing, using logon and logoff scripts, and working with administrative templates.

- **Chapter 11, "Configuring Group Policy Preferences,"** covers the policy options included in Group Policy Objects for client-side preferences in both Windows and Control Panel. This includes deploying printers, defining network drive mappings, configuring Internet Explorer settings, and redirecting the user profile folder.

Part IV: Implementing Active Directory Certificate Services (AD CS)

- **Chapter 12, "Installing and Configuring Active Directory Certificate Services,"** covers the basics of how to properly install and configure the Active Directory Certificate Services role service. This chapter covers when to use online versus offline certificate authorities (CAs) and how to set up a standalone CA for security purposes. It also covers how to properly back up and recover AD CS for disaster recovery and business continuity.

- **Chapter 13, "Managing Certificates,"** covers how to use AD CS to create and issue certificates by using certificate templates in the directory. This includes manual certificate enrollment as well as autoenrollment using Group Policy.

Part V: Implementing Identity Federation and Access Solutions

- **Chapter 14, "Installing and Configuring Active Directory Federation Services,"** covers how to install and properly configure Active Directory Federation Services for use as a claims-based authentication provider. This chapter provides details on configuring a relying party trust, using multi-factor authentication, and authenticating against third-party LDAP directories.

- **Chapter 15, "Implementing Web Application Proxy,"** covers the Microsoft provided reverse proxy server Web Application Proxy (WAP). It includes installation and setup instructions and details on how to properly configure WAP to authenticate incoming requests using an AD FS server.

- **Chapter 16, "Installing and Configuring Active Directory Rights Management Services,"** covers the basic installation and setup for an Active Directory Rights Management Services (AD RMS) server. This includes managing service connection points (SCP), AD RMS templates, exclusion policies, and backing up and restoring AD RMS.

- **Chapter 17, "Final Preparation,"** identifies tools for final exam preparation and helps you develop an effective study plan. It contains tips on how to best use the web-based material to study.

Part VI: Appendices

- **Appendix A, "Answers to "Do I Know This Already?" Quizzes and Q&A Questions,"** includes the answers to all the questions from Chapters 1 through 16.

- **Glossary of Key Terms**

Elements Available on the Book Website

- **Appendix B, "Memory Tables,"** contains the key tables and lists from each chapter, with some of the contents removed. You can print this appendix and, as a memory exercise, complete the tables and lists. The goal is to help you memorize facts that can be useful on the exams. This appendix is available in PDF format at the book website; it is not in the printed book.

- **Appendix C, "Memory Tables Answer Key,"** contains the answer key for the memory tables in Appendix B. This appendix is available in PDF format at the book website; it is not in the printed book.

- **Appendix D, "Study Planner,"** is a spreadsheet available from the book website. It has major study milestones, where you can track your progress through your study.

Companion Website

Register this book to get access to the Pearson Test Prep practice test software and other study materials plus additional bonus content. Check this site regularly for new and updated postings written by the author that provide further insight into the more troublesome topics on the exam. Be sure to check the box that you would like to hear from us to receive updates and exclusive discounts on future editions of this product or related products.

To access this companion website, follow these steps:

1. Go to www.pearsonITcertification.com/register and log in or create a new account.

2. Enter the ISBN: **9780789757036**.

3. Answer the challenge question as proof of purchase.

4. Click on the **Access Bonus Content** link in the Registered Products section of your account page to be taken to the page where your downloadable content is available.

Please note that many of our companion content files can be very large, especially image and video files.

If you are unable to locate the files for this title by following the preceding steps, please visit www.pearsonITcertification.com/contact and select the **Site Problems/ Comments** option. Our customer service representatives will assist you.

Pearson Test Prep Practice Test Software

As noted previously, this book comes complete with the Pearson Test Prep practice test software containing two full exams. These practice tests are available to you either online or as an offline Windows application. To access the practice exams developed with this book, please see the instructions on the card inserted in the sleeve in the back of the book. This card includes a unique access code that enables you to activate your exams in the Pearson Test Prep software.

Accessing the Pearson Test Prep Software Online

The online version of this software can be used on any device with a browser and connectivity to the Internet including desktop machines, tablets, and smartphones. To start using your practice exams online, simply follow these steps:

1. Go to http://www.PearsonTestPrep.com.

2. Select **Pearson IT Certification** as your product group.

3. Enter your email/password for your account. If you don't have an account on PearsonITCertification.com or CiscoPress.com, you need to establish one by going to PearsonITCertification.com/join.

4. In the **My Products** tab, click the **Activate New Product** button.

5. Enter the access code printed on the insert card in the back of your book to activate your product.

6. The product is now listed in your My Products page. Click the **Exams** button to launch the exam settings screen and start your exam.

Accessing the Pearson Test Prep Software Offline

If you want to study offline, you can download and install the Windows version of the Pearson Test Prep software. There is a download link for this software on the book's companion website, or you can just enter this link in your browser: www.pearsonitcertification.com/content/downloads/pcpt/engine.zip.

To access the book's companion website and the software, simply follow these steps:

1. Register your book by going to PearsonITCertification.com/register and entering the ISBN: **9780789757036**.

2. Respond to the challenge questions.

3. Go to your account page and select the **Registered Products** tab.

4. Click on the **Access Bonus Content** link under the product listing.

5. Click the **Install Pearson Test Prep Desktop Version** link under the Practice Exams section of the page to download the software.

6. When the software finishes downloading, unzip all the files on your computer.

7. Double-click the application file to start the installation and follow the on-screen instructions to complete the registration.

8. Once the installation is complete, launch the application and click the **Activate Exam** button on the My Products tab.

9. Click the **Activate a Product** button in the Activate Product Wizard.

10. Enter the unique access code found on the card in the sleeve in the back of your book and click the **Activate** button.

11. Click **Next** and then click the **Finish** button to download the exam data to your application.

12. You can now start using the practice exams by selecting the product and clicking the **Open Exam** button to open the exam settings screen.

Note that the offline and online versions sync together, so saved exams and grade results recorded on one version are available to you on the other as well.

Customizing Your Exams

Once you are in the exam settings screen, you can choose to take exams in one of three modes:

- Study Mode
- Practice Exam Mode
- Flash Card Mode

Study Mode allows you to fully customize your exams and review answers as you are taking the exam. This is typically the mode you would use first to assess your knowledge and identify information gaps. Practice Exam Mode locks certain customization options, as it is presenting a realistic exam experience. Use this mode when you are preparing to test your exam readiness. Flash Card Mode strips out the answers and presents you with only the question stem. This mode is great for late stage preparation when you really want to challenge yourself to provide answers without the benefit of seeing multiple choice options. This mode does not provide the detailed score reports that the other two modes do, so it should not be used if you are trying to identify knowledge gaps.

In addition to these three modes, you can select the source of your questions. You can choose to take exams that cover all the chapters, or you can narrow your selection to just a single chapter or the chapters that make up specific parts in the book. All chapters are selected by default. If you want to narrow your focus to individual chapters, simply deselect all the chapters and then select only those on which you want to focus in the Objectives area.

You can also select the exam banks on which to focus. Each exam bank comes complete with a full exam of questions that cover topics in every chapter. The two exams printed in the book are available to you as well as two additional exams of unique questions. You can have the test engine serve up exams from all four banks or just from one individual bank by selecting the desired banks in the exam bank area.

You can make several other customizations to your exam from the exam settings screen, such as the time of the exam, the number of questions served up, whether to randomize questions and answers, whether to show the number of correct answers for multiple answer questions, or whether to serve up only specific types of questions. You can also create custom test banks by selecting only questions that you have marked or questions on which you have added notes.

Updating Your Exams

If you are using the online version of the Pearson Test Prep software, you should always have access to the latest version of the software as well as the exam data. If you are using the Windows desktop version, every time you launch the software, it checks to see whether there are any updates to your exam data and automatically downloads any changes that were made since the last time you used the software. This requires that you be connected to the Internet at the time you launch the software.

Sometimes, due to many factors, the exam data may not fully download when you activate your exam. If you find that figures or exhibits are missing, you may need to manually update your exams.

To update a particular exam you have already activated and downloaded, simply select the **Tools** tab and select the **Update Products** button. Again, this is only an issue with the desktop Windows application.

If you want to check for updates to the Pearson Test Prep exam engine software, Windows desktop version, simply select the **Tools** tab and select the **Update Application** button. This ensures you are running the latest version of the software engine.

This chapter covers the following topics:

- **Identity and Active Directory 2016**: This section describes how Microsoft has rolled its identity products together under the umbrella of Active Directory.

- **Active Directory Domain Services (AD DS)**: This section describes the major components that make up AD DS, the largest and most frequently used service in Active Directory.

- **Active Directory Federation Services (AD FS)**: This section describes how Microsoft's federated identity service AD FS allows authentication outside the boundaries of the network.

- **Active Directory Certificate Services (AD CS)**: This section explains the structure of AD CS, the public key infrastructure service built into Microsoft Active Directory.

- **Active Directory Rights Management Services (AD RMS)**: This section describes how AD RMS is used to protect sensitive information and documents as they are transmitted both in and out of the organization.

CHAPTER 1

Introducing Active Directory 2016

Every year information security becomes a more important part of an IT professional's skill-set. The computers that our businesses, schools, charities, and even our homes now rely upon are gathering more data, expected to perform more complex tasks, and increasingly subject to the threat of data theft or loss, whether malicious or accidental. At the same time, a dynamic and global workforce also expects to have secure access to these systems and data from a wide range of devices and locations. We need new and inventive ways to authenticate with and authorize access to computer systems that provide flexibility and range while minimizing security risks. With the introduction of Windows Server 2016, Microsoft has changed its certification strategy to reflect this growing need and introduced exam 70-742: Identity with Windows Server 2016.

With exam 70-742 Microsoft has built a certification that specifically addresses installing and configuring the security services collected under the Active Directory umbrella. Active Directory has grown as a product to include many new and modern security services that deal with the challenges IT organizations face. These services include Active Directory Domain Services for authenticating and authorizing users on the network, Federation Services for extending that authentication outside the boundaries of the network, Certificate Services for creating and managing public key infrastructure, and Rights Management Services to help protect and control information even as it's transmitted around and outside the company.

Understanding the role each of these services plays, and how each is structured, is an important first step to understanding how to deploy and manage a secure Windows Server environment.

"Do I Know This Already?" Quiz

The "Do I Know This Already?" quiz allows you to assess whether you should read this entire chapter thoroughly or jump to the "Exam Preparation Tasks" section. If you are in doubt about your answers to these questions or your own assessment of your knowledge of the topics, read the entire chapter. Table 1-1 lists the major headings in this chapter and their corresponding "Do I Know

This Already?" quiz questions. You can find the answers in Appendix A, "Answers to the 'Do I Know This Already?' Quizzes."

Table 1-1   "Do I Know This Already?" Section-to-Question Mapping

Foundation Topics Section	Questions
Identity and Active Directory 2016	1
Active Directory Domain Services (AD DS)	2-5
Active Directory Federation Services (AD FS)	6-7
Active Directory Certificate Services (AD CS)	8
Active Directory Rights Management Services (AD RMS)	9-10

CAUTION   The goal of self-assessment is to gauge your mastery of the topics in this chapter. If you do not know the answer to a question or are only partially sure of the answer, you should mark that question as wrong for purposes of the self-assessment. Giving yourself credit for an answer you correctly guess skews your self-assessment results and might provide you with a false sense of security.

1. Which Active Directory service is used to store users, computers, and other objects on the network?

    a. Active Directory Federation Services

    b. Group Policy Objects

    c. Active Directory Rights Management Services

    d. Active Directory Domain Services

2. Which of the following are components of the AD DS directory? (Choose all that apply.)

    a. Object

    b. Organizational unit

    c. Tree

    d. Domain

3. Installing AD DS causes the server to be promoted to which of the following?

   a. Domain controller

   b. Global catalog

   c. FSMO server

   d. Member server

4. The first domain controller in a forest serves as which of the following?

   a. Operations master

   b. Forest root

   c. Master domain controller

   d. Forest master

5. Which of the following settings cannot be configured with Group Policy?

   a. Registry settings

   b. Security settings

   c. Domain settings

   d. Group Policy preferences

6. AD FS makes assertions about user identities using which of the following techniques?

   a. Group Policy Objects

   b. Active Directory Certificate Services

   c. Identity provider

   d. Claims token

7. Which of the following two systems exchange identity information in a federated identity deployment?

   a. Active Directory and Windows Server

   b. AD FS and AD RMS

   c. Relying party and identity provider

   d. Federator and consumer

8. Which of the following describes the AD CS role as a certificate provider and validator?

    a. Certificate authority

    b. Domain controller

    c. Identity provider

    d. Public key certificate

9. Which of the following does AD RMS attach to a document to describe the permissions and restrictions for the document?

    a. Client licensor certificate (CLC)

    b. Publishing license (PL)

    c. RD RMS client

    d. Group Policy Object

10. Which of the following does AD RMS attach to a document to encrypt the data?

    a. Client licensor certificate (CLC)

    b. Publishing license (PL)

    c. RD RMS client

    d. Group Policy Object

Foundation Topics

Identity and Active Directory 2016

You walk into your office in the morning, sit down at your desk, and sign in to your computer using your username and password. The computer validates that those credentials are correct. You start up Outlook and download your emails from the server. You try to print one email in particular, but you're informed that email cannot be printed due to its containing sensitive information. You open a web browser and browse to your timesheet application. Even though this application is hosted by a third-party organization, the app recognizes you and loads your specific timesheet.

How did the computer know whether your credentials were correct? How did Outlook know which emails were yours? How did the server know that you were allowed to download these emails? How did Outlook know you were not allowed to print that email, and how did the timesheet website know who you were?

The answer to all the above questions is Active Directory. Active Directory is a core component of the Microsoft Windows Server environment. In its simplest deployment, Active Directory is a database (or directory) of all the users, computers, folders, printers, and other objects connected to your network. Software components on the network reference that directory when authenticating and authorizing access to their systems. In the previous example, the email server Microsoft Exchange validates who you are and which emails are associated with your entry in Active Directory before allowing you to download and review those emails. Because of its tightly coupled nature with Windows Server and other Microsoft server products, this validation is often completely transparent and seamless. Users are checked and verified all day long and are never the wiser.

This book covers Microsoft Exam 70-742: Identity with Windows Server 2016. While the title doesn't explicitly reference Active Directory, everything that Windows Server does with respect to identity management, authentication, and authorization is wrapped up in the Active Directory suite of products. Whether it's directly managing users, groups, and security permissions with Active Directory Domain Services, synchronizing to the cloud with Azure Active Directory, or creating public key encryption certificates with Certificate Services, it's all a part of Active Directory. The 70-742 exam could be titled The Active Directory exam because it never loses its focus on that product.

If you're preparing to take this exam, you are most likely familiar with the basic usage of Active Directory, namely, its role as a database for objects and security groups on the network. In early iterations of Active Directory that is all it was, but now that service has a specific title, Active Directory Domain Services, and is only one component of Active Directory as a whole.

Over the past two decades Active Directory has grown to include a number of different services. Each of these services offers features and functionality for specific use in an enterprise, but they all address the challenges of identity management, authentication, and authorization.

Active Directory is made up of the five services outlined in Table 1-2.

Table 1-2 Active Directory Services

Active Directory Service	Description
Active Directory Domain Services (AD DS)	Active Directory Domain Services is a specialized type of database called a directory. This directory stores information about objects on the network including users, computers, servers, printers, and just about any other object you can imagine. AD DS is also the service that allows access to and makes available the information stored in the directory.
Active Directory Federation Services (AD FS)	Active Directory Federation Services allows the configuration and management of Single Sign-On (SSO) access to resources located both within and outside the organization's logical information boundaries. AD FS replaces more traditional trust mechanisms that allow two different organizations to share or expose resources to specific individuals or groups within each other's organization.
Active Directory Certificate Services (AD CS)	Active Directory Certificate Services is a customizable service for issuing and managing public key certificates for software security systems that employ public key technologies. AD CS can be used to create secure VPN tunnels, to provide SSL for HTTP traffic, and even for encrypted file system storage.
Active Directory Rights Management Services (AD RMS)	Active Directory Rights Management Services allows you to protect and control the distribution of information both within your organization and outside it. Trade secrets, classified information, or even regulated data located on common documents such as emails and presentations can be protected against unauthorized access, viewing, printing, or modification with AD RMS.
Active Directory Lightweight Directory Services (AD LDS)	Like its name implies, Active Directory Lightweight Directory Services is a sparser version of AD DS. AD LDS provides much of the same functionality of AD DS but does not require the deployment of domains, controllers, and forests. It's ideal for directory-enabled applications, and in fact you can run multiple instances of AD LDS on a single machine for each application that requires it. This feature is not covered in the Microsoft 70-742 exam, so we will not be discussing it in detail in this book.

Active Directory Domain Services (AD DS)

Active Directory Domain Services (AD DS) is the oldest and probably the most popular service in the Active Directory family. As previously mentioned, it is a data store known as a directory used for looking up information. The closest analogy might be a phone book, where you can look up information such as an address or phone number about a specific person. AD DS is not very different, comprised at the most basic level of *objects*, which are like the individual people found in the phone book analogy.

> **NOTE**   When Active Directory was introduced to Windows in 2000 Server, it was comprised exclusively of the features and functionality that now make up AD DS. AD DS is the most widely used and largest piece of Active Directory. Consequently, when someone refers to "Active Directory" they are usually referring just to AD DS. To avoid confusion in this book we always refer to AD DS explicitly when we're discussing these features and reserve the phrase "Active Directory" for the product suite as a whole.

The most obvious and common use case for AD DS is to provide authentication for users on the network. Authentication is the process by which a system verifies that the user is who he claims to be, for example, by typing in a username and password. When a user sits down and signs in to the computer, that computer verifies the credentials entered against AD DS and receives a token in exchange. As the user tries to perform actions or access resources on the network, the AD DS token indicates what permissions and restrictions the user has.

Perhaps unsurprisingly, this book (and the associated exam) spends more time with AD DS than any of the other products in Active Directory. Between Domain Services and Group Policy Objects (GPO), more than half of the material covered falls under the AD DS heading. A foundational understanding of this technology is crucial for success in working with Active Directory.

To that end we'll spend some time now covering the logical building blocks of the directory managed by AD DS beginning with objects. The entire directory follows a tree structure, where a single-parent many-child relationship exists. This hierarchy is important for understanding AD DS as you see in the following sections.

Object

Objects are the specific items being catalogued in AD DS. Common objects found in a directory are users, computers, printers, folders, and even files. These objects are grouped into containers, usually *organizational units*, which in turn are grouped into higher order containers themselves. An object is made up of a collection of *attributes*, which are key-value pairs of information. An example of an attribute key would be "Given Name," and every object in the directory would have a different value for that attribute. AD DS is dynamic and extensible, which means that not all objects share the same attributes, and as an administrator we can define new attributes or even classes of attributes.

A *class* is a signifier for an object that defines which attributes an object will have. So an object of class "User" would have "Given Name" and "E-mail-Addresses" as attributes, while an object of class "Document" would not. The collective classes and their attribute definitions are known as the Active Directory schema. This schema is applied to the entire forest and can be customized by an administrator. Customizing the schema can cause serious problems and is only recommended for advanced users.

Containers and Organizational Units

The AD DS directory is organized into a tree structure where objects can have multiple children but only one parent. Any object in the directory that has children objects is known as a *container*. Forests, trees, and domains are all specialized types of containers, although not usually referred to as such. More common objects like users and computers can also have child objects and consequently can also be containers, although that's not typically how they're used. Containers are used to provide structure and separation to the objects in a directory. A company may have thousands of user objects in its directory, but it wouldn't be very useful to have them all lumped into one list. Containers can break them up by geographic region, organizational type, or even physical location within a building.

There is a class in the default schema known as a container, but this type of object is almost never used directly. Instead, the majority of the time objects are grouped into organizational units (OUs). OUs are a specific type of container that can have Group Policy Objects applied to them. For this reason, OUs are used almost exclusively in AD DS implementations. Group Policy Objects can be used to apply security and permissions to every object within a container.

For example, a directory could have an OU named "Third Floor" and within that container two child OUs named "Users" and "Printers." This would allow for all the users who sit on the third floor to be grouped together with all the printers that are also on that floor, and access to those printers could be granted to any users who shared the OU with them. Furthermore, the "Third Floor" OU could have "Milwaukee" as its parent OU, and a separate administrator could be assigned to that OU to delegate user management authority.

Domains

At the root of all AD DS installations is the *domain*. While a domain is not the top-most level of the Active Directory structure (there are still trees and forests), it is the structural element required to run AD DS. The domain is the lowest level of namespace in the directory, which means that many attributes must be unique across all objects within a domain. While a domain can and should contain one or more OUs (and those OUs likely have OUs within them), the OUs do not create separate namespaces, only the domain does.

A namespace in AD DS often looks similar to a DNS name. Recommended practice strongly encourages you to name your domains as you would fully qualified DNS names. This ensures compatibility with DNS and eases the configuration of client computers. At a minimum a domain should have two labels. One example might be the domain **certguide.com**. The two labels in this example are **certguide** and **com**, separated by the period. All the objects in this domain would be said to belong to **certguide.com**. If a second domain was created, say **benfinkel.com**, this domain would not share a namespace with the first, and consequently objects in **benfinkel. com** could duplicate attributes already found in **certguide.com**.

When AD DS is installed onto a Windows Server, that server becomes the *domain controller (DC)* where the directory is stored. All objects registered with that domain are stored in the database on the DC, and the DC is responsible for answering all authentication requests, object queries, and other activity performed against the di-rectory. A DC is authoritative for one, and only one, domain. If a second domain is to be created, it requires its own DC.

Domain Trees and Forests

Often an organization needs only a single domain. As the company grows and becomes more complex, however, the need for multiple domains can arise. A com-mon solution is to split the organization along geographic lines and have a different domain for each region the company operates in. When more than one domain is being used in AD DS, this is known as a domain *tree*. Trees are collected under a single parent domain and share a namespace with that parent domain. For example, the domains **west.certguide.com** and **east.certguide.com** would make up a tree along with the parent domain **certguide.com**. Domains organized into a tree in this fashion share a trust relationship that allows objects in one domain to access objects in the other.

West.certguide.com and **east.certguide.com** share what is known as a *contiguous namespace* because they both share the same parent domain. Objects in one of these domains would need to be unique across both, since every object in either domain is also in the top-level **certguide.com** domain as well.

A *forest* is a collection of one or more domain trees that do not share a contiguous namespace. For example, the domains **certguide.com** and **benfinkel.com** would make up a forest. Each domain might have its own child domains and define its own trees. When you first create a new Active Directory installation, the first domain you create is known as the forest root domain. The root domain has special properties (such as containing the configuration information for the entire forest). This means that even in a simple installation with one domain and no child domains, the concepts of forest and trees still exist.

The most important concept to take away from all this is the hierarchical nature of the AD DS directory. Each object, OU, and domain in the directory has one and only one parent, while each parent may have multiple children. As we progress through this book, we look much more closely at each of these concepts and the implications of how to install and configure them.

Group Policy Objects (GPOs)

Group Policy Objects (GPOs) are used to define the security allowances and restraints for users and computers on the network. The policies defined in GPOs are then automatically applied to and enforced on the network by Group Policy. GPOs can be applied to individual computers, users, domains, and of course organizational units. GPOs can configure values for

- Registry settings
- Security settings
- Group policy preferences
- Software installation

These areas cover a wide range of permissions and settings from power management to screen saver settings to scheduled task and script execution. There are thousands of possible setting configurations available for GPOs to control both the behavior of workstations on the network as well as the experience for users.

GPOs make the process of managing environments for a large organization feasible. Not only can administrators create a set of policies, control over the policies can be delegated to authorized administrators for specific domains and organizational units. This allows a central IT service to define high-level policies for the entire organization while more specific policies can be custom tailored by and for different parts of the organization. These policies are then applied automatically even as users join or leave those portions of the company. As long as their AD DS entries are moved appropriately, they'll receive the appropriate policy restrictions.

Active Directory Federation Services (AD FS)

As services have transitioned from corporate-owned data centers to external hosts in "the cloud," the need for extending authentication to third-party partners has grown substantially in the last few years. Active Directory Federation Services (AD FS) allows you to implement *identity federation* to address this need. This means that users can sign in to an application owned by a partner organization using the same credentials they used to sign in to their own local network. AD FS does this in a secure fashion and enables us to use AD DS as the identity provider without unnecessary exposure.

Identity Federation

Identity federation is a process that enables authentication across organizational and platform boundaries. AD DS, which we described previously as providing authentication, is restricted by its organization and network. If an application needs to authenticate you against AD DS, it must be running on a system connected to the physical network where the AD DS server is and have permission to authenticate in that domain. It is much more common today to access applications and websites owned and managed by third-party vendors and other sources running in their own data center outside our network infrastructure.

Accessing third-party applications like this can create management and security problems because we typically would require a separate set of credentials for each application that a user needs to access. Just imagine the collection of usernames and passwords you have for all the websites you log in to, and now imagine an enterprise with thousands of employees each having to maintain their own separate list. With identity federation, that third-party application can "trust" (or rely on) our AD FS server and identify the user based on the claims provided by that server.

For example, imagine that your company uses a third-party web-based application for employees to enter their weekly timesheet. If employees want to access the application and enter their time for the week or review their existing data, they need to authenticate themselves to the application. With AD FS the timesheet application becomes known as a *relying party (RP)* because it trusts and relies upon the company's AD FS server. The AD FS server in turn is known as the *identity provider (IdP)*. The timesheet application asks the AD FS server (over a secure HTTP connection) who you are, and you continue into the application without having to key in an additional username and password.

Importantly, this structure allows the RP to keep control over authorization. Authorization is the process by which a system decides what an authenticated user is and is not allowed to do. The RP relies on AD FS to provide authentication services, but authorization remains in the jurisdiction of the RP. Once your authentication has been confirmed it is up to the RP to authorize your access. This separation means that the RP, which owns the services or data being accessed, is still in control of who can and cannot access them.

Claims-Based Authentication

AD FS works using claims-based authentication. This means that when a user accesses or logs in to the relying party, AD FS provides a token with *claims* about the user. As long as the trust relationship has been established, the relying party can then decide what the user is or is not allowed to do based on the provided claims. This is a vast improvement in security because the organization does not have to expose user credentials (only claims), and the relying party has complete control over access to and use of their own resources.

Single Sign-On (SSO)

The end goal of implementing AD FS is to enable Single Sign-On (SSO) for users in an organization. SSO is the process whereby a user is not required to even enter credentials a second time to access a third-party application. By utilizing the trust relationship and claim token system described previously, AD FS can extend the organization's AD DS authentication to those third parties. Once a user has logged in to the local domain, the user's token can be handed back and forth between the AD FS server and the relying party completely transparently to the user. The user simply accesses the application and with no further prompts or roadblocks is granted the appropriate access.

Active Directory Certificate Services (AD CS)

Active Directory Certificate Services (AD CS) allows for the creation and management of *public key infrastructure (PKI)* certificates for use in an organization. These certificates can be used to encrypt files on the network, create secure VPN tunnels, set up SSL for intranet applications, and even identify individual users or computers.

While not a large or complicated service, AD CS does allow for additional layers of security and identity verification often required for highly sensitive information or regulatory compliance. PKI is a complex topic in its own right and outside the scope of this book, but at a basic level AD CS creates public-private key pairs and binds the identity of a person or device to the private key. The server role that AD CS uses for this is known as a *certificate authority (CA)*.

With the certificate authority role installed, you can manage the creation, distribution, backup, recovery, and revocation of digital certificates for the domain. You can have multiple CAs installed in a domain; however, one CA at the top is known as the *root CA.* Underneath the root CA there can be one or more *subordinate CAs.* Those subordinate CAs can have subordinate CAs of their own, and when they do they become known as *intermediate CAs.*

AD CS offers two types of CA: enterprise and stand-alone. Enterprise CAs are integrated with AD DS, and in fact the certificates they create are stored in the directory. They can also use certificate templates to fill in default information for requested certificates and can enable accounts in the AD DS directory to request and receive certificates without the involvement of an administrator.

Stand-alone CAs do not use AD DS or certificate templates. All information for a requested certificate must be included in the request, and all requests are held in a pending queue until an administrator approves or rejects them.

Active Directory Rights Management Services (AD RMS)

Document and information security is a paramount concern for organizations in all industries today. Even modestly sized organizations deal with protected data such as private financial documents, intellectual property, executive management communications, and human resource details. Even trained employees sometimes make careless mistakes: printing a document with employee salaries and forgetting it at the printer or forwarding an email with internal financial numbers to a group email chain.

Active Directory Rights Management Services (AD RMS) helps to prevent these mistakes, as well as more proactive attempts at malicious information theft, from compromising company data. AD RMS allows users to encrypt common document formats like emails and Microsoft Office documents and selectively specify who, when, and where that data can be decrypted. This protection is embedded into the document itself, meaning that even entities outside the organization cannot decrypt the data without first contacting and being approved by the originating AD RMS server. These protections extend to certain actions such as editing or printing, which allows for fine-grained control over the use of sensitive company documents.

AD RMS Clients

When choosing to protect a document, the user uses an AD RMS client to request a *client licensor certificate (CLC).* The CLC is used to encrypt the document as well as create and sign a *publishing license (PL).* The PL describes who can decrypt the document and under what circumstances. The PL is bound to the encrypted document so that even if the document is sent outside the boundaries of the organization's network the restrictions remain in place.

When a user receives and wants to view content protected this way, the user needs to first use a rights-enabled application. Microsoft Office is the most common option and has supported RMS since 2003. Other applications such as Adobe Acrobat and Internet Explorer can become rights-enabled with third-party software. The application handles communicating with the AD RMS server and determining whether the recipient meets the policies set forth in the PL. When it does meet those requirements, it receives an end-user license, which ensures that the user honors all conditions indicated by the PL. This means that the client application can continue to restrict content as necessary even if it loses connectivity to the AD RMS server.

AD RMS Server

The AD RMS server component handles the creation of CLCs when users are publishing protected content and the issuance of end-user licenses when requests are made. The AD RMS server is also responsible for authorizing the usage of protected content. For this reason AD RMS servers run as Web Service components on Microsoft Internet Information Services. As web servers, the AD RMS server can be contacted from both a company's internal intranet and, if desired, the public Internet. AD RMS also utilizes Microsoft SQL Server and integrates closely with AD DS.

Exam Preparation Tasks

As mentioned in the section "Book Features" in the Introduction, you have a few choices for exam preparation: the exercises here; Chapter 17, "Final Preparation"; and the exam simulation questions in the Pearson Test Prep Software Online.

Review All Key Topics

Review the most important topics in this chapter, noted with the Key Topics icon in the outer margin of the page. Table 1-3 lists a reference of these key topics and the page number on which each is found.

Table 1-3 Key Topics for Chapter 1

Key Topic Element	Description	Page Number
Table 1-2	Services in the Active Directory product suite	8
Paragraph	Description of objects in a directory	9
Paragraph	Description of organizational units in a directory	10
Paragraph	How a computer becomes a domain controller	11
Paragraph	Introduction to Group Policy Objects (GPOs)	12
Paragraph	Explanation of claims-based authentication	14
Paragraph	Description of AD RMS clients	15
Paragraph	Description of AD RMS servers	16

Complete Tables and Lists from Memory

Print a copy of Appendix B, "Memory Tables" (found on the book website), or at least the section for this chapter, and complete the tables and lists from memory. Appendix C, "Memory Tables Answer Key," also on the website, includes completed tables and lists to check your work.

Define Key Terms

Define the following key terms from this chapter and check your answers in the glossary:

objects, attributes, containers, organizational units (OUs), domains, domain controllers, namespace, tree, forest, Group Policy Object, identity federation, relying party, identity provider, claims, authentication, authorization, certificate, certificate authority, client licensor certificate, publishing license

End-of-Chapter Review Questions

The answers to these questions appear in Appendix A. For more practice with exam format questions, use the Pearson Test Prep Software Online.

1. What are the five core services in the Active Directory product suite?

2. You have been tasked with reducing the risk of sensitive corporate information being leaked via email and document sharing. Of particular importance is the protection of documents that leave the corporate network. What Active Directory product would you research?

3. A number of users at your organization are working remotely and connecting to your office network via VPN. As an added measure of security, you would like them to provide some additional metric of identification when they log in. Which Active Directory product would you research?

   a. AD DS

   b. AD FS

   c. AD RMS

   d. AD CS

4. What are some benefits of implementing Group Policy Objects (GPOs) on your directory? (Choose all that apply.)

   a. Define security at the organization, group, or individual level

   b. Organize users and computers into separate hierarchies in the directory

   c. Apply security systemically without manual intervention

   d. Federated identity authentication to third-party services

5. Employees in the Finance department are using a new vendor-hosted financial analysis software suite in their daily activities. Rather than maintain a separate logon and password for each user in the department, you could consider which Active Directory product to extend your identity authentication to the vendor product?

This chapter covers the following topics:

- **Installing a New Forest**: This section describes the steps required to install a new forest, domain, and the first domain controller.

- **Adding or Removing a Domain Controller from a Domain**: This section describes how to add a new writeable domain controller to an existing domain.

- **Upgrading a Domain Controller**: This section explains how and when to upgrade the operating system of a domain controller.

- **Installing AD DS on a Server Core Installation**: This section describes the PowerShell command required to install AD DS and promote a domain controller on a Server Core installation.

- **Installing a Domain Controller with Install from Media (IFM)**: This section describes how and when you would use the Install from Media option for installing a domain controller.

- **Installing and Configuring a Read-Only Domain Controller (RODC):** This section explains the purpose of read-only domain controllers in the deployment and how to perform a staged RODC install.

- **Configuring Domain Controller Cloning:** This section explains how to successfully clone a domain controller installed in a virtual machine instance.

- **Resolving DNS SRV Record Registration Issues**: This section explains the required DNS records for an Active Directory domain and how to verify they are set up properly.

- **Configuring a Global Catalog Server**: This section explains the global catalog server and how to install it on additional domain controllers.

- **Transferring and Seizing Operations Master Roles**: This section explains how to transfer FSMO roles from one domain controller to another.

CHAPTER 2

Installing and Configuring Domain Controllers

Until you have a domain controller (DC), you don't really have a domain. The processes of installing Active Directory Domain Services (AD DS), creating a new forest, and promoting a server to domain controller are all closely related to one another. When you install your first DC, most of the required processes happen automatically through the Server Manager Wizard or PowerShell. This doesn't mean that installing DCs is always simple and straightforward.

As your organization grows and becomes more complex, so do your network and your domain structure. In this chapter we start with a basic domain controller installation but quickly get into various advanced installations.

"Do I Know This Already?" Quiz

The "Do I Know This Already?" quiz allows you to assess whether you should read this entire chapter thoroughly or jump to the "Exam Preparation Tasks" section. If you are in doubt about your answers to these questions or your own assessment of your knowledge of the topics, read the entire chapter. Table 2-1 lists the major headings in this chapter and their corresponding "Do I Know This Already?" quiz questions. You can find the answers in Appendix A, "Answers to the 'Do I Know This Already?' Quizzes."

Table 2-1   "Do I Know This Already?" Section-to-Question Mapping

Foundation Topics Section	Questions
Installing a New Forest	1-3
Adding or Removing a Domain Controller from a Domain	4-5
Upgrading a Domain Controller	6
Installing AD DS on a Server Core Installation	7-8
Installing a Domain Controller with Install from Media (IFM)	9
Installing and Configuring a Read-Only Domain Controller (RODC)	10
Configuring Domain Controller Cloning	11

Foundation Topics Section	Questions
Resolving DNS SRV Record Registration Issues	12
Configuring a Global Catalog Server	13
Transferring and Seizing Operations Master Roles	14-15

CAUTION   The goal of self-assessment is to gauge your mastery of the topics in this chapter. If you do not know the answer to a question or are only partially sure of the answer, you should mark that question as wrong for purposes of the self-assessment. Giving yourself credit for an answer you correctly guess skews your self-assessment results and might provide you with a false sense of security.

1. You are planning the new domain structure for your organization. It has become clear that you will need multiple domains for the different lines of business you support. These domains will be children to your parent domain **corp. com**. The namespaces for the child domains must be

   a. Contiguous

   b. Multi-forest

   c. Non-contiguous

   d. Forest root

2. What GUI tool do you use to install AD DS on a Windows Server 2016 with Desktop Experience?

   a. Local Server

   b. Active Directory Administration Center

   c. Active Directory Domains and Trusts

   d. Server Manager

3. You are setting up Active Directory Domain Services on your network for the first time. You have successfully installed AD DS on the server. What is the next step to perform to complete the operation?

   a. Transfer an FSMO role.

   b. Promote to a domain controller.

   c. Prepare installation media for IFM.

   d. Enable the Schema Admin snap-in.

4. Which of the following services can be enabled on a new writeable domain controller being installed in an existing domain? (Choose two answers.)

    a. Global Catalog server

    b. DNS server

    c. Higher forest functional level

    d. Higher domain functional level

5. Before you can uninstall AD DS from a domain controller, you must first perform which of the following tasks?

    a. Raise the forest functional level.

    b. Transfer the domain naming master role to it.

    c. Demote it from a domain controller.

    d. Log on to the Primary Domain Controller (PDC) FSMO role server.

6. Which of the following are valid operating systems you can upgrade to Windows Server 2016? (Choose two answers.)

    a. Windows Server 2012 R2

    b. Windows 10

    c. Windows Server 2008 R2

    d. Windows Server 2012

7. Which PowerShell command is used to install AD DS on Windows Server 2016?

    a. **Add-WindowsFeature**

    b. **Install-ADDSForest**

    c. **Install-WindowsFeature**

    d. **Install-ServerManagerRole**

8. Which PowerShell command is used to promote a server to a domain controller?

    a. **Add-WindowsFeature**

    b. **Install-ADDSForest**

    c. **Install-WindowsFeature**

    d. **Install-ServerManagerRole**

9. Which command-line utility is used to create the media for an Install from Media (IFM) installation?

   a. **dcpromo**

   b. **Install-WindowsFeature**

   c. **adprep**

   d. **ntdsutil**

10. You are preparing to set up a read-only domain controller at a retail branch office. The personnel performing the setup of the controller are third-party vendors that you do not want to grant administrative access to your network. You can safely deploy this server by which of the following methods?

    a. Staging the installation with a pre-created account

    b. Using Install from Media (IFM) to securely transmit the directory

    c. Sharing your credentials temporarily

    d. You cannot; installing a new domain controller requires administrative access.

11. Which Active Directory group must the server object be a member of before the virtual machine can be successfully cloned?

    a. Users

    b. Computers

    c. Cloneable Domain Controllers

    d. Domain Controller Admins

12. Which types of DNS records are required for Active Directory to function properly? (Choose all that apply.)

    a. SRV

    b. A

    c. MX

    d. CNAME

13. The object attributes stored in the global catalog (GC) can be modified by

    a. Transferring the GC to a Windows Server 2016 domain controller

    b. Modifying the forest schema

    c. Moving the Schema Master FSMO server into the Cloneable Domain Controllers group

    d. Installing the GC on a second writeable domain controller in the domain

14. Which utility is used to seize the PDC role in Active Directory Domain Services?

    a. Active Directory Domains and Trusts

    b. Active Directory Users and Computers

    c. Active Directory Schema Snap-In

    d. Flexible Single Master Operations

15. The utility to seize the domain naming master role in Active Directory Domain Services is:

    a. Active Directory Domains and Trusts

    b. Active Directory Users and Computers

    c. Active Directory Schema Snap-In

    d. Flexible Single Master Operations

Foundation Topics

Installing a New Forest

It has been said that the journey of a thousand miles begins with a single step. Moving an organization, even a modestly sized one, onto Active Directory Domain Services (AD DS) can feel like such a journey. This section outlines the basic process for taking that first step, beginning with guidance on how to plan your domain structure, including some best practices. Installing a new forest means nothing more than creating your first domain. With Windows Server 2016 Desktop Experience this process is no more difficult than walking through a GUI wizard using the Server Manager included in Windows Server. First you learn how to install the appropriate server role, AD DS, and then how to promote the server to a domain controller.

Planning the Domain

When planning to deploy AD DS in your organization, there are several key decisions to make ahead of time. Deciding on the structure and layout of your forest, including how many domains and trees there will be and how their *namespace*s will be structured, is a good first step.

You want to design a domain structure that matches the structure of your organization but also reflects the management model for your IT department. A smaller organization with a single geographic location and a centralized IT department may only need a single domain, while a more complex or dispersed organization might need to structure multiple domains in multiple trees. Recall that even in a simple single-domain setup, there is still the concept of a forest, tree, and forest root domain.

In general, consider one of the following three domain structures:

- **Single domain**: A single domain in a single tree. Good for small organizations with a single centralized IT department for administration.

- **Multi-domain**: Multiple domains organized into a single tree. Good for organizations with central IT administration over a widespread or geographically diverse physical presence.

- **Multi-tree**: Multiple domains spread across more than one domain tree. This complicated but powerful structure can allow a large enterprise to delegate administration to various geographic regions of the organization while still centrally managing critical components and infrastructure.

In certain cases, it may also make sense to have multiple forests in your AD DS deployment. If your organization has acquired or taken ownership of outside organizations or if there are subsidiary or independently managed companies within the enterprise, then separate forests might be appropriate. These are typically unusual cases, however, and only recommended for advanced administrators.

When planning the structure of your domain, start with a single domain and add domains that can be justified by your IT or organizational structure. Remember that each additional domain requires at least one additional domain controller (and often more than one for redundancy purposes) and consequently incurs capital and administrative costs.

Once you've decided on your domain structure, you want to consider how to arrange the domain namespace. As discussed in Chapter 1, "Introducing Active Directory 2016," the namespace is a DNS name used to reference the domain and all its objects on the network. A DNS name typically has at least two labels, such as **certguide.com**, where "certguide" is the first label and "com" is the second. While it is possible to deploy a domain with a *single-label* namespace, Microsoft strongly discourages the practice.

NOTE A large number of objects and the need to delegate administration are not good reasons to justify adding domains. A domain can create roughly 2.15 billion objects during its lifetime, a limit no one is likely to encounter, and administration can be delegated at the OU level if needed. More appropriate justifications include isolating replication across geographical boundaries or separating production, test, and development infrastructure.

This namespace represents the root domain for a tree. If that is the only domain you are deploying, it also represents the namespace for all the objects in the domain. If you are deploying a domain tree, the child domains from this root require contiguous namespaces, for example, **east.certguide.com**, **west.certguide.com**. Objects in their respective domains belong to the namespace of their domain.

Regardless of the number of domains and namespaces, they need to be registered with *service records* in the DNS server. Having the appropriate records in the DNS server is critical for communication across the network. Later in this chapter we discuss how to troubleshoot issues that might arise from those records.

Installing AD DS from Server Manager

There are two methods for installing AD DS and promoting your server to a domain controller. The first method, using the installation wizard in Server Manager, requires a "Desktop Experience" version of Windows Server 2016 to be installed. With the desktop experience, administrators have access to a full GUI interface for Windows Server. If you are using Server Core instead, you need to use the PowerShell commands covered later in this chapter.

For those who are familiar with installing AD DS on Windows Server 2008 or 2012, very little has changed. The process should be familiar. If you are new to Windows Server, the installation wizard is an ideal place to start as it walks you through all the options and key decisions during installation.

To begin, you need to be logged in to the Windows Server as a local administrator. Then follow this process to install AD DS:

Step 1.   Start Server Manager from either the Start Menu or the Taskbar.

Step 2.   From the Dashboard Quickstart pane, click **Add roles and features**.

Step 3.   The Add Roles and Features Wizard starts. Click **Next** on the Before You Begin page and ensure **Role-based or feature-based installation** is selected on the Installation Type page. Click **Next**.

Step 4.   On the Server Selection page ensure that the **Select a server from the server pool** option is chosen and then click to highlight the current server from the list. Click **Next**.

Step 5.   On the Server Roles page, check the box next to **Active Directory Domain Services**. If prompted to Add Features that are required... review the role services that must be installed for AD DS to work and ensure **Include management tools** (if applicable) is checked. Click **Add Features** to return to the Server Roles page (see Figure 2-1).

Step 6.   Click **Next**.

Step 7.   Review the features that have been selected for you on the Features page. You can check any additional features you want to install at this time. Click **Next**.

Step 8.   Review the information on the AD DS page. Click **Next**.

Step 9.   Review the confirmation page for all the services and features you chose to install. Do not check the box to **Restart the destination server automatically** if any other users are currently relying on the server. Click **Install**.

Step 10.   The server displays an installation progress page. Note the option at the bottom of the page to **Export configuration settings**, which generates an XML file you can use with PowerShell to install the same roles and features on another server (see Figure 2-2).

Figure 2-1   The Add Roles and Features Wizard Indicating Additional Services to Be Installed as Requirements for AD DS

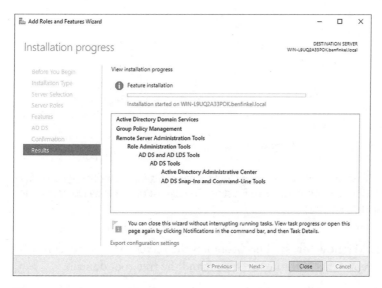

Figure 2-2   The Add Roles and Features Wizard in the Process of Installing AD DS

Promoting the Server to Domain Controller

Installing AD DS is only the first step. Once the server successfully runs the Add Roles and Features Wizard, you are prompted with a link to **Promote this server to a domain controller**. If you want to perform the promoting at a later point, click **Close**.

Step 1.   Click the link to **Promote this server to a domain controller**. This launches the Active Directory Domain Services Configuration Wizard.

Note the three choices (see Figure 2-3):

- Add a domain controller to an existing domain

- Add a new domain to an existing forest

- Add a new forest

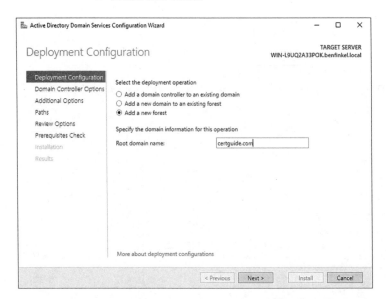

Figure 2-3   The Active Directory Domain Services Configuration Wizard Prompting for the Type of Deployment: Adding a Domain Controller to an Existing Domain, Adding a New Domain to an Existing Forest, or Creating a New Forest

Step 2.   Select **Add a new forest**. This promotes the server to a domain controller that represents both the forest root and the tree root domain.

Step 3.   Type the fully qualified DNS name of the domain to create, for example, **certguide.com**. Click **Next**.

Step 4.   On the Domain Controller Options page you have a number of choices to make. Review the following choices and then click **Next** (see Figure 2-4):

- **Forest and Domain function level**: These are essentially choices about compatibility for your domain. Choosing an earlier version of Windows Server allows older versions of Server to act as domain controllers but prevents you from using newer features. We cover these levels in more detail later in the chapter.

- **Domain Name System (DNS) server**: This installs the DNS Server role onto the domain controller, which is required for AD DS to properly function. If you want to integrate the server into an existing DNS infrastructure, uncheck this box and configure that in the next page.

- **Global Catalog (GC)**: This option is checked and disabled for the first domain in a forest. This DC must also be a GC.

- **Read-only domain controller (RODC)**: This option is unchecked and disabled for the first domain in a forest. This DC cannot be an RODC.

- **Directory Services Restore Mode (DSRM) password**: This password can be used to repair or restore the directory in certain troubleshooting situations. It must adhere to the server's password policies. Key one in and document it in a secure location.

Figure 2-4   The Active Directory Domain Services Configuration Wizard Domain Controller Options Page with a Variety of Key Options to Choose During Promotion

Step 5. If you selected to install DNS server on the previous page, the DNS Options page displays. Unless you're integrating into an existing DNS infrastructure, you receive a message indicating that the delegation for this DNS server cannot be created and the **Create DNS Delegation** option is disabled. Click **Next**.

Step 6. The Additional Options page provides you the opportunity to type in the NetBIOS name for the domain. It should default to the leftmost label on the domain DNS name specified in Step 4. This will be used for legacy NetBIOS communications on the network. Click **Next**.

Step 7. The Paths page allows you to override the default locations for the database, its transaction log, and the SYSVOL folder. In larger installations it can make sense to separate the SYSVOL from the two database folders, as heavy use of Group Policy can grow this share quite large. Click **Next**.

Step 8. Review the options on the Review Options page for all the choices you made. Take particular note of the View Script button in the lower right, which allows you to view the PowerShell script that would perform the exact same configuration you just set up. Save this script somewhere you can find it. Click **Next**.

Step 9. The wizard displays a Prerequisites Check page that displays any notable information, errors, or warnings. Read this information carefully and prepare for any resolutions you might need to perform. The bottom of the results box should read **All prerequisite checks passed successfully. Click 'Install' to begin installation**. Click **Install**.

Step 10. The installation takes a few moments to complete, and progress is listed in the operation results box (see Figure 2-5). As a final step, the server requires a reboot.

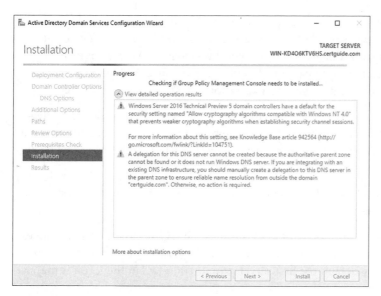

Figure 2-5   The Active Directory Domain Services Configuration Wizard Finalizing and Promoting the Server to a Domain Controller. Warnings and Errors Are Listed in the Box Labeled **View detailed operation results**.

Adding or Removing a Domain Controller from a Domain

It's almost certain that you will want to add an additional domain controller to your existing infrastructure at some point. Additional controllers can have authentication traffic balanced across them to avoid overloading a single server, can offer redundancy for disaster recovery purposes, and can be installed geographically close to regional offices for reduced latency. Even a small network will likely need a second domain controller for failover purposes in the event of a system failure on the primary controller. This section walks through the considerations you should take into account when planning to add domain controllers to the domain.

Multimaster Replication and FSMO Roles

Active Directory Domain Services takes advantage of a replication scheme known as *multimaster replication*. In a traditional master-slave replication setup, a single master server receives all changes to the data and replicates those changes to its slaves. This method can help to ensure consistency but introduces its own challenges. That single master is a single point of failure and can be difficult to set up for failover or redundancy. Communication from that single master can also be problematic if the subordinate servers are widespread.

Multimaster replication, in contrast, allows multiple servers to receive updates and propagate those changes to all other masters. Because AD DS is often deployed across multiple organizational and geographical boundaries, AD DS implements multimaster replication. A domain in AD DS can have multiple domain controllers, and all those DCs can be considered a master for the purposes of replication.

In some situations, however, AD DS requires a single master controlling information for the entire domain or forest. There are five of these functions, and the server that is the master for any one of these five roles is known as the *Flexible Single Master Operations (FSMO)* role owner.

The five FSMO roles (two of which are masters for the entire forest, not just a single domain) are as follows:

- **Schema master (forest-wide)**: This role is the DC allowed to make changes to the directory schema. No other server in the forest can process or update the schema. By default the first server promoted to DC in the forest is the schema master.

- **Domain naming master (forest-wide)**: This role is the DC allowed to make changes to the forest-wide namespace, including adding, moving, or removing domains. By default the first server promoted to DC in the forest is the domain naming master.

- **Primary domain controller (PDC) emulator (domain-wide)**: The PDC is a holdover from the days of Windows NT when there was only a single domain controller. The PDC emulator also performs a number of other functions on the domain, which you can read about here: https://msdn.microsoft.com/en-us/library/cc223749.aspx.

- **Relative identifier (RID) master (domain-wide)**: This role maintains a universal (within the domain) list of unique RIDs that are a component of the security identifier (SID) all security-enabled objects in AD DS receive. The SID must be unique across all objects in a domain, and the RID master FSMO server helps ensure that uniqueness.

- **Infrastructure master (domain-wide)**: The infrastructure master role is used to maintain references to objects from other domains. For example, if users from Domain 1 are members of a group in Domain 2, the Domain 2 infrastructure master maintains references to the users from Domain 1.

Forest and Domain Functional Levels

Microsoft introduced *functional levels* as a way for administrators to control and ensure minimum functionality across an entire forest and domain. Forest functional levels and domain functional levels combine to ensure that every DC in the domain meets a minimum operating system requirement.

For example, if the forest functional level is Windows 2003 and the domain functional level is Windows 2003, then DCs in the domain can be any version of Windows from 2003 onward. An arrangement like this, however, would mean that features from newer versions of Windows Server could not be used since not all DCs would be able to support them. If the administrator decided to raise the domain functional level to Windows Server 2012, then first all DCs in that domain would need to be upgraded to Windows Server 2012 or newer. At that point the domain functional level could be raised and Windows Server 2012 domain features would be available. The same is true for the forest functional level. Upgrading all the DCs in the forest is required before the forest functional level can be raised.

When a new domain is added to an existing forest, you need to take note of the forest and domain functional levels and choose a version of Windows Server that will be supported.

Adding a New Domain Controller to an Existing Domain

To add a new domain controller to an existing domain, you first need to install AD DS on the server according to the steps described earlier in the chapter. When you reach the end of the install process you should be prompted with a link to **Promote this server to a domain controller**.

Step 1. Click the link to **Promote this server to a domain controller**. This launches the Active Directory Domain Services Configuration Wizard.

Note the three choices:

■ Add a domain controller to an existing domain

■ Add a new domain to an existing forest

■ Add a new forest

Step 2. Select **Add a domain controller to an existing domain**. This allows you to choose an existing domain name (see Figure 2-6).

Step 3. Type the fully qualified domain name of an existing domain in the **Domain** text box. Click **Select**.

Step 4. Type in administrator credentials for the target domain. Be sure to use the fully qualified domain user name, for example, **certguide\ Administrator** or **Administrator@certguide.com**.

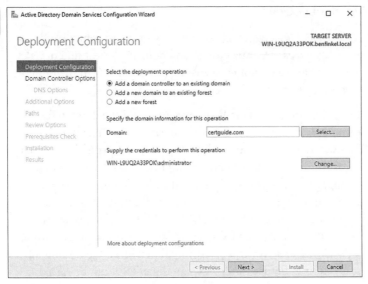

Figure 2-6 The Active Directory Domain Services Configuration Wizard Prompting for the Type of Deployment. In This Case, the Selected Option, **Add a domain controller to an existing domain**, Prompts for Additional Details.

Step 5. A dialog prompts you to select one domain from the forest. Click to highlight the domain you want and click **OK**. Click **Next**.

Step 6. On the Domain Controller Options page you have a number of choices to make. Review the following choices and then click **Next**.

- **Domain Name System (DNS) server**: This installs the DNS server role onto the domain controller, which is required for AD DS to properly function. If you want to integrate the server into an existing DNS infrastructure, uncheck this box and configure that in the next page.

- **Global Catalog (GC)**: For additional DCs in the domain, this can be either installed or not. It's recommended to install the GC on every DC for redundancy and feature purposes.

- **Read-only domain controller (RODC)**: This box turns the DC into a read-only controller, effectively acting as a slave to the active writeable DCs in the domain. See details for this option later in the chapter.

- **Site name**: Choose a site name from the list provided. Sites can be used to represent the physical topology of the domain. Read more here: https://technet.microsoft.com/en-us/library/cc754697(v=ws.11). aspx.

- **Directory Services Restore Mode (DSRM) password**: This password can be used to repair or restore the directory in certain troubleshooting situations. It must adhere to the server's password policies. Key one in and document it in a secure location.

Step 7.   If you selected to install DNS server on the previous page, the DNS options page displays. Unless you're integrating into an existing DNS infrastructure, you receive a message indicating that the delegation for this DNS server cannot be created and the **Create DNS Delegation** option is disabled. Click **Next**.

Step 8.   The Additional Options page offers two options to configure with regards to replication. Because a domain and DC already exist, the directory must be initially replicated from another DC to this server:

- **Install from media**: This option is used if you do not want the initial replication of the directory to happen over the network. Checking this box allows you to choose the media where the directory has been saved. See more details later in this chapter.

- **Replicate from**: Even if you are installing from media, some data will need to replicate to this server. Choose a specific source server here, or allow AD DS to choose by selecting **Any domain controller**.

Step 9.   The Paths page allows you to override the default locations for the database, its transaction log, and the SYSVOL folder. In larger installations, it can make sense to separate the SYSVOL from the two database folders, as heavy use of Group Policy can grow this share quite large. Click **Next**.

Step 10.   The wizard displays a Prerequisites Check page, which displays any notable information, errors, or warnings. Read this information carefully and prepare for any resolutions you need to perform. The bottom of the results box should read **All prerequisite checks passed successfully. Click 'Install' to begin installation**. Click **Install.**

Step 11.   The installation takes a few moments to complete, and progress is listed in the operation results box. As a final step, the server requires a reboot.

Demoting a Server from Domain Controller

When you want to remove AD DS from a server and thereby revoke its status as a domain controller, Server Manager allows you to do this easily.

Step 1. Start Server Manager from either the Start Menu or the Taskbar.

Step 2. From the Dashboard Quickstart pane, click **Add Roles and Features**. The Add Roles and Features Wizard starts. Click the link to **Start the Remove Roles and Features Wizard**.

Step 3. The Remove Roles and Features Wizard launches. You can also launch this wizard by selecting the Local Server in Server Manager and pulling down the **Tasks** drop-down next to the Roles and Features panel.

Step 4. Click **Next** on the Before You Begin page.

Step 5. On the Server Selection page, ensure that the **Select a server from the server pool** option is chosen, and then click to highlight the current server from the list. Click **Next**.

Step 6. On the Server Roles page, uncheck **Active Directory Domain Services**. If prompted to "Remove Features that require..." review the role services that must be removed when AD DS is removed and ensure **Remove management tools** is checked. Click **Remove Features** to return to the Server Roles page.

Step 7. A dialog prompts you indicating that you must demote the domain controller before you can continue. Click the link to **Demote this domain controller** (see Figure 2-7).

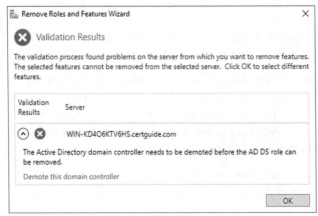

Figure 2-7 The Remove Roles and Features Wizard Presents a Validation Error. The AD DS Role Cannot Be Removed Until the Server Has Been Demoted from a Domain Controller to a Member Server.

Step 8. A domain administrator account should be listed as the credentials to perform this operation. If not, click **Change** and type in the correct credentials. Be sure to use the fully qualified domain user name—for example, **certguide\Administrator** or **Administrator@certguide. com**. Select **Force the removal of this domain controller** if previous attempts to demote the controller have failed. Click **Next**.

Step 9. The warnings page tells you about roles such as DNS or GC that are required for AD DS. Check the **Proceed with removal** box and then click **Next**.

Step 10. Type a new password for the local Administrator account and then click **Next**.

Step 11. Review the options on the Review Options page for all the choices you made. Take particular note of the View Script button in the lower right, which allows you to view the PowerShell script that would perform the same configuration you just set up. Save this script somewhere you can find it. Click **Demote.**

Step 12. After the demotion completes, the server reboots. You need to perform Steps 1 through 6 again to fully remove AD DS from this server.

Upgrading a Domain Controller

Most users will not be deploying a fresh Windows Server 2016 directory in their network environment but rather integrating Windows Server 2016 with an existing AD DS deployment. The recommended method for upgrading the DCs in a domain is to promote new DCs that run newer versions of Windows Server and demote existing DCs running legacy versions. This is preferable to upgrading the operating system on an existing DC.

Table 2-2 lists the valid upgrade paths if you want to upgrade an existing server.

Table 2-2 Windows Server 2016 Upgrade Paths

If you are running...	You can upgrade to:
Windows Server 2012 Standard	Windows Server 2016 Standard or Datacenter
Windows Server 2012 Datacenter	Windows Server 2016 Datacenter
Windows Server 2012 R2 Standard	Windows Server 2016 Standard or Datacenter
Windows Server 2012 R2 Datacenter	Windows Server 2016 Datacenter
Windows Server 2012 R2 Essentials	Windows Server 2016 Essentials

The primary tasks in preparing a domain to accept a newer version of Windows Server revolve around the forest and domain. As mentioned earlier, upgrading existing DCs to newer versions of Windows Server is a prerequisite to upgrading the functional level of the forest or domain. If you want to take advantage of the new features and functionality of AD DS, you need to first upgrade each of your servers and then raise the forest and domain functional levels.

To raise the functional level for the forest:

Step 1.   Log on to the forest root domain controller.

Step 2.   Start Server Manager from either the Start Menu or the Taskbar.

Step 3.   From the navigation menu choose **Local Server**.

Step 4.   Right-click the server and click **Active Directory Administrative Center**.

Step 5.   Select the domain you want to raise in the navigation pane (see Figure 2-8).

Step 6.   Click **Raise the forest functional level** in the Tasks pane (see Figure 2-8).

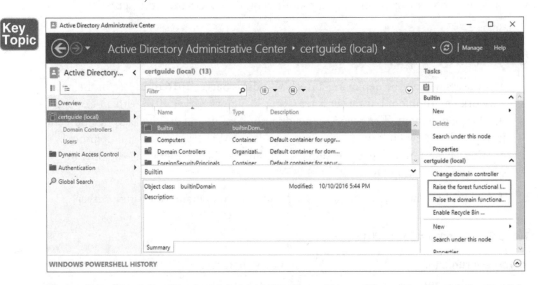

Figure 2-8   The Active Directory Administrative Center Primary View with a Domain (certguide) Chosen on the Navigation Pane, a Container (Builtin) Highlighted in the Main Pane

Step 7.   The available functional levels are listed in the drop-down. Choose **Windows Server 2016** and click **OK**.

Step 8.   A warning dialog appears. Click **OK.**

The domain functional level can be raised in the same way, except during Step 6 choose **Raise the domain functional level** from the Tasks pane (see Figure 2-8).

When you first promote a Windows Server 2016 server to a domain controller, the promotion wizard runs a utility known as *adprep* on the schema master FSMO server and the infrastructure master FSMO server. In earlier iterations of Windows Server you needed to run this step yourself, but it is now integrated into the promotion process.

If you still want to perform the adprep functions manually prior to promoting your server, you can read more about it here: https://technet.microsoft.com/en-us/library/cc731728(v=ws.11).aspx.

Installing AD DS on a Server Core Installation

Windows Server has been a notorious resource hog for many years. This has become particularly apparent with the rise of lightweight Linux alternatives that can run with much less memory and take up less hard drive space. With the release of Windows Server 2008, and with every release since then up to and including Windows Server 2016, Microsoft has offered a minimal installation known as Server Core. Server Core is a low-maintenance server that drastically reduces the footprint of the OS. Working with Server Core has unique challenges, but promoting a Server Core installation to a domain controller still requires the same two basic steps as the Desktop Experience version of Windows Server: Installing AD DS and promoting the server.

Installing AD DS with PowerShell

The Server Manager utility in Windows Server makes it easy to launch and run GUI wizards for installing AD DS roles and services. Server Core eschews much of the overhead that the Windows Server Desktop Experience version includes; most notably Server Core lacks any GUI shell. All configuration and maintenance on Server Core is performed with remote utilities, the command-line interface, or PowerShell. You cannot use the Server Manager Wizard to install AD DS on a Server Core machine.

The command to install roles and services in PowerShell is as follows:

```
Install-WindowsFeature [-Name] <Feature[]>'
[-ComputerName <String> ]'
[-Credential <PSCredential> ]'
[-IncludeAllSubFeature]'
[-IncludeManagementTools]'
[-LogPath <String> ]'
```

```
[-Restart]'
[-Source <String[]> ]'
[-Confirm]'
[-WhatIf]'
[ <CommonParameters>]
```

You can find the full documentation for the **Install-WindowsFeature** cmdlet here:
https://technet.microsoft.com/en-us/library/jj205467(v=wps.630).aspx.

To specify AD DS as the feature to install, you need to supply *AD-Domain-Services*
for the -Name parameter. All other parameters are optional, although Microsoft
recommends using the **-IncludeManagementTools** option to ensure all management tools are also installed.

Step 1.   At the Server Core command line, type **Powershell** and press **Enter**.

Step 2.   From the PowerShell prompt type the following command and press
Enter.

```
Install-WindowsFeature -Name AD-Domain-Services
IncludeManagementTools
```

Step 3.   Server Core runs through the install process for AD DS and returns a
table output with a Success value of True upon completion.

Promoting a Server to Domain Controller with PowerShell

Just as with a GUI installation of AD DS, after the server roles and services have
been installed, you need to promote the server to a domain controller. As above, the
AD DS Configuration Wizard is not available in Server Core; instead you need to
use PowerShell commands.

The command to promote a server to a domain controller is as follows:

```
Install-ADDSForest -DomainName <String>'
[-CreateDnsDelegation]'
[-DatabasePath <String> ]'
[-DnsDelegationCredential <PSCredential> ]'
[-DomainMode <DomainMode> ]'
[-DomainNetbiosName <String> ]'
[-Force]'
[-ForestMode <ForestMode> ]'
[-InstallDns]'
[-LogPath <String> ]'
[-NoDnsOnNetwork]'
[-NoRebootOnCompletion]'
```

```
[-SafeModeAdministratorPassword <SecureString> ]'
[-SkipAutoConfigureDns]'
[-SkipPreChecks]'
[-SysvolPath <String> ]'
[-Confirm]'
[-WhatIf]'
[ <CommonParameters>]
```

You can find the full documentation for the **Install-ADDSForest** cmdlet here: https://technet.microsoft.com/en-us/library/hh974720(v=wps.630).aspx.

The **-DomainName** parameter is the only required parameter for this command. All other parameters are optional and use the default settings observed during the promotion steps performed with the Configuration Wizard earlier in this chapter. If you do not include the **-SafeModeAdministratorPassword** in the command you are prompted to key one in during the installation process. If you saved the output from the View Script button during the GUI version of this process, you can see how the choices made translate to the PowerShell cmdlet.

Step 1. At the Server Core command line, type **Powershell** and press **Enter**.

Step 2. From the PowerShell prompt, type the following command and press **Enter**.

```
Install-ADDSForest -DomainName corecertguide.com
```

Step 3. At the **SafeModeAdministratorPassword** prompt, type in the desired Directory Services Restore Mode password and press **Enter** (see Figure 2-9).

Figure 2-9 The Install-ADDSForest cmdlet Prompting for the SafeModeAdministratorPassword

Step 4. Retype the password to confirm and press **Enter**.

Step 5. Read the prompt and press **Y** when you are ready to continue. The PowerShell window provides progress updates for the promotion process (see Figure 2-10). Note the server reboots upon completion.

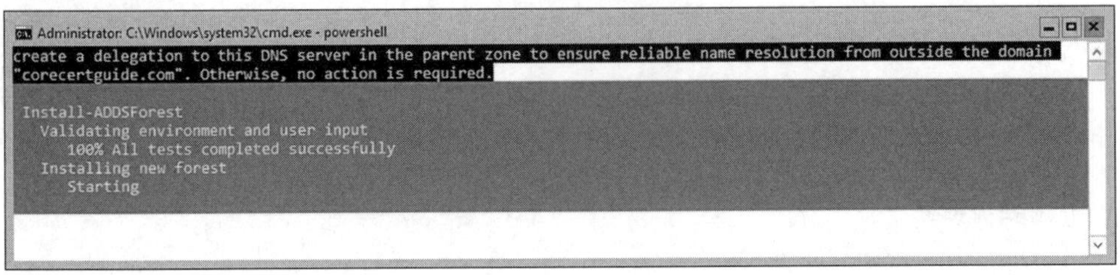

Figure 2-10   The **Install-ADDSForest** PowerShell cmdlet in the Process of Promoting a Member Server to a Domain Controller

Once the server finishes rebooting, the installation and promotion are complete.

Installing a Domain Controller with Install from Media (IFM)

Microsoft Windows Server has the capability to install AD DS and promote a machine to a domain controller from physical media. This is known as *Install from Media (IFM)* and has the benefit of reducing traffic over your network. When additional domain controllers are installed into an existing domain, a sizable amount of data needs to be replicated from the current directory to the directory being created on the new DC. If you need to set up multiple DCs at once, or if the controllers are being created at office locations that have significant latency to the home office (for instance, a VPN tunnel over the public Internet), then using IFM can improve the process and reduce the amount of data replicated over the network.

Creating the Media for Installation

It is important to note that IFM does not preclude all replication traffic over the network. There are still important reasons for the target server to be able to communicate with and download information from the source server during installation. Most notably, any directory changes that have occurred since the media was created need to be synchronized to the target server. For this reason you should aim to use the media created as soon as possible.

Before you begin this process, ensure that you have enough free space on the target location to store the entire directory (and SYSVOL if it's being included).

To create the media to be used during installation:

Step 1.   Log on to a source domain controller. (This must be a full writeable DC. IFM media cannot be created from an RODC).

Step 2.   Open a command prompt.

Step 3.   Type **ntdsutil** and press **Enter**.

Step 4.   At the prompt type **activate instance ntds** and press **Enter**.

Step 5.   At the prompt type **ifm** and press **Enter**.

Step 6.   At the prompt type **create full c:\IFM** and press **Enter** (see Figure 2-11).

```
Select Administrator: Command Prompt - ntdsutil                              —   □   ×

C:\>ntdsutil
ntdsutil: activate instance ntds
Active instance set to "ntds".
ntdsutil: ifm
ifm: create full c:\IFM
Creating snapshot...
Snapshot set {d62e7f25-8c1d-481f-b1ba-231f4a638cc1} generated successfully.
Snapshot {5ad0fa8b-b627-4052-97b2-24edfe30af2a} mounted as C:\$SNAP_201610261845_VOLUMEC$\
Snapshot {5ad0fa8b-b627-4052-97b2-24edfe30af2a} is already mounted.
Initiating DEFRAGMENTATION mode...
     Source Database: C:\$SNAP_201610261845_VOLUMEC$\Windows\NTDS\ntds.dit
     Target Database: c:\IFM\Active Directory\ntds.dit

                 Defragmentation  Status (% complete)

         0    10   20   30   40   50   60   70   80   90   100
         |----|----|----|----|----|----|----|----|----|----|
         ....................................................

Copying registry files...
Copying c:\IFM\registry\SYSTEM
Copying c:\IFM\registry\SECURITY
Snapshot {5ad0fa8b-b627-4052-97b2-24edfe30af2a} unmounted.
IFM media created successfully in c:\IFM
ifm: _
```

Figure 2-11   The ntdsutil Command-line Utility Creates a Folder for an IFM Installation.

The process completes and writes the directory data to the folder specified in Step 6. You can copy this data to any location including network shares and external hard drives to be accessed during the deployment of the target domain controller.

There are four options for the command indicated in Step 6:

- **Create full**: This creates a file used to deploy a writeable domain controller.

- **Create RODC**: This creates a file used to deploy a read-only domain controller.

- **Create Sysvol full**: This creates a file used to deploy a writeable domain controller and includes the SYSVOL in the target location.

- **Create Sysvol RODC**: This creates a file used to deploy a read-only domain controller and includes the SYSVOL in the target location.

You must use the correct option for the desired target server. A file created with **create full** cannot be used to deploy an RODC or vice versa. You also must create the media from the same version of Windows Server as your target. Media created on Windows Server 2012 R2 cannot be used to deploy on Windows Server 2016.

Deploying a Domain Controller Using IFM

Once the media has been prepared, deploying a domain controller using IFM is straightforward.

For a GUI installation, follow the instructions detailed earlier in the chapter in the section, "Adding a New Domain Controller to an Existing Domain." At Step 8, perform the following tasks:

Step 1. Check the box labeled **Install from media**.

Step 2. A **Path:** text box appears. Type or browse to the top-level folder for the media.

Step 3. Click **Verify** to ensure the media is valid and recognizable for the type of DC being promoted (see Figure 2-12).

Step 4. Choose a specific source server from the **Replicate from** pull-down box. This server is used to synchronize and replicate additional data, including any changes to the directory since the media was created. If you have no preference you can leave it as Any domain controller (see Figure 2-12).

 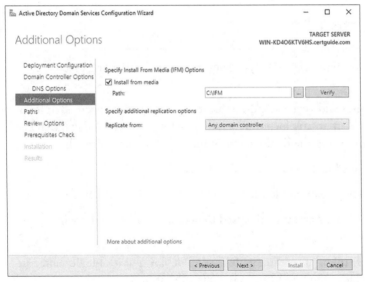

Figure 2-12   The Active Directory Domain Services Configuration Wizard Additional Options Page Allows You to Choose Where the Media Is Located for an IFM Installation.

Step 5. Click **Next**.

Step 6. Continue on with the installation as described earlier in the section "Adding or Removing a Domain Controller from a Domain."

Installing and Configuring a Read-Only Domain Controller (RODC)

Read-only domain controllers (RODC) are a type of domain controller that Microsoft introduced with Windows Server 2008. Like the name implies, an RODC is effectively a slave to the writeable master DCs in the domain. An RODC hosts only a portion of the entire directory and cannot update or propagate changes to the directory itself. This makes the RODC more secure in certain scenarios.

RODCs are meant to be deployed in locations where physical security is not as robust as the organization may like, for example, at a remote site where the server also hosts software or applications that require staff to frequently log on to the domain controller interactively. This can create an unacceptable security risk on a writeable domain controller. RODCs are also suitable for sites where the staff has little knowledge of IT procedures or network bandwidth is at a premium.

To deploy an RODC, there must be at least one writeable domain controller running Windows 2008 or higher in the domain. There are two ways to deploy an RODC controller:

- **Staged**: A dual-step installation where an AD DS Domain Administrator prepares the installation on the source controller and then a user finalizes the installation on the remote server without administrator or elevated rights.

- **Non-staged**: This method installs the RODC in a single step by one user with Domain Administrator credentials.

Using the staged installation method, a user with AD DS Domain Administrator rights performs the first stage by creating an account in the directory for the RODC. Permission to execute the second stage, attaching the RODC to that account, can be delegated to a group or user that doesn't otherwise have administrative rights on the directory. In this way, the second stage can be performed at a remote location without unnecessarily granting elevated rights to users that do not otherwise need them.

The administrator who creates the RODC account during stage 1 can also choose to specify no delegation for second stage permissions. In this case only a member of the Domain Admins or Enterprise Admins groups can execute stage 2 and complete the installation.

To perform a staged RODC installation, follow these steps:

Step 1.   Log on to the source domain controller as a member of the Domain Admins group.

Step 2.   Start Server Manager from either the Start Menu or the Taskbar.

Step 3.   From the navigation menu choose **AD DS**.

Step 4.   Right-click the server and click **Active Directory Users and Computers**.

Step 5.   Right-click the **Domain Controllers** OU and click **Pre-create Read-only Domain Controller account...** (see Figure 2-13).

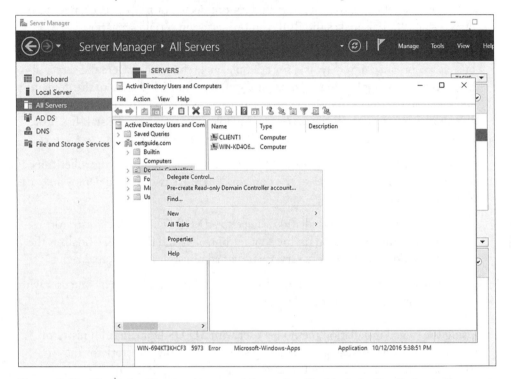

Figure 2-13   The Active Directory Users and Computers Tool Includes the Option to Pre-create a Read-only Domain Controller Account in the Context Menu of the Domain Controllers Folder.

Step 6.   On the welcome screen, click **Next**.

NOTE   If you need to modify the Password Replication Policy (PRP), click the **Use advanced mode installation** box before continuing. Read more about PRP here: https://technet.microsoft.com/en-us/library/rodc-guidance-for-administering-the-password-replication-policy(v=ws.10).aspx.

Step 7.   On the Network Credentials page choose credentials that will be used during the RODC installation. The RODC needs to impersonate this user to perform admin activities since the user you delegate to will not have the authority. Leave **My current logged on credentials** selected or select **Alternate credentials** and click **Set** to choose which user to impersonate (see Figure 2-14).

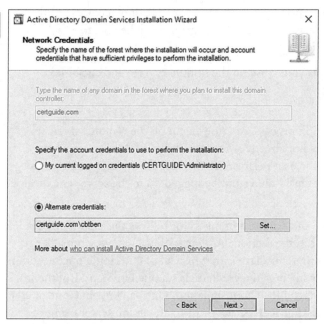

Figure 2-14 The Active Directory Domain Services Installation Wizard Requires Credentials to Be Used During the RODC Installation. Either the Current User Can Be Chosen or an Alternate User from the Domain.

Step 8.   On the Specify the Computer Name page, type the name of the computer that will become the RODC. Note this server must NOT already be a member of the domain. Click **Next**.

Step 9.   On the Select a Site page, select an existing site from the list. Click **Next**.

Step 10.   After a moment the Additional Domain Controller Options page displays. Review the following selections and then click **Next**.

- **DNS server**: Select this box to install DNS on the RODC. This box is checked by default so that users in the remote office can perform name resolution. If you want to uncheck this box, DNS records need to be manually created in an existing on-site DNS server.

- **Global Catalog**: Select this box to add the global catalog to the domain controller. This is necessary for users to be able to log on to the domain when access to the main DC site is offline.

- **Read-only domain controller (RODC)**: When pre-creating an RODC account this option is selected and disabled.

Step 11.   On the Select Users, Computers, and Groups page, type the name of the user or group you want to delegate stage 2 permissions to. You can only type in one security principal. If this is left blank, only members of the Domain Admins or Enterprise Admins groups will be able to attach the RODC server. Click **Next**.

Step 12.   Review the options you chose on the Summary page and click **Next**.

Step 13.   Click **Finish**.

Stage 2, the RODC installation process, can now begin on the remote server. It is important that the server is not already a member server of the domain when this process is started. Also, the user performing this stage must have access to the credentials supplied during Step 11 above but be logged on to the server as a local administrator account.

To attach the RODC server, the remote administrator follows the same steps described earlier in this chapter in the section "Adding a New Domain Controller to an Existing Domain." The difference here is that instead of entering Domain Admin credentials at Step 5, you would enter the credentials supplied in Step 11 of the instructions for performing a staged RODC installation. On the Domain Controller Options page, select **Use existing RODC account** to attach the server using the settings chosen previously.

Installing a DC as an RODC without staging is as simple as following the steps in the earlier section "Adding a New Domain Controller to an Existing Domain." At Step 7, you would simply check the **Read-only domain controller** box.

Configuring Domain Controller Cloning

Virtual machines are an ideal environment for domain controllers. DCs tend to use few resources, benefit from the security and network isolation VMs can provide, and are often being promoted or demoted in a larger domain. There are challenges when using virtualization with Active Directory though. AD DS relies heavily on time synchronization for secure encryption techniques, generation of unique IDs, and other critical functions. Typical features for virtual machines, such as snapshots and cloning, can cause numerous potential problems in the directory because of their impact on time synchronization.

Microsoft recognizes the value of virtualization, and especially the value that virtual cloning can provide for efficient deployment of additional DCs in a domain.

Requirements to Clone a Virtual Domain Controller

There are a few basic requirements needed to take advantage of cloning a virtual DC:

- The hypervisor software must support a feature known as VM-GenerationID. Most later hypervisors do, including all versions of Hyper-V since Windows 2012 and VMware vSphere 5.1 and later.

- The source virtual DC must be running Windows Server 2012 or later.

- The DC owner of the PDC FSMO role must be accessible on the network and running Windows Server 2012 or later.

- The source virtual DC must be a member of the **Cloneable Domain Controllers** group in AD DS.

- An XML configuration file with all the settings the cloned DC will take when it boots named DCCloneConfig.xml. This file includes network settings, DNS, WINS, the AD Site name, the new DC name, and more.

Creating DCCloneConfig.xml

The DCCloneConfig.xml file is used by the cloned DC when it first boots up. The settings in this file tell the cloned DC how to configure itself. While this file can be created from scratch by hand, it is strongly recommend that you use the **New-ADDCCloneConfig** cmdlet in PowerShell to produce the file or modify an existing config previously produced this way.

The command to create the config file is as follows:

```
New-ADDCCloneConfigFile -IPv4Address <String>'
-IPv4DNSResolver <String[]>'
-IPv4SubnetMask <String>'
-Static'
[-AlternateWINSServer <String> ]'
[-CloneComputerName <String> ]'
[-IPv4DefaultGateway <String> ]'
[-Path <String> ]'
[-PreferredWINSServer <String> ]'
[-SiteName <String> ]'
[ <CommonParameters>]
```

You can find the full documentation for the **New-ADDCCloneConfigFile** here: https://technet.microsoft.com/en-us/library/jj158947(v=wps.630).aspx.

To create the config file, follow these steps:

Step 1.   Log on to the virtual machine hosting the DC to be cloned.

Step 2.   Start Server Manager from either the Start Menu or the Taskbar.

Step 3.   From the navigation menu choose **AD DS**.

Step 4.   Right-click the server and click **Active Directory Users and Computers**.

Step 5.   Select the **Users** OU, right-click **Cloneable Domain Controllers**, and choose **Properties**.

Step 6.   Choose the **Members** tab and click **Add…**

Step 7.   Type the name of the source DC for cloning and click **OK** (see Figure 2-15).

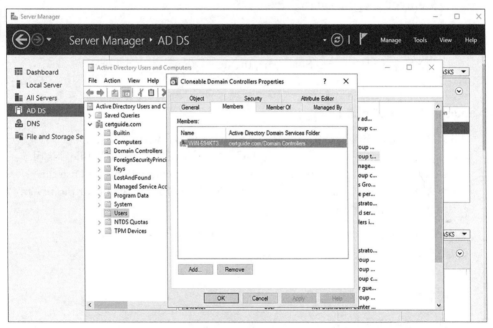

Figure 2-15   The Members Tab of the Properties for the Cloneable Domain Controllers Group Indicates Any Computers That Have Been Added to It.

The domain controller is now a member of the Cloneable Domain Controllers group. The remaining steps that follow will not function if you do not perform this process first. It's also recommended that you re-move the DC from this group once cloning is complete.

Step 8.   Open a command prompt and type **PowerShell** and press **Enter**, or start the PowerShell ISE.

Step 9.   From the PowerShell prompt type the following command and press **Enter**:

Get-ADDCCloningExcludedApplicationList

This lists all software running on the DC that may potentially interfere with DC cloning. Review the list, validate with the appropriate vendors that the listed applications are safe to clone, and then rerun the command with the **-GenerateXml** parameter:

```
Get-ADDCCloningExcludedApplicationList -GenerateXml
```

This adds all the applications to an "allow list" so that cloning can continue.

Step 10.   From the PowerShell prompt type the following command and press **Enter**:

```
New-ADDCCloneConfigFile -IPv4Address desired IP Address
-IPv4DefaultGateway desired IP gateway -IPv4SubnetMask
255.255.255.0 -IPv4DNSResolver DNS server IP1,DNS server IP2
-Static
```

> **NOTE**   IP addresses will be specific to your network configuration.

Step 11.   If the server passes validation, you see a message indicating **All preliminary validation checks passed** and are notified that the DCCloneConfig.xml file was created in the C:\Windows\NTDS folder (see Figure 2-16).

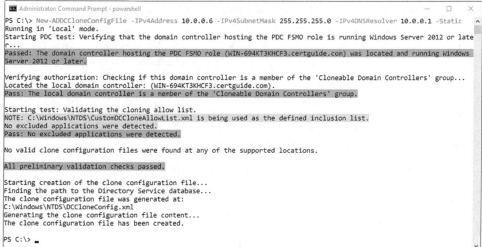

Figure 2-16   PowerShell Creating the DCCloneConfig.xml File

Exporting and Importing the Cloned DC

The final step is to export your VM in the hypervisor and import the clone into a new VM. Follow the instructions for your hypervisor software to perform this task.

Resolving DNS SRV Record Registration Issues

Active Directory Domain Services relies heavily on DNS to locate domain controllers. Specifically, it requires a set of SRV locator records on the DNS server. If those records are not present or are entered incorrectly, users will not be able to connect to and authenticate against AD DS.

If you are running the DNS server on your domain controller with the Microsoft DNS service, you can use the DNS Management Console to verify that the appropriate zones and resource records are there.

Table 2-3 lists the DNS records required for proper Active Directory functionality.

Table 2-3 *DNS Records Required for Active Directory*

Type	DNS Record	Requirements
SRV	_ldap._tcp.pdc._msdcs.<DnsDomainName>	One per domain
SRV	_ldap._tcp.gc._msdcs.<DnsForestName>	At least one per forest
A	_gc._msdcs.<DnsForestName>	At least one per forest
CNAME	<DsaGuide>._msdcs.<DnsForestName>	One per domain controller
SRV	_kerberos._tcp.dc._msdcs.<DnsDomainName>	At least one per domain
SRV	_ldap._tcp.dc._msdcs.<DnsDomainName>	At least one per domain
A	<DomainControllerFQDN>	One per domain controller (Domain controllers that have multiple IP addresses can have more than one A resource record.)

If you have integrated your DC with an existing DNS infrastructure, use the management tools provided to validate these records.

Read more here: https://msdn.microsoft.com/en-us/library/bb727055.aspx.

Configuring a Global Catalog Server

The global catalog (GC) plays a critical role in searches and queries performed against the directory. It is a catalog of all objects in the AD DS forest. Along with a catalog of all objects, it contains a subset of the attributes for each object. In complex AD DS implementations, querying the GC first before querying against the directory itself can often return the desired results. In a multi-forest domain, querying the GC first is required. The subset of attributes that the GC stores can be modified in the Active Directory schema, but this is recommended only for advanced users.

Every domain controller in the domain can potentially store the GC, but it is up to you to determine how many GCs there should be for your implementation. Microsoft recommends the following basic guidelines:

- Even in a simple deployment, install at least two GCs for redundancy purposes. The domain will not function if the only GC goes down.

- Consider a GC at each site in a multi-site network. Having a GC that local computers can easily reach can reduce network latency.

- GCs replicate across the network separately from directory replication, so the more GCs you have the more replication traffic there will be.

To promote an existing domain controller to a global catalog server, follow these steps:

Step 1.   Log on to the domain controller.

Step 2.   Start Server Manager from either the Start Menu or the Taskbar.

Step 3.   From the navigation menu choose **AD DS**.

Step 4.   Right-click the server and click **Active Directory Sites and Services**.

Step 5.   Expand the **Sites** container and expand the site the current DC is located in.

Step 6.   Expand the **Servers** container and expand the entry for the DC.

Step 7.   Right-click **NTDS Settings** and select **Properties**.

Step 8.   On the General tab check the **Global Catalog** box and then click **Apply**.

Transferring and Seizing Operations Master Roles

The Flexible Single Master Operations (FSMO) roles described earlier in this chapter are important pieces for a functioning AD DS deployment. Occasionally you may need to transfer the role from one DC to another. For example, if a controller is being retired or shut down, you will want to transfer the role to another DC prior to that. If the need arises to move those roles from their current DC, there are different management tools required for each role. Table 2-4 summarizes those tools.

Table 2-4   Tools to Transfer Operations Roles

Role	Tool
RID	Active Directory Users and Computers
PDC	Active Directory Users and Computers
Infrastructure master	Active Directory Users and Computers
Domain naming master	Active Directory Domains and Trusts
Schema master	Active Directory Schema Snap-In

To change the RID, PDC, or infrastructure master role, you need to "seize" it from the current master:

Step 1.   Log on to the domain controller that you want to host the role.

Step 2.   Start Server Manager from either the Start Menu or the Taskbar.

Step 3.   From the navigation menu choose **AD DS**.

Step 4.   Right-click the server and click **Active Directory Users and Computers**.

Step 5.   Right-click the domain in the left-hand pane and select **Operations Masters**.

Step 6.   On the Operations Masters dialog, choose the tab for the role you want to seize (RID, PDC, and Infrastructure are available).

Step 7.   Note the current master is listed, and the current machine name is in the second text box. To seize the role click **Change**.

Step 8.   Click **Yes** to confirm.

Step 9.   Once the transfer is complete click **OK**.

To change the domain naming master you need to "seize" it from the current master:

Step 1.   Log on to the domain controller that you want to host the role.

Step 2.   Start Server Manager from either the Start Menu or the Taskbar.

Step 3.   From the navigation menu choose **AD DS**.

Step 4.   Right-click the server and click **Active Directory Domains and Trusts**.

Step 5.   Right-click the Active Directory Domains and Trusts in the left-hand pane and select **Operations Masters**. (Note: Right-click on the top-level node that reads Active Directory Domains and Trusts, not on the domain itself.)

Step 6.   Note the current master is listed, and the current machine name is in the second text box. To seize the role click **Change**.

Step 7.   Click **Yes** to confirm.

Step 8.   Once the transfer is complete click **OK**.

To change the schema master, you first need to activate the Schema snap-in:

Step 1.   Log on to the domain controller that you want to host the role.

Step 2.   Open a command prompt.

Step 3.   Type **regsvr32 schmmgmt.dll** and press **Enter**.

Step 4.   Click **OK** on the success dialog.

Step 5.   At the command prompt type **mmc** and press **Enter**.

Step 6.   The MMC window launches. Click **File** and then select **Add/Remove Snap-in**.

Step 7.   Select the **Active Directory Schema** snap-in from the list of Available snap-ins on the left and then click **Add.**

Step 8.   Click **OK**.

Step 9.   On the MMC window click to select the **Active Directory Schema** snap-in. Two folders, classes and attributes, should show up on the right.

Step 10.   Right-click the **Active Directory Schema** and select **Operations Master**.

Step 11.   Note the current master is listed, and the current machine name is in the second text box. To seize the role click **Change**.

Step 12.   Click **Yes** to confirm.

Step 13.   Once the transfer is complete click **OK**.

Exam Preparation Tasks

As mentioned in the section "Book Features" in the Introduction, you have a few choices for exam preparation: the exercises here; Chapter 17, "Final Preparation"; and the exam simulation questions in the Pearson Test Prep Software Online.

Review All Key Topics

Review the most important topics in this chapter, noted with the Key Topics icon in the outer margin of the page. Table 2-5 lists a reference of these key topics and the page number on which each is found.

Table 2-5   Key Topics for Chapter 2

Key Topic Element	Description	Page Number
List	Types of domain structure you can plan for	26
Figure 2-1	Additional Windows Features required by AD DS	29
Figure 2-4	Important options to choose when promoting a server to DC	31
List	List of FSMO roles	34
Figure 2-6	Choosing appropriate credentials to join the domain	36
Figure 2-7	How to demote a server before removing AD DS	38
Table 2-2	Windows Server 2016 Upgrade Paths	39
Figure 2-8	How to raise the forest functional level	40
Command	The PowerShell command to install AD DS	41
Command	The PowerShell command to promote a server to a DC	42
Figure 2-11	Creating the media for an IFM installation	45
List	The options available when creating IFM media	45
Figure 2-12	Selecting the IFM option during DC promotion	46
List	Staged versus Non-Staged RODC installation	47
Figure 2-14	Choosing the appropriate credentials for a staged installation	49
Command	The PowerShell command to create the DCCloneConfig.xml file	51
Figure 2-15	Adding the server to the Cloneable Domain Controllers group	52
Figure 2-16	Output from the New-ADDCCloneConfigFile command	53
Table 2-3	Required DNS records for Active Directory	54
Paragraph	Explanation of the Global Catalog (GC)	55
Table 2-4	List of the FSMO roles and utility used to transfer them	56

Complete Tables and Lists from Memory

Print a copy of Appendix B, "Memory Tables" (found on the book website), or at least the section for this chapter, and complete the tables and lists from memory. Appendix C, "Memory Tables Answer Key," also on the website, includes completed tables and lists to check your work.

Define Key Terms

Define the following key terms from this chapter and check your answers in the glossary:

> single domain, multi-domain, multi-forest, Desktop Experience, Server Core, Server Manager, promotion, FSMO, forest functional level, domain functional level, demotion, IFM, RODC, staged installation, cloning, global catalog

End-of-Chapter Review Questions

The answers to these questions appear in Appendix A. For more practice with exam format questions, use the Pearson Test Prep Software Online.

The next five questions apply to the following scenario:

You have been tasked with implementing Active Directory Domain Services at your company. Your company has two offices: a central office with 150 employees and a regional office with 45 employees. They are connected via VPN over WAN. IT personnel at the regional office will manage and maintain user accounts there.

1. You need to plan for a domain strategy. Which option would be most appropriate?

    a. Install a separate forest at each site managing their own domain and establish a two-way transitive trust between the forests.

    b. Install a single-domain forest and separate objects into OUs based on their physical location in the central or regional office.

    c. Install a multi-domain forest and hire remote IT administrators to manage the domain for the regional office.

    d. Install a multi-domain forest and use only an RODC at the regional office for the second domain.

2. You have promoted a server to a domain controller for the company domain. You would like another domain controller on the network, but your manager is hesitant about the cost. What factors would justify the additional expense? (Choose all that apply.)

   a. Redundancy in the event of a failure of the first DC

   b. Enabling remote administration for IT staff in the regional office

   c. Increased security through segmentation of data

   d. Improved performance during periods of high usage

3. Reviewing your AD DS plan, you decide that the second DC must contain the global catalog as well as function as the domain naming master. Which two steps must be performed? (Choose two.)

   a. Install a copy of the domain naming master to the second DC.

   b. Transfer the global catalog to the second DC.

   c. Transfer the domain naming master to the second DC.

   d. Install a copy of the Global Catalog on the second DC.

4. Your company has grown over the past six months, and the need for a third DC has come up. You have chosen to utilize Server Core for this server. You need to ensure all prerequisites for AD DS are installed. What is the full command you'll use to install the AD DS role on the server?

5. Now that the AD DS role has been installed, you need to promote the server. You must ensure that DNS is also installed. What PowerShell command will you use to promote the server to a domain controller in your existing domain?

6. What is the command-line utility used to create IFM media?

7. What is the correct order of steps below to perform a staged RODC installation?

   a. Install AD DS on the remote server.

   b. Specify credentials for the remote server to impersonate.

   c. Promote the server to a domain controller.

   d. Pre-create an RODC account on an existing domain controller.

8. You are preparing to clone a VM operating as a domain controller on your network. What is the command to discover if there is any software running that may potentially interfere with the process?

   a. **New-ADDCClongConfigFile**

   b. **Get-ADDCCloningExcludedApplicationList**

   c. **Get-ADDCCloningValidationList**

   d. **DCClongConfig.xml**

9. You have installed AD DS into your existing environment and chosen to con-tinue using the existing DNS infrastructure that is already supported by your network. How can you ensure the DNS hosts have the proper records installed for AD DS?

    a. Run gpupdate /force.

    b. Install AD DS on the DNS hosts.

    c. Manually add the required records to the DNS host(s).

    d. Run the djoin utility.

10. Which types of DNS records are required in the DNS host for the domain controller to function properly? (Choose all that apply.)

    a. SRV

    b. A

    c. CNAME

    d. MX

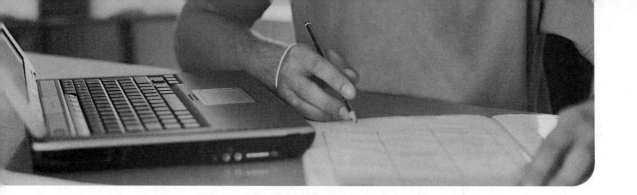

This chapter covers the following topics:

- **Creating, Copying, Configuring, and Deleting Users and Computers**: This section covers how to use the Active Directory Administrative Center to work with user and computer accounts in AD DS.

- **Automating the Creation of Active Directory Accounts**: This section covers how to use Windows PowerShell to work with user and computer accounts in AD DS.

- **Performing Bulk Active Directory Operations**: This section introduces the csvde and ldifde utilities for bulk exporting and importing of objects in AD DS.

- **Configuring User Rights**: This section introduces the Group Policy Management Editor and demonstrates how to change basic user permissions.

- **Implementing Offline Domain Join**: This section describes the process of an offline domain join and how to use the djoin utility.

- **Managing Inactive and Disabled Accounts**: This section discusses locked and disabled accounts and how to use Windows PowerShell to manage those accounts.

CHAPTER 3

Creating and Managing Active Directory Users and Computers

Once you've successfully installed a domain controller (or multiple domain controllers), your Active Directory Domain Services directory is up and running. Even in the default state, there is a lot that can be done with a directory, but you'll almost certainly be ready to start creating user account objects. By creating users and computers, you can populate the directory with the most common type of object you'll run into, namely, the people who work at your organization.

This chapter covers the basics for creating user account objects in your AD DS directory so that those people can log on to the network. We also discuss how to pre-create a computer account in the directory so that the computer those users use is recognized as they join the domain. Finally, we look at various scripting utilities that can be used to ease and automate this process.

"Do I Know This Already?" Quiz

The "Do I Know This Already?" quiz allows you to assess whether you should read this entire chapter thoroughly or jump to the "Exam Preparation Tasks" section. If you are in doubt about your answers to these questions or your own assessment of your knowledge of the topics, read the entire chapter. Table 3-1 lists the major headings in this chapter and their corresponding "Do I Know This Already?" quiz questions. You can find the answers in Appendix A, "Answers to the 'Do I Know This Already?' Quizzes."

Table 3-1 Do I Know This Already?" Section-to-Question Mapping

Foundation Topics Section	Questions
Creating, Copying, Configuring, and Deleting Users and Computers	1-3
Automating the Creation of Active Directory Accounts	4-5
Performing Bulk Active Directory Operations	6-7

Foundation Topics Section	Questions
Configuring User Rights	8
Implementing Offline Domain Join	9
Managing Inactive and Disabled Accounts	10-11

CAUTION   The goal of self-assessment is to gauge your mastery of the topics in this chapter. If you do not know the answer to a question or are only partially sure of the answer, you should mark that question as wrong for purposes of the self-assessment. Giving yourself credit for an answer you correctly guess skews your self-assessment results and might provide you with a false sense of security.

1. Which of the following tools can be used to create users in Active Directory Domain Services? (Choose all that apply.)

   a. Active Directory Administrative Center

   b. dcpromo.exe

   c. Active Directory Users and Computers

   d. Windows PowerShell

2. An account with the "Protect from accidental deletion" flag checked can still be deleted by doing which of the following?

   a. Using the **-Force** option with Windows PowerShell

   b. Using the Active Directory Administrative Center

   c. Deleting the account from a member of the Domain Admins group.

   d. Editing the account and unchecking **Protect from accidental deletion**

3. The finance department has just hired ten temporary employees for seasonal work. You need to create user accounts for all ten individuals with the same restricted access. One efficient way to go about this would be to perform which of the following?

   a. Delegate user creation to a manager in finance.

   b. Use a template account.

   c. Provide an RODC to the finance department.

   d. Share a single account among all ten temps.

4. What is the cmdlet to create a new user in the directory?

   a. New-ADUser

   b. Create-ADUser

   c. New-ADAccount

   d. Create-ADAccount

5. What is the cmdlet to query the directory for a user?

   a. Query-ADUser

   b. Get-ADUser

   c. Query-ADAccount

   d. Get-ADAccount

6. Which command-line utilities can be used to extract directory information from AD DS? (Choose all that apply.)

   a. djoin

   b. dcpromo

   c. csvde

   d. ldifde

7. If a mode is not specified for **csvde**, in what mode does it operate?

   a. export

   b. query

   c. update

   d. import

8. If an account does not have a policy specified for it, what policy will be applied?

   a. Group Policy Object (GPO)

   b. No Policy

   c. Default Domain Policy

   d. Default Forest Policy

9. What is the utility to start the offline domain join process?

   a. dcpromo

   b. csvde

   c. ldifde

   d. djoin

10. What is the PowerShell cmdlet to enable and disable AD DS accounts?

   a. **Set-ADAccountPassword**

   b. **Enable-ADUser**

   c. **Set-ADUser**

   d. **Disable-ADAccount**

11. What is the PowerShell cmdlet to reset an account password?

   a. **Set-ADAccountPassword**

   b. **Enable-ADUser**

   c. **Set-ADUser**

   d. **Disable-ADAccount**

Creating, Copying, Configuring, and Deleting Users and Computers

When you first install a new forest and domain, Active Directory Domain Services populates the directory with a collection of default users and groups. Of course, those will bear no relationship to your actual organization. Most likely the first step you need to perform in a new domain is to introduce user and computer accounts for the personnel in your organization who will be connecting to the network.

Without a user account in the directory, a user cannot log on to the network and view file shares, connect to printers, download emails, or perform other secure network-enabled tasks. Without a computer account in the directory, a computer is not allowed to log on either, meaning both the user and the computer the user wants to log on from must be established in the directory for a successful logon.

NOTE   When a user signs in to a domain, the user typically has the rights to join the computer as well, which will create the computer account in the directory if it doesn't already exist. Creating the computer account ahead of time is still a good idea since you can assign it to the proper OU and security groups before it connects.

Users can be created using the GUI interface on Windows Server 2016 Desktop Experience with either the legacy Active Directory Users and Computers (ADUC) tool or the newer Active Directory Administrative Center (ADAC) tool. On Server Core or in cases of remote administration, Microsoft PowerShell can be used to perform all these same functions. In fact, the Active Directory Administrative Center just invokes PowerShell in the background to complete its tasks.

These tools look and function similarly to one another, but this book focuses on the Active Directory Administrative Center whenever appropriate and utilizes the legacy tools only in cases where it's required.

Creating and Configuring a New User

To create a new user account in Active Directory Domain Services:

Step 1.   Log on to a writeable domain controller.

Step 2.   Start Server Manager from either the Start Menu or Taskbar.

Step 3.   From the context menu at the top of the panel, click **Tools** and then select **Active Directory Administrative Center**.

Step 4.   On the left-hand panel select the domain you want to add users to. The
right-hand panel displays the top-level containers that are created in a
directory by default (see Figure 3-1).

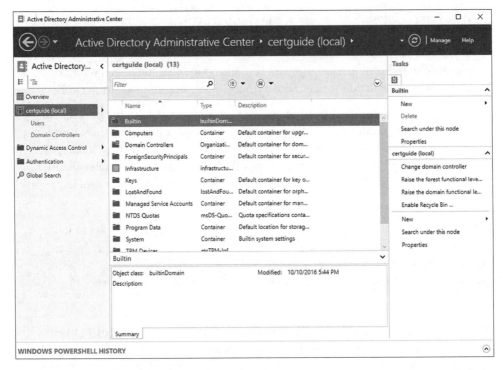

Figure 3-1   The Active Directory Administrative Center with a Domain Highlighted. The Default
Domain Containers Can Be Seen Listed in the Central Panel.

Step 5.   Double-click the container or organizational unit you want to add the
user to. This is typically either Users or a custom OU you have created.

Step 6.   On the Tasks panel click **New**; then select **User**.

Step 7.   You are presented with a dialog box of information to fill out about the
user you want to create. All these values are attributes on a User object in
AD DS. Some of the more common fields are covered here (see Figure
3-2).

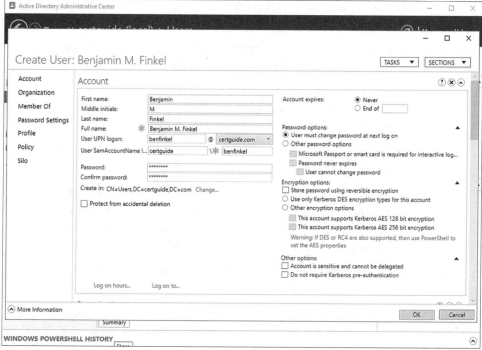

Figure 3-2   The Create User Dialog Box from the Active Directory Administrative Center

- **First, Middle, and Last name**: These are simple text values that relate to the user's name.

- **User UPN logon**: This is the username the user can use to log on with the DNS-style domain name. Note how similar it is to an email address.

- **User SamAccountName logon**: This is the username the user can use to log on with the legacy-style NetBIOS logon format.

- **Password**: Enter an initial password for the user. It must meet any defined password policies for the domain.

- **Create in**: Indicates the OU and domain you chose to create this user in. You can change this here, and the object will be created elsewhere in the directory.

- **Protect from accidental deletion**: Check this box to prevent the user object from being deleted. If an administrator wants to delete the object, the administrator must configure the account and uncheck this box.

- **Log on hours…**: Click this link to set specific days and times when the user is allowed to log on to the network.

- **Log on to…**: Click this link to specify computer objects in the directory the user can use to log on to the network.

- **Account expires**: This setting allows you to create a temporary account with a set expiration date. This is useful for temp workers or staff that you only want to grant access for a specified period of time.

- **Password options**: Use these settings to dictate what choices the user has with his password.

- **Encryption options**: Use these settings to override the default storage settings for passwords. Note that selecting the **Store password using reversible encryption** option reduces security since by default passwords are stored with a one-way hash.

- **Other options**: Use these settings to configure additional nonstandard options for user accounts.

Step 8. You can select the different tabs from the left side of the wizard to configure additional attributes or simply scroll the right-hand panel down to each section.

- **Organization**: Basic demographic details about the user including phone numbers, mailing address, and job title. Including this information in the directory is useful for searching and query purposes.

- **Member Of**: This panel allows you to add the user to existing Group objects in the directory. Groups are covered in further detail in Chapter 4, "Creating and Managing Active Directory Groups and Organizational Units." Click **Add** to bring up the basic directory search dialog box. Type in **Domain** and click **Check Names** to see a list of groups that begin with Domain that the user can be added to. Double-click **Domain Users** to add that to the group list, and then click **OK**.

- **Password Settings**: Use this to apply user or group-specific password settings that override the domain password settings. This is covered in further detail in Chapter 5, "Configuring Service Authentication and Account Policies."

- **Profile**: This panel allows you to specify:

  - **Profile path**: This can be used to store the user's profile folders (e.g., My Documents, Desktop, etc.) so they follow the user regardless of what computer the user logs on to.

> - **Home folder**: Allows you to map a drive on the user's computer to a network share where the user can store and retrieve files from anywhere on the network.
>
> - **Log on script**: Allows you to specify a command-line script to execute when the user logs on to the network.

Step 9.   Click **OK**.

The user has now been added to the directory and can log on using the username and password specified during step 7. If you chose **User must change password at next log on,** when the user logs on she is forced through a password change process.

The same dialog box used during user creation can be accessed any time by

- Double-clicking the user object in ADAC

- Right-clicking the user object and choosing **Properties** in ADAC

- Selecting the user object in ADAC and clicking **Properties** in the Tasks panel

From there you can change or adjust any of the settings for the user object.

Creating and Configuring a New Computer

Creating a computer object is similar to creating a user object. Recall from Chapter 1, "Introducing Active Directory 2016," that objects have a class, and that class defines which attributes an object will have. Computers are a separate class from users; consequently, the configuration options in the dialog are different, although they do share many attributes (as do many object classes in AD DS).

To create a new computer account in Active Directory Domain Services:

Step 1.   Log on to a writeable domain controller.

Step 2.   Start Server Manager from either the Start Menu or Taskbar.

Step 3.   From the context menu at the top of the panel click **Tools** and then select **Active Directory Administrative Center**.

Step 4.   On the left-hand panel select the domain you want to add users to. The right-hand panel displays the top-level containers that are created in a directory by default.

Step 5.   Double-click the container or organizational unit you want to add the user to. This is typically either Computers or a custom OU you have created.

Step 6.   On the Tasks panel click **New** and then select **Computer**.

Step 7.   You are presented with a dialog box of information to fill out about the computer object you want to create. All these values are attributes on a computer object in AD DS. Some of the more common fields are covered here (see Figure 3-3):

Figure 3-3   The Create Computer Dialog Box from Active Directory Administrative Center

- **Computer name**: Type in the name of the new computer account here.

- **Computer (NetBIOS) name**: This defaults to be the same as the name typed above. The NetBIOS name is used for backward compatibility and should always be the same as the object name.

- **Create in**: Indicates the OU and domain you choose to create this computer in. You can change this here, and the object will be created elsewhere in the directory.

- **User or Group**: This setting indicates which group or user is allowed to modify the local computer settings to join that computer to the domain. If the computer is being set up at a remote location by administrators who are not members of the Domain Admins group you may need to change this.

- **Assign this computer account as a Pre-Windows 2000 computer**: This should be checked if the computer is running an operating system from pre-Windows 2000 (e.g., Windows NT).

- **Protect from accidental deletion**: Check this box to prevent the computer object from being deleted. If an administrator wants to delete the object, the administrator must configure the account and uncheck this box.

Step 8. You can select the different tabs from the left side of the wizard to configure additional attributes or simply scroll the right-hand panel down to each section.

- **Managed By**: Click **Edit** to find a user account in the directory that will be associated with the computer object. These values can then be searched or queried for.

- **Member Of**: This panel allows you to add the computer to existing Group objects in the directory. Groups are covered in further detail in Chapter 4.

Step 9. Click **OK**.

The computer object is now in the directory, and users can log on to the network using that computer. Computers are matched to their directory entry by the Computer Name field chosen in step 7 in the preceding list. The first time the computer joins the domain the user performing the join must be a member of the group chosen during step 7.

The same dialog box used during computer creation can be accessed any time by

- Double-clicking the computer object in ADAC

- Right-clicking the computer object and choosing **Properties** in ADAC

- Selecting the computer object in ADAC and clicking **Properties** in the Tasks panel

Copying Users

Building out each new object in Active Directory Domain Services from scratch might be a time-consuming process. It's also not very efficient, especially when you may have users that share many properties from account to account. For instance, every time a new user is hired by the accounting department, that user likely needs almost everything set up the same as other users in the accounting department. In this case, instead of creating a new user from scratch it can be easier to simply copy an existing object and then only modify the specific attributes that need to change.

Copying objects is not supported in Active Directory Administrative Center, so you need to use the Active Directory Users and Computers (ADUC) tool to perform this operation. Don't worry; it's just as easy to use.

To copy a user or computer account

Step 1.   Log on to a writeable domain controller.

Step 2.   Start Server Manager from either the Start Menu or Taskbar.

Step 3.   From the context menu at the top of the panel, click **Tools** and then select **Active Directory Users and Computers**.

Step 4.   On the left navigation panel, expand the domain you want to manage; select the container or OU where the object you want to copy resides.

Step 5.   In the right panel, right-click the object you want to copy and select **Copy**.

> **NOTE**   Because ADAC and ADUC are simply tools that provide a window into the same source directory, anything you've done in one tool is immediately visible in the other. In this case you should see the users and computers you just created in their respective OUs.

Step 6.   The Copy Object Wizard pops up, prompting you for basic user information that is either expected to be or needs to be filled in to make this object unique. Fill in these values and then click **Next** (see Figure 3-4).

   - **User logon name**: This is the same value as the **User UPN logon** from the User Options dialog in ADAC.

   - **User logon name (pre-Windows 2000)**: This is the same value as the **User SamAccountName logon** from the User Options dialog in ADAC.

Step 7.   The Copy Object Wizard displays password settings prompts. These are the equivalent settings as their counterparts in the User Options dialog in ADAC. Type in the initial user password and confirm it. Check any additional settings you want to enable and click **Next**.

Step 8.   Review your choices on the final page of the wizard and click **Finish**.

The user object has now been copied into the same location in the directory as the original user object.

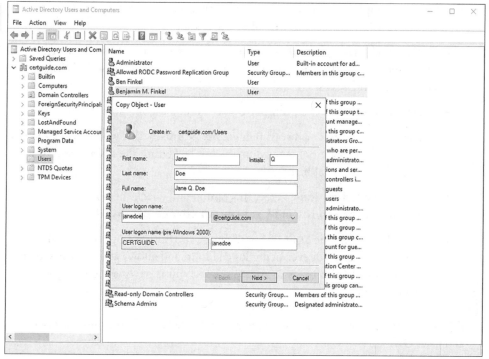

Figure 3-4   The Copy Object - User Wizard Prompting for Values to Apply to the New User Object

Configuring Templates

Using existing users can be useful as a source for copying and creating new user accounts, but it does have some drawbacks. There may not be a suitable user in the directory that you want to copy from. There may also be users with additional security permissions that you do not typically want to grant to new users. In the earlier example, if the source user account for the new hire was a manager or department head, their account may well have access to network objects that new hires should not have. If you forget to remove that group member or revoke that access after copying the user, you have a potential security problem on your hands.

As a solution, one option is to create a template account. A template account is nothing more than a user account that doesn't represent an actual user on the network, cannot be activated or logged on to, and is used only as a source for copying and creating new user accounts. This template account can exist once in the directory, or multiple copies can be created in each OU. The template account can have just the base level of permissions and security group membership that new user accounts should receive.

To create the template account, follow the instructions for creating a new user account earlier in this chapter with the following specifics:

- **Full Name**: Type **_Template** as the user's name. Using the underscore character ensures the object will sort to the top of the list in both ADAC and ADUC, making it easy to find.

- **User UPN logon**: Type **_template** as the user's logon name.

- **Password**: Leave the password field blank. Normally this would be a violation of the password policies for the domain, but by setting the following settings you are able to leave it blank:

- **Other password options**: Select this option and check the boxes for **Password never expires** and **User cannot change password**.

- **Log on hours…**: Click this link and choose the option **Logon Denied**. This prevents the user from ever being logged in to and allows you to save with a blank password. This helps to ensure the account is never accidentally enabled and logged on to.

Select any other settings or group membership desired for the base user template and click **OK**.

You can now use this template user account as a source for copying, as described earlier in this chapter.

Deleting Objects

Objects can easily be removed from the directory using the ADAC:

Step 1.   Log on to a writeable domain controller.

Step 2.   Start Server Manager from either the Start Menu or Taskbar.

Step 3.   From the context menu at the top of the panel click **Tools** and then select **Active Directory Administrative Center**.

Step 4.   On the left-hand panel select the domain you want to delete objects from. The right-hand panel displays the top-level containers that are created in a directory by default.

Step 5.   Double-click the container or organizational unit you want to delete the object from.

Step 6.   Select the object in the right-hand pane and then click **Delete** from the Tasks menu (see Figure 3-5).

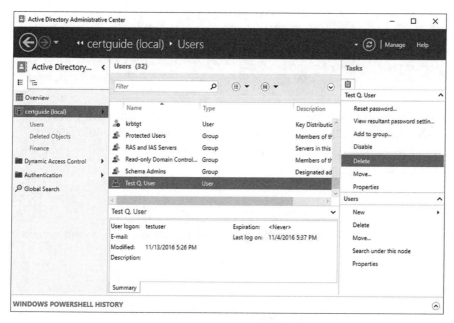

Figure 3-5 Deleting an Object from the Directory Using Active Directory Administrative Center

Alternatively, you can right-click the object and select **Delete** from the context menu.

Step 7.   If the object had **Protect object from deletion** checked, you will not be able to delete it until you edit the properties and uncheck that box.

Automating the Creation of Active Directory Accounts

The GUI is a useful tool for working with Active Directory Domain Services, and the legacy utilities such as Active Directory Users and Computers offer the full suite of functionality that AD DS offers. There are also times when you may want to programmatically script your activities in the AD DS directory that a user interface does not allow for.

Working with Server Core, for instance, requires everything to be done from the command line. Attaching AD DS operations onto other scripted functions or scheduled tasks is also not possible with the GUI tools.

Windows PowerShell is a task-based command-line shell and scripting language designed especially for system administration. PowerShell includes an Active Directory module that contains all the cmdlets used for administering Active Directory. This module is installed onto your Windows Server system when you install the AD DS role (see Chapter 2, "Installing and Configuring Domain Controllers").

> **NOTE**   While we cover a number of different PowerShell cmdlets throughout this book, you can read the most up-to-date documentation for every PowerShell cmdlet here: https://technet.microsoft.com/en-us/library/ee617195.aspx.

To import this module into your current PowerShell script or environment, type **Import-Module ActiveDirectory** or launch **Active Directory Module for Windows PowerShell** from Administrative Tools to get a PowerShell prompt with the module already imported.

Working with Users

There are three basic cmdlets for working with users in PowerShell, as outlined in Table 3-2.

Table 3-2   PowerShell cmdlets for Working with Users

PowerShell cmdlet	Description
Get-ADUser	Returns one or more AD user accounts
Set-ADUser	Updates the properties of an AD user account
New-ADUser	Creates a new Active Directory user
Remove-ADUser	Deletes a user from the directory

The **Get-ADUser** cmdlet has three different parameter sets: Identity, Filter, and LDAPFilter. Filter and LDAPFilter are used to search for and retrieve multiple users from the directory, whereas Identity is the default parameter set and returns a single user account.

The PowerShell command to retrieve a user by identity from the directory is

```
Get-ADUser [-Identity] <ADUser>'
```

For the identity parameter you can supply the object name, DistinguishedName, SamAccountName, SID, or ObjectGUID. See the example that follows and the results in Figure 3-6.

```
Get-ADUser cbtben
```

```
Select Administrator: Command Prompt - powershell                          —    □    ×
PS C:\> Get-ADUser cbtben


DistinguishedName : CN=Ben Finkel,CN=Users,DC=certguide,DC=com
Enabled           : True
GivenName         : Ben
Name              : Ben Finkel
ObjectClass       : user
ObjectGUID        : 0378a100-4872-4bd4-ac13-d9fcc27b9f80
SamAccountName    : cbtben
SID               : S-1-5-21-4245515385-270232610-2476381508-1103
Surname           : Finkel
UserPrincipalName : cbtben@certguide.com


PS C:\> _
```

Figure 3-6   The **Get-ADUser** cmdlet Returning Basic Properties About a User

When you use the Filter or LDAPFilter parameter set, you may also supply a set of search parameters as referenced here:

```
Get-ADUser [-Filter]'
[-SearchBase <string>]'
[-SearchScope {<Base> | <OneLevel> | <Subtree>}]
```

The **-SearchScope** parameter specifies the scope of the search. Possible values are

- Base (0)

- OneLevel (1)

- Subtree (2)

A Base query only searches the path supplied in the **SearchScope** parameter. OneLevel specifies the base path plus the immediate children. A scope of Subtree will search recursively through all descendants of the SearchBase.

The **-SearchBase** parameter specifies where to search the directory. The value is supplied in X.500 format, for example:

```
-SearchBase "cn=Users,dc=certguide,dc=com"
```

The **Set-ADUser** cmdlet can be used either with a specified **-Identity** parameter or with an existing ADUser object instance.

> **NOTE**   The full cmdlet reference for **Set-ADUser** is too long to print in this book in its entirety. We have indicated the most useful or interesting properties. The full documentation can be found here: https://technet.microsoft.com/en-us/library/ee617215.aspx.

The PowerShell command to modify an existing AD user is

```
Set-ADUser [-Identity] <ADUser>'
[-Replace <hashtable>]'
[-CannotChangePassword <System.Nullable[bool]>]'
[-ChangePasswordAtLogon <System.Nullable[bool]>]'
[-City <string>]
[-DisplayName <string>]'
[-Enabled <System.Nullable[bool]>]'
[-HomeDirectory <string>]'
[-HomeDrive <string>]'
[-PasswordNeverExpires <System.Nullable[bool]>]'
[-ProfilePath <string>]'
[-SamAccountName <string>]'
[-UserPrincipalName <string>]'
```

For the **-Identity** parameter you can supply the object name, DistinguishedName, SamAccountName, SID, or ObjectGUID. Enabled must be set to either true or false to enable or disable the account. Refer to the following example:

Set-ADUser has many common properties of a user object built into it. If you're not sure whether the cmdlet takes the property you need to set as a parameter, the **-Replace** parameter allows you to specify any attribute on the user object with a simple PowerShell hashtable. For example, the following command searches the Finance OU and replaces the title of each user object found with the value **"Manager"**:

```
Get-ADUser -Filter -SearchScope 0 -SearchBase "ou=Finance,dc=certguide
,dc=com" | Set-ADUser -Replace @{title="Manager"}
```

> **NOTE** This example relies on stock PowerShell features such as hashtables and the pipe (|) command. You need to know these common PowerShell features for the exam. Take care to brush up before you sit for the test.

> **NOTE** The **Set-ADUser** cmdlet can also take an AD User object variable if the **-Instance** switch is supplied.

The **New-ADUser** cmdlet has a single property set, but it can take almost all the attributes for a User Account that can be specified in the GUI.

> **NOTE**   The full cmdlet reference for **New-ADUser** is too long to print in this book in its entirety. We have indicated the most useful or interesting properties. The full documentation can be found here: https://technet.microsoft.com/en-us/library/ee617253.aspx.

The PowerShell command to add a user to the directory is as follows:

```
New-ADUser [-Name] <string>'
[-AccountPassword <SecureString>]'
[-CannotChangePassword <System.Nullable[bool]>]'
[-ChangePasswordAtLogon <System.Nullable[bool]>]'
[-Description <string>]'
[-DisplayName <string>]'
[-EmailAddress <string>]'
[-Enabled <System.Nullable[bool]>]'
[-HomeDirectory <string>]'
[-HomeDrive <string>]'
[-OtherAttributes <hashtable>]'
[-PasswordNeverExpires <System.Nullable[bool]>]'
[-ProfilePath <string>]'
[-SamAccountName <string>]'
[-ScriptPath <string>]'
[-UserPrincipalName <string>]
```

Consider the following example:

```
$pw = ConvertTo-SecureString Password123 -AsPlainText -Force
New-ADUser "Jane Doe" -AccountPassword $pw -UserPrincipalName janedoe
```

The **Remove-ADUser** cmdlet is straightforward. It has one parameter set and takes an identity parameter similar to **Get-ADUser** to identify the user to remove.

The PowerShell command to remove a user from the directory is as follows:

```
Remove-ADUser [-Identity] <ADUser>'
[-AuthType {<Negotiate> | <Basic>}]'
[-Credential <PSCredential>]'
[-Partition <string>]'
[-Server <string>]'
[-Confirm]'
[-WhatIf]'
[<CommonParameters>]
```

Consider the following example:

```
Remove-ADUser janedoe
```

Working with Computers

As outlined in Table 3-3, there are three basic cmdlets for working with computers in PowerShell.

Table 3-3   PowerShell cmdlets for Working with Computers

PowerShell cmdlet	Description
Get-ADComputer	Returns one or more AD computer objects
New-ADComputer	Creates a new Active Directory computer
Remove-ADComputer	Deletes a computer from the directory

The Computer cmdlets work similarly to the cmdlets for users. There are three parameter sets for **Get-ADComputer**: Identity, Filter, and LDAPFilter. Filter and LDAPFilter are used to search for and retrieve multiple computers from the directory, whereas Identity is the default parameter set and returns a single computer object.

The PowerShell command to retrieve a computer from the directory is as follows:

```
Get-ADComputer [-Identity] <ADComputer>
```

For the **-Identity** parameter you can supply the DistinguishedName, SamAccountName, SID, or ObjectGUID. See the example that follows and the results in Figure 3-7.

```
Get-ADComputer CLIENT1
```

```
Administrator: Command Prompt - powershell                                    —   □   ×

PS C:\> Get-ADComputer CLIENT1


DistinguishedName : CN=CLIENT1,CN=Computers,DC=certguide,DC=com
DNSHostName       : CLIENT1.certguide.com
Enabled           : True
Name              : CLIENT1
ObjectClass       : computer
ObjectGUID        : 795c4868-082e-42bf-97e7-7749c608c688
SamAccountName    : CLIENT1$
SID               : S-1-5-21-4245515385-270232610-2476381508-1105
UserPrincipalName :



PS C:\> _
```

Figure 3-7   The **Get-ADComputer** cmdlet Returning Basic Properties About a Computer

The **New-ADComputer** cmdlet has a single property set, but it can take almost all the attributes for a computer account that can be specified in the GUI.

> **NOTE**   The full cmdlet reference for **New-ADComputer** is too long to print in this book in its entirety. We have indicated some of the common properties. The full documentation can be found here: https://technet.microsoft.com/en-us/library/ee617245.aspx.

The PowerShell command to add a computer to the directory is as follows:

```
New-ADComputer [-Name] <string>
[-OperatingSystem <string>]'
[-OperatingSystemVersion <string>]'
[-SAMAccountName <string>]
[-UserPrincipalName <string>]
```

Consider the following example:

```
New-ADComputer CLIENT2
```

The **Remove-ADComputer** cmdlet is straightforward. It has one parameter set and takes an identity parameter similar to **Get-ADComputer** to identify the computer to remove.

The PowerShell command to remove a computer from the directory is

```
Remove-ADComputer [-Identity] <ADUser>
```

Consider the following example:

```
Remove-ADComputer CLIENT2
```

Performing Bulk Active Directory Operations

Unfortunately, most organizations will not be small enough to manage user and computer accounts on a one-by-one basis. This is especially true when first setting up an AD DS directory. Working with accounts on an individual basis is simply too time consuming and error prone.

The PowerShell cmdlets discussed earlier in this chapter can allow for bulk operations, but manipulating data into a format that is friendly for PowerShell is not easy. Even then, scripts to perform data parsing, validation, and import still need to be written.

Microsoft has provided a few different tools that you can use to extract or insert data to and from the directory without having to write your own scripts.

The two following utilities are available from the command line:

- **csvde**: The Comma Separated Value Data Exchange (csvde.exe) utility allows you to export data from your AD DS directory into a comma separated file format (csv) or import a csv file into your AD DS directory.

- **ldifde**: The LDAP Data Interchange Format Data Exchange (ldifde) utility allows you to create, modify, and delete directory objects. It can also facilitate the exchange of data from other directory sources that support LDAP.

Comma Separated Value Data Exchange (csvde)

The **csvde** utility works with csv files to extract or insert data to and from AD DS. csv files are plain text files where each value is separated by the comma character and a record is on its own line. This is a popular file format for passing structured data between systems.

The first line in a csv file is known as the header, and it contains the names of each attribute in the same order as the data in each of the subsequent lines. See this example:

```
objectClass,dn,givenName,sn,samAccountName
user,johndoe,John,Doe,johndoe
user,janedoe,Jane,Doe,janedoe
```

Files in this format can be produced either by hand, or more likely with a common application such as Microsoft Excel, which can easily save a workbook in csv format. This is also the file format that is produced when **csvde** is used to export data from AD DS.

> **NOTE**   If the value of an attribute includes a comma, it can confuse the format by introducing too many commas into a line. Be sure that any value that uses a comma has surrounding quotation marks. Read more here: https://technet.microsoft.com/en-us/library/cc732101(v=ws.11).aspx.

Table 3-4 lists some common parameters for the **csvde** tool.

Table 3-4   Common Parameters for **csvde**

Parameter	Description
-i	Specifies import mode. If not specified, the default mode is export.
-f *<FileName>*	Identifies the import or export file name.
-j *<Path>*	Sets the log file location. Useful for troubleshooting.
-d *<BaseDN>*	Sets the distinguished name of the search base for data export.
-l *<LDAPAttributeList>*	Sets the list of attributes to return in the results.
-r *<LDAPFilter>*	Creates an LDAP search filter for data export.

To see **csvde** in action:

Step 1.   Log on to a domain controller.

Step 2.   Open a command prompt.

Step 3.   Type the following command and press **Enter** (see Figure 3-8).

```
csvde -f output.csv -d "CN=users, DC=certguide, DC=com" -r
"(objectclass=user)"
```

```
Administrator: Command Prompt - powershell                                    —   □   X
PS C:\> Csvde -f output.csv -d "CN=users, DC=certguide, DC=com" -r "(objectclass=user)"
Connecting to "(null)"
Logging in as current user using SSPI
Exporting directory to file output.csv
Searching for entries...
Writing out entries
.......
Export Completed. Post-processing in progress...
7 entries exported

The command has completed successfully
PS C:\> _
```

Figure 3-8   The **csvde** Utility Extracting a Subset of Objects from the Directory to a File

NOTE   The values *certguide* and *com* are based on the examples from installing a new forest in Chapter 2. If you chose a different domain name, you need to modify the command to match your domain name. For example, a domain name of myCorp.local would be *CN=users, DC=mycorp, DC=local*. Read more about formatting distinguished names (DNs) here: https://msdn.microsoft.com/en-us/library/aa366101(v=vs.85).aspx.

Step 4.   A file named output.csv has been created at your current location. Type **notepad output.csv** to view that file, or open it with the editor of your choice.

The preceding example can be modified to import a csv file by adding the **-i** parameter to the command.

LDAP Data Interchange Format Data Exchange (ldifde)

Similar to **csvde**, **ldifde** allows you to both export data into plain text files and import data from those files. The primary difference between the two utilities is that **ldifde** uses a format known as line-separated. In this file format each attribute is defined on its own line of text, and each record is separated from the previous record with a blank line.

The line-separated format repeats the attribute name on each line where it's used. Consider the following example:

```
dn: CN=Users,DC=certguide,DC=com
changetype: add
name: johndoe
objectClass: user
givenName: John
sn: Doe
samAccountName: johndoe

dn: CN=Users,DC=certguide,DC=com
changetype: add
name: janedoe
objectClass: user
givenName: Jane
sn: Doe
samAccountName: janedoe
```

Take notice of the **changetype** attribute listed in the example. This attribute is used to define what type of operation is being performed on the data. Valid values for **changetype** are

- Add
- Modify
- Delete

Table 3-5 lists some common parameters for the **ldifde** tool.

Table 3-5   Common Parameters for **ldifde**

Parameter	Description
-i	Specifies import mode. If not specified, the default mode is export.
-f *<FileName>*	Identifies the import or export file name.
-j *<Path>*	Sets the log file location. Useful for troubleshooting.
-d *<BaseDN>*	Sets the distinguished name of the search base for data export.
-l *<LDAPAttributeList>*	Sets the list of attributes to return in the results.
-r *<LDAPFilter>*	Creates an LDAP search filter for data export.

To see **ldifde** in action:

Step 1.   Log on to a domain controller.

Step 2.   Open a command prompt.

Step 3.   Type the following command and press **Enter**.

```
ldifde -f output2.csv -d "CN=users, DC=certguide, DC=com" -r
"(objectclass=user)"
```

Step 4.   A file named output.csv has been created at your current location. Type **notepad output2.csv** to view that file or open it with the editor of your choice.

> **NOTE**   Full documentation, including a listing of all parameters, for the **csvde** and **ldifde** commands can be found here: https://technet.microsoft.com/en-us/library/cc732101(v=ws.11).aspx and here: https://technet.microsoft.com/en-us/library/cc731033(v=ws.11).aspx.

Configuring User Rights

Getting user objects into the directory is, of course, only half the story. Those users once defined need to have permissions for a variety of tasks granted or restricted. The whole promise of Active Directory is to provide a central place for administration of users' permissions on the network. As you see in later chapters, the real power to perform this security administration comes from using Group Policy Objects.

It makes sense to take a short look at how you can quickly and easily take advantage of some of the user rights assignment features that exist in Active Directory Domain Services already. You need to launch the Group Policy Management utility and from there browse to an existing policy and launch the Group Policy Management Editor utility:

Step 1.   Log on to a domain controller.

Step 2.   Open a command prompt.

Step 3.   Type **gpmc** and press **Enter**.

Step 4.   The Group Policy Management utility launches. Expand the Forest, Domains, domain node, and Group Policy Objects node to expose the **Default Domain Policy**.

Step 5.   Right-click the **Default Domain Policy** and select **Edit**.

Step 6.   The Group Policy Management Editor utility launches. Expand the Computer Configuration, Policies, Windows Settings, Security Settings, and Local Policies nodes to expose the **User Rights Assignment** node.

Step 7.   Select the **User Rights Assignment** node, and a list of the possible policies is displayed in the right-hand panel (see Figure 3-9).

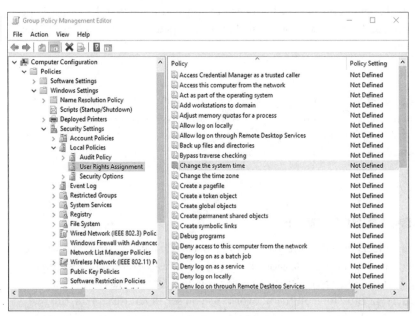

Figure 3-9   The Group Policy Management Editor Utility Displaying Some of the Options Available for User Rights Assignment

Step 8.   Right-click a policy, such as **Change the system time**, and click **Properties**.

Step 9.   Click the **Explain** tab to display some brief documentation about the policy.

Step 10.   Click the **Security Policy Setting** tab.

Step 11.   Check the box labeled **Define these policy settings**.

Step 12.   Click **Add User or Group**.

Step 13.   Click **Browse**.

Step 14.   Type **Domain Admins** and click **Check Names**.

The words "Domain Admins" will appear underlined, indicating it was found in the directory. (If it does not appear underlined, click **Advanced** and **Find Now** to browse the directory for the group.)

Step 15.   Click **OK**.

Step 16.   Click **OK**.

Step 17.   The group should now be listed in the **Security Policy Setting** tab (see Figure 3-10). Click **OK**.

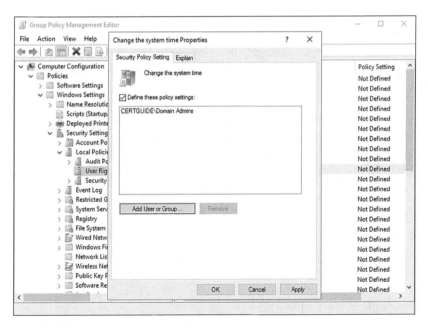

Figure 3-10   The Properties Dialog for a User Right Indicating Which Domain Users the Right Is Applied to

The Policy Setting for the policy you chose should now reflect that group name. On the domain, this Group Policy (Default Domain Policy) applies to all users and groups that don't have an overriding policy attached to them. Users and members of groups that have this policy attached can now change the system time on their local desktop only if they are a member of the Domain Admins group.

Implementing Offline Domain Join

Offline domain join is a feature that Microsoft rolled out in Windows 7 and Windows Server 2008. Offline domain join allows the client machine to join to an Active Directory domain without having network connectivity to that domain. There are a few different use cases for this feature:

- **Deploying virtual machines in a data center**: Offline domain join makes it possible for VMs to be joined to the domain when they are initially provisioned and started. No additional restart or network traffic is required, which can reduce the time required for wide-scale deployments.

- **Improved domain join using an RODC**: With Windows 2008 the possibility to domain join a computer using RODC was rolled out. This multistep process can be cumbersome and error prone. Offline domain join simplifies and streamlines the join process in this situation, saving time and potential error.

- **Rapid enterprise deployments**: Rolling out deployments using tools such as Windows System Image Manager allows you to include the offline domain join instructions in the image. All the necessary information can be supplied in an xml configuration file.

To perform an offline domain join, you must first create a provision file with instructions for joining the domain. That file is then copied onto the client computer that will be joining the domain, and the join is performed. The same utility is used to both create the file and perform the join operation: **djoin.exe**.

The syntax for the **djoin.exe** command to create the provision file is as follows:

```
djoin /provision
/domain <domain_name>
/machine <destination computer>
/savefile <filename.txt>
[/machineou <OU name>]
[/dcname <name of domain controller>]
[/reuse]
[/downlevel]
[/defpwd]
```

```
[/nosearch]
[/printblob]
[/rootcacerts]
[/certtemplate <name>]
[/policynames <name(s)>]
[/policypaths <Path(s)>]
```

Notable parameters include

- **/provision**: Tells **djoin** to provision an account in AD DS for the computer.

- **/domain** *<domain_name>*: The name of the domain to join.

- **/machine** *<destination computer>*: The name of the computer being joined.

- **/savefile** *<filename.txt>*: The name of the provision file to create.

- **/machineou** *<OU Name>*: An OU to provision the computer account into. The default is the Computers container.

An example:

```
djoin /provision /domain certguide.com /machine Client3 /savefile C:\
Client3Join.txt
```

Once this operation completes, there will be an entry for the specified machine name in the directory, and the file will be written to the specified location. This file needs to be manually copied to the target machine before the second step can proceed.

The syntax for the **djoin.exe** command to perform the join operation follows:

```
djoin /requestodj
/loadfile <filename.txt>
/windowspath <path to the Windows directory of the offline image> /
localos
```

Notable parameters include

- **/requestodj**: Requests a domain join at the next start.

- **/loadfile** *<filename.txt>*: The name of the provision file created earlier.

- **/windowspath** *<path to the windows directory of the offline image>*: Specifies the path to the Windows directory. If you are using the */localos* parameter, you can use %systemroot% or %windir% for this value.

- **/localos**: Joins the local OS instead of an offline image.

An example:

```
djoin /requestodj /loadfile c:\Client3Join.txt /windowspath %windr% /
localos
```

Once this operation completes, the computer will be joined to the domain on the next restart.

> **NOTE**   More details about the use cases for offline domain join and the syntax of djoin.exe can be read here: https://technet.microsoft.com/en-us/library/offline-domain-join-djoin-step-by-step(v=ws.10).aspx.

Managing Inactive and Disabled Accounts

When it comes to removing users from the network, user accounts can easily be deleted from the directory. This prevents the account from being used to log on to the network and accessing any protected resources. However, there are significant downsides to deleting objects. A deleted account may not be recoverable in the instance that it was deleted accidentally. If a user has left the organization for temporary leave, then the account will need to be rebuilt when the user returns.

Instead, AD DS offers the option to disable and lock accounts. This has all the same security benefits of deleting an object without the downsides. The entire object remains in the directory intact and can be reenabled as needed to allow access once again. These disabled accounts can even be reused for new or temporary employees who require the same access as the previous employee.

Accounts can also be locked, which is slightly different from being disabled. A locked account was typically put into that state by some trigger being tripped, such as too many failed logon attempts. Locked accounts cannot be used to log on to the network until an administrator has unlocked them. Locked accounts will have event log entries that display what specifically triggered the lock.

Accounts can be disabled or reenabled both via the Active Directory Administrative Center (ADAC) and the Active Directory Users and Computers (ADUC) utility. Simply right-click the object and choose to disable or enable from the context menu.

Accounts may also be enabled and disabled with PowerShell. Table 3-6 lists the cmdlets for enabling and disabling accounts.

Table 3-6 PowerShell cmdlets for Enabling and Disabling Accounts

PowerShell cmdlet	Description
Enable-ADAccount	Enables a disabled Active Directory account
Disable-ADAccount	Disables an Active Directory account

The PowerShell command to enable an account is as follows:

```
Enable-ADAccount [-Identity] <ADAccount>
```

For the **-Identity** parameter, you can supply the DistinguishedName, SamAccountName, SID, or ObjectGUID:

```
Enable-ADAccount cbtben
```

The PowerShell command to enable an account is as follows:

```
Disable-ADAccount [-Identity] <ADAccount>
```

For the **-Identity** parameter, you can supply the DistinguishedName, SamAccountName, SID, or ObjectGUID.

Consider the following example:

```
Disable-ADAccount cbtben
```

Automating Unlocking of Disabled Accounts Using Windows PowerShell

An easier way to deal with locked and disabled accounts is to use Windows PowerShell. The PowerShell commands can be run on either Windows Server Desktop Experience or Windows Server Core.

The cmdlet for enabling and disabling an account is **Set-ADUser**. It can be used to update most of the attributes found on a user account, but the typical parameters are listed here:

```
Set-ADUser [-Identity] <ADUser>'
[-Enabled <System.Nullable[bool]>]
```

For the **-Identity** parameter, you can supply the object name, DistinguishedName, SamAccountName, SID, or ObjectGUID. Enabled must be set to either true or false to enable or disable the account. Consider the following example:

```
Set-ADUser -Identity janedoe -Enabled $false
```

> **NOTE**   **Set-ADUser** can take a wide variety of parameters to update any user account attribute. See the complete documentation here: https://technet.microsoft.com/en-us/library/ee617215.aspx.

The cmdlet for unlocking an account is **Unlock-ADAccount**:

```
Unlock-ADAccount [-Identity] <ADAccount>
```

For the **-Identity** parameter, you can supply the object name, DistinguishedName, SamAccountName, SID, or ObjectGUID.

Automating Password Resets Using Windows PowerShell

Another common security task you may run into is user accounts that require the password to be reset, either because the user forgot the password or the account is being assigned to a new user. This can again be easily done via the ADAC or ADUC utilities in Windows Server Desktop Experience or with PowerShell.

The PowerShell cmdlet to reset a user account password is **Set-ADAccountPassword**:

```
Set-ADAccountPassword [-Identity] <ADAccount>'
[-NewPassword <SecureString>]'
[-OldPassword <SecureString>]'
[-Reset <switch>]
```

For the **-Identity** parameter, you can supply the object name, DistinguishedName, SamAccountName, SID, or ObjectGUID. When the Reset switch is included you do not need to use the OldPassword parameter. Consider the following example:

```
$pw = ConvertTo-SecureString Password123 -AsPlainText -Force
Set-ADAccountPassword -NewPassword $pw -Reset
```

Exam Preparation Tasks

As mentioned in the section "Book Features" in the Introduction, you have a few choices for exam preparation: the exercises here; Chapter 17, "Final Preparation"; and the exam simulation questions in the Pearson Test Prep Software Online.

Review All Key Topics

Review the most important topics in this chapter, noted with the Key Topics icon in the outer margin of the page. Table 3-7 lists a reference of these key topics and the page number on which each is found.

Table 3-7   Key Topics for Chapter 3

Key Topic Element	Description	Page Number
Figure 3-2	New user properties in the ADAC	69
List	Different ways to access user properties	71
Figure 3-3	New computer properties in the ADAC	72
List	Different ways to access computer properties	73
Figure 3-4	User copy options dialog	75
Table 3-2	PowerShell cmdlets for working with users	78
Table 3-3	PowerShell cmdlets for working with computers	82
List	Bulk AD DS utilities	84
Table 3-4	Common parameters for **csvde**	85
Table 3-5	Common parameters for **ldifde**	87
Figure 3-9	User rights in the group policy management editor	88
List	Use cases for offline domain join	90
List	Common parameters for djoin /provision	91
List	Common parameters for djoin /requestodj	91
Table 3-6	PowerShell cmdlets for enabling/disabling accounts	93
Command	PowerShell cmdlet to enable/disable a user account	93
Command	PowerShell cmdlet for a password reset	94

Complete Tables and Lists from Memory

Print a copy of Appendix B, "Memory Tables" (found on the book website), or at least the section for this chapter, and complete the tables and lists from memory. Appendix C, "Memory Tables Answer Key," also on the website, includes completed tables and lists to check your work.

Define Key Terms

Define the following key terms from this chapter and check your answers in the glossary:

user, computer, object, ADAC, ADUC, UPN, Profile path, Home older, template account, comma separated values (CSV), line-separated values, disabled account, locked account, deleted account

End-of-Chapter Review Questions

The answers to these questions appear in Appendix A. For more practice with exam format questions, use the Pearson Test Prep Software Online.

1. You need to update the City property for all the users in the East OU. Which PowerShell script will accomplish this?

   a. **Set-ADUser -SearchBase "OU=East,dc=certguide,dc=com" -Property @{City="Springfield"}**

   b. **Get-ADUser -Filter -SearchBase "OU=East,dc=certguide,dc=com" -SearchScope subtree | Set-ADUser -Replace @{City="Springfield"}**

   c. **Get-ADUser -Filter *east.certguide.com | Set-ADUser -Replace @{City="Springfield"}**

   d. **Set-ADUser -Replace @{City="Springfield"} | Get-ADUser -Filter -SearchBase "OU=East,dc=certguide,dc=com" -SearchScope subtree**

2. You need to create and manage 30 new user accounts in the East OU. All these accounts will belong to the same security groups and use the same UPN suffix. What is the most effective way to accomplish this?

   a. Assign each user to a new distribution group.

   b. Copy a similar OU in the directory with a similar user structure.

   c. Create and configure a template user; then copy that to create each new user.

   d. Run **Set-ADUser** in a looping PowerShell script.

3. The DNS-style logon name for a user account is known as the _____.

4. The _____ _____ (two words) is used to store the user's personal folders such as My Documents on the network.

5. Complete the blanks in the following script to disable the user janedoe:

    Import-Module _____

    $usr = _____ **janedoe**

    $usr._____ = $false

    Set-ADUser -Instance _____

6. What is the command to import a csv file, newUsers.csv, into the directory?

7. A remote office has purchased 20 new computers to install and join to the domain. They will be brought online during the maintenance window for the domain when all DCs are unavailable. What steps should be performed to successfully join these computers to the domain?

    a. Install a new RODC at the remote office and join the new computers to that domain controller.

    b. Run the following command on a domain controller:

       djoin /provision /domain certguide.com /machine _<machine name>_ **/ savefile C:\offlinejoin.txt**

       Run the following command on the client computers:

       djoin /requestodj /loadfile c:\offlinejoin.txt /windowspath %SystemRoot% /localos

    c. Run both of these commands on the domain controller:

       djoin /provision /domain certguide.com /machine _<machine name>_ **/ savefile C:\offlinejoin.txt**

       Djoin /requestodj /loadfile c:\offlinejoin.txt /windowspath %SystemRoot% /localos

    d. Wait until the maintenance period has ended and then run dcpromo on each client computer.

8. Write a PowerShell script to reset the password for each user account in the East OU and all of its child containers.

This chapter covers the following topics:

- **Creating, Copying, Configuring, and Deleting Groups and OUs**: This section describes the processes for creating, copying, and configuring security groups and organizational units (OUs).

- **Configuring Group Nesting**: This section describes how to properly nest security groups to ensure waterfalling permissions are properly applied using the IGDLA method.

- **Delegating the Creation and Management of Groups and OUs**: This section describes how to delegate permissions for creating and managing groups and OUs without unnecessarily granting administrative access.

- **Managing Group Membership Using Group Policy**: This section describes how to use Group Policy and Group Policy Objects (GPOs) to systematically add and remove members to and from security groups.

- **Managing Default Active Directory Containers**: This section describes how to adjust the default directory container for new user and computer objects.

CHAPTER 4

Creating and Managing Active Directory Groups and Organizational Units

Groups and organizational units (OUs) represent two common yet different containers to sort and organize objects in Active Directory. Groups provide a way to collectively assign security and permissions to objects that belong to a given group. OUs represent a structured element in the directory that groups objects, usually so that Group Policy can deal with them collectively.

This chapter covers the creation and management of groups and OUs, including when and where to use one versus the other. This chapter also looks at the delegation of permissions for adding and removing users from these containers, automating with PowerShell and Group Policy, and working with default containers.

"Do I Know This Already?" Quiz

The "Do I Know This Already?" quiz allows you to assess whether you should read this entire chapter thoroughly or jump to the "Exam Preparation Tasks" section. If you are in doubt about your answers to these questions or your own assessment of your knowledge of the topics, read the entire chapter. Table 4-1 lists the major headings in this chapter and their corresponding "Do I Know This Already?" quiz questions. You can find the answers in Appendix A, "Answers to the 'Do I Know This Already?' Quizzes."

Table 4-1   "Do I Know This Already?" Section-to-Question Mapping

Foundation Topics Section	Questions
Creating, Copying, Configuring, and Deleting Groups and OUs	1-6
Configuring Group Nesting	7
Delegating the Creation and Management of Groups and OUs	8
Managing Group Membership Using Group Policy	9
Managing Default Active Directory Containers	10

CAUTION   The goal of self-assessment is to gauge your mastery of the topics in this chapter. If you do not know the answer to a question or are only partially sure of the answer, you should mark that question as wrong for purposes of the self-assessment. Giving yourself credit for an answer you correctly guess skews your self-assessment results and might provide you with a false sense of security.

1. Which type of object is used by Active Directory Domain Services to add structure to the directory?

    a. Groups

    b. OUs

    c. Users

    d. Computers

2. Which type of object is used by Active Directory Domain Services to assign authorization on the network?

    a. Groups

    b. OUs

    c. Users

    d. Computers

3. Which scope of group is used if you need to both include objects from and assign permissions to multiple domains across the forest?

    a. Security

    b. Domain local

    c. Universal

    d. Global

4. Which cmdlet is used to create a new group in the directory?

    a. **Create-ADGroup**

    b. **Add-ADGroupMember**

    c. **New-Group**

    d. **New-ADGroup**

5. Which cmdlet is used to create a new OU in the directory?

   a. **New-ADGroup**

   b. **New-ADOrganizationalUnit**

   c. **Create-ADOrganizationalUnit**

   d. **New-ADOU**

6. Which cmdlet is used to add a new member to a group?

   a. **New-GroupMember**

   b. **Create-ADGroupMember**

   c. **Add-ADGroupMember**

   d. **New-ADUser**

7. Following the IGDLA method, which scope of group should be granted access to resources?

   a. Global

   b. Domain local

   c. Security

   d. Universal

8. You want to assign all the IT help desk staff the rights to reset passwords for a remote office. Which option would you choose?

   a. Delegate common tasks to a domain local group that contained the IT help desk staff.

   b. Create a custom task and assign it to the IT help desk staff.

   c. Make the IT help desk staff administrators on the network.

   d. Create a child domain for the remote site and grant the IT help desk staff administrative rights to that domain.

9. Which element of a GPO should you edit to assign domain users membership in a local group?

   a. Domain default policy

   b. Account policies

   c. Local policies

   d. Restricted groups

10. What is the name of the utility Microsoft provides to change the default location for new computers?

   a. djoin

   b. redircmp

   c. redirusr

   d. dcpromo

Foundation Topics

Creating, Copying, Configuring, and Deleting Groups and OUs

Groups and organizational units (OUs) are fairly straightforward entities to work with. They both consist of little more than a name and a list of one or more objects that belong to them. It's important to understand how and when to use a group, or an OU, or both, to organize your directory structure. You also need to know the various ways you can create and manage groups and OUs, including using PowerShell to script out the process. Finally, there are subtle but important configuration details, particularly for groups, that you will want to get correct to successfully use groups and OUs.

Active Directory Groups and Active Directory OUs

For new, and even experienced Active Directory administrators, the difference between OUs and groups can be difficult to grasp. At first blush they seem to accomplish similar goals. They are very different features, though, and part of a successful implementation of AD DS is using groups and OUs appropriately.

Organizational Units

Organizational units are part of the structure of your directory. Recall from Chapter 1, "Introducing Active Directory 2016," that at the top of your directory is a forest, and the first domain is a child of that forest. Objects such as user accounts are then created as children of that domain forming a tree structure. However, a domain often represents thousands or tens of thousands of users, computers, and other network objects. Having them all lumped together under one parent would be neither effective nor helpful for administration. Instead, domain administrators create organizational units within the domain and create the network objects as children of the OUs. In fact, OUs can be nested, creating as large and complex a structure as needed (see Figure 4-1).

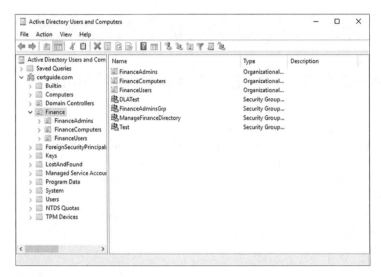

Figure 4-1   An Example of a Simple OU Structure. The Finance OU at the Top of the Domain Contains Three Child OUs: FinanceUsers, FinanceComputers, and FinanceAdmins.

One of the first steps in creating a new directory is to plan out what your domain and OU structure will be. The structure of your OUs should map to your organization's structure in some fashion. An OU to represent each region your business operates in is common. So are departmental OUs that reflect different lines of business. Combining these two is a typical scenario as well for companies large enough to require it. There are two major reasons for creating an OU:

- **Delegation**: Administration for an OU and the objects beneath it can be delegated to different administrators in your organization. It may make sense to create an OU for a U.S. office and one for the UK and delegate administrative duties to a different individual for each of those OUs. That way IT staff in one region can manage users for their region and not impact user objects in another region.

- **Group Policy**: The security rights assigned by Group Policy Objects (GPOs) can be applied to an OU. Creating an OU for a department, such as Finance, allows administrators to customize the GPOs for every user object found in that OU while creating a different policy to be applied to user objects in another OU such as Information Technology.

Similar to the advice given in Chapter 1 for planning your domain structure, you should start simple with your OU structure and then grow it as needed. You can be a little more cavalier, however, since the impact of creating and rearranging OUs is less severe than with domains, and most organizations find they need to restructure their OUs as they grow and change.

Groups

Groups in Active Directory are also used as a tool for organizing user and computer objects but in a different fashion than OUs. Groups are objects that exist as collections of users to identify those users to outside services. Unlike OUs, groups do not typically have children objects in the directory. Instead, other objects can become a member of the group. Membership in a group is used by outside services to authorize or control access.

For example, there may be a file server on the network with a folder meant for users in the Finance department, and another meant only for executives in the Finance department. Allowing users from other departments to see any of the files stored in those folders would be problematic. In this scenario the AD DS administrator would create two groups in the directory, such as FinanceUsers and ExecutiveFinanceUsers. The administrator of the file server could then restrict access to the folders to the appropriate groups (a trivial task if the file server in question is running Windows Server). Users could then be granted access to either folder by being made a member of the appropriate group, or revoked access by removing their membership.

> **NOTE**   Almost all Microsoft Server products have built-in tools to allow for managing security with AD DS. It is also common for third-party products to allow for authorization based on AD DS. If you're writing or creating your own software in a Microsoft Windows environment, it behooves you to take advantage of AD DS for securing your custom software as well.

In this fashion, groups allow for central management of user security on the network. As new hires join the organization, they can be assigned membership to the appropriate groups and are then seamlessly granted authorization to any of the network services that rely on those groups. Similarly, if a user leaves a department or the organization, the simple act of removing the user from the group ensures the user no longer has access to secured network resources.

Group Types

Groups have one of two different types:

- **Security**: A security group functions just as described previously. It has its own Security Identifier (SID) and can be used to grant permissions to network resources.

- **Distribution**: A distribution group is a simpler type of group. It does not have an SID and consequently is not used to assign permissions. Instead, it is used to identify a collection of users for email distribution lists with Microsoft Exchange or Outlook.

Group Scope

Groups belong to one of three scopes:

- **Universal**: Groups with a universal scope can have as a member any user account from any domain within the forest, as well as other global or universal groups in the forest. Universal groups can grant permissions to any resource in the forest.

- **Global**: Groups with a global scope can have as a member any user account as well as other global groups from the same domain. Permissions are also limited to the resources in the domain.

- **Domain local**: Groups with a domain local scope can have as a member any user account in the forest or any other trusted domain or forest. They are limited to assigning permissions to resources in their own domain. This allows a domain administrator to control access to local domain resources for users in other domains in the forest.

It is important to note that there are many built-in groups in AD DS that are created and populated automatically when various events occur or manually by directory administrators. This includes groups such as **Domain Users**, which contains all the user accounts in the domain, or **Remote Desktop Users**, which represents users that can use Remote Desktop to access servers on the network. You are encouraged to review these groups and use them as a part of your security strategy. More details about these groups can be read here: https://technet.microsoft.com/en-us/library/dn579255(v=ws.11).aspx.

Table 4-2 compares groups and OUs.

Table 4-2   AD DS Groups Versus Organizational Units

Feature	Groups	Organizational Units
Object membership	Objects can be members of unlimited groups.	Objects are the child of one and only one OU.
Usage	Outside service authorization.	Group Policy and AD DS administration delegation.
Can become a member of a group?	Yes.	No.
Has a Security Identifier (SID)?	Security groups do; distribution groups do not.	No.

Working with Active Directory Groups

The process for creating groups is similar to the process for creating users and computers outlined in Chapter 3, "Creating and Managing Active Directory Users and Computers." You can use either Active Directory Administrative Center (ADAC) or Active Directory Users and Computers (ADUC) to create a group account:

Step 1. Log on to a writeable domain controller.

Step 2. Start Server Manager from either the Start Menu or Taskbar.

Step 3. From the context menu at the top of the panel click **Tools** and then select **Active Directory Administrative Center**.

Step 4. On the left-hand panel select the domain you want to add a group to. The right-hand panel displays the top-level containers that are created in a directory by default.

Step 5. Right-click the container you want to add a group to and select **New > Group**.

Step 6. The Create Group dialog appears with the following properties (see Figure 4-2).

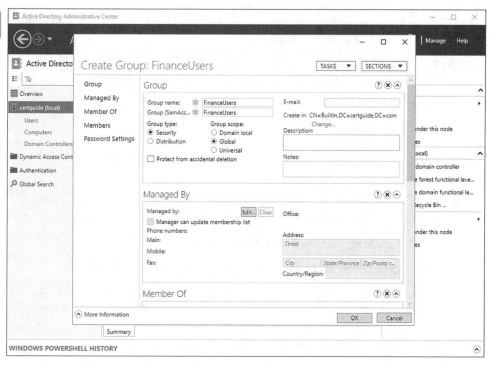

Figure 4-2 The Create Group Dialog Box from Active Directory Administrative Center (ADAC)

- **Group name**: The name of the object in the directory.

- **Group (SamAccountName)**: The pre-windows 2000 NetBIOS name. This will populate with the value keyed into the **Group name.**

- **Group type**: Select a type based on the descriptions listed earlier. Typically this will be **Security**.

- **Group scope**: Select a scope based on the descriptions listed earlier.

- **Protect from accidental deletion**: Checking the box prevents the group from being deleted from the directory until an administrator edits the properties of the object and unchecks this box.

- **E-mail**: Specify the email address of the person who manages this group.

Step 7.   The **Managed By** section of the dialog allows you to specify a user account in the directory that manages this security group. This does not confer any security on that user and is used only for reference.

Step 8.   The **Member Of** section of the dialog allows you to specify one or more existing groups that this group will become a member of. Group membership is inherited, so any members of this group would then inherit the permissions of the parent group(s) specified here. See more about group nesting later in this chapter.

Step 9.   The **Members** section of the dialog allows you to add users or groups as members of this group. More on group membership is covered later in this chapter (see Figure 4-3).

Step 10.   Click **OK**.

The group can now be found in the container chosen during Step 4, and accounts can be added to or removed from it as needed.

As with most AD DS directory objects, the properties and attributes set up during group creation can be configured at any time by

- Double-clicking the group object in ADAC

- Right-clicking the group object and choosing **Properties** in ADAC

- Selecting the group object in ADAC and clicking **Properties** in the Tasks panel

As long as the **Protect from accidental deletion** flag is not checked, you can delete a group by simply right-clicking and choosing **Delete**. You are prompted to confirm, and then the object (and its membership) is removed.

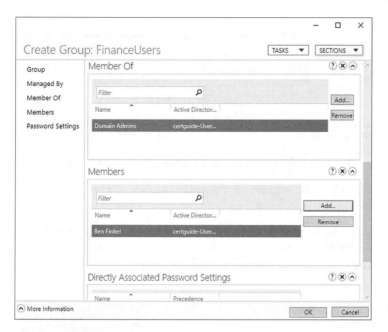

Figure 4-3   The Create Group Dialog Box Showing the Group as a Member of Another Group and Having a Member Added to It

Working with Active Directory OUs

Creating new organizational units is just as easy as creating other objects in the directory. The process for organizational units is similar to the process for creating users, computers, and groups. You can use either Active Directory Administrative Center (ADAC) or Active Directory Users and Computers (ADUC) to create an organizational unit:

Step 1.   Log on to a writeable domain controller.

Step 2.   Start Server Manager from either the Start Menu or Taskbar.

Step 3.   From the context menu at the top of the panel click **Tools** and then select **Active Directory Administrative Center**.

Step 4.   On the left-hand panel select the domain you want to add an OU to. The right-hand panel displays the top-level containers that are created in a directory by default.

Step 5.   Right-click either the domain itself or an existing OU to serve as the parent to the OU you want to create and select **New > Organizational Unit**.

NOTE Many of the default top-level containers, such as Users, cannot have an OU added to them via the context menu. It's best to leave those containers as-is and create your own hierarchy of OUs starting at the domain.

Step 6. The Create Organizational Unit dialog appears. It has few fields to fill out (see Figure 4-4):

- **Name**: The only required field, the OU Name, is typed in here.

- **Address**: If the OU represents a physical location, the relevant information can be typed here.

- **Protect from accidental deletion**: Checking this box prevents the OU from being deleted from the directory until an administrator edits the properties of the object and unchecks this box.

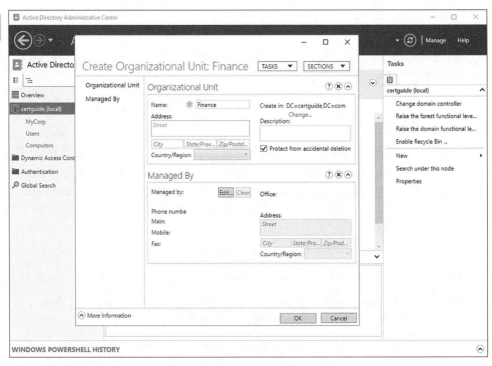

Figure 4-4   The Create Organizational Unit Dialog in Active Directory Administrative Center (ADAC)

Step 7.   The **Managed By** section of the dialog allows you to specify a user account in the directory that manages this security group. This does not confer any security on that user and is used only for reference.

Step 8.   Click **OK**.

The OU is now available in the directory, and objects can be created or moved into it.

As with most AD DS directory objects, the properties and attributes set up during OU creation can be configured at any time by

- Right-clicking the group object and choosing **Properties** in ADAC

- Selecting the group object in ADAC and clicking **Properties** in the Tasks panel

Double-clicking doesn't work for OU objects because the default action for double-clicking is to navigate the user interface into the OU itself, rather than edit the object properties.

As long as the **Protect from accidental deletion** flag is not checked, you can delete an OU by simply right-clicking and choosing **Delete**. If there are objects located in the OU when you attempt to delete, you receive a confirmation dialog. Clicking **Yes** deletes those children objects from the directory as well.

Automate Groups and OUs with PowerShell

Similar to creating users and computers with PowerShell, there are important PowerShell cmdlets for working with groups and OUs. See Table 4-3 for a quick breakdown of these cmdlets.

Table 4-3   Group and OU PowerShell Cmdlets

Cmdlet	Operation	Required Parameter(s)
New-ADGroup	Creates a new Active Directory group object	**-Name** **-GroupScope**
Add-ADGroupMember	Adds a user or group as a member of an Active Directory group	**-Identity** **-Members**
Remove-ADGroup	Removes an Active Directory group object	**-Identity**

Cmdlet	Operation	Required Parameter(s)
Remove-ADGroupMember	Removes a user or group from an Active Directory group	**-Identity** **-Members**
New-ADOrganizationalUnit	Creates a new Active Directory OU	**-Name**
Remove-ADOrganizationalUnit	Removes an Active Directory OU	**-Identity**

The PowerShell cmdlet to create a new group is

```
New-ADGroup [-Name] <string>'
[-GroupScope] <System.Nullable[Microsoft.ActiveDirectory.Management.
ADGroupScope]>'
[-DisplayName <string>]'
[-GroupCategory <System.Nullable[Microsoft.ActiveDirectory.Management.
ADGroupCategory]>]'
[-SamAccountName <string>]'
[-Path <string>]
```

The **-GroupScope** parameter specifies the scope. Possible values are

- *DomainLocal* (0)

- *Global* (1)

- *Universal* (2)

The **-GroupCategory** parameter specifies the type. Possible values are

- *Distribution* (0)

- *Security* (1)

The **-Path** parameter can be used to specify where in the directory to create the group. It takes a string formatted as an X.500 path. When no path is specified, a default path is used (typically the default Users container).

Consider an example of creating a group with PowerShell:

```
New-ADGroup FinanceUsers -GroupScope Global -GroupCategory Security
-Path "ou=Finance,dc=certguide,dc=com"
```

You can find complete documentation here: https://technet.microsoft.com/en-us/library/ee617258.aspx.

The PowerShell cmdlet to add a member to a group is

```
Add-ADGroupMember [-Identity] <ADGroup>'
[-Members] <ADPrincipal[]>'
```

For the identity parameter you can supply the object name, DistinguishedName, SamAccountName, SID, or ObjectGUID. This identifies the group having members added.

For the members parameter you can supply the object name, DistinguishedName, SamAccountName, SID, or ObjectGUID. Multiple objects can be included as a comma separated list. This identifies the object or objects being added as members.

Consider an example of adding a group member with PowerShell:

```
Add-ADGroupMember FinanceUsers -Members cbtben,janedoe
```

Complete documentation can be found here: https://technet.microsoft.com/en-us/library/ee617210.aspx.

The PowerShell cmdlet to remove a group is

```
Remove-ADGroup [-Identity] <ADGroup>
```

For the identity parameter you can supply the object name, DistinguishedName, SamAccountName, SID, or ObjectGUID.

An example of removing a group with PowerShell:

```
Remove-ADGroup FinanceUsers
```

Complete documentation can be found here: https://technet.microsoft.com/en-us/library/ee617228.aspx.

The PowerShell cmdlet to remove a member from a group is

```
Remove-ADGroupMember [-Identity] <ADGroup>'
[-Members] <ADPrincipal[]>'
```

For the identity parameter you can supply the object name, DistinguishedName, SamAccountName, SID, or ObjectGUID. This identifies the group having members removed.

For the members parameter you can supply the object name, DistinguishedName, SamAccountName, SID, or ObjectGUID. Multiple objects can be included as a comma separated list. This identifies the object or objects being removed as members.

An example of removing a group member with PowerShell:

```
Remove-ADGroupMember FinanceUsers -Members cbtben,janedoe
```

Complete documentation can be found here: https://technet.microsoft.com/en-us/library/ee617242.aspx.

The PowerShell cmdlet to create a new OU is

```
New-ADOrganizationalUnit [-Name] <string>'
[-Path <string>]
```

The **-Path** parameter can be used to specify where in the directory to create the OU. It takes a string formatted as an X.500 path. When no path is specified a default path is used (typically the top of the domain).

Consider an example of creating an OU with PowerShell:

```
New-ADOrganizationalUnit FinanceExecutives -Path "ou=Finance,dc=certg
uide,dc=com"
```

You can find complete documentation here: https://technet.microsoft.com/en-us/library/ee617237.aspx.

The PowerShell cmdlet to remove an OU is

```
Remove-ADOrganizationalUnit [-Identity] <ADGroup>'
[-Recursive <switch>]
```

For the identity parameter you can supply the object name, DistinguishedName, SamAccountName, SID, or ObjectGUID.

The **-Recursive** switch must be included if the OU has any children objects.

Consider an example of removing an OU with PowerShell:

```
Remove-ADOrganizationalUnit "ou=Finance,dc=certguide,dc=com"
-Recursive
```

You can find complete documentation here: https://technet.microsoft.com/en-us/library/ee617239.aspx.

Converting Group Scope and Type

It is important to create groups with the appropriate scope when they are first made, but in the event you want to convert the group from one scope to another there are restrictions to be aware of. Generally, domain local and global groups can only be converted to universal groups, while universal groups can be converted to either domain local or global. There are restrictions, however, laid out in Table 4-4.

Table 4-4 Group Type Conversion Paths

Type	Can Convert to
Domain local	Universal, as long as it does not contain another domain local group as a member
Global	Universal, as long as it is not a member of another group
Universal	Domain local or global, as long as it does not contain other universal groups as a member

If the requirements are met, groups can be converted using the ADUC or ADAC utility. Navigate to the group you want to convert, right-click, and select Properties. Change the group type using the interface described previously. If the group fails one of the tests outlined in Table 4-4, you receive an error message indicating the problem.

Group type can be converted from a security group to a distribution group or vice versa in the same fashion. There are no restrictions on converting the group type; however, when converting from a security to a distribution type any permissions granted to the group will no longer apply. These permissions do not leave the directory, however, and can be reapplied simply by converting the group type back to a security group.

Configuring Group Nesting

One often overlooked feature of AD DS groups is the ability to nest them inside one another. Nesting a group means nothing more than making one group a member of another. To nest a group, you follow the same process as making a user a member: Either edit the object and choose which groups it is a member of, or edit the group and choose which objects are to be members.

IGDLA

When a group is nested, members of the nested group gain all the security and rights associated with the parent group. In other words, permission waterfalls down to members of the top level group but also members of any nested groups. This does present some possible challenges:

- **Unintended permissions**: If groups are nested too deeply, an administrator may not realize the full implication of adding a member to a group. That member may be receiving inappropriate security permissions from a parent, or even higher-level, group.

- **Overcomplication**: Tracking and maintaining what objects have access to which resources can quickly spiral out of control and become an undocumentable mess.

For these reasons it is encouraged to follow a sound nesting strategy that does not create multiple layers of groups. One popular strategy is known as identities, global groups, domain local groups, and access (IGDLA) (see Figure 4-5).

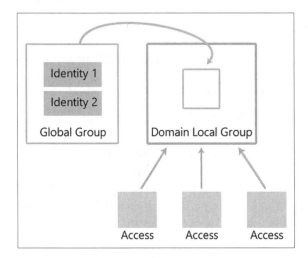

Figure 4-5   The IGDLA Layout: Identities Added to Global Groups Which Are Added to Domain Local Groups Which Have Access Permissions Assigned

- **Identities**: Users or computers (identity objects) are made members of global groups.

- **Global groups**: Global groups represent their members' roles in the organization. These groups in turn are made members of domain local groups.

- **Domain local groups**: Domain local groups represent management rules for permissions to resources on the network. Domain local groups are granted access.

- **Access**: Access to network resources is assigned to the domain local group, which in turn grants it to member global groups and then is granted to the identities in the global groups.

With IGDLA the purpose of a group is defined by its group scope. Global groups are role groups that represent their members' roles in the organization. FinanceUsers or HRTemps are examples of such groups. Domain local groups are rule groups that represent a rule or set of rules for access on the network. Examples of a rule group might be FinanceFolderReadWrite or HRDatabaseReadOnly.

By adding the user accounts to the role groups and granting permissions to the rule groups, network access can be effectively, clearly, and efficiently managed.

> **NOTE**   IGDLA represents only one of a few different strategies for nesting AD DS groups. You can read more about other strategies here: http://blogs.msmvps.com/acefekay/2012/01/06/using-group-nesting-strategy-ad-best-practices-for-group-strategy/.

Enumerating Group Membership

A challenge that can arise with group nesting is the ability to accurately report on which users are in fact members of which groups. The basic tools provided with the ADUC and ADAC can only show one level of membership. That is to say, you can see who is directly a member of a group, but not any members of nested groups. You need to drill down into each member group to see individual membership. This can be time consuming and error prone.

Instead, Windows PowerShell offers the **Get-ADGroupMember** cmdlet:

```
Get-ADGroupMember [-Identity] <ADGroup>'
[-Recursive <switch>]
```

For the **-Identity** parameter you can supply the object name, DistinguishedName, SamAccountName, SID, or ObjectGUID.

The **-Recursive** parameter is what allows you to enumerate all the members of child objects as well. Specifying this switch displays all the objects that do not have any child objects.

An example of enumerating the top-level members of a group:

```
Get-ADGroupMember "ManageFinanceDirectory"
```

An example of enumerating the childless members of a group:

```
Get-ADGroupMember "ManageFinanceDirectory" -Recursive
```

See Figure 4-6 for an example of how the first example displays only the role group in the ManageFinanceDirectory group, but the second example displays the member(s) of the role group instead.

Figure 4-6   Comparing the Output of the Get-ADGroupMember cmdlet Both With and Without the **-Recursive** Flag. Notice the Group Listed When the Flag Was Excluded Is Not Listed When the Flag Is Used.

> **NOTE**   Using the **-Recursive** switch displays all childless objects throughout the entire membership tree. So users that had been directly added to the top-level group would be displayed along with any other childless objects regardless of how complex or how deeply the groups were nested.

Delegating the Creation and Management of Groups and OUs

The ability to separate and delegate authority over domain objects into the appropriate scope is one of the major benefits of creating a sound OU hierarchical structure. Permissions for the administration of the directory itself can be granted to varying security groups but limited to only the portion of the directory those groups should be managing.

Imagine a geographically diverse organization. The IT services at the home office in the United States may not need or want to manage the AD DS objects for a satellite office in London. In this scenario, an organizational unit for the London office can be created and IT staff in London can be granted permission to perform administrative tasks but only within the London OU. Administrators grant those permissions using the IGDLA structure defined earlier in this chapter.

AD DS allows the delegation of permissions and authority at a granular level. Dozens of individual permissions can be enabled or restricted, and those permissions can be customized for each OU and security group. Powerful built-in security groups, such as Enterprise Admins, can even have their permissions curtailed for further security regulation, which is often needed in lines of business with complex regulatory requirements.

Permissions can be delegated with the Active Directory Users and Computers utility.

To delegate basic permissions:

Step 1. Log on to a writeable domain controller.

Step 2. Start Server Manager from either the Start Menu or Taskbar.

Step 3. From the context menu at the top of the panel, click **Tools** and then select **Active Directory Users and Computers**.

Step 4. On the left-hand panel right-click the OU you want to delegate permissions for and select **Delegate Control**.

Step 5. The Delegation of Control Wizard starts. Click **Next**.

Step 6. Click **Add**.

Step 7. The standard Select Users, Computers, or Groups dialog appears. Type the name of the user or group you want to delegate control to. Click **Check Names**. If the user or group is found, the name will be underlined.

Step 8. Click **OK**.

Step 9. Note the selected object is now listed on the dialog. Click **Next**.

Step 10. The Tasks to Delegate window allows you to choose which permissions will be granted (see Figure 4-7). For now leave **Delegate the following common tasks** selected. Select the **Create, delete, and manage groups** box and any others you want. Click **Next**.

Step 11. Review the permissions that have been granted and click **Finish**. You may also click **Back** to make any desired adjustments.

The entities selected when searching the directory during Step 7 have now been delegated the permissions that were chosen in Step 10, but only over the OU being delegated and any of its child objects.

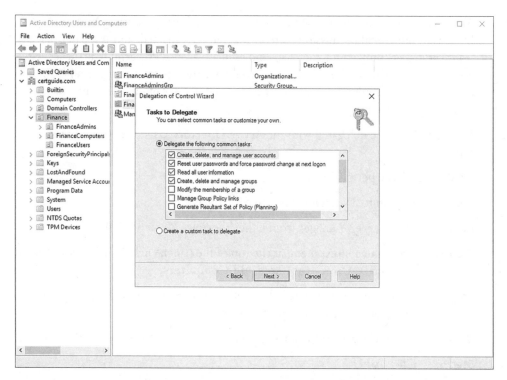

Figure 4-7 The Tasks to Delegate Step During the Delegation of Control Wizard. The **Delegate the following common tasks** Option Enables the Choices in the Selection Box.

NOTE This is the perfect place to practice IGDLA structure. First, create a new global group and place the desired users into it. Second, create a new domain local group and place the first group into that. Follow the steps outlined previously to delegate new permissions. When searching for an entity to delegate to, select the domain local group you just created and continue.

If you want to delegate more granularly, or delegate advanced operations such as the creation of OUs, you need to create a custom task to delegate.

Follow the same steps just covered, but during Step 10, do the following:

Step 10. The Tasks to Delegate window allows you to choose which permissions will be granted. Select **Create a custom task to delegate**. Click **Next** (see Figure 4-8).

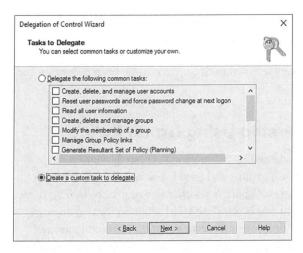

Figure 4-8   The Tasks to Delegate Step During the Delegation of Control Wizard. Selecting **Create a custom task to delegate** Enables Further Choices Once You Click **Next**.

Step 11.   Select **This folder, existing objects in this folder, and creation of new objects in this folder**. Click **Next**.

Step 12.   Select **Creation/deletion of specific child objects**. The **Permissions** list box updates with additional choices.

Step 13.   Scroll down the **Permissions** list box to find **Create Organizational Units**. Select that check box and the check box below it for **Delete Organizational Units**. Click **Next** (see Figure 4-9).

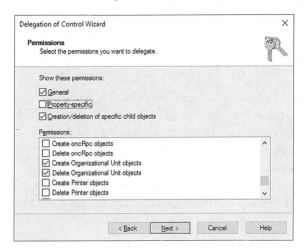

Figure 4-9   The Permissions Step of the Delegation of Control Wizard. This Is Displayed Only if You Chose to Create a Custom Task Earlier in the Wizard.

Step 14.   Review the permissions that have been granted and click **Finish**. You may also click **Back** to make any desired adjustments.

The users or members of the groups selected in Step 7 have now been delegated the permissions chosen in Step 13.

Managing Group Membership Using Group Policy

So far the discussion of groups has been limited to groups created in and managed by AD DS. These groups are domain groups and used for reference by other systems on the network for authorization. There is another tier of groups in Microsoft Windows known as local groups (not to be confused with domain local groups). Every Windows installation, both desktop and server versions, has a collection of default local groups defined. These local groups affect user permissions on the machine only and don't have any bearing on permissions on the network itself.

NOTE   If you go looking for local groups on a domain controller, you won't find any. This is because on any domain controller the local groups are replaced wholesale by the network groups defined in the directory. Local groups can be found on desktop clients and other member servers not functioning as a domain controller.

Managing membership to these groups is an important task for administrators. For example, you may want certain IT staff in the organization to always be added to the local Backup operators group when they log on to a server in the network, and a different set of staff to be added to the local Administrators group. This can, of course, be completed by logging in to each server and manually adding a specific domain user or domain group to the correct local group. For any nonmarginal number of computers in the organization, this would quickly become an unwieldly task.

Microsoft addresses this challenge by allowing Group Policy Objects to manage membership in local groups. This makes a certain amount of sense. If you recall in Chapter 3, Group Policy was used to manage user rights on individual computers. Managing user membership on those same computers falls into a similar category. By editing the GPO and modifying the Restricted Groups settings, you can define a policy of which domain objects get added to which local groups. Like all GPOs, this policy will be applied automatically and consistently across the computers in the domain.

To add all Enterprise Admins to the local Administrators group:

Step 1.   Log on to a domain controller.

Step 2.   Open a command prompt.

Step 3.   Type **gpmc** and press **Enter**.

Step 4.   The Group Policy Management utility launches. Expand the Forest, Domains, domain node, and Group Policy Objects node to expose the **Default Domain Policy**.

Step 5.   Right-click the **Default Domain Policy** and select **Edit**.

Step 6.   The Group Policy Management Editor utility launches. Expand the Computer Configuration, Policies, Windows Settings, and Security Settings to expose the **Restricted Groups** node (see Figure 4-10).

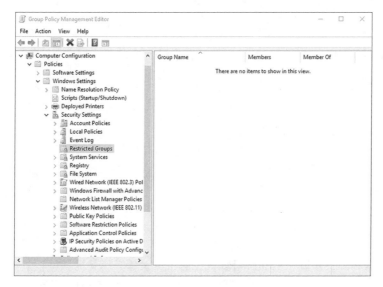

Figure 4-10   The Group Policy Management Editor with the Restricted Groups Node Exposed

Step 7.   Right-click the **Restricted Groups** node and select **Add Group**.

Step 8.   Click **Browse**.

Step 9.   Type **Administrators** and click **Check Names**. The word should underline, indicating the group was found. Click **OK**.

Step 10.   Click **OK**.

Step 11.   The Administrators Properties dialog opens, allowing you to select domain objects to become a member of this group and any groups this group should be made a member of. Click **Add** at the top, next to the **Members of this group** box.

Step 12.   Click **Browse**.

Step 13.   Type **Enterprise Admins** and click **Check Names**. The word should underline, indicating the group was found. Click **OK**.

Step 14.   **Enterprise Admins** will now be displayed as a member of the group (see Figure 4-11). Click **OK**.

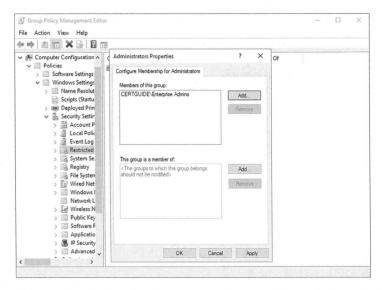

Figure 4-11   Designating Members of a Restricted Group via Group Policy Objects in the GPME

Step 15.   Click **OK** on the Administrators Properties dialog.

For any computer to which this GPO applies, the domain group Enterprise Admins will be added to the local Administrators group. Network users who belong to the Enterprise Admins group will in turn receive local administrator privileges on those computers.

Managing Default Active Directory Containers

Chapter 3 demonstrated various methods for creating user and computer objects, often without noting where in the directory those objects should be created. AD DS creates a number of default containers when a domain is first created, and by default that is where new objects are created in the directory. Two containers in particular, Users and Computers, are where new user and computer objects are placed, respectively.

Now that you know how to create OUs that reflect the structure of your organization, the process of onboarding new users and computers may need to change.

Specifically there are two command-line utilities that Microsoft provides to redirect the default location for new user and computer objects:

- **Redircmp**: Changes the default container for new computer objects
- **Redirusr**: Changes the default container for new user objects

The only requirement to use these utilities is a domain functional level of at least Windows Server 2003.

An example of each utility follows:

```
redircmp ou=FinanceComputers,ou=Finance,dc=certguide,dc=com
redirusr ou=FinanceUsers,ou=Finance,dc=certguide,dc=com
```

Once either of these commands has been run, the message "Redirection was successful" will be returned, and the specified container will be the default location for newly created objects.

Exam Preparation Tasks

As mentioned in the section "Book Features" in the Introduction, you have a few choices for exam preparation: the exercises here; Chapter 17, "Final Preparation"; and the exam simulation questions in the Pearson Test Prep Software Online.

Review All Key Topics

Review the most important topics in this chapter, noted with the Key Topics icon in the outer margin of the page. Table 4-5 lists a reference of these key topics and the page number on which each is found.

Table 4-5   Key Topics for Chapter 4

Key Topic Element	Description	Page Number
Paragraph	Description of organizational unit (OU) objects	103
Paragraph	Description of group objects	105
List	Possible group scopes	106
Table 4-2	AD DS groups versus organizational units	106
Figure 4-2	Create Group dialog box	107
Figure 4-4	Create Organizational Unit dialog box	110
Table 4-3	Group and OU PowerShell cmdlets reference	111
Table 4-4	Group type conversion paths	115
List	Description of IGDLA acronym	116

Key Topic Element	Description	Page Number
Command	**Get-ADGroupMember** cmdlet	117
Paragraph	Managing local group membership with GPO	122
List	Default AD container utilities	125

Complete Tables and Lists from Memory

Print a copy of Appendix B, "Memory Tables" (found on the book website), or at least the section for this chapter, and complete the tables and lists from memory. Appendix C, "Memory Tables Answer Key," also on the website, includes completed tables and lists to check your work.

Define Key Terms

Define the following key terms from this chapter and check your answers in the glossary:

organizational unit (OU), group, group type, group scope, group nesting, IGDLA, delegation, local group, default containers

End-of-Chapter Review Questions

The answers to these questions appear in Appendix A. For more practice with exam format questions, use the Pearson Test Prep Software Online.

1. You are responsible for building the AD DS directory for the Finance department at your organization. You have been delegated authority over the Finance OU. There are three general security profiles to manage: Managers, General Staff, and Temp employees. How would you organize the directory tree to facilitate administration?

   a. Create three global security groups in the Finance OU for each security profile. Assign users as members of the correct security group.

   b. Delegate administration of each Manager's subordinate employees to that manager user. Allow them to organize the directory as they see fit.

   c. Create the users in the Finance OU. Create GPOs for each security profile. Assign those GPOs to the appropriate user objects.

   d. Create three child OUs of the Finance OU for the security profiles. Place user objects into the correct OU for their employee type. Create and assign GPOs to each child OU that reflects the needs of each security profile.

2. The two primary benefits to create organizational units (OUs) in the directory that mirror organizational structure and administrative goals are (Choose two.)

    a. Delegation of administration for individual OUs to users.

    b. Securing the directory from regional administrators operating outside their boundaries.

    c. Applying GPOs to OUs eases and automates the application of security policies.

    d. Isolating directory corruption and potential malware threats.

3. The two types of AD DS groups are _____ and _____ (two words).

4. Your directory currently has a Global Security group. You need to convert that group to a domain local group. What steps would you perform to accomplish this? (Choose three.)

    a. Convert the group to a domain local group.

    b. Delete and re-create the group.

    c. Disable the member accounts in the group.

    d. Convert the group to a universal group.

    e. Ensure the group is not a member of another group.

5. Write a PowerShell command to create a new security group with a global scope named FinanceFolderAccess.

6. There are 45 user accounts in the FinanceUsers OU. You need to make all these accounts members of the new FinanceFolderAccess group. How would you accomplish this?

    a. **Get-ADUser -Filter -SearchScope subtree -SearchBase "OU= FinanceUsers,dc=certguide,dc=com" | Add-ADGroupMember FinanceFolderAccess**

    b. **Get-ADUser -Filter -SearchScope subtree -SearchBase "OU=FinanceUsers,dc=certguide,dc=com" | Add-ADPrincipalGroupMembership -MemberOf FinanceFolderAccess**

    c. Manually add each user to the group

    d. Add the FinanceUsers OU as a member of the group

7. The Finance department has two shared network folders. One is for all Finance users to share, and the second is reserved for managers in the Finance department. Managers have access to both, but non-Managers cannot access the managers' share due to the sensitivity of the information. How would you organize your OUs, groups, and permissions to most effectively manage this? (Hint: IGDLA)

8. A group meant to contain identity accounts such as users or computers is known as a _____.

9. Your directory has an OU for the Finance department named Finance. That OU has three direct children, FinanceManagers, FinanceUsers, and FinanceTemps. Due to growth in the size of the department, you have decided to delegate password administration for the Users and Temps to Amy while retaining control over the Managers OU yourself. Which of the following tasks should you perform?

   a. Run the Delegation of Control Wizard on the Finance OU and delegate Amy's user account the **Reset user passwords and force password change at next logon** task. Disallow permission inheritance on the FinanceManagers OU.

   b. Run the Delegation of Control Wizard on the certguide.com domain object and delegate Amy's user account the **Reset user passwords and force password change at next logon** task. Disallow permission inheritance on the Finance OU.

   c. Run the Delegation of Control Wizard on the FinanceUsers and FinanceTemps OUs and grant Amy's account **Read and Create All Child Objects** permissions.

   d. Run the Delegation of Control Wizard on the Finance OUs and grant Amy's account **Read and Create All Child Objects** permissions. Disallow permission inheritance on the FinanceManagers OU.

10. You plan to install a number of new computers in the Finance department to support all the new hires. You'll be using a script but want to ensure that all the new computer objects are placed into a specific OU, FinanceComputers, located in the Finance OU of your domain certguide.com. What command should you run before adding the computer objects to the domain?

This chapter covers the following topics:

- **Creating and Configuring Service Accounts**: This section describes how to create and manage service accounts that have both local and network access.

- **Configuring Kerberos Constrained Delegation (KCD)**: This section describes how to set up Kerberos Constrained Delegation (KCD) for applications running on the domain.

- **Configuring Default Domain Account Policies**: This section describes how to configure the Account Policies found in the Default Domain Policy object that always take precedence in the domain.

- **Configuring and Applying Password Settings Objects (PSOs)**: This section describes how to configure Password Settings Objects (PSOs), which are used to set up fine-grained password policy.

CHAPTER 5

Configuring Service Authentication and Account Policies

In most cases, user accounts are meant to be used by actual users on the network. Individuals sitting at keyboards log in with the account information and are granted or denied access. In some cases, however, user accounts are needed for software and services that run continually without user interaction. These services still need access to resources on the network and have accounts that must be managed by Active Directory administrators. In general terms, accounts used for this purpose are called *service accounts*.

This chapter describes how to grant permissions to local services accounts, which are defined on one computer and used only by software on that computer. It also describes how to create various types of managed service accounts, which are defined in Active Directory and available to all computers and services joined to the domain. Finally, this chapter describes how to manage password settings, such as complexity requirements and expiration, for different levels in the directory.

"Do I Know This Already?" Quiz

The "Do I Know This Already?" quiz allows you to assess whether you should read this entire chapter thoroughly or jump to the "Exam Preparation Tasks" section. If you are in doubt about your answers to these questions or your own assessment of your knowledge of the topics, read the entire chapter. Table 5-1 lists the major headings in this chapter and their corresponding "Do I Know This Already?" quiz questions. You can find the answers in Appendix A, "Answers to the 'Do I Know This Already?' Quizzes."

Table 5-1 "Do I Know This Already?" Section-to-Question Mapping

Foundation Topics Section	Questions
Creating and Configuring Service Accounts	1-4
Configuring Kerberos Constrained Delegation (KCD)	5-6
Configuring Default Domain Account Policies	7-8
Configuring and Applying Password Settings Objects (PSOs)	9-10

CAUTION   The goal of self-assessment is to gauge your mastery of the topics in this chapter. If you do not know the answer to a question or are only partially sure of the answer, you should mark that question as wrong for purposes of the self-assessment. Giving yourself credit for an answer you correctly guess skews your self-assessment results and might provide you with a false sense of security.

1. Which service account context authenticates to the domain as a machine account and has limited access on the local machine?

   a. Local service

   b. Network service

   c. Local system

   d. Group Managed Service Account

2. Which password options should be selected for a service account? (Choose two.)

   a. Password never expires

   b. User must change password at next logon

   c. Minimum password history of 12

   d. User cannot change password

3. Which service account context authenticates to the domain as an anonymous account and has limited access on the local machine?

   a. Local service

   b. Network service

   c. Local system

   d. Group Managed Service Account

4. Which PowerShell cmdlet is used to create a new Group Managed Service Account (gMSA) in AD DS?

   a. **Install-ADServiceAccount**

   b. **Add-ADComputerServiceAccount**

   c. **New-ADServiceAccount**

   d. **Add-ADServiceAccount**

5. With Kerberos Delegation, an application attempts to access another service under which security context?

   a. Group Managed Service Account

   b. User account

   c. Virtual service account

   d. Network service

6. Which delegation option for a computer object enables Kerberos Constrained Delegation?

   a. Trust this computer for delegation to specified services only

   b. Trust this computer for delegation to any service

   c. Do not trust this computer for delegation

   d. Trust all computer and user objects for specified services

7. Which scope of Group Policy Object (GPO) will override the Account Policies for the Default Domain Policy?

   a. Forest

   b. Domain

   c. Organizational unit

   d. The Account Policies specified in the Default Domain Policy cannot be overridden with a GPO.

8. Which Password Policy setting is used to ensure that users do not evade the password history requirement by changing their passwords multiple times in a row?

   a. Maximum password age

   b. Minimum password age

   c. Account lockout threshold

   d. Minimum password length

9. A user object has a PSO with a precedence of 20 applied directly to the user object. The user also belongs to a security group that has a PSO with a precedence of 3 applied to it. Which PSO will the system apply to the user?

   a. Neither; the system will produce an error.

   b. The PSO applied to the security group.

   c. PSOs cannot be applied to security groups, only users.

   d. The PSO directly applied to the user object.

10. Which security group has permission to create and modify PSOs by default?

   a. Domain Admins

   b. Enterprise Admins

   c. Domain Users

   d. Everyone

Foundation Topics

Creating and Configuring Service Accounts

A large part of modern computing, whether in the context of a corporate network or simply on your home computer, is executables and processes running in the background. These are applications that provide a service of some kind, often in response to specific events but also on repeating schedules or even on demand. Even the most basic installations of Windows have dozens of these services running in the background (see Figure 5-1).

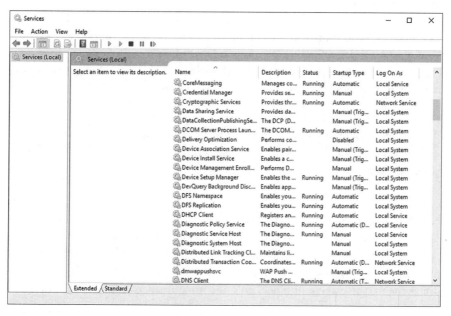

Figure 5-1   The Services App Showing Some of the Services Running on a Windows Computer

This is doubly true for enterprise servers. A lot of a server's primary functionality comes in the form of services because servers are designed to run quietly on the network without stopping or shutting down. The server roles that have been installed earlier in this book, such as AD DS and DNS, execute as services. You can see these services listed by running the Services app from Control Panel on a domain controller.

Service Accounts

To properly execute and access resources on the computer, a service needs an account to impersonate, often called a logon context. The credentials for this account are saved in the properties of the service, and it walks through the logon process with those credentials when it starts up and uses those credentials to perform the tasks it needs to perform. This account, known as the service account, is typically one of three built-in service accounts in the Windows OS:

- Local system

- Local service

- Network service

The local system account provides maximum access to the local computer the service is running on and can log on to an Active Directory Domain Services domain impersonating the computer account in the domain. This high-level of access is not used very often; it violates the principle of least privilege.

> **NOTE**   The principle of least privilege is a maxim for deploying secure software that requires any identity to only have as much access as is needed to perform its function and no more than that.

Services also sometimes run under the local service account. The context of local service provides minimal access to the system and authenticates to an AD DS domain as an anonymous user. In between these two extremes is the network service account, which still provides minimal access to the system but authenticates to the network as the machine account. See Table 5-2 for a breakdown of these accounts.

Table 5-2   Properties of Built-In Service Accounts

Account	Local Access	Network Authentication
Local System	Maximum	Machine account
Local Service	Minimum	Anonymous
Network Service	Minimum	Machine account

One challenge for these service accounts that arises in a networked environment is access to network resources. For example, how would you grant access to a service that needed to access a shared folder on a file server? What if the service needed to read or write to a database hosted on another server? One solution would be to grant permissions to the machine account in AD DS (via the IGDLA method) and use either the local system or network service account. This introduces administration tasks if the service is ever spun up on another computer since every computer has a different machine account. The current trend of immutable infrastructure and containerization would make that process almost completely untenable as computers with random names were frequently spun up and shut down.

Instead, the recommended solution is to create an account in AD DS specifically for the service to log on as, known as a service account. This account is no different from a typical user account with the exception of a few password strategies. To prevent having to constantly update the service configuration, the password for a service account is set once on creation and set to never expire.

To create a service account in AD DS, follow these same steps as outlined in Chapter 3, "Creating and Managing Active Directory Users and Computers":

Step 1.   Log on to a writeable domain controller.

Step 2.   Start Server Manager from either the Start Menu or Taskbar.

Step 3.   From the context menu at the top of the panel, click **Tools** and then select **Active Directory Administrative Center**.

Step 4.   On the left-hand panel select the domain you want to add users to. The right-hand panel displays the top-level containers that are created in a directory by default.

Step 5.   Double-click the container or organizational unit you want to add the user to. This is typically either Users or a custom OU you have created.

Step 6.   On the Tasks panel click **New** and then select **User**.

Step 7.   You are presented with a dialog box of information to fill out about the user you want to create.

Step 8.   Be sure to choose the **Other password options** button and check the **Password never expires** and **User cannot change password** boxes (see Figure 5-2).

Step 9.   You may make this account a member of any security groups it requires at this stage. You may also perform that task later if those groups have not yet been created.

Step 10.   Click **OK**.

This account can now be used for the logon context for a service running on a member client or server. The service will gain any permissions granted to the account in the domain just as if a user were using the account (see Figure 5-3).

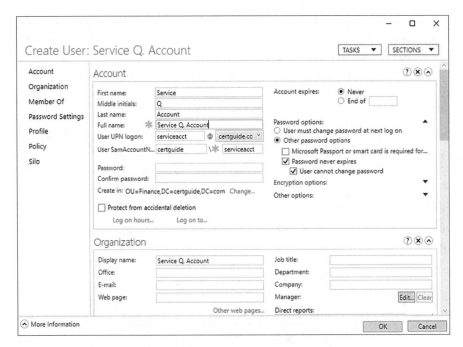

Figure 5-2   The Create User Dialog with Appropriate Password Options Selected for a Service Account

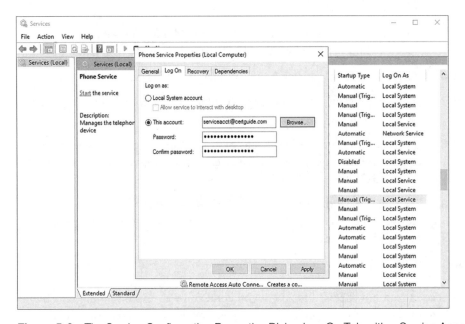

Figure 5-3   The Service Configuration Properties Dialog Log On Tab with a Service Account User Set as the Authentication Context

Managed Service Accounts

Service accounts created by the method described previously do introduce a significant security flaw. Passwords should have a routine expiration set for them. If you flag the password to reset in AD DS, however, you'll be constantly updating service configurations with the new password. The officially recommended solution was to simply produce a long and complex password to reduce the likelihood of a security breach.

With Server 2008 R2, Microsoft introduced the concept of Standard Managed Service Accounts (sMSAs). An sMSA is a special class of object in AD DS that can have its password updated automatically by the computer it represents. Windows recycles the password routinely (every 30 days by default) to a new 240 byte (120 character) cryptographically random password. sMSAs cannot be locked out and cannot be used for interactive logons. Technically, an administrator can set the MSA password to a known value, although this would be an unusual situation likely only used in troubleshooting scenarios.

Creating an sMSA is a four-step process:

Step 1.   Create the account.

Step 2.   Associate it with a computer.

Step 3.   Install the account on the computer that was associated.

Step 4.   Configure the service to use the sMSA.

The first three steps cannot be performed with any of the existing GUI tools; you need to use PowerShell. Table 5-3 displays the PowerShell cmdlets for working with service accounts.

Table 5-3   PowerShell Cmdlets for Working with Service Accounts

Cmdlet	Description
New-ADServiceAccount	Create a service account.
Add-ADComputerServiceAccount	Associate a service account with a computer account.
Install-ADServiceAccount	Install a service account on a member server.
Add-KDSRootKey	Create a Root Key in the Key Distribution Service (KDS).

The PowerShell cmdlet to create the service account is

```
New-ADServiceAccount [-Name] <string>`
-RestrictToSingleComputer`
[-Enabled <System.Nullable[bool]>]
```

The -**RestrictToSingleComputer** switch indicates this account will be a Standard Managed Service Account and not a Group Managed Service Account (gMSA), covered later in this chapter.

> **NOTE**   The default location for a managed service account is a top-level OU in the domain named **Managed Service Accounts**. You can supply the -**Path** parameter to specify an alternate location as described in the official documentation: https://technet.microsoft.com/en-us/library/hh852236(v=wps.630).aspx.

The PowerShell cmdlet to associate the account with a computer account is

```
Add-ADComputerServiceAccount [-Identity] <ADComputer>`
[-ServiceAccount] <ADServiceAccount[]>`
```

For the -**Identity** parameter you can supply the object name, DistinguishedName, SamAccountName, SID, or ObjectGUID. This cmdlet can also take a computer object from the PowerShell pipeline from a cmdlet such as **Get-ADComputer** (covered in Chapter 3).

For the -**ServiceAccount parameter** you can supply the object name, DistinguishedName, SamAccountName, SID, or ObjectGUID.

The Powershell cmdlet to install a managed service account on a member server or client is

```
Install-ADServiceAccount [-Identity] <ADGroup>
```

For the -**Identity** parameter you can supply the object name, DistinguishedName, SamAccountName, SID, or ObjectGUID.

To create and install an sMSA:

Step 1.   Log on to a writeable domain controller.

Step 2.   Launch a PowerShell IDE or command prompt.

Step 3.   Type the following command and press **Enter**:

```
New-ADServiceAccount -Name msaClient1
-RestrictToSingleComputer -Enabled $true
```

Step 4.   When the prompt returns, type the following command and press **Enter**:

```
Add-ADComputerServiceAccount -Identity CLIENT1
-ServiceAccount msaClient1
```

The account has now been created and associated with a computer.

Step 5.   Log on to the computer specified in Steps 3 and 4.

Step 6.   Launch a PowerShell IDE or command prompt.

NOTE Depending on which operating system you are trying to set up, you may need to install the Active Directory module for Windows PowerShell, import the module in your PowerShell context, or both. See further instructions here: https:// blogs.technet.microsoft.com/ashleymcglone/2016/02/26/install-the-active-directory-powershell-module-on-windows-10/.

Step 7.   Type the following command and press **Enter**:

```
Install-ADServiceAccount -Identity msaClient1
```

The account can now be used when configuring services. Note that the password can be left blank (the computer will manage it), and the account name ends with a USD ($) sign (see Figure 5-4).

Figure 5-4   The Service Configuration Properties Dialog Log On Tab with a gMSA Set as the Authentication Context

Group Managed Service Accounts (gMSAs)

As good an idea as Standard Managed Services Accounts are, they still have significant flaws in their implementation. Most obvious is the single-host rule. sMSAs can only be associated with and used on one host computer. sMSAs also cannot be used in scheduled tasks, nor are they supported in Microsoft SQL Server or Exchange.

Microsoft's solution to these problems is the Group Managed Service Account (gMSA). gMSAs work similarly to sMSAs but rely on Microsoft's Key Distribution Service (KDS) to produce a private key. This key is used to produce passwords when necessary on each host that wants to use the gMSA.

Creating the gMSA is a three-step process: Create the KDS Root Key (only has to be done once per forest), create the gMSA, and configure the gMSA on the hosts.

The PowerShell cmdlet to create the KDS Root Key is

```
Add-KdsRootKey -EffectiveImmediately
```

This straightforward cmdlet produces a new KDS Root Key in Microsoft Group Key Distribution Service in Active Directory. This only needs to be run once for any given forest.

The PowerShell cmdlet to create the gMSA is the same cmdlet used to create the sMSA but with a different parameter set:

```
New-ADServiceAccount [-Name] <String>`
-DNSHostName <String>`
[-PrincipalsAllowedToRetrieveManagedPassword <ADPrincipal[]> ]
[-Enabled <Boolean> ]`
```

For this parameter set you need to specify a DNS name for the account. Typically this is based on the domain name and the name of the account, for example, <acct name>.certguide.com.

The **-PrincipalsAllowedToRetrieveManagedPassword** parameter allows you to specify an AD DS computer account, or more likely a security group, that is allowed to retrieve the password and consequently use the gMSA.

Installing a gMSA is the same process as described previously for installing an sMSA.

To create and install a gMSA:

Step 1.   Log on to a writeable domain controller.

Step 2.   Create a new security group named **gMSAGroup** using the process described in Chapter 4, "Creating and Managing Active Directory Groups and Organizational Units."

Step 3. Add any computer accounts from the directory as members of **gMSA-Group** that will be using this gMSA.

Step 4. Launch a PowerShell IDE or command prompt.

Step 5. Type the following command and press **Enter**:

```
Add-KDSRootKey -EffectiveImmediately
```

Step 6. Type the following command and press **Enter**:

```
New-ADServiceAccount -Name gMSAAcct -DnsHostName gMSAAcct.
certguide.com -PrincipalsAllowedToRetrieveManagedPassword
gMSAGroup -Enabled $true
```

Step 7. Log on to one of the hosts that was granted access to the security group created in step 2. Be aware the host may need to be restarted after being added to the group.

Step 8. Launch a PowerShell IDE or command prompt.

Step 9. Type the following command and press **Enter**:

```
Install-ADServiceAccount -Identity gMSAAcct
```

The account can now be used when configuring services. Note that the password can be left blank (the computer will manage it), and the account name ends with a USD ($) sign.

Virtual Service Accounts

With Windows Server 2008 R2, Microsoft introduced another type of service account known as a virtual service account. A virtual service account can be thought of as a locally managed service account. There are three primary features of a virtual service account:

- **No password management required**: The local computer that uses the virtual service account handles all password management.

- **Accesses the domain as the computer account**: A service running under a virtual service account authenticates against an AD DS domain as the computer account that it's running on, similar to the local network service account.

- **Is a specifically named account**: The virtual service account has a unique name, that of the service using it, instead of a computer-wide name such as local service or network service.

The use case for a virtual service account is to provide administrators with an account like network service but with a specific name. With this type of account you can grant permissions to the virtual service account to protected local resources. If you used the network service account instead, every service on the machine running as network service would then have access to those resources. Instead, the virtual service account can be granted permission, and only that service gains those permissions.

Installing a virtual service account is straightforward. No domain or directory interaction is required. Simply configure the service to run under a security context with a logon of NT Service*<service name>*. Leave the password blank when using this account as the security context (see Figure 5-5).

<service name> is the name of the service as displayed in the Windows Service Properties General tab.

Figure 5-5   The Service Properties Dialog Log On Tab with a Virtual Service Account Set as the Authentication Context

Configuring Kerberos Constrained Delegation (KCD)

A complex and potentially confusing topic, Kerberos Constrained Delegation (KCD) is ultimately fairly straightforward. Kerberos Delegation is about allowing one application or service to delegate authentication to another service. This process becomes Kerberos Constrained Delegation when you limit, or constrain, the services that can be delegated to. An example is the easiest way to grasp it.

Imagine the common scenario of a web application, running in IIS, that allows users to read and write to an SQL Server database. When an application like this is deployed, you must address the question of how to grant the web application permission to access the database. One solution is to simply use a local account in the SQL Server and code those credentials into the web application. Another option is having a dedicated service account with read and write access to the database.

Both of these solutions push important access management back onto the web application. Different users likely have different access levels to the data in the database, but from the perspective of the database all queries are presented with the same user credentials (those of the local account or service account). If you want to restrict a specific group of users from viewing a subset of data, the application has to programmatically enforce this restriction. This leads to administrative interfaces programmed at the application level to control authorization to the data in the database.

An alternative to this process is to use Kerberos Delegation, sometimes inaccurately called pass-through authentication. With Kerberos Delegation the web application attempts to access the database in the context of, or impersonating, the user currently using the application. As long as that user is a domain user account and delegation has been set up properly, then the database can manage authorization with its own internal tools.

Constrained Delegation

Constraining Kerberos Delegation allows you to prevent the authorized service from having full access to network resources when delegating. The permission to delegate is instead constrained to a list of available services limiting delegation to only the services it needs to access.

To set up Kerberos Delegation:

Step 1. Log on to a writeable domain controller.

Step 2. Start Server Manager from either the Start Menu or Taskbar.

Step 3. From the context menu at the top of the panel click **Tools** and then select **Active Directory Administrative Center**.

Step 4. Navigate to the computer object you want to set up delegation for (e.g., in the scenario above the computer hosting the web application).

Step 5. Right-click the computer object and select **Properties**.

Step 6.   On the left-hand panel select **Delegation** or scroll down the Details pane until the Delegation section is shown.

Step 7.   Review the three options (see Figure 5-6).

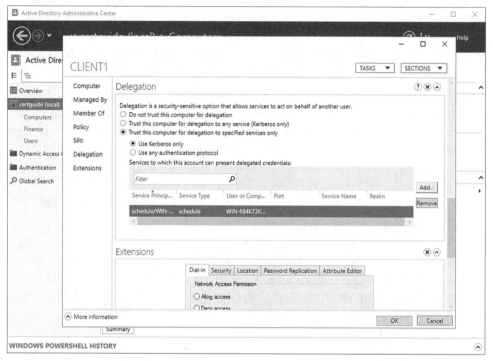

Figure 5-6   The Delegation Configuration Page for a Computer Object. Select **Trust this computer for delegation to specified services only** to Enable Kerberos Constrained Delegation. The Services Are Specified Below That Selection.

- **Do not trust this computer for delegation**: This is the default state for all objects in AD DS and prevents delegation.

- **Trust this computer for delegation to any service (Kerberos only)**: This enables basic Kerberos Delegation. This option exists for backward compatibility purposes but otherwise should be avoided.

- **Trust this computer for delegation to specified services only**: This enables Kerberos Constrained Delegation. Notice that once this option is chosen a red alert indicates you must also select at least one service to constrain delegation to.

Step 8.   Click the **Add...** button next to the list of **Services to which this account can present delegated credentials**.

Step 9.   The Add Services dialog appears. Click **Add Users or Computers…** to open the standard directory search window.

Step 10.   Type the name of a computer object on the network and click **OK**.

Step 11.   Browse the list of available services on that computer. You may need to expand the window for better visibility (see Figure 5-7).

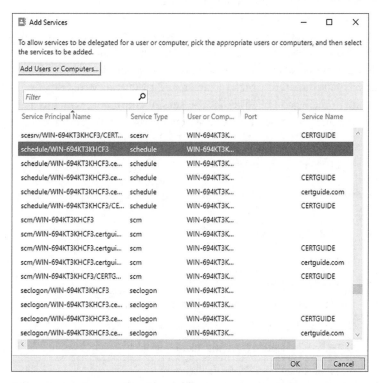

Figure 5-7   The Add Services Dialog for Specifying Service(s) to Constrain Delegation to

Step 12.   Select a service and click **OK**.

Step 13.   You are returned to the computer object properties with the chosen service listed in the delegation section. Click **OK**.

Kerberos Constrained Delegation has now been enabled for the computer chosen during Step 4.

Managing Service Principal Names (SPNs)

In the preceding scenario, the delegating identity is a web application and not a computer. Web applications do not execute in the context of a computer account and instead use something known as an application pool where an identity can be specified. It is this application identity, or potentially any other service account identity, that you want to enable delegation on for most services. Unfortunately, if you look at the properties for user accounts in the directory, you do not see the option to configure delegation.

This is because user accounts do not have a Service Principal Name (SPN). An SPN is used by a service instance to uniquely identify it on the domain. SPNs are used by Kerberos authentication to associate a service instance with a service logon account. Computers create their own SPN when they join the domain, and many services create an SPN if they add their account to the domain. If you want to add an SPN to a service account you have created, which in turn gives it the ability to delegate to other services on the domain, you need to use the **setspn** command, which is a command-line utility installed with AD DS. The syntax for the **setspn** command is as follows:

```
setspn <Computer> [-l] [-r] [-d <SPN>] [-s <SPN>]
```

Table 5-4 details **setspn** command parameters.

Table 5-4 Parameters of the setspn Command

Parameter	Description
<Computer>	The AD object for which to configure the SPN
-l	Lists the currently registered SPNs for the object
-r	Resets the default SPN registrations for the object
-d *<SPN>*	Deletes the specified SPN for the object
-s *<SPN>*	Adds the specified SPN for the object

To create an SPN for a service account in the directory:

Step 1. Log on to a writeable domain controller.

Step 2. Launch a command prompt window.

Step 3. Type the following command to create an SPN on an existing service account (see Figure 5-8):

```
setspn -s http/app.certguide.com <service account>
```

For the *<service account>* parameter, type the fully qualified domain name you used earlier in this chapter when creating a service account, for example, *certguide\serviceacct*

```
C:\>setspn -s http/app.certguide.com certguide\serviceacct
Checking domain DC=certguide,DC=com

Registering ServicePrincipalNames for CN=Service Q. Account,OU=Finance,DC=certguide,DC=com
        http/app.certguide.com
Updated object

C:\>_
```

Figure 5-8   The **setspn** Command and Its Output Upon Successful Completion

If you open ADAC or ADUC and view the properties of the account, you now see the Delegation section available for configuration just as previously described.

Configuring Default Domain Account Policies

Generally, the settings defined in Group Policy Objects (GPOs) are applied in a cascading or waterfall fashion. Because different GPOs can be applied at different levels whenever a GPO is applied, the settings in that GPO append to and override the settings from the previous GPO. There is a specific order or application for this cascade.

One notable exception to this order is the Account Policies found in the Default Domain Policy. These settings override all other GPOs on the domain and consequently represent the policies for every object on the network.

NOTE   In Windows Server 2008, Microsoft introduced a feature called Fine-Grained Password Policies (FGPP), which allows you to specify different policies for different sets of users in the same domain. An introduction to FGPP is covered later in this chapter, or you can read more about FGPP here: https://technet.microsoft.com/en-us/library/cc770842(v=ws.10).aspx.

There are three categories of policy settings in the Account Policies node of the Default Domain Policy. They are

- **Password Policy Settings**: The complexity and age requirements for user passwords in the domain

- **Account Lockout Policy Settings**: The rules that can be tripped to cause a user account to be locked out

- **Kerberos Policy Settings**: The settings for the Kerberos authentication that occurs when users access resources on the network

All these policy settings are used for the purpose of securing your network against malicious intrusion. Most of the settings should be familiar to you, such as minimum password length and account lockout threshold. Configuring these policies is an important part of a robust security plan and may be required for regulatory compliance purposes as well.

Configuring Domain and Local User Password Policy Settings

To configure the Domain Default Password Policy settings, you need to start the Group Policy Management Editor:

Step 1. Log on to a writeable domain controller.

Step 2. Launch a command prompt window.

Step 3. Type **gpmc** and press **Enter.**

Step 4. The Group Policy Management utility launches. Expand the Forest, Domains, domain node, and Group Policy Objects node to expose the **Default Domain Policy**.

Step 5. Right-click the **Default Domain Policy** and select **Edit**.

Step 6. The Group Policy Management Editor utility launches. Expand the Computer Configuration, Policies, Windows Settings, Security Settings, Account Policies node and select **Password Policy**.

Step 7. The panel on the right displays the following Password Policies (see Figure 5-9).

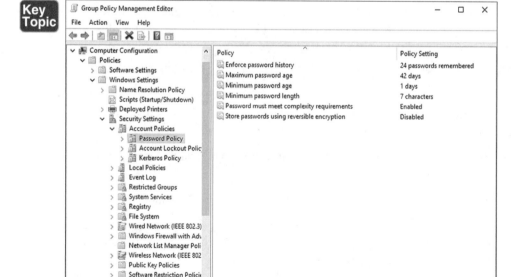

Figure 5-9 The Password Policy Settings in the Default Domain Policy

- **Enforce password history**: This setting determines how many new unique passwords must be associated with a user account before an old password can be reused. It can be between 0 and 24.

- **Maximum password age**: This setting determines the period of time (in days) that a password can be used before the system forcefully expires it and requires the user to change it.

- **Minimum password age**: This setting determines the period of time (in days) that a password must be in use before it can be changed. Using this setting prevents a user from quickly cycling through the password history count to reuse an old password right away.

- **Minimum password length**: This setting determines the fewest number of characters that a password may contain.

- **Password must meet complexity requirements**: This setting forces user passwords to meet a number of different complexity requirements. These requirements are detailed on the **Explain** tab of the Setting Property dialog.

- **Store passwords using reversible encryption**: This setting determines how AD DS stores passwords. Contrary to what you might think, it is more secure to leave it disabled. When disabled, passwords are stored with one-way encryption, which is less vulnerable to attack.

Step 8.   You can modify any of the policy settings by double-clicking the setting or right-clicking and selecting **Properties**.

Step 9.   The property page for each setting also includes an **Explain** tab that details exactly what the setting does.

Configuring Account Lockout Policy Settings

To configure the Domain Default Account Lockout Policy settings, you need to start the Group Policy Management Editor:

Step 1.   Log on to a writeable domain controller.

Step 2.   Launch a command prompt window.

Step 3.   Type **gpmc** and press **Enter.**

Step 4.   The Group Policy Management utility launches. Expand the Forest, Domains, domain node, and Group Policy Objects node to expose the Default Domain Policy.

Step 5.   Right-click the **Default Domain Policy** and select **Edit**.

Step 6.   The Group Policy Management Editor utility launches. Expand the Computer Configuration, Policies, Windows Settings, Security Settings, Account Policies node and select **Account Lockout Policy.**

Step 7.   The panel on the right displays the following Account Lockout Policies (see Figure 5-10).

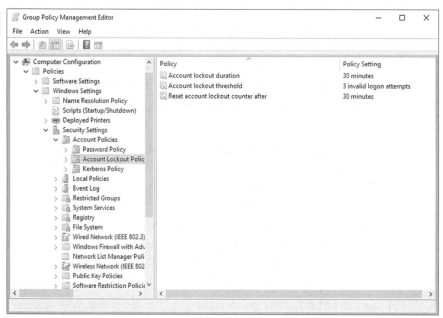

Figure 5-10   The Account Lockout Policy Settings in the Default Domain Policy

- **Account lockout duration**: This setting determines the period of time (in minutes) a locked-out account remains locked out before automatically becoming unlocked. Setting this to 0 causes accounts to lock out indefinitely until an administrator explicitly unlocks it.

- **Account lockout threshold**: This setting determines the number of failed logon attempts that causes a user account to be locked out. Setting this to 0 allows for indefinite tries—that is, the account will never be locked out.

- **Reset account lockout count after**: This setting determines the period of time (in minutes) after a failed logon attempt before the counter is reset to 0 bad attempts. This setting must be less than or equal to the Account lockout duration.

Step 8.   You can modify any of the policy settings by double-clicking the setting or right-clicking and selecting **Properties**.

Step 9.   The property page for each setting also includes an Explain tab that details exactly what the setting does.

Configuring Kerberos Policy Settings Within Group Policy

The Kerberos Policy settings are almost never adjusted by administrators. These settings are used by the software on the network to exchange Kerberos tickets for authentication and authorization. Microsoft does want you to be aware of where they are configured in the unlikely event you need to troubleshoot an issue with them.

To configure the Domain Default Kerberos Policy settings, you need to start the Group Policy Management Editor:

Step 1.   Log on to a writeable domain controller.

Step 2.   Launch a command prompt window.

Step 3.   Type **gpmc** and press **Enter**.

Step 4.   The Group Policy Management utility launches. Expand the Forest, Domains, domain node, and Group Policy Objects node to expose the Default Domain Policy.

Step 5.   Right-click the **Default Domain Policy** and select **Edit**.

Step 6.   The Group Policy Management Editor utility launches. Expand the Computer Configuration, Policies, Windows Settings, Security Settings, Account Policies node and select **Kerberos Policy**.

Step 7.   The panel on the right displays the following Kerberos Policies (see Figure 5-11):

- **Enforce user logon restrictions**: This setting determines whether the Key Distribution Center validates every request for a session ticket against the user rights policy. Disabling it is not recommended but can improve the speed of network access.

- **Maximum lifetime for service ticket**: This setting determines the period of time (in minutes) that a session ticket is valid. This setting must be greater than 10 minutes and less than or equal to the setting for Maximum lifetime for user ticket.

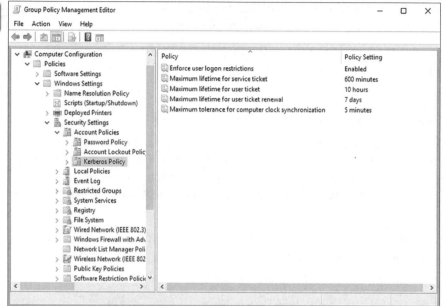

Figure 5-11   The Kerberos Policy Settings in the Default Domain Policy

- **Maximum lifetime for user ticket**: This setting determines the period of time (in hours) that a user's ticket-granting ticket is valid.

- **Maximum lifetime for user ticket renewal**: This setting determines the period of time (in days) during which a user's ticket-granting ticket may be renewed.

- **Maximum tolerance for computer clock synchronization**: This setting determines the maximum allowable time difference (in minutes) between the clock on the client computer and the clock on the authenticating server.

Step 8.   You can modify any of the policy settings by double-clicking the setting or right-clicking and selecting **Properties**.

Step 9.   The property page for each setting also includes an **Explain** tab that details exactly what the setting does.

Configuring and Applying Password Settings Objects (PSOs)

Microsoft's one-size-fits-all approach to password policy settings in AD DS was a point of contention for system administrators for many years. It didn't always make sense to apply one single password policy to every user in the directory. For example, the high level of network access and permissions that IT staffs have can justify stringent password policies. Those same policies may not be appropriate for staff such as retail employees or temporary workers.

Microsoft introduced the concept of Fine-Grained Password Policy (FGPP) with Windows Server 2008. FGPP allows administrators to create Password Settings Objects (PSOs) that override the password policy settings from the Default Domain Policy. PSOs can then be applied to either user account objects or security groups in the directory.

PSOs can be found in the Password Settings container in the System container, both of which are created by default on a new domain. It is important to note that while you can see PSOs in the Active Directory Users and Computers utility, PSOs can only be created and managed with the newer Active Directory Administrative Center (ADAC).

PSO Precedence

One important concept for working with PSOs is precedence. PSOs, like other Group Policy Objects in AD, can run into conflict when more than one apply to the same object. To resolve conflicts, GPOs follow the LSDOU methodology for applying settings, which stands for Local, Site, Domain, and OU. With LSDOU, policies applied later take precedence over policies applied earlier. PSOs have a different order for conflict resolution.

1. PSOs override the settings from the Default Domain Policy GPO. Any object that has a PSO applied always uses the settings from the PSO instead of the GPO.

2. PSOs applied directly to user objects override PSOs applied to security groups. If a user has a PSO inherited from the user's membership in a security group and a PSO applied directly to it, the directly applied PSO is used.

3. Lower precedence values override higher precedence values. When creating a PSO you must indicate a numeric precedence. When two (or more) PSOs come into conflict that are not resolved above, the PSO with the lower value is used.

Creating PSOs

To create and apply a PSO:

Step 1. Log on to a writeable domain controller.

Step 2. Start Server Manager from either the Start Menu or Taskbar.

Step 3. From the context menu at the top of the panel click **Tools** and then select **Active Directory Administrative Center**.

Step 4. On the left-hand panel select the domain you want to create PSOs for. The right-hand panel displays the top-level containers created in a directory by default.

Step 5. Double-click the **System** container to expose its child objects.

Step 6. Double-click the **Password Settings Container** to expose any existing PSOs.

Step 7. From the Tasks panel on the right, select **New > Password Settings**.

Step 8. The Password Settings dialog box presents the following configuration options, as shown in Figure 5-12. (They mirror the Password policy and Account lockout policy settings from Group Policy.)

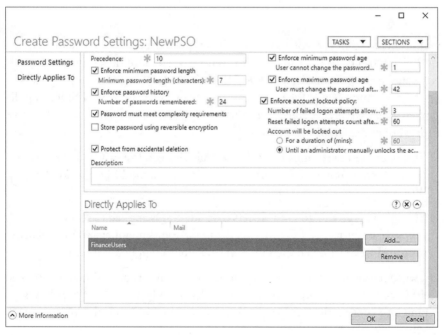

Figure 5-12 The Create Password Settings Dialog When Creating a New PSO

- **Name**: The name of the object in the directory.

- **Precedence**: The precedence order for the PSO. Used to resolve conflicts.

- **Enforce minimum password length**: This setting determines the fewest number of characters that a password may contain.

- **Enforce password history**: This setting determines how many new unique passwords must be associated with a user account before an old password can be reused. It can be between 0 and 24.

- **Password must meet complexity requirements**: This setting forces user passwords to meet a number of different complexity requirements.

- **Store password using reversible encryption**: This setting determines how AD DS stores passwords. Contrary to what you might think, it is more secure to leave it disabled. When disabled, passwords are stored with one-way encryption, which is less vulnerable to attack.

- **Enforce minimum password age**: This setting determines the period of time (in days) that a password must be in use before it can be changed. Using this setting prevents a user from quickly cycling through the password history count to reuse an old password right away.

- **Enforce maximum password age**: This setting determines the period of time (in days) that a password can be used before the system forcefully expires it and requires the user to change it.

- **Enforce account lockout policy**: This setting enables the lockout policies. Without it the user account can never become locked out.

- **Number of failed logon attempts allowed**: This setting determines the number of failed logon attempts that causes a user account to be locked out.

- **Reset failed logon attempts count after (mins)**: This setting determines the period of time (in minutes) after a failed logon attempt before the counter is reset to 0 bad attempts. This setting must be less than or equal to the **For a duration of (mins)** setting.

- **For a duration of (mins)**: This setting determines the period of time (in minutes) a locked-out account remains locked out before automatically becoming unlocked.

- **Until an administrator manually unlocks the account**: This setting disables the preceding duration setting and causes accounts to be permanently locked until they are specifically unlocked.

Step 9.   The **Directly Applies To** section is used to declare which user objects or security groups this PSO will be applied to. Click **Add** to bring up the default directory search window to find a group or user.

Step 10.   Type the name of a user or group and click **Check Names**. If the name is found it will be underlined in the dialog. Click **OK**.

Step 11.   Click **OK**.

The PSO is now shown in ADAC and is being actively enforced for all users chosen during Step 10.

Delegating Password Settings Management

By default the creation and management of PSOs is limited to members of the Domain Admins group. This is because only Domain Admins have create child and delete child permissions on the Password Settings Container. You can delegate these permissions to other groups if needed.

To delegate management of a PSO to a user or group:

Step 1.   Log on to a writeable domain controller.

Step 2.   Start Server Manager from either the Start Menu or Taskbar.

Step 3.   From the context menu at the top of the panel click **Tools** and then select **Active Directory Administrative Center**.

Step 4.   On the left-hand panel select the domain you want to create PSOs for. The right-hand panel displays the top-level containers created in a directory by default.

Step 5.   Double-click the **System** container to expose its child objects.

Step 6.   Double-click the **Password Settings Container** to expose any existing PSOs.

Step 7.   Right-click the PSO you want to delegate management for and select **Properties**.

Step 8.   Scroll down to the **Extensions** section.

Step 9.   The Security extension displays various groups. Selecting a group displays the permissions for that group in the bottom half of the extension (see Figure 5-13). Click **Add**.

Step 10. Type the name of a user or group you want to delegate permissions to and click **Check Names**. If the object is found it will be underlined. Click **OK**.

Step 11. The object has been added to the list. Select it and check the **Write** box.

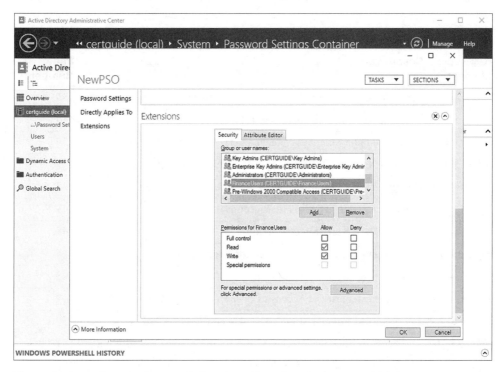

Figure 5-13 A Security Group with Read and Write Permissions on a PSO

Step 12. Click **OK**.

The user or group chosen in Step 10 now has permissions to modify the chosen PSO.

Exam Preparation Tasks

As mentioned in the section "Book Features" in the Introduction, you have a few choices for exam preparation: the exercises here; Chapter 17, "Final Preparation"; and the exam simulation questions in the Pearson Test Prep Software Online.

Review All Key Topics

Review the most important topics in this chapter, noted with the Key Topics icon in the outer margin of the page. Table 5-5 lists a reference of these key topics and the page number on which each is found.

Table 5-5   Key Topics for Chapter 5

Key Topic Element	Description	Page Number
List	The three built-in local service account contexts	136
Table 5-2	The properties of built-in service accounts	136
Paragraph	Description of a Standard Managed Service Account (sMSA)	139
Table 5-3	PowerShell cmdlets for working with service accounts	139
Paragraph	Description of a Group Managed Service Account (gMSA)	142
List	The features of a virtual service account	143
Paragraph	Description of Kerberos Delegation	145
Figure 5-6	The delegation configuration page for a computer object	146
Table 5-4	Parameters of the **setspn** command	148
List	The three categories of Account Policies in Group Policy	149
Figure 5-9	The Password Policy settings in the Default Domain Policy	150
Figure 5-10	The Account Lockout Policy settings in the Default Domain Policy	151
Figure 5-11	The Kerberos Policy settings in the Default Domain Policy	152
List	The steps used to determine PSO precedence	155
Figure 5-12	The Create Password Settings dialog when creating a new PSO	156

Complete Tables and Lists from Memory

Print a copy of Appendix B, "Memory Tables" (found on the book website), or at least the section for this chapter, and complete the tables and lists from memory. Appendix C, "Memory Tables Answer Key," also on the website, includes completed tables and lists to check your work.

Define Key Terms

Define the following key terms from this chapter and check your answers in the glossary:

> service accounts, Standard Managed Service Account (sMSA), Group Managed Service Account (gMSA), virtual service account, Kerberos Constrained Delegation (KCD), Service Principal Names (SPNs), Account Policies, password history, password complexity, lockout threshold, Password Settings Objects (PSOs), PSO precedence

End-of-Chapter Review Questions

The answers to these questions appear in Appendix A. For more practice with exam format questions, use the Pearson Test Prep Software Online.

1. The Human Resources department has recently installed a new software system. This application needs access to the general ledger SQL Server database for processing payroll. The GL database runs on a separate server from the HR system. How would you configure the security context for the HR system to provide access while minimizing exposure of the GL database?

    a. Create a virtual service account on the machine running the HR system and configure the system to run under that security context.

    b. Create a Group Managed Service Account and provision both machines as principals allowed to retrieve the password. Configure the SQL Service for the GL to run under the gMSA security context. Grant the gMSA permissions to access the HR application service.

    c. Create a Group Managed Service Account and add the HR machine to a security group provisioned as a principal allowed to retrieve the password. Configure the HR application service to run under the gMSA security context. Grant the gMSA permissions to access the SQL Server for the GL.

    d. Create Standard Managed Service Accounts for both the HR system and the GL system. Configure each service to run under its respective sMSA. Grant the HR sMSA permissions to access the SQL Server for the GL.

2. What is the command to add an SPN of type http to a service account named srvFinance?

3. Your organization has grown fairly large. Your home office on the East Coast has been supplemented with a remote office out West. The IT staff in the remote office will be handling all the AD DS services for their on-site users. Which steps would be most appropriate to grant that IT staff the needed permissions? (Choose all that apply.)

    a. Add the user accounts for the remote IT staff to the Domain Admins security group.

    b. Create separate OUs for the East and West objects, and delegate full permissions to the West OU for the remote IT staff.

    c. Create a Password Setting Object for the users in the West OU and delegate permissions for that PSO to the remote IT staff.

    d. Install and configure a new domain for the remote office. Add the user accounts for the remote IT staff to the Domain Admins security group on that new domain.

4. What is the command to create a new gMSA named srvFinance in the domain certguide.com with a group named grpFinance allowed to retrieve the password for it?

This chapter covers the following topics:

- **Configuring Active Directory Snapshots**: This section describes how to build point-in-time snapshots of the Active Directory database.

- **Backing Up and Restoring Active Directory and SYSVOL**: This section describes how to properly back up and restore both the Active Directory database and the SYSVOL database for proper disaster recovery procedures.

- **Managing Active Directory Offline**: This section describes basic management tasks that can be performed while the Active Directory service is in an offline state.

- **Cleaning Up Metadata**: This section describes how to clear leftover directory metadata from computer objects that were not properly removed from the directory.

- **Configuring Replication to Read-Only Domain Controllers (RODCs)**: This section describes how to configure database replication to Read-Only Domain Controllers (RODCs).

- **Monitoring and Managing Replication**: This section describes the tools used to monitor the state of replication and troubleshoot any problems that occur.

CHAPTER 6

Maintaining Active Directory

Once Active Directory Domain Services has been deployed in your infrastructure, it is a mission-critical system. Users depend on it to perform their jobs every day. AD DS has a role in everything from logging on to the network and accessing file systems and databases to powering Rights Management Services and Certificate Services. Your users cannot afford to lose connectivity or access to AD DS for any amount of time.

This criticality means that proper system maintenance, especially data storage, backup, archival, and restoration, is just as important as any other administrative task. This chapter covers the many ways in which your AD DS installation can be configured for these tasks to meet the requirements of your disaster recovery and business continuity planning procedures.

"Do I Know This Already?" Quiz

The "Do I Know This Already?" quiz allows you to assess whether you should read this entire chapter thoroughly or jump to the "Exam Preparation Tasks" section. If you are in doubt about your answers to these questions or your own assessment of your knowledge of the topics, read the entire chapter. Table 6-1 lists the major headings in this chapter and their corresponding "Do I Know This Already?" quiz questions. You can find the answers in Appendix A, "Answers to the 'Do I Know This Already?' Quizzes."

Table 6-1 "Do I Know This Already?" Section-to-Question Mapping

Foundation Topics Section	Questions
Configuring Active Directory Snapshots	1-2
Backing Up and Restoring Active Directory and SYSVOL	3-4
Managing Active Directory Offline	5-6
Cleaning Up Metadata	7
Configuring Replication to Read-Only Domain Controllers (RODCs)	8-9
Monitoring and Managing Replication	10

CAUTION   The goal of self-assessment is to gauge your mastery of the topics in this chapter. If you do not know the answer to a question or are only partially sure of the answer, you should mark that question as wrong for purposes of the self-assessment. Giving yourself credit for an answer you correctly guess skews your self-assessment results and might provide you with a false sense of security.

1. Which utility would you use to create a current snapshot of the AD DS directory?

    a. **repadmin**

    b. **ntdsutil**

    c. **dsamain**

    d. PowerShell

2. Which utility would you use to host a snapshot of the AD DS directory?

    a. **repadmin**

    b. **ntdsutil**

    c. **dsamain**

    d. PowerShell

3. Which feature must be installed on the domain controller to back up AD DS?

    a. Domain Name Server (DNS)

    b. Global catalog

    c. WINS Server

    d. Windows Server Backup

4. A domain controller becomes corrupted and must be restored from an earlier backup. You need all changes made to the directory to be replicated to the restored server after restoration. Which type of restore should you perform?

    a. Authoritative

    b. Single master

    c. Nonauthoritative

    d. Multimaster

5. Which of the following operations will successfully bring the AD DS service offline? (Choose all that apply.)

    a. Reboot in DSRM.

    b. Remove the controller from the domain controllers container.

    c. Use the **ntdsutil** utility.

    d. Stop the AD DS service.

6. Which utility is used to perform an offline defragmentation of the AD DS directory?

    a. **repadmin**

    b. **ntdsutil**

    c. **dsamain**

    d. PowerShell

7. How is metadata cleared from the directory for a controller that was not demoted gracefully?

    a. Recover with an authoritative restore.

    b. Re-promote it to a domain controller and then demote it gracefully.

    c. Use **ntdsutil**.

    d. Delete the computer object from the domain controllers container.

8. Which write operations will an RODC forward to a writeable domain controller? (Choose all that apply.)

    a. Security Group Membership change

    b. LastLogonTimeStamp

    c. Password changes

    d. Password Replication Policies

9. Which accounts have their passwords cached on an RODC by default?

    a. Domain Users

    b. Enterprise Admins

    c. Domain Admins

    d. No accounts are cached by default.

10. Which utility is used to monitor the status of replication events on the domain?

   a. repadmin

   b. ntdsutil

   c. dsamain

   d. PowerShell

Foundation Topics

Configuring Active Directory Snapshots

One of the most basic ways to create a backup of your Active Directory Domain Services directory is to use snapshots. If you're familiar with other database technologies, the term *snapshot* is probably familiar to you as well. A snapshot is a read-only copy of the directory as it was at the point in time when the snapshot was created. Snapshots are useful to get a glimpse into the previous state of your directory without the more involved hassle of restoring from a backup.

Two different command-line tools are required for working with snapshots **ntdsutil** and **dsamain**. In the **ntdsutil** command you use the **snapshots** menu to create, manage, and mount a snapshot. Mounting a snapshot means attaching the binary data to the file system in the OS so that it can be viewed. With **dsamain** you run a small LDAP server connected to that mount point. Once it'sloaded in **dsamain,** you can view the information inside the directory snapshot with utilities like Active Directory Users and Computers.

NTDSUTIL Snapshot Menu

You can review all the options of the **ntdsutil** snapshot menu by starting **ntdsutil**, typing **snapshot** to navigate into the snapshot menu, and typing **?** to bring up the options for that menu.

Some important **ntdsutil** snapshot options to be aware of include

- **Create**: Creates a new snapshot of the active directory at the current moment.

- **Mount %s**: Mounts a snapshot into the file system. The **%s** parameter is the index number of a snapshot, such as **2**, which can be reviewed with the **list** command.

- **List all**: Lists all the snapshots in the system. Each snapshot typically takes up two lines and has its index number for mount, unmount, and delete commands listed on the last row.

Creating and Mounting a Snapshot

To create and mount the snapshot (see Figure 6-1):

Step 1.   Log on to a writeable domain controller.

Step 2.   Launch a command prompt.

Step 3.   Type **ntdsutil** and press **Enter**.

Step 4.   At the **ntdsutil** prompt type **activate instance ntds** and press **Enter**.

Step 5.   At the **ntdsutil** prompt type **snapshot** and press **Enter**.

Step 6.   At the snapshot menu prompt type **create** and press **Enter**.

Step 7.   A snapshot is created representing the current state of the directory. Type **list all** and press **Enter** to see a list of all snapshots that have been created.

Step 8.   At the snapshot prompt type **mount 1** and press **Enter**.

Step 9.   At the snapshot prompt type **quit** and press **Enter**.

Step 10. At the **ntdsutil** prompt type **quit** and press **Enter**.

```
Administrator: Command Prompt                                    —    □    ×

C:\>ntdsutil
ntdsutil: activate instance ntds
Active instance set to "ntds".
ntdsutil: snapshot
snapshot: create
Creating snapshot...
Snapshot set {81038297-9f70-4fee-a634-65bdccef09d4} generated successfully.
snapshot: list all
 1: 2016/11/10:17:30 {81038297-9f70-4fee-a634-65bdccef09d4}
 2:   C: {399b06a8-abf1-477c-b348-0cdc11488d05}

snapshot: mount 1
Snapshot {399b06a8-abf1-477c-b348-0cdc11488d05} mounted as C:\$SNAP_201611101730_VOLUMEC$\
snapshot: quit
ntdsutil: quit

C:\>
```

Figure 6-1   The ntsdutil Snapshot **create**, **list**, and **mount** Commands. Notice the Snapshot Listed in **list all** Has Two Lines Associated with It.

The snapshot has been created and mounted onto the file system at the location indicated after Step 8. If you want to browse that snapshot you can do so with Windows Explorer. Take note that there is an ntds.dit file located in the snapshot in the /Windows/NTDS folder (see Figure 6-2).

At this point, the snapshot has been mounted, but its directory is not being hosted yet for viewing.

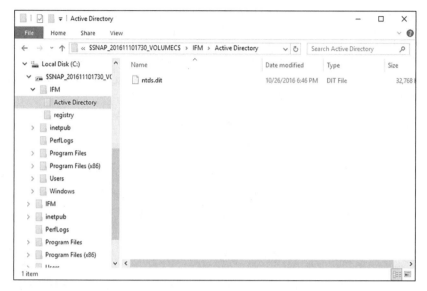

Figure 6-2   The Snapshot of the ntds.dit File in the Mounted Snapshot Folder

Hosting a Snapshot

Even though the snapshot is loaded in the file system, it cannot be accessed via typical directory browsing tools until it is being hosted. When you host a snapshot, a server (**dsamain** in this case) listens on a specified port for LDAP queries and responds to those queries similar to a regular directory.

The **dsamain** utility provides hosting for snapshots. Table 6-2 outlines the common parameters for **dsamain**.

Table 6-2   Common Parameters for **dsamain**

Parameter	Description
-dbpath *<filepath>*	Specifies the file path to the .dit database file to host
-ldapport *<number>*	Specifies an ldap port number to listen on
-logpath *<path>*	Specifies the path to write log output files to

To host the snapshot:

Step 1.   Log on to the same domain controller where the snapshot was created. (Or just continue to use the same command prompt window used to create and mount the snapshot.)

Step 2.   Launch a command prompt.

Step 3.   Type the following command. You need to replace the name of the volume with the name of your mounted volume (see Figure 6-3).

```
dsamain -dbpath "C:\$SNAP_201611101730_VOLUMEC$\Windows\
NTDS\ntds.dit" -ldapport 10000
```

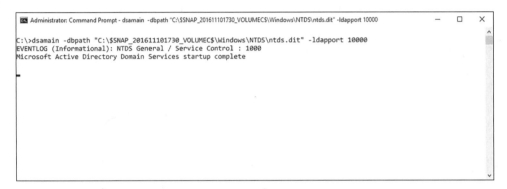

Figure 6-3   The **dsamain** Utility Actively Hosting on Port 10000

Step 4.   The directory is now hosted at the port indicated with the **-ldapport** switch. Leave this window open in the background to keep the **dsamain** server running.

Step 5.   Launch Active Directory Users and Computers (ADUC).

Step 6.   Right-click **Active Directory Users and Computers** on the left-hand navigation pane and select **Change Domain Controller**.

Step 7.   Select the **This domain Controller or AD LDS instance** option and then click in the list box below where it reads **<Type a Directory Server name[:port] here>**.

Step 8.   Type **localhost:10000** and press **Enter**.

Step 9.   When the **Status** reads "Online," the server is connected and recognized. Click **OK**.

ADUC is now connected to and browsing the read-only snapshot you created earlier. You can see the entire directory structure, although you will not be able to make any changes.

To stop the server and shut down everything:

Step 1.   Close ADUC.

Step 2.   Return to the command prompt where **dsamain** is running and press **Ctrl+C** on your keyboard. You are notified that the service was shut down successfully.

Step 3.   Type **ntdsutil** and press **Enter**.

Step 4.   Type **snapshot** and press **Enter**.

Step 5.   Type **unmount 2** and press **Enter**.

Backing Up and Restoring Active Directory and SYSVOL

Snapshots are a great way to get a capture of the current state of the directory. They are useful when you know you'll be performing some maintenance or otherwise effecting changes in the system and you want to have a previous known good version readily available for comparison. Snapshots are not a valid backup process or disaster recovery plan. There is no way to schedule or automate snapshots, and they can only be used to manually view and recover AD DS information.

Backing Up Active Directory

For a true backup process, you need to use the built-in Windows Server Backup utility supplied by Microsoft. This is the same utility used to back up any Windows Server, and you should already be familiar with it.

Using the Server Backup utility, AD DS will be automatically included in any full backups that are run with the service. Generally, you want to be running regularly scheduled full backups for your server. If you want to create a custom backup that is sure to include the AD DS directory, follow these steps:

Step 1.   Log on to a writeable domain controller.

Step 2.   From the Start Menu launch **Server Manager**.

Step 3.   Click **Tools** > **Windows Server Backup**.

Step 4.   Right-click **Local Backup** in the navigation pane on the left-hand side and select **Backup Once**.

Step 5.   Choose **Different Options** and click **Next**.

Step 6.   Choose **Custom** and click **Next**.

Step 7.   On the **Select Items for Backup** step, click **Add Items**.

Step 8. Select **System state**, which includes all the components and services on which Active Directory is dependent. Notably this includes the SYSVOL (see Figure 6-4).

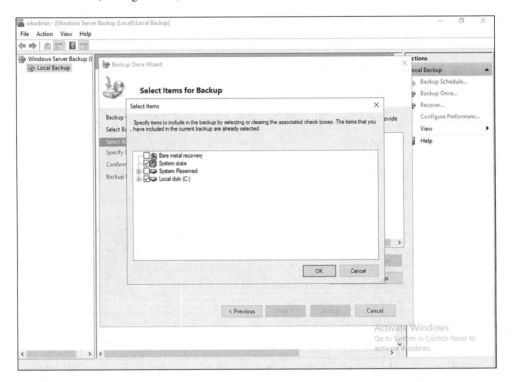

Figure 6-4 The Windows Server Backup Utility Selecting the System State and C: Drive for Backup

Step 9. Click **OK**.

Step 10. Select **Local drives** if you have a separate drive from the one NTDS is installed on. If no drive is available select **Remote shared folder**. Click **Next**.

Step 11. Specify the location to store the backup image and click **Next**.

Step 12. Review the choices made and click **Backup**.

AD DS has now been successfully backed up.

Restoring Active Directory

Once you have AD DS backed up you can plan to restore the directory in case the need arises. There are two approaches to restoring a domain controller. The first, and simpler of the two, is restoration through reinstallation and replication. With this method you are replacing or reinstalling Windows Server completely. Promoting that clean install to a domain controller causes it to replicate the current directory from another domain controller in the domain.

You can also restore Active Directory by restoring the System State data from backup media created with the Windows Server Backup tool. There are two methods for this restoration process:

- **Nonauthoritative**: A nonauthoritative restore means that after the domain controller is restored from backup media, it relies upon normal replication to bring its directory current with the rest of the domain. A nonauthoritative restore is typically used when a server fails in some capacity and must be restored from backup.

- **Authoritative**: With an authoritative restore the domain controller being restored immediately becomes authoritative and replicates its current state to the other domain controllers on the domain. Even if the restored data is older than the current replicas, the restored data takes precedence. An authoritative restore is used when you want to bring the directory back to a previously known state, such as before objects were erroneously deleted.

Nonauthoritative Restore

The default method for restoring a directory with the Windows Server Backup tool is nonauthoritative. If you restore the data using this tool, and no other, the domain controller will detect it hasn't been updated since the backup and start automatically receiving replication updates from its replication partners. Any directory changes that occurred after the backup took place will be applied to the restored domain controller.

You cannot restore an Active Directory that is online; you must place the domain controller into Directory Services Restore Mode (DSRM). To reboot in DSRM:

Step 1.   Launch Windows Administrative Tools from the Start Menu.

Step 2.   Launch the System Configuration tool.

Step 3.   Select the **Boot** tab.

Step 4.   In the **Boot options** section, select the **Safe boot** box and the **Active Directory repair** option. Click **OK** (see Figure 6-5).

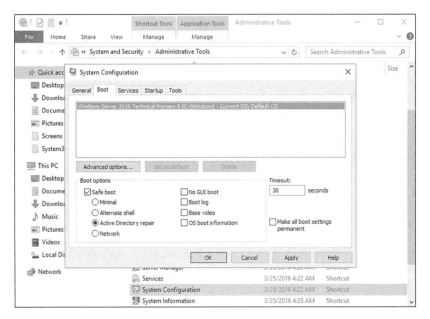

Figure 6-5   The System Configuration Menu for Booting in DSRM Mode

Step 5.   You may be told the computer needs to restart. Click **OK** or manually restart the server.

Step 6.   After the server reboots, on the logon screen select **Other user.**

Step 7.   For the user name type **.\Administrator** and for the password enter the DSRM password chosen when the server was promoted to a domain controller.

NOTE   If it has been a while since you promoted the server and you don't recall the DSRM password, you're not alone. This is a common occurrence, and AD DS has a method to reset the password using **ntdsutil**, covered later in this chapter.

Step 8.   From the Start Menu launch **Server Manager**.

Step 9.   Click **Tools > Windows Server Backup**.

Step 10.   Select **Local Backup** from the left-hand navigation pane.

Step 11.   Right-click **Local Backup** and select **Recover**.

Step 12.   Select **A backup stored on another location** and click **Next**.

Step 13.   Choose either **Local drives** or **Remote shared folder** depending on where you stored your custom backup in the previous section. Click **Next**.

Step 14.   Choose the location of the backups and click **Next**.

Step 15.   If you chose a remote shared folder, type the fully qualified username and password of a domain user with access to the location and click **OK**.

Step 16.   The recovery wizard lists all the backups found in that location. Select the backup you want to recover based on date and click **Next**.

Step 17.   Select **System state** to restore Active Directory Domain Services and click **Next** (see Figure 6-6).

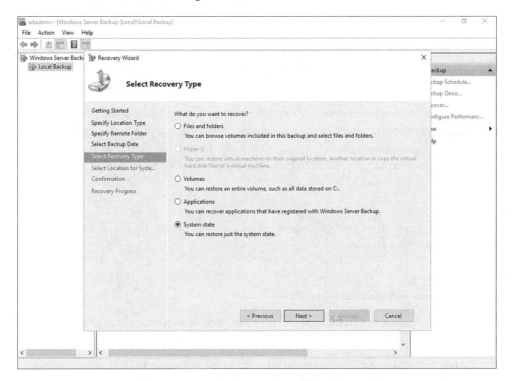

Figure 6-6   The Recovery Wizard Being Used to Restore the System State for AD DS

Step 18.   Select **Original Location** and click **Next.**

Step 19.   Review the warning and click **OK**.

Step 20.   If you chose a remote shared folder, you receive another warning. Review this warning and click **OK**.

Step 21.   Review the details of the recovery and click **Recover**.

Step 22.   Review the warning and click **Yes**.

Once the recovery is complete, you need to turn off DSRM mode. Repeat the steps to turn it on but uncheck the **Safe boot** option and restart the server. After the server finishes rebooting, any directory updates will replicate from another domain controller to this one.

Authoritative Restore

An authoritative restore begins similarly to the nonauthoritative restore process but diverges significantly at the end. When you perform an authoritative restore you first perform a recovery from backup media and then designate either the entire directory, a subtree, or individual objects in the restored directory to take precedence over other instances of those objects elsewhere in the forest. In other words, the recovered directory becomes authoritative for all its replication partners and replicates its version of the data to those partners even if it contains older data.

One common use case for an authoritative restore is to recover objects accidentally deleted from the directory. After the restore completes but prior to restarting the controller and bringing it online, you designate the deleted objects as authoritative. Those objects are then replicated from the recovered controller to its replication partners.

> **NOTE** An authoritative restore does not have an effect on objects created after the backup from which you are restoring.

To perform an authoritative restore:

Step 1.   Follow the steps from the previous section to perform a nonauthoritative restore.

Step 2.   Reboot the domain controller while remaining in DSRM. This ensures the domain controller remains offline.

Step 3.   Launch a command prompt.

Step 4.   Type **ntdsutil** and press **Enter**.

Step 5.   At the **ntdsutil** command prompt, there are two different types of restore:

- To authoritatively restore the entire directory type **restore database** and press **Enter**.

- To authoritatively restore only a portion type **restore subtree** *<subtree distinguished name>* (e.g., **restore subtree** *ou=Finance,dc=certguide,dc= com*).

Step 6.   Once the restore completes, at the **ntdsutil** command prompt type **quit** and press **Enter**.

Step 7.   Reboot the domain controller in normal mode by following the directions covered previously.

The domain controller then replicates any changes in the specified restore scope to its partner controllers in the domain.

> **NOTE**   If you perform a full directory authoritative restore you may want to copy the SYSVOL directory manually. Follow the steps under **Authoritative Restoration of the Entire Active Directory Database** found on this document: https://technet. microsoft.com/en-us/library/cc961934.aspx.

Configuring and Restoring Objects by Using the Active Directory Recycle Bin

One way in which Microsoft attempts to simplify the process of recovering accidentally deleted objects is the creation of a Recycle Bin or Deleted Objects container. Just like the Recycle Bin on Windows file system, the Active Directory Recycle Bin is a staging area where deleted objects are placed. If the delete was inadvertent or needs to be reversed for any reason a domain admin can simply view the deleted objects container and restore the object.

To use the AD Recycle Bin, the domain must be at the forest functional level of 2008 R2 or higher. You must also first enable the Recycle Bin:

Step 1.   Log on to a writeable domain controller.

Step 2.   From the Start Menu launch **Server Manager**.

Step 3.   Select **Tools > Active Directory Administrative Center**.

Step 4.   On the left-hand navigation pane select the domain you want to enable Recycle Bin for.

Step 5.   On the right-hand Tasks pane, click **Enable Recycle Bin** (see Figure 6-7).

Step 6.   You receive a warning that this process is irreversible. Click **OK**.

Step 7.   You receive a notification to refresh AD Administrative Center. Click **OK** and close and reopen ADAC.

There now is a **Deleted Objects** container at the top level of the domain.

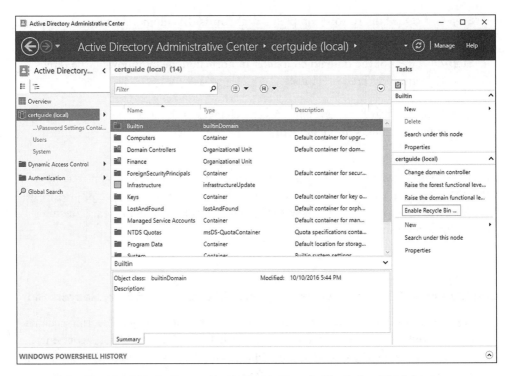

Figure 6-7   The ADAC Tasks Pane with the Enable Recycle Bin Option Highlighted

Step 8.   Browse to an object, right-click it, and select **Delete**.

Step 9.   Click **Yes** to confirm.

Step 10.   Browse to the **Deleted Objects** container to see the deleted object.

Step 11.   Right-click the object in the container and select **Restore**.

The object you deleted in Step 8 is restored to its original location. Notice the context menu for the deleted object also contained an option **Restore To**. This option allows you to restore the object completely intact but in a different location in the directory.

NOTE   You can enable AD Recycle Bin on your directory with the **Enable-ADOptionalFeature** PowerShell cmdlet. Read more about that here: https://technet.microsoft.com/en-us/library/ee617209.aspx.

Managing Active Directory Offline

Many tasks can only be performed while the AD DS service is in an offline state. Prior to Windows Server 2008 R2, an administrator could only place AD DS into an offline state by restarting in Directory Services Restore Mode (DSRM) as described earlier in this chapter. This process is time consuming and cumbersome and not always ideal if the domain controller in question needs to be running to perform other tasks on the network.

Instead, the AD DS service can now be brought offline using the same method for any other service in Windows. To stop the AD DS service with the GUI, perform the following steps:

Step 1.   Log on to a writeable domain controller.

Step 2.   From the Start Menu launch **Server Manager**.

Step 3.   Select **Tools > Services**.

Step 4.   Right-click the service **Active Directory Domain Services** and select **Stop**.

Step 5.   A dialog appears warning you of dependent services that must also be stopped. Click **Yes** (see Figure 6-8).

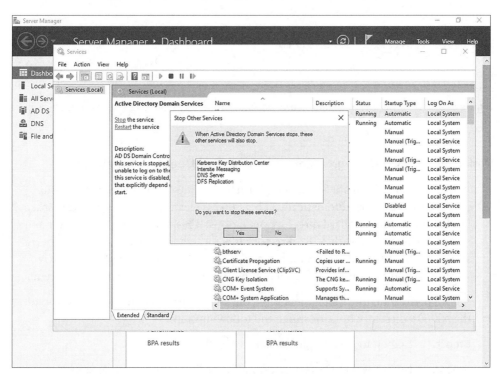

Figure 6-8   The Dependent Services Confirmation Dialog Presented When Stopping Active Directory Domain Services

The service is now in a stopped state. You can also use the command prompt to stop a service with the **net stop** command:

Step 1.   Log on to a writeable domain controller.

Step 2.   Launch a command prompt.

Step 3.   Type **net stop ntds** and press **Enter**.

Step 4.   Review the list of dependent services that will also be stopped. Type **Y** and press **Enter** (see Figure 6-9).

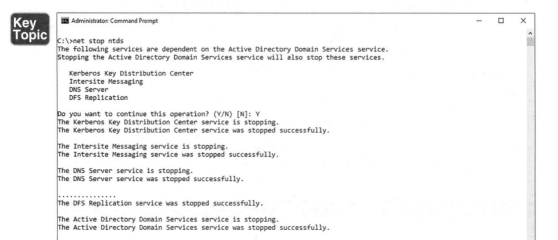

Figure 6-9   Using **net stop** to Shut Down the Active Directory Domain Services Service

Performing Offline Defragmentation of an Active Directory Database

Active Directory Domain Services performs an online defragmentation of its database every 12 hours automatically. This process cleans up and releases free space left behind during standard directory operations. This online defragmentation only recaptures free space within the directory file, though; it does not shrink the overall size of the file. If a major object move or other operation has occurred, you may want to perform an offline defragmentation to recapture space on the file system.

Before performing the defragmentation, ensure you have an up-to-date backup of the AD DS directory by performing the following steps:

Step 1.   Log on to a writeable domain controller.

Step 2.   Bring the AD DS service offline according to the previous steps.

Step 3.   Launch a command prompt.

Step 4.   Type **ntdsutil** and press **Enter**.

Step 5.   At the **ntdsutil** prompt type **activate instance ntds** and press **Enter**.

Step 6.   At the **ntdsutil** prompt type **files** and press **Enter**.

Step 7.   At the files prompt type **compact to C:\defrag** and press **Enter**.

> **NOTE**   The location you choose to compact to in Step 7 must have enough space for the defragmentation operation. If it does not, the compact will fail.

Step 8.   Once the operation completes, review the instructions for copying the ntds.dit file and deleting log files (see Figure 6-10).

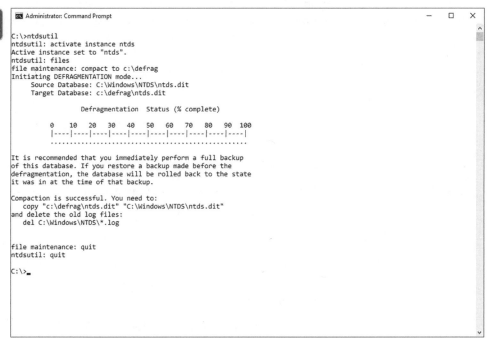

Figure 6-10   The **ntds** Offline Defragmentation Utility

Step 9.   At the file maintenance prompt type **quit** and press **Enter**.

Step 10.   At the **ntdsutil** prompt type **quit** and press **Enter**.

A compacted version of the ntds.dit file (the directory database file) now exists in the location specified in Step 7. Copy this file and overwrite the current ntds.dit file, by default installed at C:\Windows\NTDS. Delete the log files as instructed by **ntdsutil** and reboot the computer.

Cleaning Up Metadata

If a domain controller in the forest fails or is otherwise corrupted for some reason, the easiest thing to do is usually to simply rebuild it from scratch. The replacement controller receives an up-to-date directory via replication from the other controllers in the domain. When you do this, or if a DC is removed from the network for any reason without first being demoted, metadata about that controller needs to be manually removed from the directory.

In earlier versions of Windows Server, cleaning this metadata out of the directory was a multistep process facilitated through **ntdsutil**. You can still clean metadata in this fashion, but since Windows Server 2012, the clean-up process can be completed with the GUI using Active Directory Users and Computers. All that is required is to delete the domain controller object from the directory the same as you would any other object as described in the following list. Additional confirmations are requested by ADUC.

Step 1.   Log on to a writeable domain controller.

Step 2.   From the Start Menu launch **Server Manager**.

Step 3.   Select **Tools > Active Directory Users and Computers**.

Step 4.   Navigate to the domain where you want to clean up metadata.

Step 5.   Select the **Domain Controllers** container on the left-hand navigation pane.

Step 6.   Right-click the controller being removed from the directory and select **Delete**.

Step 7.   Click **Yes** at the confirmation prompt.

Step 8.   You receive a warning dialog box. Check the **Delete this Domain Controller anyway** box and click **Delete** (see Figure 6-11).

Step 9.   If the controller was a global catalog, you receive another confirmation prompt. Click **Yes**.

Step 10. If the controller held any FSMO roles, you receive another confirmation prompt. Click **OK** to move the role(s) to the controller indicated.

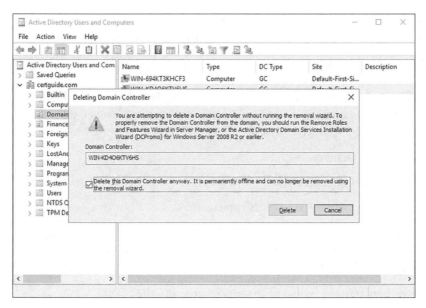

Figure 6-11 The Confirmation Dialog for Deleting a Domain Controller from ADUC Instead of Gracefully Demoting It

The DC is now removed from the directory. If you attempt to start up that controller after cleaning the metadata for it, you receive an error trying to log on.

Configuring Replication to Read-Only Domain Controllers (RODCs)

Read-Only Domain Controllers (RODCs) were introduced in Chapter 2, "Installing and Configuring Domain Controllers." An RODC is a useful variant for both security purposes as well as replication load. The name "read-only" can be misleading. An RODC is read-only specifically for the purposes of replication from other controllers in the domain. Replication to RODCs is a one-way operation. Updates are only replicated to an RODC, and the RODC never sends out updates. Because inbound replication is a single-threaded operation, other writeable domain controllers do not need to poll RODCs for updates, which simplifies and reduces the replication load on the network.

This structure means that any accidental deletion of data or corruption of files on an RODC can be easily remedied by receiving replication updates or simply repromoting the server to an RODC. There is no fear of lost updates or changes that haven't replicated to other partners yet.

Because RODCs are typically used to service users and applications at remote sites, they can still receive attempted writes from those users. When a user or application attempts to perform a write operation on an RODC, one of the three following things can occur:

- The RODC forwards the write request to a writeable domain controller and then receives the update via standard replication from its partners. RODCs only forward a limited set of writes, including

    - Password changes

    - LastLogonTimeStamp

    - Service Principal Name (SPN) updates

- The RODC sends a referral for a writeable domain controller to the originating application. The application can then target a writeable domain controller with the desired update.

- The write operation fails and an error is returned to the client.

Configuring Password Replication Policy (PRP) for RODC

One of the ways in which RODCs improve security is by not storing passwords in their local directory. RODCs are often installed at remote locations or in perimeter networks (DMZs) where there is a greater risk of data being compromised. Locations like that also have a greater risk of losing their network connectivity to writeable replication partners. If that happens, users cannot authenticate against the RODC until the connectivity has been restored. A domain controller that cannot be used for authentication has lost most of its value to the organization.

To mitigate the impact of losing network connectivity to a writeable domain controller, you can choose to cache account passwords on the RODC. Caching a password allows the RODC to save, for specified users, the last password used during an authentication event. If the RODC is unable to communicate with a writeable domain controller, it can use those cached passwords to authenticate users and computers. RODCs can be configured to either allow or deny accounts to cache passwords through the Password Replication Policies (PRPs).

Two default security groups are created in the domain when an RODC is first installed (see Figure 6-12):

- **Allowed RODC Password Replication Group**: This group contains users, computers, and other security groups that can be cached on the RODC. By default it is empty and must be populated by an administrator.

- **Denied RODC Password Replication Group**: This group contains users, computers, and other security groups that can never have their passwords cached on the RODC. By default it includes a number of high-security members such as Domain Admins, Schema Admins, and Cert Publishers.

In the event an account ends up in both groups, the **Denied** group takes precedence.

NOTE Caching passwords on the RODC obviously circumvents one of its key security features. If an RODC is compromised in any way, those cached passwords may also be compromised. In this event it is recommended that you immediately remove the RODC from the domain and reset the passwords for any accounts cached on the RODC. AD DS makes this easy by presenting the option to reset all passwords for both user and computer accounts that were cached when you delete the computer object from the Domain Controllers container.

The recommended way to allow or deny user or computer accounts caching on an RODC is to simply use the default groups provided by AD DS. To explicitly allow or deny accounts:

Step 1. Log on to a writeable domain controller.

Step 2. From the Start Menu launch **Server Manager**.

Step 3. Click **Tools > Active Directory Users and Computers**.

Step 4. On the left-hand navigation pane expand the domain and select **Domain Controllers**.

Step 5. In the right-hand pane right-click the RODC you want to configure and select **Properties**.

Step 6. Select the **Password Replication Policy** tab (see Figure 6-12).

Step 7. Click **Add**.

Step 8. Choose either **Allow passwords** or **Deny passwords** depending on whether you are allowing or denying caching.

Step 9. Use the standard directory search box to find the account(s) you want to add to the list. Click **Check Names**, and valid accounts are underlined. Click **OK**.

Step 10. The account(s) are now listed in the **Password Replication Policy** tab with the appropriate setting.

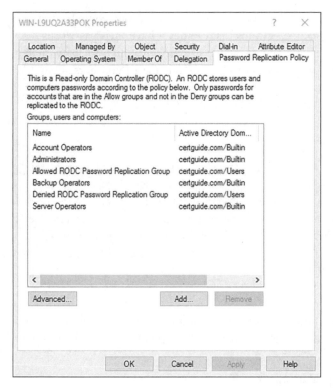

Figure 6-12   The Password Replication Policy Tab of a Read-Only Domain Controller in ADUC

You can also choose to prepopulate an account password on the RODC, effectively caching it before the account has first logged on. This is useful in scenarios when you are aware the connectivity to a writeable domain controller will be interrupted but an account still needs to authenticate to the RODC. To prepopulate a password:

Step 1.   Add the user to the default Allow security group or follow the steps from the previous list to allow the RODC to cache the user account. You cannot prepopulate an account that isn't already allowed.

Step 2.   From the **Password Replication Policy** tab click **Advanced**.

Step 3.   Click **Prepopulate Passwords**.

Step 4.   Use the standard directory search box to find the account you want to prepopulate. Click **Check Names**, and valid accounts are underlined.

Step 5.   Review the confirmation dialog box (see Figure 6-13). Click **Yes**.

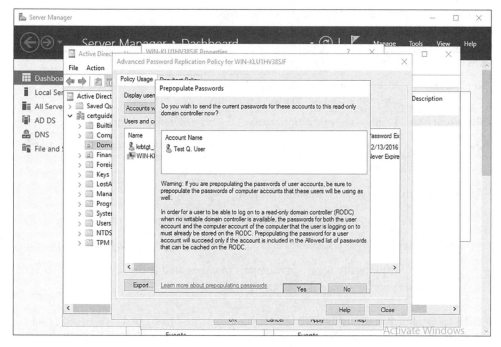

Figure 6-13   List of Accounts Whose Passwords Will Be Prepopulated on an RODC

The **repadmin** tool can be used with the /prp switch to effect many of these same changes. The documentation for the /prp switch can be found here: https://technet. microsoft.com/en-us/library/cc835090(v=ws.11).aspx#BKMK_View. The next section covers usage of **repadmin**.

Monitoring and Managing Replication

Replication between domain controllers generally happens without problems; however, due to the potentially complex nature of multimaster replication and the rules governing how AD DS handles replication and conflict resolution between many masters, there is occasionally a problem. Troubleshooting issues with replication is always a headache for AD DS admins.

The command-line tool for troubleshooting replication is **repadmin**, and it is installed by default with the AD DS server role. The basic syntax for **repadmin** is

```
repadmin <cmd> <args>
```

The *<args>* that **repadmin** can take depend on which option is chosen for the *<cmd>* parameter. Table 6-3 lists some of the key *<cmd>* parameter options.

Table 6-3 Common *<cmd>* Parameters for **repadmin**

Command	Description
/prp	Lists and modifies the Password Replication Policy for RODCs
/ReplSummary	Identifies domain controllers that are failing inbound or outbound replication and summarizes the results
/ShowRepl	Displays the replication status of the current domain controller
/Queue	Displays the inbound replication requests currently waiting to be processed

The **repadmin** /prp switch has the following arguments:

- **Add**: Adds a specified entry to the Allowed List for password caching
- **Delete**: Removes a specified entry from the Allowed List for password caching
- **View**: Displays the security principals in a specified list or displays the current PRP setting for a specified account

To use **repadmin** to display the list of accounts whose passwords are already cached on an RODC, run the following command from a command prompt of any domain controller (see Figure 6-14):

```
repadmin /prp view <RODC-server-name> reveal
```

where *<RODC-Server-name>* is the name of the RODC you want to query.

Figure 6-14 The **/prp** Switch of **repadmin** Displaying All Accounts with Passwords Cached on the Specified RODC

The **repadmin /replsummary** switch has the following arguments:

- **/bysrc**: Summarizes the replication status for all domain controllers that a given source replicates to
- **/bydest**: Summarizes the replication status for all domain controllers that a given destination replicates from
- **/errorsonly**: Shows on the domain controllers where there is an error

To get a summarized list of the current replication status, run the following command from a command prompt of any domain controller (see Figure 6-15):

repadmin /replsummary

```
Administrator: Command Prompt                                              —    □    ×
C:\>repadmin /replsummary
Replication Summary Start Time: 2016-11-15 17:34:04

Beginning data collection for replication summary, this may take awhile:
  .....


Source DSA         largest delta    fails/total %%    error
  WIN-694KT3KHCF3          42m:26s     0 /   5    0
  WIN-VBKTP3RJQD3          42m:08s     0 /   5    0


Destination DSA    largest delta    fails/total %%    error
  WIN-694KT3KHCF3          42m:08s     0 /   5    0
  WIN-VBKTP3RJQD3          42m:26s     0 /   5    0



C:\>_
```

Figure 6-15   A Replication Summary Complete with No Errors

The **repadmin /showrepl** switch has the following arguments:

- **/repsto**: Lists the partner domain controllers with which the targeted domain controllers perform outbound replication to

- **/verbose**: Displays additional information

- **/csv**: Displays the results in comma separated value format

To see a replication status report, run the following command from a command prompt of any domain controller:

repadmin /showrepl /verbose

The **repadmin /queue** switch does not take parameters. It is generally run as is:

repadmin /queue

NOTE   Full documentation for the repadmin utility can be found here: https://technet.microsoft.com/en-us/library/cc770963(v=ws.11).aspx.

There are a handful of useful PowerShell cmdlets for replication management as well, listed in Table 6-4.

Table 6-4   PowerShell Replication Cmdlets

Cmdlet	Description
Get-ADReplicationFailure	Returns all failures associated with a given domain controller
Get-ADReplicationPartnerMetadata	Returns the replication metadata for a set of one or more replication partners
Get-ADReplicationUpToDatenessVector Table	Displays the highest Update Sequence Number (USN) for the specified domain controller

All three of these cmdlets are typically run with only a single parameter, **-Target**, like so:

```
Get-ADReplicationFailure -Target localhost
```

Using *localhost* for the target specifies the current machine the cmdlet is being run from. You can also pass any fully qualified domain name into the **-Target** parameter.

Upgrading SYSVOL Replication to Distributed File System Replication (DFSR)

With the release of Windows 2000 and Server 2003, Microsoft relied on a technology known as NT File Replication Service (FRS) to replicate updates to the SYSVOL between domain controllers. With the release of Server 2008, the replication technology was upgraded to Distributed File System Replication (DFSR).

DFSR includes a number of efficiency and security improvements over FRS. Unfortunately, if your domain was originally a 2000 or 2003 domain and you have not gone through this migration process, you are still relying on FRS. Even if you've upgraded the forest and domain functional levels to 2008 or higher the migration process must be performed for older installations. Microsoft highly recommends migrating from FRS to DFSR for SYSVOL replication.

NOTE   A full listing of pros and cons for migrating to DFSR can be found here: https://blogs.technet.microsoft.com/askds/2010/04/22/the-case-for-migrating-sysvol-to-dfsr/.

The migration for SYSVOL is done with the **dfsrmig** command-line utility. The syntax for **dfsrmig** is straightforward:

```
dfsrmig [/SetGlobalState <state>
 | /GetGlobalState
 | /GetMigrationState]]
```

To migrate you need to run this command iteratively. First with the **/SetGlobalState** parameter, then with the **/GetMigrationState** parameter, and then repeating:

Step 1.   Log on to a writeable domain controller.

Step 2.   Launch a command prompt.

Step 3.   Type **dfsrmig /SetGlobalState 1** and press **Enter**.

Step 4.   All DCs in the domain are now migrating to state 1. Type **dfsrmig /GetMigrationState 3** and press **Enter**.

Step 5.   If the migration to state 1 is complete you receive a message indicating that. If not, wait one minute and rerun Step 4 until you receive a message indicating All domain controllers have migrated successfully to the Global state ('Prepared').

Step 6.   Type **dfsrmig /SetGlobalState 2** and press **Enter**.

Step 7.   Repeat Step 5 until you receive the success message.

Step 8.   Type **dfsrmig /SetGlobalState 3** and press **Enter**.

Step 9.   Repeat Step 5 until you receive the success message (see Figure 6-16).

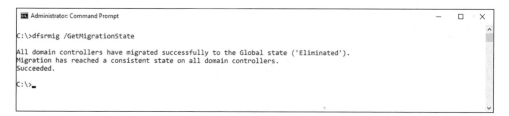

```
Administrator: Command Prompt                                        —   □   ×

C:\>dfsrmig /GetMigrationState

All domain controllers have migrated successfully to the Global state ('Eliminated').
Migration has reached a consistent state on all domain controllers.
Succeeded.

C:\>_
```

Figure 6-16   The Final Migration State of SYSVOL to DFSR. All Domain Controllers Have Migrated Successfully.

The SYSVOL has now been successfully migrated.

Exam Preparation Tasks

As mentioned in the section "Book Features" in the Introduction, you have a few choices for exam preparation: the exercises here; Chapter 17, "Final Preparation"; and the exam simulation questions in the Pearson Test Prep Software Online.

Review All Key Topics

Review the most important topics in this chapter, noted with the Key Topics icon in the outer margin of the page. Table 6-5 lists a reference of these key topics and the page number on which each is found.

Table 6-5   Key Topics for Chapter 6

Key Topic Element	Description	Page Number
List	Important snapshot menu options in **ntdsutil**	169
Table 6-2	Common parameters for **dsamain**	171
Paragraph	The Windows Backup utility for backing up AD DS	173
List	The two types of restore that you can perform on AD DS	175
Paragraph	Description of a nonauthoritative restore	175
Paragraph	Description of an authoritative restore	178
Paragraph	Explanation of the AD DS Recycle Bin	179
Figure 6-9	Using net stop to shut down the Active Directory Domain Services service	182
Figure 6-10	The ntds offline defragmentation utility	183
Paragraph	How to clean metadata out of AD DS	184
List	How an RODC handles attempted write operations	186
Paragraph	Explanation of Password Replication Policy (PRP)	186
Table 6-3	Common <*cmd*> parameters for **repadmin**	190
Table 6-4	PowerShell replication cmdlets	192
Paragraph	Migrating from FRS to DFSR for SYSVOL replication	192

Complete Tables and Lists from Memory

Print a copy of Appendix B, "Memory Tables" (found on the book website), or at least the section for this chapter, and complete the tables and lists from memory. Appendix C, "Memory Tables Answer Key," also on the website, includes completed tables and lists to check your work.

Define Key Terms

Define the following key terms from this chapter and check your answers in the glossary:

snapshot, mounting a snapshot, hosting a snapshot, system state, authoritative restore, nonauthoritative restore, defragmentation, metadata, Password Replication Policy (PRP), Distributed File System Replication (DFSR)

End-of-Chapter Review Questions

The answers to these questions appear in Appendix A. For more practice with exam format questions, use the Pearson Test Prep Software Online.

1. You are preparing to roll out a major batch update to your AD DS directory. The update will touch 1,500 different objects across multiple OUs. Part of your post-change validation strategy is to compare random accounts from the update and validate them against their pre-update status. How would you best perform the comparison?

    a. Disconnect a read-only domain controller from the network prior to rolling out the change. Use that RODC as a snapshot of the pre-change state of the directory for comparison.

    b. Perform a full backup of the directory prior to rolling out the change. After the change has been put in place perform an authoritative restore and validate the accounts against their pre-change state.

    c. Capture a snapshot of the directory prior to rolling out the change. After the change has been put in place, mount the snapshot and browse it to compare accounts to their pre-change state.

    d. Perform a full backup of the directory prior to rolling out the change. After the change has been put in place perform a nonauthoritative restore and validate the accounts against their pre-change state.

2. You have been using **ntdsutil** to create many snapshots over the past month while various directory updates have been performed. You no longer need those snapshots and would like to reclaim the space they're taking up. What command would you perform to remove the snapshots?

3. An RODC in a remote location used exclusively for hosting AD DS for the users at that location has a hard disk failure. Once a new drive is in place you have been tasked with restoring the authentication services on that machine. What would be the best approach?

   a. Reinstall Windows Server and the AD DS role. Promote the server to a DC in the existing domain.

   b. Reinstall Windows Server and the AD DS role. Perform an authoritative restore from a recent backup using Windows Server Backup.

   c. Reinstall Windows Server and the AD DS role. Perform a nonauthoritative restore from a recent backup using Windows Server Backup.

   d. Clone an existing RODC on the network and ship it to the remote site.

4. You administer an RODC located in the network DMZ to allow for authentication from users outside the network. This machine also hosts a number of web applications accessible from outside the network as well as their supporting databases. There is a hard disk failure, and once a replacement drive is in place you have been tasked with restoring the services on that machine. What would be the best approach?

   a. Reinstall Windows Server and the AD DS role. Promote the server to a DC in the existing domain.

   b. Reinstall Windows Server and the AD DS role. Perform an authoritative restore from a recent backup using Windows Server Backup.

   c. Reinstall Windows Server and the AD DS role. Perform a nonauthoritative restore from a recent backup using Windows Server Backup.

   d. Clone an existing RODC on the network and ship it to the remote site.

5. A junior staffer just informed you that he accidentally deleted an entire OU with over 100 active user and computer accounts. What steps could you perform to recover the directory?

6. An RODC in a remote location used exclusively for hosting AD DS for the users at that location has a hard disk failure. Once a new drive is in place you have been tasked with restoring the authentication services on that machine. You choose to install a fresh copy of Windows Server with the AD DS role and promote the server to a controller on the domain. What must you do before you can promote this "new" server?

This chapter covers the following topics:

- **Deploying Windows Server 2016 Domain Controllers Within a Pre-Existing Active Directory Environment**: This section describes how to deal with common issues and tasks when deploying a Windows Server 2016 domain controller into an existing Active Directory environment.

- **Configuring Trusts**: This section describes how to create and manage trusts between domains, trees, and forests.

- **Configuring Sites**: This section describes how to organize domain controllers into sites and manage subnets associated with those sites.

CHAPTER 7

Configuring Active Directory in a Complex Enterprise Environment

Setting up and configuring Active Directory consists of more than just installing Active Directory Domain Services and promoting a few member servers. You usually need to integrate it with an existing Active Directory deployment and make decisions about whether you want to upgrade Windows Server OS versions and domain and forest functional levels. Enterprise installations that consist of many domain controllers, domains, and trees also need to have a sound site and trust management plan in place.

This chapter covers considerations when you are upgrading OS, domain, and forest functional levels. It also introduces the concept of trusts and describes how to manage trust relationships, and how and why to organize domain controllers into sites.

"Do I Know This Already?" Quiz

The "Do I Know This Already?" quiz allows you to assess whether you should read this entire chapter thoroughly or jump to the "Exam Preparation Tasks" section. If you are in doubt about your answers to these questions or your own assessment of your knowledge of the topics, read the entire chapter. Table 7-1 lists the major headings in this chapter and their corresponding "Do I Know This Already?" quiz questions. You can find the answers in Appendix A, "Answers to the 'Do I Know This Already?' Quizzes."

Table 7-1 "Do I Know This Already?" Section-to-Question Mapping

Foundation Topics Section	Questions
Deploying Windows Server 2016 Domain Controllers Within a Pre-Existing Active Directory Environment	1-3
Configuring Trusts	4-6
Configuring Sites	7-9

CAUTION   The goal of self-assessment is to gauge your mastery of the topics in this chapter. If you do not know the answer to a question or are only partially sure of the answer, you should mark that question as wrong for purposes of the self-assessment. Giving yourself credit for an answer you correctly guess skews your self-assessment results and might provide you with a false sense of security.

1. Your forest currently runs at functional level 2008 R2. You would like to raise it to forest functional level 2016. Which of the following steps do you need to first perform? (Choose two.)

   a. Take the forest offline.

   b. Ensure the domain functional levels are at least 2012.

   c. Ensure the domain functional levels are at least 2016.

   d. Upgrade all domain controllers in the forest to Windows Server 2016.

2. Which tool is used to raise forest and domain functional levels?

   a. Active Directory Domains and Trusts

   b. Active Directory Users and Computers

   c. Active Directory Sites and Services

   d. Active Directory Administrative Center

3. Your forest currently runs at functional level 2008 R2. You would like to raise it to forest functional level 2016. Which of the following methods would you choose to ensure Server 2016 was running on all domain controllers? (Choose two.)

   a. Run an in-place upgrade to Server 2016 on any Server 2012 or 2012 R2 servers.

   b. Run an in-place upgrade to Server 2016 on any Server 2008 R2 or later servers.

   c. Demote all Server 2008 R2 servers and promote Server 2016 servers in their place.

   d. Leave all servers at their current OS and raise the forest functional level.

4. What are the two parties in a trust relationship named? (Choose two.)

   a. Outgoing domain

   b. Trusting domain

   c. Trusted domain

   d. Receiving domain

5. Which direction is the trust when the local domain is trusting and the remote domain is trusted?

   a. One-way incoming

   b. Two-way

   c. One-way outgoing

   d. All-way

6. Which type of trust would you create if a domain in one forest needs to trust a domain in another forest, exclusive of all other domains in either forest?

   a. Realm trust

   b. Forest trust

   c. Two-way transitive trust

   d. External trust

7. Your network includes three domain controllers on the 10.0.1.0/24 subnet and a fourth in the 10.0.0.0/24 subnet. All four controllers are located in the same data center. What would be the appropriate configuration for these controllers to manage replication?

   a. Create a separate site for each subnet and place the servers in their respective sites.

   b. Create a single site with two subnets and place all four servers in the same site.

   c. Create a separate site for each server with a site link for all four.

   d. Create a separate site for each subnet and place the servers in their respective sites with transitive trusts between the sites.

8. Which tool is used to manage sites and subnets in Windows Server 2016?

   a. Active Directory Domains and Trusts

   b. Active Directory Users and Computers

   c. Active Directory Sites and Services

   d. Active Directory Administrative Center

9. Which PowerShell cmdlet would you use to create a new subnet?

   a. **New-ADReplicationSubnet**

   b. **Add-ReplicationSubnet**

   c. **New-ADReplicationSite**

   d. **New-ADReplicationSiteLink**

Foundation Topics

Deploying Windows Server 2016 Domain Controllers Within a Pre-Existing Active Directory Environment

Chances are you won't be installing Windows Server 2016 into a brand new forest. Most of the time you'll be working with an existing legacy domain that was originally built on earlier versions of Windows Server. Even if the plan is to ultimately replace all the domain controllers with Server 2016, that's not likely to happen all at once, but rather over time in various stages.

Adding Server 2016 domain controllers to an existing AD DS deployment can be done as long as the existing domain functional level is set to Windows Server 2003 or higher. Recall from Chapter 2, "Installing and Configuring Domain Controllers," that even if you do promote a Server 2016 server to a DC on the domain you will not be able to take advantage of the newest features until the domain functional level is also raised to 2016. The domain functional level is dependent on the least recent version of Windows Server running on a domain controller. If there is still a Windows Server 2003 DC on the domain, the domain functional level will be limited to 2003 until that controller is upgraded or removed. Similarly, the forest functional level is limited by the lowest domain functional level in the forest. As long as a domain at functional level 2003 exists in the forest, the forest functional level is limited.

Upgrading Existing Domains and Forests

There are two general approaches to upgrade the domains and forests of an existing AD DS deployment:

- **OS upgrade**: If all the existing servers are running at least Windows Server 2012, you can perform an in-place upgrade of the operating system on each controller to Server 2016. Any domain controllers running an earlier version of the Windows Server OS, such as 2008 R2, will not be upgradable this way.

- **Replacement controllers**: You can introduce new Windows Server 2016 servers as domain controllers on the domain, transfer the Flexible Single Master Operations (FSMO) roles to those new servers, and then decommission (demote) the domain controllers running earlier versions of Windows Server. This method is generally preferred by system administrators.

A combination of the two processes can be performed as well. Whichever is chosen, once the domain controllers running the older versions of Windows Server have been upgraded or decommissioned, the domain and forest functional levels can be raised to Windows Server 2016. Prior to Windows Server 2012, a system administrator also needed to run the adprep utility to prepare the existing Active Directory environment. This is no longer the case; the domain will be prepared automatically when the first server running Windows Server 2016 is promoted to a domain controller on the domain.

Configuring Domain and Forest Functional Levels

Once the server upgrades have been performed, it is easy to raise the domain and forest functional levels.

To raise the domain functional level:

Step 1.   Log on to a writeable domain controller.

Step 2.   From the Start Menu launch **Server Manager**.

Step 3.   Click **Tools > Active Directory Domains and Trusts**.

Step 4.   Select the domain you want to raise from the left-hand navigation pane. Right-click the domain and select **Raise Domain Functional Level** (see Figure 7-1).

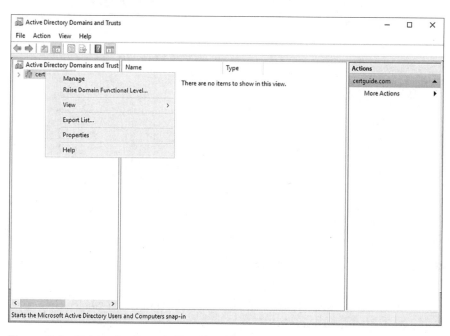

Figure 7-1   Raising the Domain Functional Level

Step 5. Choose the desired functional level from the pull-down labeled **Select an available domain functional level**.

Step 6. Click **Raise**.

The domain is raised to the chosen functional level. If the domain is already at the highest possible level, you are notified in the dialog box and there is no option to select a different functional level.

Raising the forest functional level is similar:

Step 1. Log on to a writeable domain controller.

Step 2. From the Start Menu launch **Server Manager**.

Step 3. Click **Tools > Active Directory Domains and Trusts**.

Step 4. In the left-hand navigation pane, right-click **Active Directory Domains and Trusts** and select **Raise Forest Functional Level** (see Figure 7-2).

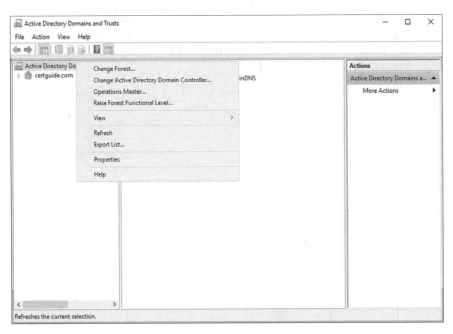

Figure 7-2 Raising the Forest Functional Level

Step 5. Choose the desired functional level from the pull-down labeled **Select an available forest functional level**.

Step 6. Click **Raise**.

The forest is raised to the chosen functional level. If the forest is already at the highest possible level, you are notified in the dialog box and there is no option to select a different functional level.

Configuring Multiple User Principal Name (UPN) Suffixes

When logging on to the domain, the user supplies his username and password. The necessary domain information can be gathered from the domain membership of the computer that the user is logging on from. When more than one domain or forest is present, the user may need to specify the User Principal Name (UPN) to log on. A UPN includes both the user's account name and the UPN suffix that is the name of the domain they are authenticating against. It is formatted similarly to an email address and is often exactly the same as the user's email address. A UPN is structured like so:

<username> @ <upn suffix>

By default, all users are configured to use the UPN suffix of the forest root domain. For example, if user ben.finkel has an account in the west.certguide.local domain, which is itself a child of the certguide.local domain, that user's UPN would be ben.finkel@certguide.local.

In many instances it might be desirable to provide an alternate logon UPN suffix for users. Using the previous example, certguide.local might not be ideal, and you might prefer certguide.com. You can configure additional UPN suffixes for a forest using the Active Directory Domains and Trusts tool:

Step 1. Log on to a writeable domain controller.

Step 2. From the Start Menu launch **Server Manager**.

Step 3. Click **Tools** > **Active Directory Domains and Trusts**.

Step 4. In the left-hand navigation pane, right-click **Active Directory Domains and Trusts** and select **Properties**.

Step 5. Type the name of the alternate suffix in the **Alternative UPN suffixes** box and click **Add** (see Figure 7-3).

Step 6. Click **OK**.

You can now configure users to use that UPN suffix on the properties page of the user object in either Active Directory Users and Computers (ADUC) or Active Directory Administrative Center (ADAC).

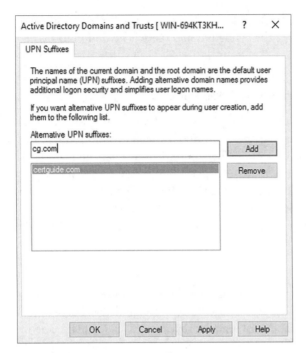

Figure 7-3   Adding a New UPN Suffix to a Forest

Configuring Trusts

When more than one domain exists in a tree, or across multiple trees or multiple forests, the need can arise to have one domain grant access to its objects to a user from another domain. Just because users have been split into a separate domain does not mean that they don't need access to resources in other domains. For example, users in a production domain may need to access resources in a domain dedicated to testing. For a domain to recognize an object from another domain, a trust relationship must exist between the two domains.

In a trust relationship there are two parties:

- **The trusted domain**: The trusted domain hosts the user accounts or security principals to which you want to grant access.

- **The trusting domain**: The trusting domain hosts the resources to which access is being granted.

If a security group in west.certguide.com is being granted read access to a file share in east.certguide.com, then west is the trusted domain and east is the trusting domain.

Some of these trust relationships exist by default in your AD DS deployment. By design all domains in the same tree have a two-way, transitive trust relationship with their parent domain. A two-way trust means that each domain trusts the other domain, or put another way, each domain is both trusted and trusting for each other. A transitive trust means that trust is passed between the domains in a chainlike manner.

For example, imagine the domains west.na.certguide.com and east.eu.certguide.com. They have a contiguous namespace and consequently exist in the same domain tree. While there is not a direct trust between the two, each has a two-way transitive trust with its parent domain (na.certguide.com and eu.certguide.com respectively). Those domains in turn have a two-way transitive trust with their common parent, certguide.com. By the transitive property this means that the two original domains have a trust relationship established by traversing the structure of the domain.

Three directions of trust can be established between domains, as described in Table 7-2.

Table 7-2 *Trust Relationship Directions*

Trust Direction	Description
One-way outgoing	The local domain is the trusted domain and the remote domain is the trusting domain. Unidirectional.
One-way incoming	The local domain is the trusting domain and the remote domain is the trusted domain. Unidirectional.
Two-way	Both domains are trusted and trusting. Bidirectional.

As mentioned, trust relationships can also be transitive. A nontransitive trust exists only between the two domains in the relationship and does not extend any further. A one-way trust is nontransitive by default. Most two-way trusts are transitive, although you can create two separate one-way trusts to create a nontransitive two-way trust in effect.

It is important to understand that trusts do not by themselves grant access or permissions. All the trust does is allow the trusting domain to recognize and accept the authentication from the trusted domain. Access to resources in the trusting domain still have to be explicitly granted.

Configuring Forest, External, Realm, and Shortcut Trusts

Forest trusts create a trust between two different forests just like domain trusts. Forest trusts can be either one-way or two-way and are always transitive, so all the resources in the trusting forest are accessible by users in the trusted forest. The forests on both sides of the trust must be at a minimum forest functional level of Windows Server 2003. Two types of authentication are available for forest trusts:

- **Forest-wide authentication**: This is the default configuration. With forest-wide authentication, all users in the trusted forest are authenticated automatically in the trusting forest. This is generally used when the two forests represent different divisions of the same organization.

- **Selective authorization**: When selective authorization is configured, users from the trusted forest have to be explicitly granted "Allow To Authenticate" permission in the trusting forest. This is a suitable option when the two forests in question belong to separate entities or need tighter control due to regulation.

An external trust is similar in that it exists between two forests and can be uni- or bidirectional, but an external trust is nontransitive. With an external trust, no other domain in either forest is included in the trust relationship. External trusts can be used to create a trust relationship with a forest that is not running at the Windows Server 2003 or higher functional level such as a Windows 2000 domain. Realm trusts are used to create a trust between an AD DS domain and a non-Windows Kerberos realm. Kerberos security is popular and can be found in both Linux and Apple Macintosh environments.

A shortcut trust is created between two domains that exist in the same forest and possibly even the same domain tree. While two-way trust is already enabled between domains such as these, the authentication traffic has to traverse up and then down the tree to successfully authenticate users. With a shortcut trust the authentication traffic can skip that traversal and authenticate directly between the two domains, potentially saving time and network traffic.

To create a trust relationship, determine which domain will be the trusting domain and begin there. If creating a two-way trust, you can start in either domain:

Step 1. Log on to a writeable domain controller in the trusting domain.

Step 2. From the Start Menu launch **Server Manager**.

Step 3. Click **Tools > Active Directory Domains and Trusts**.

Step 4. In the left-hand navigation pane, right-click the trusting domain and select **Properties**.

Step 5. Select the **Trusts** tab (see Figure 7-4).

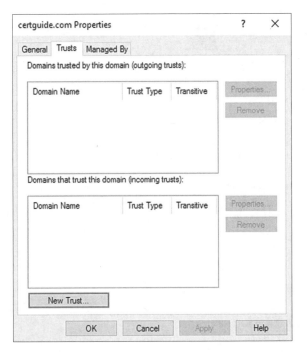

Figure 7-4   The Trusts Tab of the Domain Properties Dialog in Active Directory Domains and Trusts

Step 6.   Click **New Trust**.

Step 7.   The New Trust Wizard launches. Click **Next**.

Step 8.   Type the name of the remote trust you want to create a relationship with and click **Next**.

Step 9.   The next page of the wizard depends on the type of trust you're creating:

- For an unrecognized domain, you are presented with the option to create a realm trust or retype the domain. If you choose a realm trust you are then able to choose transitive or nontransitive.

- For a recognized domain you have the option to create an external trust or a forest trust.

Step 10.   Choose the trust direction and click **Next** (see Figure 7-5).

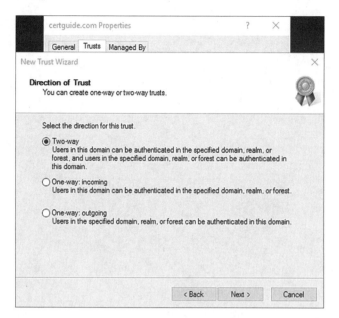

Figure 7-5   Selecting a Trust Direction in the New Trust Wizard

Step 11.   The Sides of Trust option displays, allowing you to create the trust in both domains if you have credentials, or just in the current domain. If you choose to only create the trust in the current domain, you need to manually create the other side of the trust. Click **Next**.

Step 12.   If you chose both sides of the domain, supply Domain Admin credentials for the remote domain and click **Next**.

Step 13.   Select **Forest-Wide** or **Selective** authentication and click **Next**.

Step 14.   If you chose a two-way trust, choose **Forest-Wide** or **Selective** authentication for the other side of the trust and click **Next**.

Step 15.   Click **Next**.

Step 16.   Click **Finish**.

The trust can now be viewed in either domain (see Figure 7-6).

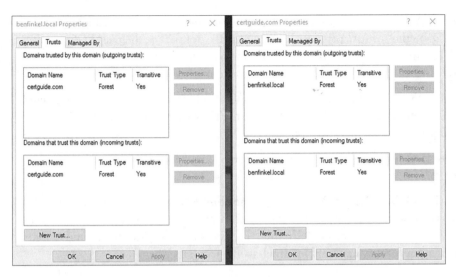

Figure 7-6   Side-by-Side View of the Trusts Tab from Both Domains in a Two-Way Trust

For trust communication to work between two domains or forests, the following ports must be open to network traffic (see Table 7-3).

Table 7-3   Network Ports for Trust Communication

Port	Used by...
387 UDP and TCP	LDAP
445 TCP	Microsoft SMB
88 UDP	Kerberos
135 TCP	Trust endpoint resolution

Configuring SID Filtering

Security identifiers (SIDs) are a critical piece of cross-domain authentication. When a security principal is presented to a trusting domain, its token includes all the associated SIDs for that principal. This includes SIDs for any security group membership that principal might have. If a user object in a trusted domain is a member of security groups in other domains in the trusting forest, they could inadvertently be granted elevated privileges. When those other security groups were granted additional privileges, the remote security object gains those privileges when it authenticates to the trusting domain.

When SID filtering is enabled, the trusting domain filters out, essentially ignoring, all SIDs in the security principal's token that are not part of the trusted domain. This ensures that any membership the principal might have in other domains is ignored and elevated privileges are not inadvertently granted.

SID filtering is a critical security feature and should not be disabled without sound justification. To disable SID filtering, run the following command from the command prompt of the trusting domain:

```
netdom trust <trusting domain> /domain:<trusted domain> /
EnableSIDHistory:Yes
```

The **/EnableSIDHistory:Yes** switch on **netdom** tells the trusted domain that the security principal can use all the SIDs it has in its history to access resources. This has the effect of disabling SID filtering. To re-enable SID filtering, a similar command is run setting the **/EnableSIDHistory** switch to **No**:

```
netdom trust <trusting domain> /domain:<trusted domain> /
EnableSIDHistory:No
```

You can learn more about the **netdom** command here: https://technet.microsoft.com/en-us/library/cc835085(v=ws.11).aspx.

Configuring Name Suffix Routing

When a cross forest trust is created, by default any UPN suffix in the trusted domain can be authenticated for resources in the trusting domain. You can disable or prevent this for individual name suffixes or for name suffix branches with name suffix routing. For example, if your domain is trusting in a relationship with certguide.com, you might want to exclude users in west.certguide.com from the relationship. By disabling name suffix routing for that domain or branch, you would prevent those users from authenticating in your domain.

Name suffix routing is configured in the properties panel of a trust from Active Directory Domains and Trusts:

Step 1.   Log on to a writeable domain controller in the trusting domain.

Step 2.   From the Start Menu launch **Server Manager**.

Step 3.   Click **Tools** > **Active Directory Domains and Trusts**.

Step 4.   In the left-hand navigation pane, right-click the trusting domain and select **Properties**.

Step 5.   Select the **Trusts** tab.

Step 6.   Select the trust you want to configure and click **Properties**.

Step 7.   Select the **Name Suffix Routing** tab (see Figure 7-7).

Figure 7-7   The Name Suffix Routing Tab of the Trust Properties Dialog in Active Directory Domains and Trusts

Step 8.   Select the domain name to configure routing for and click **Edit**.

Step 9.   Underneath the **Name Suffixes to exclude from routing to** <domain> box click **Add**.

Step 10.   Type the name suffix you want to exclude and click **OK**.

Step 11.   Click **OK**.

Configuring Sites

Domain infrastructure does not always line up with the geographical realties of modern-day organizations. Your sales department may be headquartered in the United States with a secondary office in London and various satellites around the world. All those users may well want to authenticate to the sales domain, but which domain controller will their authentication request be handled by? Authenticating a user in Australia to a server in the UK doesn't make much sense, nor does replicating traffic from New York to Berlin when it could much more easily be replicated from a geographically closer server. In other words, the physical layout of the organization may not match the logical structure of the domain.

Active Directory Domain Services addresses this challenge with a concept known as *sites*. Sites in AD DS represent the physical structure of your network. A site typically represents a physical location where hosts share a fast local network connection. A building or campus sharing a direct connection would be an example of a site. Sites are made up of one or more subnets. AD DS can use sites as well as subnets and site links to determine which server to route authentication and authorization requests to and to most efficiently replicate updates between domain controllers.

Configuring Sites and Subnets

A default site named *Default-First-Site-Name* is created when a forest is first created. Microsoft recommends changing this site name immediately and using a standardized naming scheme for your sites. This site name can be changed in the Active Directory Sites and Services console, which is also used to create and manage sites and subnets.

> **NOTE**   Subnetting is a complex topic covered in more depth in Microsoft's 70-741 exam. You can read about subnetting here: https://technet.microsoft.com/library/bb726997.

Sites

To create a new site:

Step 1.   Log on to a writeable domain controller.

Step 2.   From the Start Menu launch **Server Manager**.

Step 3.   Click **Tools > Active Directory Sites and Services**.

Step 4.   In the left-hand navigation pane right-click **Sites** and select **New Site**.

Step 5.   Type a name for the site and select a site link from the list. DEFAULTIPSITELINK is available by default (see Figure 7-8). The process for creating new site links is described later in this chapter. Click **OK**.

Step 6.   Review the instructions and click **OK**.

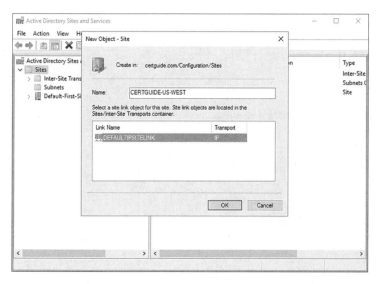

Figure 7-8   Creating a New Site in Active Directory Sites and Services. A Site Link Must Be Chosen on This Page Before Continuing.

To rename a site:

Step 1.   Log on to a writeable domain controller.

Step 2.   From the Start Menu launch **Server Manager**.

Step 3.   Click **Tools** > **Active Directory Sites and Services**.

Step 4.   In the left-hand navigation pane right-click the site to rename and select **Rename**.

Step 5.   Type the new name and press **Enter**.

To move a server between sites:

Step 1.   Log on to a writeable domain controller.

Step 2.   From the Start Menu launch **Server Manager**.

Step 3.   Click **Tools** > **Active Directory Sites and Services**.

Step 4.   In the left-hand navigation pane expand the site where the server currently resides.

Step 5.   Expand the Servers node.

Step 6.   Right-click the server to move and select **Move**.

Step 7.   In the Move Server dialog select the site to move the server to and click **OK (see Figure 7-9).**

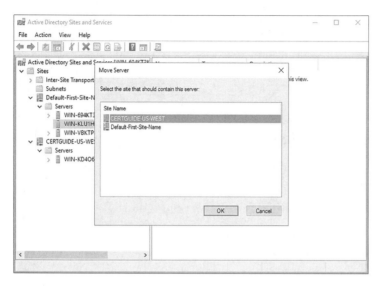

Figure 7-9 Selecting a Destination Site for a Domain Controller When Moving It in Active Directory Sites and Services

Subnets

Sites can be associated with one or more IP address ranges known as *subnets*. Subnets are used by AD DS to efficiently move replication traffic between domain controllers. Subnets and sites are the only metrics available to AD DS for determining the physical locations of domain controllers, so it's important to keep subnet information up-to-date. No subnet is required if you only have one site in your forest. If you are going to have more than one site in your forest, you must create subnets to assign IP address ranges to the various sites. You can use either IPv4 or IPv6 addresses to define a subnet. Subnets are defined with a CIDR range prefix.

To create a new subnet:

Step 1.   Log on to a writeable domain controller.

Step 2.   From the Start Menu launch **Server Manager**.

Step 3.   Click **Tools** > **Active Directory Sites and Services**.

Step 4.   In the left-hand navigation pane right-click **Subnets** and select **New Subnet**.

Step 5.   Type the subnet prefix CIDR range in the **Prefix box (see Figure 7-10).**

Step 6.   Select a site for the subnet to be associated with and click **OK**.

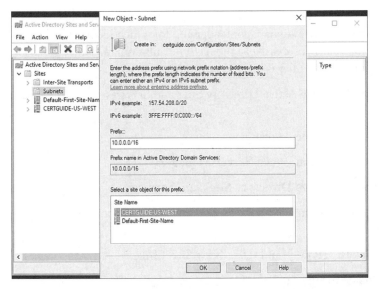

Figure 7-10   Creating a New Subnet in Active Directory Sites and Services. The Prefix Text Box Must Contain a Valid CIDR Range for the Subnet and It Must Be Associated with a Site.

A site can have multiple subnets associated with it, so you can provide both IPv4 and IPv6 subnet prefixes to a single site, or have multiple disparate subnets associated with a single site. Subnets can have their prefixes updated or moved to a new site by editing their properties in Active Directory Sites and Services.

Creating and Configuring Site Links

Administrators also have fine control over replication traffic between sites. By establishing site links and adding sites to those links, you can define how replication traffic will be prioritized around the network. Because sites may be geographically diverse and have a faster or more resilient connection to other sites, AD DS allows you to create site links to create preferred pathways for replication traffic.

A site link is comprised of three pieces:

- **Sites**: The member sites in the link. Typically there are only two sites to a link, although you can define more.

- **Cost**: The relative cost of network traffic between the sites in the link. Links with a lower cost are prioritized over links with a higher cost.

- **Schedule**: The replication schedule for the link determines how often replication occurs over the link. Schedules can be used to force replication during certain time periods or even certain days of the week.

Site links are used by AD DS to determine site coverage. For various reasons a site may not have a domain controller for a given domain. As part of Automatic Site

Coverage, domain controllers broadcast themselves as the default controller in any site that does not already have a domain controller and for which its own site has the lowest cost connection. This ensures every site has a default domain controller associated with it even if that controller is located in another site.

Site links are managed with the Active Directory Sites and Services tool. To create a site link:

Step 1.   Log on to a writeable domain controller.

Step 2.   From the Start Menu launch **Server Manager**.

Step 3.   Click **Tools > Active Directory Sites and Services**.

Step 4.   In the left-hand navigation pane expand Sites; then expand Inter-Site Transports.

Step 5.   Right-click the **IP** node and select **New Site Link**.

Step 6.   Type a name for the site link.

Step 7.   Choose sites to include in the link by selecting them from the **Sites not in this site link** box and clicking the **Add** button (see Figure 7-11).

Step 8.   Click **OK**.

Figure 7-11   Creating a New Site Link in Active Directory Sites and Services. All of the Sites Are Included in the Link.

The site is now listed under the details pane for the IP node. You can modify the default cost and schedule by right-clicking the link and selecting **Properties** (see Figure 7-12).

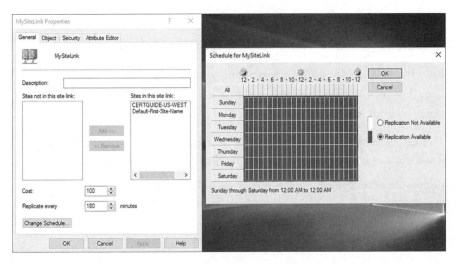

Figure 7-12 Site Link Properties and Schedule Editor from Active Directory Sites and Services

Managing Sites with PowerShell

Sites can be managed using standard PowerShell cmdlets. Table 7-4 lists the most common cmdlets used to create, delete, and update sites and site links.

Table 7-4 PowerShell Cmdlets for Managing Sites

PowerShell Cmdlet	Description
New-ADReplicationSite	Creates a new site
Remove-ADReplicationSite	Deletes an existing site
New-ADReplicationSubnet	Creates a new subnet in a site
Remove-ADReplicationSubnet	Deletes an existing subnet from a site
New-ADReplicationSiteLink	Creates a new site link
Set-ADReplicationSiteLink	Updates an existing site link
Remove-ADReplicationSiteLink	Deletes an existing site link

The PowerShell cmdlet to create a new site is

```
New-ADReplicationSite [-Name] <String>
```

All that is required is a **-Name** parameter. For example:

```
>New-ADReplicationSite -Name "CertguideWest"
```

The PowerShell cmdlet to remove a site is

```
Remove-ADReplicationSite [-Identity] <ADReplicationSite>
```

The PowerShell cmdlet to create a new subnet is

```
New-ADReplicationSubnet [-Name] <String>'
[[-Site] <ADReplicationSite> ]'
```

The **-Name** parameter specifies the IPv4 or IPv6 prefix. The **-Site** parameter specifies which site to add the subnet to. For example:

```
>New-ADReplicationSubnet -Name "10.0.0.0/16" -Site CertguideWest
```

The PowerShell cmdlet to remove a subnet is

```
Remove-ADReplicationSubnet [-Identity] <ADReplicationSubnet>
```

The **-Identity** parameter is the IPv4 or IPv6 prefix. For example:

```
>Remove-ADReplicationSubnet -Identity "10.1.0.0/24"
```

The PowerShell cmdlet to create a new site link is

```
New-ADReplicationSiteLink [-Name] <String>'
[[-SitesIncluded] <ADReplicationSite[]> ]'
[-Cost <Int32> ]'
[-ReplicationFrequencyInMinutes <Int32> ]'
[-ReplicationSchedule <ActiveDirectorySchedule> ]
```

The **-SitesIncluded** parameter specifies a comma-separated list of sites to include in the site link. You can use an ActiveDirectorySchedule object to create a specific schedule for replication. For example:

```
>New-ADReplicationSiteLink -Name "West-East" -SitesIncluded
CertguideWest,CertguideEast -Cost 50
```

The PowerShell cmdlet to update a site link is

```
Set-ADReplicationSiteLink [-Identity] <ADReplicationSiteLink>'
[-Cost <Int32> ]'
[-ReplicationFrequencyInMinutes <Int32> ]'
[-ReplicationSchedule <ActiveDirectorySchedule> ]'
[-SitesIncluded <Hashtable> ]
```

The **-SitesIncluded** parameter specifies a comma-separated list of sites to include in the site link. You can use an ActiveDirectorySchedule object to create a specific schedule for replication. For example:

```
>Set-ADReplicationSiteLink -Identity "West-East-South" -SitesIncluded
CertguideWest,CertguideEast,CertguideSouth -Cost 100
```

The PowerShell cmdlet for removing a site link is

```
Remove-ADReplicationSiteLink [-Identity] <ADReplicationSiteLink>
```

For example:

```
>Remove-ADReplicationSiteLink -Identity "West-East-South"
```

NOTE   The MCSA 70-742 exam objective "Configure Active Directory in a complex enterprise environment" includes the subtopic "Manage registration of SRV records," which overlaps slightly with a subtopic of the "Install and configure domain controllers" objective, covered in Chapter 2. You find full coverage of managing registration of SRV records in Chapter 2.

Exam Preparation Tasks

As mentioned in the section "Book Features" in the Introduction, you have a few choices for exam preparation: the exercises here; Chapter 17, "Final Preparation"; and the exam simulation questions in the Pearson Test Prep Software Online.

Review All Key Topics

Review the most important topics in this chapter, noted with the Key Topics icon in the outer margin of the page. Table 7-5 lists a reference of these key topics and the page number on which each is found.

Table 7-5   Key Topics for Chapter 7

Key Topic Element	Description	Page Number
Paragraph	Domain and forest functional levels	202
Steps	Raising the domain functional level	203
Steps	Raising the forest functional level	204
Paragraph	User principal names	205
Table 7-2	Trust relationship directions	207
List	Forest trust authorization options	208
Table 7-3	Network ports for trust communication	211
Steps	Configuring name suffix routing	212
Paragraph	Active Directory sites	214
Paragraph	Active Directory subnets	216

Key Topic Element	Description	Page Number
Paragraph	Site links	217
List	Site link properties	217
Table 7-4	PowerShell cmdlets for managing sites	219

Complete Tables and Lists from Memory

Print a copy of Appendix B, "Memory Tables" (found on the book website), or at least the section for this chapter, and complete the tables and lists from memory. Appendix C, "Memory Tables Answer Key," also on the website, includes completed tables and lists to check your work.

Define Key Terms

Define the following key terms from this chapter and check your answers in the glossary:

User Principal Name (UPN), trust, forest trust, external trust, realm trust, shortcut trust, one-way trust, two-way trust, security identifier (SID), site, subnet, site link

End-of-Chapter Review Questions

The answers to these questions appear in Appendix A. For more practice with exam format questions, use the Pearson Test Prep Software Online.

1. Your forest has three domains: certguide.com and its two children domains west.certguide.com and east.certguide.com. The west domain runs at domain functional level 2012 R2. The east domain runs at domain functional level 2008. You have been tasked with bringing the entire forest to forest functional level 2016. How would you approach raising the west.certguide.com domain?

    a. Wherever possible, demote and replace existing controllers with new Server 2016 controllers. Run in-place upgrades for servers where demotion and replacement is not an option.

    b. Perform backups of each domain controller in the domain and restore those backups to new Server 2016 servers.

    c. Raise the domain functional level to Server 2016 from each domain controller in the domain.

    d. Do nothing until the east domain has been raised.

2. Your forest has three domains: certguide.com and its two children domains west.certguide.com and east.certguide.com. The west domain runs at domain functional level 2012 R2. The east domain runs at domain functional level 2008. You have been tasked with bringing the entire forest to forest functional level 2016. How would you approach raising the east.certguide.com domain?

   a. Perform in-place upgrades of any server running Server 2008 or 2008 R2 OS.

   b. Promote servers running 2016 to controllers and demote any existing servers running 2008 R2 or earlier.

   c. Raise the domain functional level to Server 2016 from each domain controller in the domain.

   d. Do nothing until the west domain has been raised.

3. You administer a complex organization with more than a dozen different domains in the tree each representing facilities in different parts of the world. It has recently come to your attention that users in the western United States are seeing latency whenever they attempt to access a file server at the Berlin facility. What sort of trust could you implement to help with this?

   a. A realm trust between the two domains.

   b. Raise the existing trust to a two-way trust.

   c. An external trust between the two domains.

   d. A shortcut trust between the two domains.

4. What is the PowerShell command(s) to create a new site named Berlin with a subnet of the 10.0.0.0/24 prefix?

This chapter covers the following topics:

- **Introduction to Group Policy**: This section describes what Group Policy is and how to create and link Group Policy Objects (GPOs).

- **Managing Starter GPOs**: This section describes starter GPOs and how to manage them.

- **Backing Up, Importing, Copying, and Restoring GPOs**: This section describes the process of backing up, importing, copying, and restoring GPOs.

- **Delegating Group Policy Management**: This section describes how to delegate permissions to create and link GPOs to individuals and groups in the directory.

- **Detecting Health Issues Using the Group Policy Infrastructure Status Dashboard**: This section describes the Group Policy Infrastructure Status dashboard and how it is used to monitor the health and status of Group Policy updates.

- **Local Group Policies**: This section describes Local Group Policies found on member clients and servers in the domain.

CHAPTER 8

Creating and Managing Group Policy Objects (GPOs)

Group Policy and Group Policy Objects (GPOs) represent a large collection of features and functionality available in Active Directory Domain Services. The goal of Group Policy is to allow AD DS administrators to define a set of policies; target those policies to objects, sites, domains, or organizational units in the directory; and then rely on the system to enforce those policies.

There is enough material on Group Policy to fill an entire book all on its own. This book focuses on the administration and configuration of policies from the domain and forest perspective but not down to the detail of actual settings and operations on workstations. This chapter introduces the basic management features of Group Policy and GPOs.

"Do I Know This Already?" Quiz

The "Do I Know This Already?" quiz allows you to assess whether you should read this entire chapter thoroughly or jump to the "Exam Preparation Tasks" section. If you are in doubt about your answers to these questions or your own assessment of your knowledge of the topics, read the entire chapter. Table 8-1 lists the major headings in this chapter and their corresponding "Do I Know This Already?" quiz questions. You can find the answers in Appendix A, "Answers to the 'Do I Know This Already?' Quizzes."

Table 8-1 "Do I Know This Already?" Section-to-Question Mapping

Foundation Topics Section	Questions
Introduction to Group Policy	1-2
Managing Starter GPOs	3
Backing Up, Importing, Copying, and Restoring GPOs	4-5
Delegating Group Policy Management	6
Detecting Health Issues Using the Group Policy Infrastructure Status Dashboard	7
Local Group Policies	8

CAUTION   The goal of self-assessment is to gauge your mastery of the topics in this chapter. If you do not know the answer to a question or are only partially sure of the answer, you should mark that question as wrong for purposes of the self-assessment. Giving yourself credit for an answer you correctly guess skews your self-assessment results and might provide you with a false sense of security.

1. Which of the following can a Group Policy Object (GPO) be linked to? (Choose three.)

   a. Organizational units (OUs)

   b. Domains

   c. Domain controllers

   d. Sites

2. Which two utilities are most often used to manage and edit GPOs in AD DS? (Choose two.)

   a. Active Directory Administrative Console (ADAC)

   b. Active Directory Users and Computers (ADUC)

   c. Group Policy Management Editor (GPME)

   d. Group Policy Management Console (GPMC)

3. Which section of a GPO is the only one included in a starter GPO?

   a. Software Settings

   b. Administrative Templates

   c. Preferences

   d. Windows Settings

4. Where does the GPO backup folder get its name from when written to the file system?

   a. A date timestamp from the moment the backup was taken

   b. User entry

   c. The fully qualified domain name path to the GPO

   d. The GPO's ObjectID

5. Which tool is used when importing a GPO backup taken from a different domain or forest to ensure values are translated properly?

   a. GPMC

   b. Migration table

   c. GPME

   d. repadmin.exe

6. If you want to delegate the ability to create GPOs to another user in the domain, which node in the GPMC would you edit the delegation for?

   a. Starter GPOs

   b. Domain

   c. Group Policy Objects

   d. Forest

7. Which two locations store the pieces of the GPO? (Choose two.)

   a. SYSVOL

   b. Primary Domain Controller FSMO role

   c. GPMC

   d. The AD DS directory

8. What is the extension of the XML files Microsoft Active Directory uses to store Administrative Templates settings?

   a. GPO

   b. ADMX

   c. ADM

   d. XML

Introduction to Group Policy

Most often Group Policy is presented as the definition of what a user can or cannot do on the network. This is only a small part of the story. Policies can be used to determine a whole series of different configuration settings that can be applied to individual objects or collections of objects in the AD DS directory. Group Policy is tightly integrated with AD DS so that policy management can be mirrored to directory structure, especially at the organizational unit level.

The scope and functionality of Group Policy covers a few different key areas:

- Policies can be targeted to users, computers, group, sites, domains, and OUs.

- Configuration values can be set or unset under specific circumstances.

- Policies can execute scripts during logon or logoff and computer startup and shutdown.

Group Policy Objects can control the behavior of workstations and the end-user experience across the entire organization. Thousands of different settings can be managed with GPOs. Some examples of policies that can be configured with Group Policy include the ability to set the system time, disallowing installation of new software, or even preventing the system from being shut down. A GPO defines as many of these policies as the system administrator wants.

> **NOTE** Policies in a GPO are easy to set up, but due to Microsoft's choice in wording, some policies can have a confusing application, such as "Disable the display control panel." Policies are disabled by default, resulting in the option it refers to being enabled. Enabling one of these policies has the effect of disabling the option.

Management of Group Policy is performed almost entirely with the Group Policy Management Console (GPMC). This console can be launched from a command line with the **gpmc** command or from the Tools menu of the Windows Server 2016 Server Manager. The GPMC manages the creation of GPOs themselves and is the interface for viewing resultant sets of policies and linking GPOs to domains, sites, and OUs, but the settings within a GPO are configured with a utility called the Group Policy Management Editor (GPME).

In Chapter 3, "Creating and Managing Active Directory Users and Computers," we briefly modified a GPO using the GPMC and GPME when user rights assignment was discussed. The specific GPO modified was known as the Default Domain Policy. Like its name implies, the Default Domain Policy is the GPO that applies to all objects in the domain when another policy is not overriding it. Microsoft strongly recommends against using the Default Domain Policy; instead, administrators should create a custom policy and make modifications to that policy, even if it's the only policy used in the domain.

Creating Group Policy Objects

In the Group Policy Management Console, GPOs are created independently of where they'll be applied and then separately linked to the appropriate locations in the domain. This allows you to create a single GPO and apply it to different OUs or groups in the domain without having to have multiple copies of the GPO.

To create a GPO:

Step 1.   Log on to a writeable domain controller.

Step 2.   From the Start Menu launch **Server Manager**.

Step 3.   Click **Tools** > **Group Policy Management**.

Step 4.   In the left-hand navigation pane expand the **Domains** node and then the node for your domain.

Step 5.   Note the default folders available for a domain, which includes Group Policy Objects and any custom OUs in the root of your domain. Right-click **Group Policy Objects** and select **New**.

Step 6.   Type a name for the new GPO in the **Name** box (see Figure 8-1).

Step 7.   Note the option to choose a **Source Starter GPO**. By default, this is set to **(none)** and does not have any options until you create a starter GPO. Click **OK**.

Step 8.   Expand the **Group Policy Objects** node. Your new GPO should now be listed.

The GPO is created in the domain and is available to be linked by following the instructions in the next section, "Configuring GPO Links." The policy settings in the GPO are not applied until it is linked.

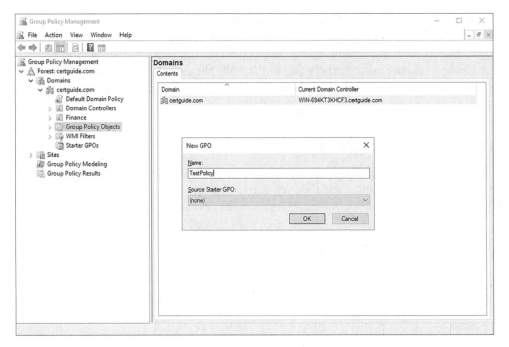

Figure 8-1   The New GPO Dialog Box Where a GPO Is Named and a Source Starter GPO Can Be Chosen

Configuring GPO Links

GPOs are not applied to any objects in the domain by default. Simply creating a GPO in the Group Policy Objects folder makes the GPO available but doesn't affect the domain. To use a GPO you must apply it or link it to a site, domain, or OU. When you link a GPO, its settings are applied to the objects in that scope.

To link an existing GPO to a node in the domain:

Step 1.   Log on to a writeable domain controller.

Step 2.   From the Start Menu launch **Server Manager**.

Step 3.   Click **Tools** > **Group Policy Management**.

Step 4.   In the left-hand navigation pane, expand the **Domains** node and then the node for your domain.

Step 5.   Right-click the domain, site, or OU you want to link a policy to and select **Link an existing GPO**.

Step 6.   Choose the domain to search for policies in the pull-down labeled **Look in this domain** and select a policy from the list below; then click **OK** (see Figure 8-2).

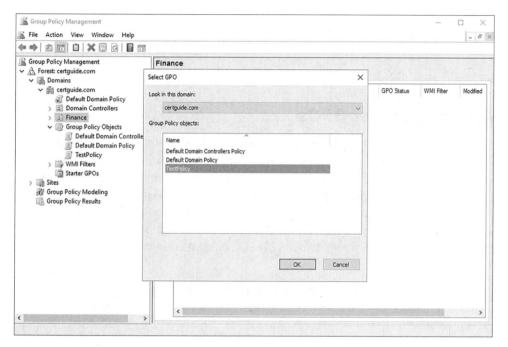

Figure 8-2   The Select GPO Dialog When Linking a GPO to a Node in the GPMC

The details pane on the right-hand side lists all the policy objects linked to the currently selected node. You can use this panel to rearrange the order that the GPOs are applied. This order determines which policy setting is ultimately effective when two or more GPOs are in conflict on the same node. You can also view which nodes a GPO is linked to. Navigate to the Group Policy Objects node of the GPME and select a GPO. The details pane on the right lists all the sites, domains, and OUs that are linked to the GPO.

When reviewing the details of a GPO link, there are two options as described in Table 8-2. You can edit either setting by right-clicking the link in the details pane and selecting the appropriate option.

Table 8-2   GPO Link Settings

Setting	Purpose
Link Enabled	Enable or disable the link. Disabled links do not apply settings to the objects in the directory.
Enforced	Forces GPO settings to override any conflicts with GPOs linked to child objects.

Managing Starter GPOs

GPOs have the potential to be large, complex configurations due to the sheer volume of potential settings that can be set. Often an organization wants to provide administrators with a template of preconfigured policy settings to reduce the time and burden when creating new policies. When you use a starter GPO to create a new GPO, all the settings, values, comments, and delegations defined in the starter GPO are included in the new GPO. Starter GPOs can also be easily exported and imported for use across domains, forests, or even entirely separate AD DS deployments.

Creating starter GPOs is just like working with regular GPOs. You create the GPO and then set the configuration values. Starter GPOs are limited to the Administrative Templates section of a GPO.

To create a starter GPO:

Step 1.   Log on to a writeable domain controller.

Step 2.   From the Start Menu launch **Server Manager**.

Step 3.   Click **Tools > Group Policy Management**.

Step 4.   In the left-hand navigation pane, expand the **Domains** node and then the node for your domain.

Step 5.   Note the default folders available for a domain, which includes Group Policy Objects and any custom OUs in the root of your domain. Right-click **Start GPOs** and select **New**.

Step 6.   Type a name for the starter GPO and any additional comments in the **Comment** box and then click **OK** (see Figure 8-3).

Step 7.   Right-click the new GPO and select **Edit**.

Step 8.   The Group Policy Starter GPO Editor launches. Note you can only edit **Administrative Template** settings for both Computer Configuration and User Configuration.

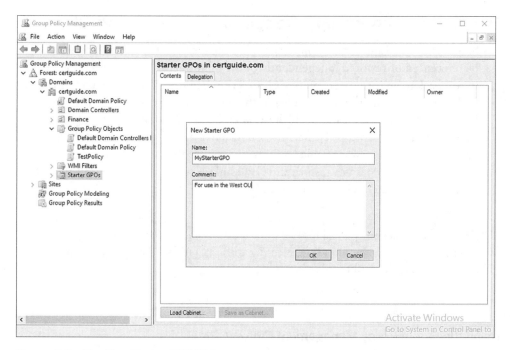

Figure 8-3   The New Starter GPO Dialog

To use the new starter GPO, create a new GPO in your domain per the instructions earlier in this chapter. During the wizard you have the option to choose a starter GPO from the domain. You can also right-click a starter GPO and select **New GPO From Start GPO**.

To export starter GPOs for use in another forest:

Step 1.   Log on to a writeable domain controller.

Step 2.   From the Start Menu launch **Server Manager**.

Step 3.   Click **Tools > Group Policy Management**.

Step 4.   In the left-hand navigation pane, expand the **Domains** node and then the node for your domain.

Step 5.   Select the **Starter GPOs** node.

Step 6.   On the right-hand details pane (not the navigation pane) select a GPO and click **Save as Cabinet...**

Step 7.   Choose a location to save the .cab file and click **Save**.

The .cab file can then be loaded in another forest using the **Load Cabinet** button.

Backing Up, Importing, Copying, and Restoring GPOs

Sometimes you want to maintain separate backups of your GPOs so that they can be referenced or restored independently of the full directory in the event you need to roll back to an earlier version of a GPO. GPME allows you to back up individual GPOs or your entire library of GPOs to the file system. Backing up a GPO creates a folder in the chosen location, which can then be imported into another GPO to override its policy settings. GPME also offers a management dialog for GPO backups where you can view available backups and restore them over their original GPO. Restoring a GPO does not restore any GPO links associated with the GPO; those have to be changed or created manually.

> **NOTE** A GPO backup is saved into a folder location named for its AD DS directory ObjectID. This ID can be found by selecting the GPO in GPME and viewing the **Unique ID** value on the **Details** tab.

Using the Group Policy Management Editor (GPME)

To back up a GPO:

Step 1. Log on to a writeable domain controller.

Step 2. From the Start Menu launch **Server Manager**.

Step 3. Click **Tools > Group Policy Management**.

Step 4. In the left-hand navigation pane expand the **Domains** node and then the node for your domain.

Step 5. Select the **Group Policy Objects** node.

Step 6. Right-click the desired GPO and select **Back up**.

Step 7. Click **Browse** to choose a location to save the backup. Be sure to choose a consistent and dedicated location that has good network connectivity to the domain (see Figure 8-4).

Step 8. Type an optional description and click **Back Up**.

Step 9. When the backup completes click **OK**.

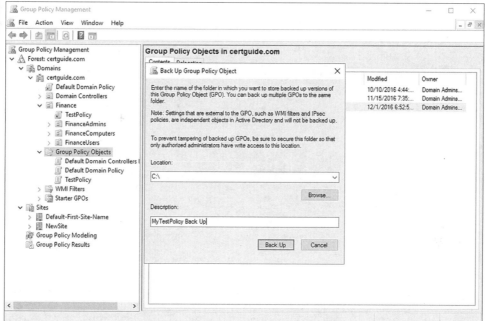

Figure 8-4 The Back Up Group Policy Object Wizard. GPMC Creates a Subfolder in the Chosen Location Named for the ObjectID of the GPO Being Backed Up.

You can back up all the GPOs in the domain by right-clicking the **Group Policy Objects** node and selecting **Back Up All**. Follow the same steps to choose a backup location as described in the preceding list.

To restore a GPO to previously backed up settings:

Step 1. Log on to a writeable domain controller.

Step 2. From the Start Menu launch **Server Manager**.

Step 3. Click **Tools** > **Group Policy Management**.

Step 4. In the left-hand navigation pane expand the **Domains** node and then the node for your domain.

Step 5. Select the **Group Policy Objects** node.

Step 6. Right-click the desired GPO and select **Restore from Backup**.

Step 7. Click **Next**.

Step 8. Click **Browse** to locate the folder where the backup is saved.

Step 9. The wizard lists all the backups found in that location for the selected GPO (see Figure 8-5). Select the desired source backup and click **Next**.

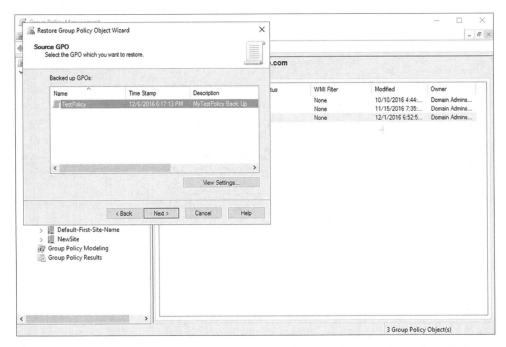

Figure 8-5   The Restore Group Policy Object Wizard. Note Any Backups for a Given GPO Are Displayed with Timestamp and Description.

Step 10.   Review the details and click **Finish**.

Step 11.   When the restore completes, click **OK**.

You can restore a GPO only from previous backups made from that same GPO object. A GPO can be overwritten with the settings of a different GPO backup by selecting **Import Settings** from the right-click context menu of a GPO. This replaces all the settings in the GPO with the settings in the selected backup.

If you want to use an existing GPO as a starting point for a new GPO, you can copy and paste a GPO in the GPME:

Step 1.   Log on to a writeable domain controller.

Step 2.   From the Start Menu launch **Server Manager**.

Step 3.   Click **Tools > Group Policy Management**.

Step 4.   In the left-hand navigation pane expand the **Domains** node and then the node for your domain.

Step 5.   Select the **Group Policy Objects** node.

Step 6.   Right-click the desired GPO and select **Copy**.

Step 7. Right-click the **Group Policy Objects** node and select **Paste**.

Step 8. Two permission options display (see Figure 8-6). Select one and click **OK**:

- **Use the default permissions for new GPOs**: Override any GPO-specific permission settings with the default new GPO permissions.

- **Preserve the existing permissions**: Retain whatever permission settings were applied to the original GPO.

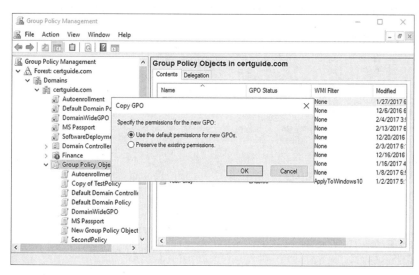

Figure 8-6 Choosing Permissions for a New GPO When Copying and Pasting in the Group Policy Management Console

Using PowerShell to Manage GPOs

All these tasks can be performed from PowerShell as well. Table 8-3 summarizes the PowerShell cmdlets for backing up, restoring, and copying GPOs.

Table 8-3 PowerShell Cmdlets for Backing Up, Restoring, and Copying GPOs

Cmdlet	Purpose
Get-GPO	Retrieves a GPO from the domain by Guid or Name
Backup-GPO	Backs up a GPO or all GPOs
Restore-GPO	Restores a GPO or all GPOs
Copy-GPO	Copies a GPO to a new GPO
Import-GPO	Imports the settings from a backup to a target GPO

The PowerShell cmdlet to get a GPO is

```
Get-GPO [-Guid] <Guid>
```

Or

```
Get-GPO [-Name] <String>
```

For most GPO cmdlets you cannot use the **–Name** parameter, since the name is not guaranteed to be unique in the domain. Instead you can use **Get-GPO** to retrieve the GPO and reference the ID property of the returned object (see Figure 8-7):

```
Get-GPO -Name TestPolicy
```

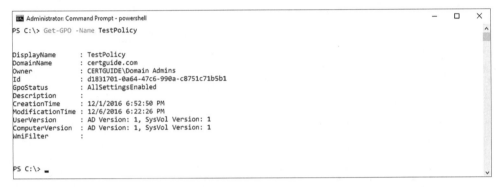

Figure 8-7   The Get-GPO PowerShell Cmdlet Returning a GPO Object Including DisplayName, DomainName, and ObjectID

The PowerShell cmdlet to back up a GPO is

```
Backup-GPO -Guid <Guid> '
-Path <String>
```

or

```
Backup-GPO [-Name] <String> '
-Path <String>
```

To back up all GPOs in the domain:

```
Backup-GPO -Path <String> [-All]
```

Backup-GPO identifies the GPO to be backed up either by Guid or Name. You can see the Guid in the details pane of a GPO in GPME, or look it up with the **Get-GPO** cmdlet. The -**Path** parameter specifies the folder on the file system to back up to. If the path does not already exist, an error is returned. You can back up all GPOs in a domain by omitting the -**Guid** and -**Name** parameters and including the -**All** switch.

```
$gpo = Get-GPO -Name TestPolicy
Backup-GPO -Guid $gpo.Id -Path C:\GPO_Backup\
```

The PowerShell cmdlet to restore a GPO is

```
Restore-GPO -Guid <Guid> '
 -Path <String>
```

or

```
Restore-GPO [-Name] <String> '
-Path <String>
```

or

```
Restore-GPO -BackupId <Guid> '
-Path <String>
```

To restore all GPOs in the domain:

```
Restore-GPO -All -Path <String>
```

Restore-GPO identifies the GPO to be backed up either by Guid, Name, or BackupId. If you use the -**Guid** or -**Name** parameter, you restore from the most recent backup. Using the -**BackupId** parameter allows you to choose a specific backup to restore from. You can see the Guid in the details pane of a GPO in GPME, or look it up with the **Get-GPO** cmdlet. The -**Path** parameter specifies the folder on the file system to restore from. If a backup in the path does not already exist, an error is returned. You can restore all GPOs in a domain by omitting the -**Guid**, -**Name**, and -**BackupId** parameters and including the **All** switch.

```
$gpo = Get-GPO -Name TestPolicy
Restore-GPO -Guid $gpo.Id -Path C:\GPO_Backup\
```

The PowerShell cmdlet to copy a GPO is

```
Copy-GPO -SourceGuid <Guid> '
-TargetName <String
```

or

```
Copy-GPO [-SourceName] <String> '
-TargetName <String>
```

Copy-GPO identifies the source GPO to copy from either by Guid or Name. You can see the Guid in the details pane of a GPO in GPME, or look it up with the

Get-GPO cmdlet. The **-TargetName** parameter is the name of the new GPO created from the source GPO.

```
$gpo = Get-GPO -Name TestPolicy
Copy-GPO -SourceGuid $gpo.Id -TargetName "NewGPO"
```

The PowerShell cmdlet to import a GPO is

```
Import-GPO -BackupId <Guid> '
-Path <String> '
-TargetGuid <Guid> '
-TargetName <String>
```

or

```
Import-GPO -BackupGpoName <String> '
-Path <String> '
-TargetGuid <Guid> '
-TargetName <String>
```

Import-GPO identifies the source backup to import from either by Guid or Name. You can see the Guid in the details pane of a GPO in GPME, or look it up with the **Get-GPO** cmdlet. The **-Path** parameter specifies the folder on the file system to restore from. If a backup in the path does not already exist, an error is returned.

The Target GPO to restore to is defined either by the **-TargetGuid** parameter or the **-TargetName** parameter. Use one or the other, but there is no need to use both.

```
$targetGpo = Get-GPO -Name OtherGPO
Import-GPO -BackupGpoName TestPolicy -Path C:\GPO_Backup\ -TargetGuid
$targetGpo.Id
```

> **NOTE**   For more information regarding Group Policy cmdlets in Windows PowerShell, see https://technet.microsoft.com/en-us/library/hh967461.aspx.

Creating and Configuring a Migration Table

Sometimes you might want to copy a GPO from one domain to another. Because GPOs contain domain-specific information, a one-to-one translation of the GPO might not work. References to security principals, UNC paths, or other domain information will not apply in the target domain. Group Policy includes a feature called a *migration table* that allows administrators to modify references during import and copy operations.

To create a migration table:

Step 1.   Log on to a writeable domain controller.

Step 2.   From the Start Menu launch **Server Manager**.

Step 3.   Click **Tools** > **Group Policy Management**.

Step 4.   Right-click the **Domains** node and select **Open Migration Table Editor**.

Step 5.   From the **Tools** menu of the Migration Table Editor, select either **Populate from GPO** or **Populate from Backup**.

Step 6.   Select the GPO or backup to populate the table from.

Step 7.   Check the **During scan, include security principals from the DACL on the GPO** box.

Step 8.   Click **OK**.

Step 9.   Review each row added to the table. Key in an appropriate destination name when needed, or leave as <Same as Source> (see Figure 8-8).

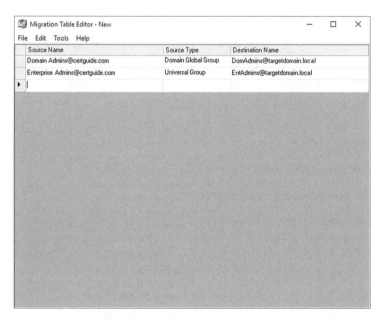

Figure 8-8   The Migration Table Editor with Two Discovered Security Principals That Need to Be Translated When Copied to a New Domain

Step 10.   Click **File** > **Save**.

Step 11.   Choose a location to save the migration table and click **Save**.

When copying a GPO between domains, the migration table can now be used to translate all defined rows into their respective counterparts in the target domain.

Resetting Default GPOs

Every domain starts with a single GPO that applies to all objects in the domain. This GPO is called the *Default Domain Policy*. As a general rule, you should leave the Default Domain Policy GPO unchanged. Any policies you want to apply to the entire domain can be made in a new GPO linked at the domain level.

Sometimes an administrator mistakenly makes changes to this policy, or previous IT staff might have edited the Default Domain Policy. While custom GPOs are backed up using the methods described previously, those backups don't often extend to the Default Domain Policy. In the event the policy needs to be reset to its original state, you can use a tool called **dcgpofix**.

Table 8-4 lists and describes the parameters for **dcgpofix**.

Table 8-4   Parameters for the **dcgpofix** Utility

Parameter	Description
-ignoreschema	If the version of **dcgpofix** being used is different from the version of the schema in the domain, this switch ignores the mismatch and restores the GPO using the schema version of **dcgpofix**.
/target { Domain | DC | Both }	Specifies whether to restore the Default Domain Policy GPO or the default domain controllers GPO or both.

To restore the Default Domain Policy GPO:

Step 1.   Log on to a writeable domain controller.

Step 2.   Open a command prompt window.

Step 3.   Type **dcgpofix** and press **Enter** (see Figure 8-9).

Step 4.   Review the first warning and type **Y** and press **Enter** to continue.

Step 5.   Review the second warning and type **Y** and press **Enter** to continue.

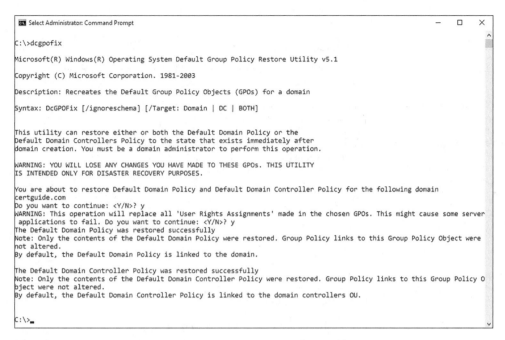

```
Select Administrator: Command Prompt                                    —    □    ×

C:\>dcgpofix

Microsoft(R) Windows(R) Operating System Default Group Policy Restore Utility v5.1

Copyright (C) Microsoft Corporation. 1981-2003

Description: Recreates the Default Group Policy Objects (GPOs) for a domain

Syntax: DcGPOFix [/ignoreschema] [/Target: Domain | DC | BOTH]


This utility can restore either or both the Default Domain Policy or the
Default Domain Controllers Policy to the state that exists immediately after
domain creation. You must be a domain administrator to perform this operation.

WARNING: YOU WILL LOSE ANY CHANGES YOU HAVE MADE TO THESE GPOs. THIS UTILITY
IS INTENDED ONLY FOR DISASTER RECOVERY PURPOSES.

You are about to restore Default Domain Policy and Default Domain Controller Policy for the following domain
certguide.com
Do you want to continue: <Y/N>? y
WARNING: This operation will replace all 'User Rights Assignments' made in the chosen GPOs. This might cause some server
 applications to fail. Do you want to continue: <Y/N>? y
The Default Domain Policy was restored successfully
Note: Only the contents of the Default Domain Policy were restored. Group Policy links to this Group Policy Object were
not altered.
By default, the Default Domain Policy is linked to the domain.

The Default Domain Controller Policy was restored successfully
Note: Only the contents of the Default Domain Controller Policy were restored. Group Policy links to this Group Policy O
bject were not altered.
By default, the Default Domain Controller Policy is linked to the domain controllers OU.

C:\>_
```

Figure 8-9   The **dcgpofix** Utility Running on a Domain Controller

Delegating Group Policy Management

In larger organizations with complex or dispersed IT staff, administration for various parts of Active Directory Domain Services is often delegated to individuals who do not otherwise have full administrative rights on the directory. Chapter 4, "Creating and Managing Active Directory Groups and Organizational Units," discussed the delegation of permissions for the creation of groups and OUs in the domain.

Group Policy Objects and Links can also be managed by domain users via delegation. Administrators can choose specific permissions in Group Policy to delegate to users in the domain. These permissions can be granted on a domain-wide basis or on individual OUs and sites. Delegation is managed via the GPMC. When you select a node from the navigation tree in the console, the Delegation tab displays with the appropriate options for the selected node. Table 8-5 details these choices.

Table 8-5   Delegation Options in GPMC

Node	Delegation Options
Domain	Link GPOs, Perform Group Policy Modeling analyses, Read Group Policy Results data
Domain Controllers	Link GPOs, Perform Group Policy Modeling analyses, Read Group Policy Results data
Organizational Unit	Link GPOs, Perform Group Policy Modeling analyses, Read Group Policy Results data
Group Policy Objects	Create GPOs
Starter GPOs	Create Starter GPOs
GPOs/Starter GPOs	Read, Edit Settings, Delete and Modify Security

To delegate the creation of GPOs:

Step 1.   Log on to a writeable domain controller.

Step 2.   From the Start Menu launch **Server Manager**.

Step 3.   Click **Tools** > **Group Policy Management**.

Step 4.   In the left-hand navigation pane, expand the **Domains** node and then the node for your domain.

Step 5.   Select the **Group Policy Objects** node.

Step 6.   In the right-hand pane select the **Delegation** tab.

Step 7.   All currently delegated security principals are listed (see Figure 8-10). Click **Add**.

Step 8.   Use the standard directory search dialog to find the user or group to delegate permission to. Click **Check Names** to validate the name. If the object is found it will be underlined. Click **OK**.

The user now has permissions to create GPOs in the domain.

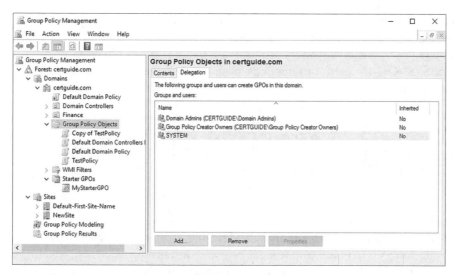

Figure 8-10   The Delegation Tab of the Group Policy Objects Node in GPMC

Detecting Health Issues Using the Group Policy Infrastructure Status Dashboard

While Group Policy generally runs quietly without any problems, occasionally the need arises to research problems that can come up. Group Policy issues are easy enough to troubleshoot in a small, simple deployment, but when an enterprise organization scales, there can be hundreds or even thousands of different GPOs for dozens of domains, trees, or forests.

When a domain has more than one domain controller deployed, Group Policy information must be replicated from one domain controller to another. Replication can be slowed down by poor network bandwidth or strict replication rules for the domain. When an organization has installations across multiple geographic regions and time zones, replication delays that cause mismatches between GPOs are expected. These delays might also reflect a problem with Group Policy.

Group Policy Infrastructure

To understand the common problems an administrator might face, it's important to understand the basic infrastructure of Group Policy. Each GPO is stored in two places on the domain controller. A portion of the GPO called the Group Policy Container is stored in the AD DS directory. The Group Policy Container is replicated along with the rest of the directory as discussed in Chapter 6, "Maintaining Active Directory," and Chapter 7, "Configuring Active Directory in a Complex

Enterprise Environment." A different part of the GPO, called the Group Policy Template, is stored in the SYSVOL, which is replicated with FRS or DFSR. Due to the differences in the way directory replication is handled versus file system replication for SYSVOL, there can be temporary mismatches in the synchronization of the data between the two.

NOTE While these individual portions of GPOs can be modified independently of one another, it is strongly discouraged. GPMC and GPME manage the GPO as a single unit, applying changes and updates to both pieces simultaneously.

Group Policy also allows for snap-ins or extensions, such as Administrative Templates, that can store data either in the directory exclusively or in both the directory and SYSVOL. One example is the Software Installation extension, which stores script files in SYSVOL and a Windows Installer package in the directory. Extensions like this must be programmed to handle the possibility of the two pieces of the GPO being out of sync. In the example of Software Installation, the script cannot be executed without the Installer package, and the installer package will fail gracefully and retry later if the script cannot be found.

Group Policy Infrastructure Status Dashboard

With Server 2012, Microsoft introduced the Group Policy Infrastructure Status Dashboard to the GPMC. This dashboard provides a more comprehensive replication check of the status of Group Policy than the previous tool, **GPOTool**. While the legacy tool is still available, its functionality is superseded by the Dashboard.

Through the Group Policy Infrastructure Status Dashboard, an administrator can launch a consistency check on the domain. This status check validates and reports any issues with the following Group Policy features:

- ACL for each Group Policy Container
- Version number attribute on each Group Policy Template
- Count of Group Policy Container objects
- ACL on each Group Policy Template
- Version number stored in the gpt.ini file in each Group Policy Container
- Count of Group Policy Template folders and files
- File hash for each file in Group Policy Template folders

To launch the Dashboard status check:

Step 1.   Log on to a writeable domain controller.

Step 2.   From the Start Menu launch **Server Manager**.

Step 3.   Click **Tools** > **Group Policy Management**.

Step 4.   In the left-hand navigation pane expand the **Domains** node and then the node for your domain.

Step 5.   In the right-hand details pane select the **Status** tab and click **Detect Now**.

The resulting report lists any domain controllers that are not fully in sync with the primary domain controller, and all the domain controllers that are in sync (see Figure 8-11). The message displayed summarizes the synchronization mismatch if there is one.

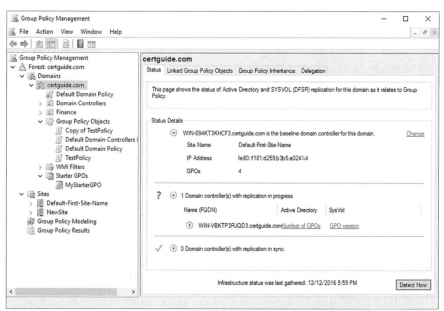

Figure 8-11   The Group Policy Status Dashboard Report After Clicking **Detect Now**, Indicating That a Replication Is Currently In Progress

NOTE   Replication issues related specifically to the AD DS directory can be researched with the **repadmin** tool discussed in Chapter 6.

Local Group Policies

Up until this point, all discussion of Group Policy in this chapter has been related to domain-wide GPOs. That is, not GPOs that necessarily apply to the entire domain but rather GPOs that are available to be linked to any OU, group, or site in the domain. Every Windows machine also has a local Group Policy Object that applies to it. You can view the local Group Policy settings in a Windows desktop by launching the Local Group Policy Editor from the Windows Control Panel.

Even in a domain environment, local Group Policies have their place—for example, on a desktop or laptop that travels to conventions and trade shows as part of a kiosk or demonstration. While out of the office, this computer would not be connected to the domain, and the local Group Policy could be used to lock out conference attendees from accessing administrative features.

In a domain, domain controllers are the only machines that do not have the capability for a local Group Policy to be applied. Local Group Policy processing can also be disabled for any machine in a domain via a domain-level GPO linked to the machine via GPMC.

Configuring Multiple Local Group Policies

Even at the local machine level, there are often use cases for multiple users and multiple security profiles. Using the previous laptop example, while it is necessary to lock down the machine while it's being used on the showroom floor, you do still want administrative users to be able to log in and have high-level access. Microsoft Windows allows for multiple local Group Policies. Local GPOs are applied at the following levels locally:

- **Local computer policy**: This local GPO applies to the computer and all users signed in to the computer. Its policy settings apply unless they are configured in the administrators, non-administrators, or user policies listed next. The local computer policy is also the only local GPO with a Computer Configuration section and is typically used for that purpose.

- **Administrators/Non-Administrators**: Users in Windows either belong to the Administrators group or they don't. If a user belongs to the administrative users group locally, the local administrators policy will apply, whereas the non-administrators policy will apply to all other users. The policy settings in this GPO apply unless they are configured in a user-specific policy.

- **User-specific policy**: These policies are defined on a user-by-user basis for local users in the Windows system. Settings configured in this policy override any other local GPOs, but only for the specified user.

To configure multiple local GPOs:

Step 1.   Log on to a Microsoft Windows desktop computer.

Step 2.   Click the **Start** button and type **mmc**; then press **Enter**.

Step 3.   Click **File > Add/Remove Snap-In**.

Step 4.   From the list of available snap-ins, select **Group Policy Objects** and click **Add**.

Step 5.   The wizard allows you to choose which GPO to load into the MMC editor. By default the local computer policy is selected. To select a different policy click **Browse**.

Step 6.   Select the **Users** tab and highlight the user or group (Administrators or Non-Administrators) you want to edit and click **OK** (see Figure 8-12).

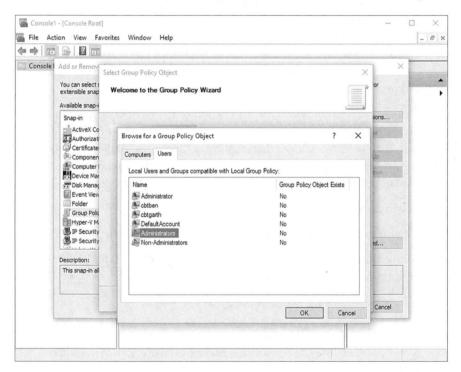

Figure 8-12   Selecting a User or Group to Add into the Local Group Policy Editor Snap-In for MMC

Step 7.   Click **Finish**.

Step 8.   The GPO is now listed in the **Selected Snap-Ins** box. You can add additional policies to the MMC editor by repeating Steps 4 through 7.

The policies are now loaded in the MMC editor, and you can modify their settings similarly to the way you would in the Group Policy Management Editor on the domain controller.

Configuring a Central Store

The Administrative Templates node of a GPO has the unique capability to be extended and customized. These customizations are stored in XML files with an *.admx* extension. Versions of Windows prior to Windows Vista used a proprietary markup language in *.adm* files. For example, Microsoft publishes an ADMX file for Microsoft Office, which includes Administrative Template settings for a wide range of features in MS Office. Everything from proofreading settings to customizing the Office ribbon can be controlled with these policy settings.

Deploying these settings is as easy as copying them into a specified folder in a Windows installation. Deploying ADMX files to each and every machine in the network, and keeping them updated as adjustments are made, would be an unmanageable chore. Microsoft uses the concept of a central store for domain-connected machines to provide a central location for ADMX files that all machines in the domain can load into their local GPOs.

The central store is created in the SYSVOL portion of the AD DS deployment. To create a central store, you need to manually create the folder and copy the desired ADMX files to that location. AD DS then replicates those files to the other domain controllers via its regular replication process. Once this is complete, domain-connected Windows machines will read that when editing GPOs.

To create a central store:

Step 1.   Log on to a writeable domain controller that has a copy of the SYSVOL.

Step 2.   Using Windows File Explorer, navigate to the SYSVOL folder (by default this is C:\Windows\SYSVOL).

Step 3.   Create the following folder in the SYSVOL folder:

FQDN\policies\PolicyDefinitions

Where *FQDN* is the fully qualified name of the domain, for example, certguide.com.

Step 4.   Copy the desired ADMX files to this location.

Computers on the domain now pull these settings into their GPO editor.

NOTE The following link offers Administrative Templates (.admx) for Windows 10 and Windows Server 2016. To explore further, see https://www.microsoft.com/en-us/download/details.aspx?id=53430.

Exam Preparation Tasks

As mentioned in the section "Book Features" in the Introduction, you have a few choices for exam preparation: the exercises here; Chapter 17, "Final Preparation"; and the exam simulation questions in the Pearson Test Prep Software Online.

Review All Key Topics

Review the most important topics in this chapter, noted with the Key Topics icon in the outer margin of the page. Table 8-6 lists a reference of these key topics and the page number on which each is found.

Table 8-6 Key Topics for Chapter 8

Key Topic Element	Description	Page Number
List	Scope of Group Policy Objects, including the domain nodes to which they can be linked	228
Paragraph	Description of GPO linking	230
Table 8-2	GPO link settings	232
Paragraph	Using a starter GPO	233
Figure 8-4	The Back Up Group Policy Object Wizard	235
Paragraph	Importing a GPO backup versus restoring it	236
Table 8-3	PowerShell cmdlets for backing up, restoring, and copying GPOs	237
Paragraph	Description and purpose of a migration table	240
Paragraph	Restoring default GPO settings with **dcgpofix**	242
Table 8-5	Delegation options in GPMC	244
Paragraph	Description of physical storage locations for GPO data	245
Figure 8-11	The Group Policy Status Dashboard report	247
List	The levels where local GPOs are applied in Windows	248
Paragraph	Description of ADMX files	250

Complete Tables and Lists from Memory

Print a copy of Appendix B, "Memory Tables" (found on the book website), or at least the section for this chapter, and complete the tables and lists from memory. Appendix C, "Memory Tables Answer Key," also on the website, includes completed tables and lists to check your work.

Define Key Terms

Define the following key terms from this chapter and check your answers in the glossary:

Group Policy, Group Policy Object (GPO), GPO link, starter GPO, Group Policy Management Console (GPMC), Group Policy Management Editor (GPME), restoring a GPO, importing a GPO, default domain GPO, delegating, local Group Policy Object, central store

End-of-Chapter Review Questions

The answers to these questions appear in Appendix A. For more practice with exam format questions, use the Pearson Test Prep Software Online.

1. As the domain admin you have created three different GPOs in the domain to apply to three different types of users: managers, users, and IT staff. The settings are not being applied to anyone's computer, however. What step would you take to ensure the GPOs you created are being used?

    a. Delete and re-create the GPOs in the proper domain.

    b. Restore the GPOs from previously known good backups.

    c. Validate network connectivity between the domain and the client desktops.

    d. Validate that the GPOs have links connecting them to their respective OUs or security groups.

2. As the domain administrator, you have created and linked GPOs to the appropriate OUs. You have also delegated GPO creation and linking abilities to the IT managers for each department. Some managers have created GPOs with settings that conflict with the policies you created. You want to ensure their settings do not override the settings you defined. Which methods would help you accomplish this? (Choose all that apply.)

   a. Set the link setting Link Enabled to **No**.

   b. Set the link setting Enforced to **Yes**.

   c. Delete the child GPOs and instruct the IT managers to re-create them without conflicts.

   d. Reorder the GPOs in GPMC to give your GPOs priority.

3. Unfortunately, a new hire on the IT staff was given incorrect permissions and modified a number of settings in the default domain GPO that are now being applied across the domain. What are the appropriate steps to take to undo the changes made? (Choose all that apply.)

   a. Run the **dcgpofix** utility.

   b. Perform a full directory restore with Windows Backup.

   c. Restore the GPO from a previously known good backup.

   d. Create a new temporary domain, back up the default domain GPO from that domain, and import it over the modified GPO in the current domain.

4. The new hire on the staff also modified a number of settings on a custom GPO linked to the Finance department's OU. You want to revert the changes made back to their original settings. What is the appropriate step to take to undo the changes made?

   a. Run the **dcgpofix** utility.

   b. Perform a full directory restore with Windows Backup.

   c. Restore the GPO from a previously known good backup.

   d. Restore the Finance department OU in the GPMC from a previously known good backup.

5. The Group Policy Infrastructure Health Status indicates that there is a problem with a remote domain controller. The remote DC has GPOs with older versions than are found on the current DC. What AD DS feature would you need to explore to find out the cause of this issue?

   a. Windows Backup

   b. AD DS replication

   c. GPO backup operations

   d. SYSVOL replication

This chapter covers the following topics:

- **Configuring Processing Order, Precedence, and Blocking of Inheritance**: This section describes how to configure the processing order of multiple GPOs applied to the same target so that conflicts can be resolved.

- **Configuring Security Filtering and Windows Management Instrumentation (WMI) Filtering**: This section describes how to filter or limit the target of a GPO by security group membership and Windows Management Instrumentation (WMI).

- **Client-Side Processing**: This section describes how GPOs are processed and applied on client computers and how to force a policy refresh when needed.

CHAPTER 9

Configuring Group Policy Processing

Creating Group Policy Objects (GPOs) is one part of working with Group Policy, but equally important are understanding how to configure and manage the processing and application of the policies defined in those objects. Sometimes multiple GPOs define the same policy differently, yet both apply to a single object in the directory. Other times, you might want to prevent or filter a policy setting from targeting an object it is otherwise configured to target.

This chapter describes the process that Group Policy uses to sort and apply multiple GPOs to containers and objects in the directory as well as the configuration options available to control that process. This includes processing order, which determines GPO precedence and blocking and filtering. It also describes the process that the client computers in the directory use to apply the actual policies described in the GPOs.

"Do I Know This Already?" Quiz

The "Do I Know This Already?" quiz allows you to assess whether you should read this entire chapter thoroughly or jump to the "Exam Preparation Tasks" section. If you are in doubt about your answers to these questions or your own assessment of your knowledge of the topics, read the entire chapter. Table 9-1 lists the major headings in this chapter and their corresponding "Do I Know This Already?" quiz questions. You can find the answers in Appendix A, "Answers to the 'Do I Know This Already?' Quizzes."

Table 9-1 "Do I Know This Already?" Section-to-Question Mapping

Foundation Topics Section	Questions
Configuring Processing Order, Precedence, and Blocking of Inheritance	1-2
Configuring Security Filtering and Windows Management Instrumentation (WMI) Filtering	3-4
Client-Side Processing	5-6

CAUTION   The goal of self-assessment is to gauge your mastery of the topics in this chapter. If you do not know the answer to a question or are only partially sure of the answer, you should mark that question as wrong for purposes of the self-assessment. Giving yourself credit for an answer you correctly guess skews your self-assessment results and might provide you with a false sense of security.

1. You have a GPO linked to a domain and a different GPO with conflicting settings linked to an OU within the domain. For the settings that are in conflict, which GPO link will apply?

   a. Domain

   b. Both

   c. Neither

   d. OU

2. You have a GPO linked to a parent OU with settings that must apply to all objects in the children OUs. How do you ensure this will happen even if another IT administrator links a conflicting GPO to a child OU?

   a. Copy the GPO link to each additional child OU.

   b. Set the parent GPO link to Enforced.

   c. Block inheritance on the parent GPO link.

   d. Revoke delegation permissions on the child OU objects.

3. In your IT Department OU you have objects for both junior IT staff and IT managers with elevated permissions. These objects are differentiated only by their membership in the respective security group. Which feature would you use if you wanted two different GPOs linked to the same OU but applied exclusively to the different user objects?

   a. Security filtering

   b. WMI filtering

   c. Loopback processing

   d. Blocking inheritance

4. Which loopback processing mode will allow only the settings from the computer object GPO and ignore the user objects GPO?

    a. Merge mode

    b. Replace mode

    c. Block mode

    d. Computer mode

5. A slow Internet connection between one site and the domain controller that serves it is causing Group Policy to limit the GPO settings applied to computers in that site. You would like to disable this feature for those machines. What GPO setting would you configure?

    a. Enable Group Policy Caching For Servers

    b. Configure Group Policy Caching

    c. Configure Group Policy Slow Link Detection

    d. Disable Detection of Slow Network Connections

6. What is the PowerShell cmdlet to remotely force a Group Policy update?

    a. **Invoke-GPUpdate**

    b. **Run-GPUpdate**

    c. **Invoke-GPOProcess**

    d. **Run-GPOProcess**

Foundation Topics

Configuring Processing Order, Precedence, and Blocking of Inheritance

There are many ways that a Group Policy Object (GPO) can be applied to a security principal. GPOs can be linked to a domain, site, or OU; inherited from a parent OU; and assigned by local Group Policy. At any of these points more than one GPO is often applied. The question that immediately comes up is how does Group Policy resolve conflicts when two or more GPOs apply the same policy setting?

The answer is simple. Group Policy walks through a specific order when processing GPOs. As GPOs are processed, Group Policy retains the most recent value for a policy setting. If a setting is configured on both a domain-wide GPO and an OU-specific GPO, the value of that setting from the OU-specific GPO is used. This does not mean that all the settings from the earlier processed GPOs are discarded. Any policy setting that is not configured on subsequent GPOs is still applied.

Processing Order and Precedence

The order of processing for Group Policy is

1. Local Group Policy Objects

2. GPOs linked to the site

3. GPOs linked to the domain

4. GPOS linked to the OU

A commonly used acronym to help you remember this is LSDOU—Local, Site, Domain, OU. GPOs are processed in this order, and the last GPO processed for a setting takes precedence, so local GPOs are processed first and can be overwritten by the others while OU links are processed last and cannot be overwritten.

Within each processing step there are additional rules as well. Administrators can link multiple GPOs to a single node such as the OU or domain. When multiple GPOs are linked to a node, the Group Policy Management Console (GPMC) indicates a Link Order value. Group Policy processes GPOs in descending order, from highest to lowest. This means that a policy with a Link Order of 1 takes precedence over policies with a higher link order (see Figure 9-1).

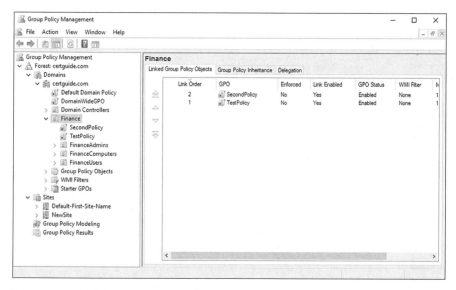

Figure 9-1   Link Order for Multiple GPO Links in the GPMC

Administrators can adjust the Link Order for GPOs at a node:

Step 1.   Log on to a writeable domain controller.

Step 2.   From the Start Menu launch **Server Manager**.

Step 3.   Click **Tools** > **Group Policy Management**.

Step 4.   In the left-hand navigation pane expand the **Domains** node and then the node for your domain.

Step 5.   In the left-hand navigation pane select the node to change the link order for.

Step 6.   The right-hand pane displays the **Linked Group Policy Objects** tab. Select a GPO and use the control buttons along the left of the policy list to adjust the order of the policies.

GPO inheritance also needs to be addressed when processing GPOs. Group Policy will "walk down the tree" when processing inheritance so that GPOs linked to the domain are processed first, followed by GPOs linked to the top-level OU, and then child GPOs. This means that, unless inheritance is blocked or a parent GPO is enforced, GPOs applied directly to an OU take precedence over inherited GPOs. This order can be seen on the Group Policy Inheritance tab shown in Figure 9-2. GPOs listed in this tab are processed in descending order by precedence, so the lower the number the higher the precedence of the GPO.

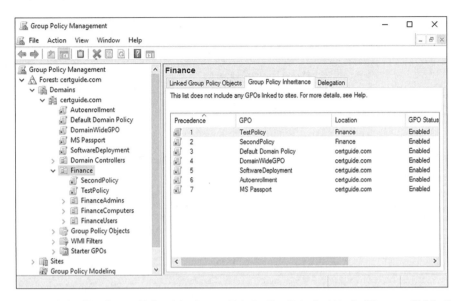

Figure 9-2   The Group Policy Inheritance Tab for the Selected Node (Finance OU) in the Group Policy Management Console

Blocking of Inheritance

When GPO administration is delegated to junior IT staff or remote administrators the vision for how and when GPOs are inherited may need to be customized. For example, the central IT department might be responsible for administering all policy settings for the primary office location contained in various top-level OUs. However, the remote IT staff responsible for administering GPOs on the remote location OU might not want domain-wide policies inherited.

Inheritance can be blocked both for an entire domain or for individual OUs. When inheritance is blocked, the node does not inherit any of the policies from GPOs linked to its parent node unless the parent GPO link is flagged as Enforced. When a GPO link is flagged as Enforced, it cannot be blocked from inheritance by children, and any of its policy settings take precedence over policies linked to children.

To block inheritance:

Step 1.   Log on to a writeable domain controller.

Step 2.   From the Start Menu launch **Server Manager**.

Step 3.   Click **Tools > Group Policy Management**.

Step 4.   In the left-hand navigation pane expand the **Domains** node and then the node for your domain.

Step 5.   Right-click the domain or OU node you want to block and select **Block Inheritance**.

Configuring Security Filtering and Windows Management Instrumentation (WMI) Filtering

Filtering GPOs allows directory administrators to further qualify which objects a given GPO link actually applies to. GPOs are linked to OUs, sites, and domains, but often security principals within these collections are further divided. The OU for a remote office might contain both IT staff as well as regular network users, or a domain will have a specific subset of users that need to be excluded from a given GPO policy. Most often the need arises when the directory structure is simply too flat to properly reflect the various roles and responsibilities of the objects it contains.

OUs and GPO links could be configured to allow for most of the required variety but introduce a fair amount of overhead and possibly redundant or conflicting structure requirements. Security group filtering and Windows management instrumentation (WMI) filtering are easy ways to take advantage of features in the directory and on Windows machines that are already in place and do not require a restricting of the directory.

Security Filtering

Security filtering simply tells Group Policy which objects to apply a GPO link to by inclusion in one or more specified security groups. For example, every GPO link by default is filtered to the Authenticated Users group. This means that Group Policy does not attempt to apply the GPO settings to any user not in that group. You can define as many additional groups as you want to further limit which objects have the policy applied (see Figure 9-3).

To set up a security filter:

Step 1.   Log on to a writeable domain controller.

Step 2.   From the Start Menu launch **Server Manager**.

Step 3.   Click **Tools > Group Policy Management**.

Step 4.   In the left-hand navigation pane expand the **Domains** node and then the node for your domain.

Step 5. Navigate to the domain, site, or OU you want to filter a GPO link for and expand the node.

Step 6. In the left-hand navigation pane select the GPO link.

Step 7. In the right-hand pane select the **Scope** tab.

Step 8. Under the **Security Filtering** section click the **Add** button.

Step 9. Use the standard Group Policy search tool to find the security group to filter by and then click **OK**.

The group is now listed in the **Security Filtering** box. Notice the Authenticated Users group was already listed there by default (see Figure 9-3). If you want to remove a filter just highlight the group and click **Remove**.

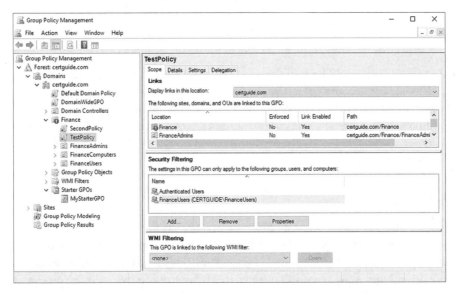

Figure 9-3 Security Filtering for a GPO Link in GPMC. Only Members of the Listed Groups Have the GPO Applied.

NOTE Security filtering is almost always done by security group, but you can also filter by both user and computer objects, although this is not recommended.

WMI Filtering

While security filtering is easy to implement, it often lacks the power or flexibility sometimes needed in enterprise environments. Windows Management Interface (WMI) filtering allows administrators to associate a WMI query with a GPO link that runs for every user or computer that the link targets. Only the directory objects that meet the filter criteria have the GPO applied. The WMI query can access any WMI-based information available on the client environment, including hardware configurations, software configurations, user profile information, and networking.

WMI filtering can be used in complex and dynamic ways. For instance, by querying for a given IP address, a GPO can be filtered to only apply to users in a specific subnet, or accessing via VPN. This means that a different set of policies can apply to an employee's laptop when the employee accesses the network from a remote location such as home as opposed to when he brings the laptop to the office and plugs in to the network itself. More commonly, WMI filtering is used to apply settings to specific versions of Windows or Server OS.

NOTE WMI queries use a subset of ANSI SQL known as WMI Query Language (WQL). The examples in this book are relatively straightforward, but WMI querying can be complex. More information is available here: https://msdn.microsoft.com/en-us/library/aa393964(v=vs.85).aspx.

WMI filters are managed in two steps: Create the filter and apply it to the link.

To create a WMI filter:

Step 1. Log on to a writeable domain controller.

Step 2. From the Start Menu launch **Server Manager**.

Step 3. Click **Tools > Group Policy Management**.

Step 4. In the left-hand navigation pane expand the **Domains** node and then the node for your domain.

Step 5. In the left-hand navigation pane right-click the WMI Filters node and select **New**.

Step 6. Type a name and optionally a description for the filter.

Step 7. Click **Add**.

Step 8. In the **Queries** box, key in the following WQL query and click **OK** (see Figure 9-4).

select * from Win32_OperatingSystem where Version like "10.%" and ProductType="1"

Step 9. Click **Save**.

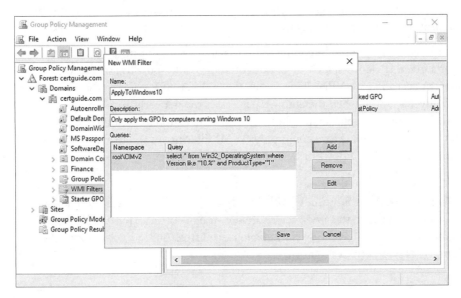

Figure 9-4 Creating a New WMI Filter Using the WQL Syntax to Query for a Specific Version of Windows

The filter is now available under the WMI Filters node to be linked to a GPO link:

Step 1. Log on to a writeable domain controller.

Step 2. From the Start Menu launch **Server Manager**.

Step 3. Click **Tools** > **Group Policy Management**.

Step 4. In the left-hand navigation pane expand the **Domains** node and then the node for your domain.

Step 5. Navigate to the domain, site, or OU you want to filter a GPO link for and expand the node.

Step 6. In the left-hand navigation pane select the GPO link.

Step 7. In the right-hand pane select the **Scope** tab.

Step 8.   Under the **WMI Filtering** section pull down the drop-down box and select the filter you just created.

Step 9.   Click **Yes**.

The filter now applies for the GPO link you selected. You can always see which
links are using a WMI filter by navigating to and selecting the filter under the WMI
Filters node (see Figure 9-5).

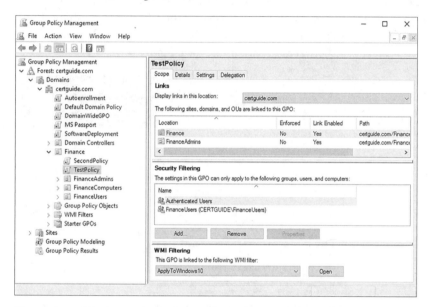

Figure 9-5   The Scope Tab of the Selected Node (TestPolicy GPO Link) in the Group Policy
Management Console. This Tab Displays All Target Links, Security Filtering, and WMI Filtering
Applied to This GPO Link.

Loopback Processing

Another way to configure when a GPO is or is not applied is to use loopback processing. Normally, GPOs are applied to users based on their location within the directory as well as the location of the computer being logged on to. A user in an OU
will have GPOs linked to that OU applied when a user logs on to a computer. The
computer might be in a separate OU and have its own GPOs applied as well. In the
event that you want to preclude or even exclude the user's GPOs with the GPOs for
the computer object, you can use loopback processing. This can be useful for pub-
licly accessible computers or computers used in group settings such as classrooms.

Loopback processing runs in two different modes:

- **Merge mode**: In merge mode the GPOs for the computer object are assigned a higher precedence (later processing) than the GPOs for the user.

- **Replace mode**: In replace mode the user's GPOs are not applied at all, only the GPOs applicable to the computer object.

Loopback processing is configured as a policy setting in a GPO itself. It can be applied via local Group Policy or a GPO. It is located in the Computer Configuration Administrative Templates, under the System \ Group Policy node. When enabling the setting you can choose between the two modes (see Figure 9-6).

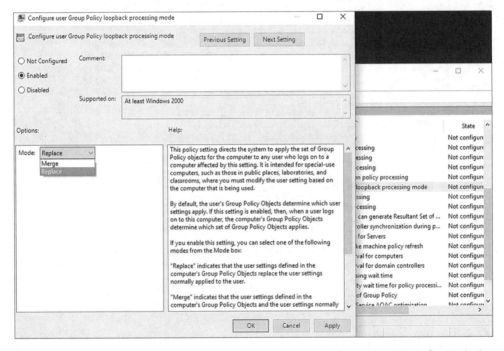

Figure 9-6 Editing the Configure User Group Policy Loopback Processing Mode Setting in the GPME

Client-Side Processing

Understanding how additional Group Policy processing occurs on the client machine is important for troubleshooting unexpected behavior. Aside from the filtering techniques described earlier in this chapter, a few additional features in Group Policy can affect how and when policy settings are processed. Slow network connections, caching, and client-side extensions are all ways to control application on the client.

Configure and Manage Slow Link Processing and Group Policy Caching

GPO settings are downloaded from a domain controller every time a user logs on to a domain-joined computer, and again routinely as long as a network connection is present. Because of this reliance on the network, a slow or intermittent network connection can cause delays when logging on and applying GPO settings. If the client machine detects that the network connection to the domain controller is too slow, it will prioritize the settings to apply and ignore noncritical settings in an effort to speed up processing. The threshold for the client to consider a network connection slow is configured via a GPO setting, as is the ability to disable slow-link processing entirely.

Two policy settings are related to slow-link processing:

- **Configure Group Policy Slow Link Detection**: This setting found in the Computer Configuration / Policies / Administrative Templates / System / Group Policy node sets the threshold for what is considered a slow link. The system uses a default of 500 kb/s when the setting is disabled or not configured.

- **Disable Detection of Slow Network Connections**: This setting is found in the Computer Configuration / Policies / Administrative Templates / System / User Profiles node and when enabled causes Group Policy to load all settings regardless of network speed. If this setting is enabled the value in the first setting is ignored.

> **NOTE**   The **Disable Detection of Slow Network Connections** setting can be tricky due to its wording. When the setting is enabled, slow network detection is disabled. Disabling the setting has the same effect as setting it to not configured: slow network detection will occur. Be careful to understand this and configure the setting properly for your desired result.

GPOs can also be cached locally, on machines running Windows 8.1, Server 2012 R2, or newer. On desktop operating systems, Group Policy stores a local cached copy of the GPO by default, while on Server OSes caching must be specifically enabled. This cached copy of the GPO is used in the event that Group Policy determines a network connection is not present or the connection times out. When a network connection is present, Group Policy routinely updates the locally cached GPO, which can then be used to process logons more quickly.

Two policy settings are related to GPO caching:

- **Enable Group Policy Caching For Servers**: This setting is located in the Computer Configuration / Administrative Templates / System / Group Policy node. This causes Group Policy to cache GPOs on Windows Server machines.

- **Configure Group Policy Caching**: This setting is located in the Computer Configuration / Administrative Templates / System / Group Policy node. Disabling this setting causes Windows client machines to stop local caching of GPOs. Enabling or not configuring this setting both have the same effect of enabling local caching.

Configure Client-Side Extension (CSE) Behavior

Group Policies are necessarily client driven. The GPOs themselves are defined in a central location, in the directory, but the actual application of the configuration changes occurs on the client machine. When a logon event occurs or the local Group Policy client applies an update, it must interpret the settings in the GPO and effect those changes locally.

The executables on the client machine that perform these configuration changes are called client-side extensions (CSEs). CSEs exist for many different categories of Group Policy settings, and their processing can be controlled via Group Policy. You can find further details about CSEs here: https://technet.microsoft.com/en-us/library/cc776182(v=ws.10).aspx.

In the Computer Configuration / Policies / Administrative Templates / System / Group Policy node are a series of configuration settings that can be set. The settings discussed previously for slow-link processing and caching are two such settings.

Each setting is preceded with the text **Configure** as seen in Figure 9-7. You can review the specifics of what a particular setting does by editing the setting and reading the supplied description.

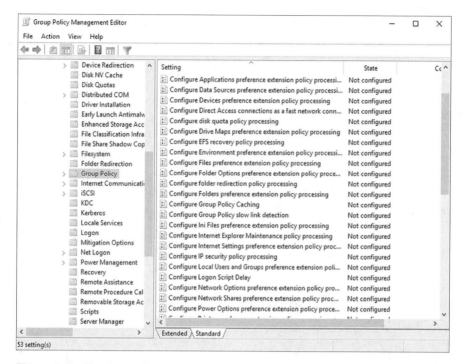

Figure 9-7 The Group Policy Node of the Computer Configuration Administrative Templates. Each Policy Labeled with Configure Allows for the Customization of How Group Policy Is Applied by the CSE.

Force a Group Policy Update

Changes to a GPO can and often do occur during the normal course of a business day. Computers will be up and running and users logged on and working while IT staff is changing settings, links, and creating new GPOs. By default policies are reviewed for changes and applied to the computer as needed in the following instances:

- Every time the machine boots up and Windows starts

- Every time a domain-authenticated user logs on

- Every 90 minutes, in a process known as a background update

Sometimes you might want to force an update to apply to a machine right away, instead of waiting for one of the previously mentioned events to occur. In this case you can force the Group Policy client to update either from the machine itself or remotely with a PowerShell cmdlet.

The utility to force a Group Policy update from the local machine is **gpupdate.exe**.

Table 9-2 lists the parameters for **gpupdate**.

Table 9-2   Parameters for the **gpupdate** Utility

Parameter	Description
/force	Ignores all processing optimizations and reapplies all settings.
/target { *computer* | *user* }	Processes only the computer settings or the settings for the current user. If this parameter is not specified, settings for both are processed.
/wait: *value*	The number of seconds that policy processing waits to finish.
/logoff	Logs off after the refresh has completed.
/boot	Restarts the computer after the refresh has completed.

To force an update from the client machine:

Step 1.   Log on to the client machine.

Step 2.   Launch a command prompt.

Step 3.   Type **gpupdate /force**.

The policy is updated and a success message is reported.

If you want to remotely force a policy refresh, the PowerShell cmdlet is **Invoke-GPUpdate**.

The syntax for **Invoke-GPUpdate** is

```
Invoke-GPUpdate [[-Computer] <String> ] '
[[-RandomDelayInMinutes] <Int32> ] '
[-Boot] '
[-Force] '
[-LogOff] '
[-Target <String> ]
```

The **-Computer** switch is used to specify the computer name on which to force the update. The value for this switch can be the NetBIOS name or the fully qualified domain name (FQDN) such as client1.west.certguide.com.

The **-RandomDelayInMinutes** switch is used to introduce a random delay before the background processing occurs. This is useful when a script is executing the cmdlet on multiple computers at the same time and you want to reduce network load.

The **-Boot** switch causes the machine to reboot when the update is completed. The **-Logoff** switch causes the machine to log off any users when the update is completed. The **-Force** switch ignores any processing optimization strategies and reapplies all GPO settings.

The **-Target** switch is used to specify either Computer or User settings to be reapplied. If it is left out the settings for both objects are applied.

To force an update on a remote computer, just run the following command from a PowerShell prompt:

```
Invoke-GPUpdate -Computer certguide\client1 -Force -Target Computer
```

Exam Preparation Tasks

As mentioned in the section "Book Features" in the Introduction, you have a few choices for exam preparation: the exercises here; Chapter 17, "Final Preparation"; and the exam simulation questions in the Pearson Test Prep Software Online.

Review All Key Topics

Review the most important topics in this chapter, noted with the Key Topics icon in the outer margin of the page. Table 9-3 lists a reference of these key topics and the page number on which each is found.

Table 9-3   Key Topics for Chapter 9

Key Topic Element	Description	Page Number
List	The order of processing for Group Policy	258
Paragraph	Blocking of inheritance	260
Paragraph	Security filtering	261
Paragraph	WMI filtering	263
List	Modes of loopback processing	266
List	Policy settings for slow-link processing	267
List	Policy settings for GPO caching	268
Paragraph	Location of CSE configuration settings within GPO	268
Table 9-2	Parameters for the gpupdate utility	270
Command	Syntax for **Invoke-GPUpdate** cmdlet	270

Complete Tables and Lists from Memory

Print a copy of Appendix B, "Memory Tables" (found on the book website), or at least the section for this chapter, and complete the tables and lists from memory. Appendix C, "Memory Tables Answer Key," also on the website, includes completed tables and lists to check your work.

Define Key Terms

Define the following key terms from this chapter and check your answers in the glossary:

processing order, inheritance, filtering, loopback processing, slow-link processing, client-side extensions (CSE)

End-of-Chapter Review Questions

The answers to these questions appear in Appendix A. For more practice with exam format questions, use the Pearson Test Prep Software Online.

1. You have created a Finance OU and split user objects into two separate child OUs: FinanceUsers and FinanceManagers. The head of the Finance department has been delegated permissions to create and link GPOs to the Finance OU and its child OUs. You have a number of GPOs linked to the domain that you would like to take precedence over any GPO links created on that OU tree. What would be the best way to do that?

   a. Set the Enforced flag to Yes for all GPOs on the domain you want to take precedence.

   b. Retain administration over the OU tree yourself and revoke the delegation.

   c. Establish a working standard so the delegated user is aware of which settings to apply.

   d. Validate that the GPOs have links connecting them to their respective OUs or security groups.

2. The Finance department has now grown so large that it has its own IT staff. These user objects are stored in a FinanceIT OU, which is in turn a child of the Finance OU. IT staff members in this OU are responsible for their own GPOs and do not want the Finance manager's GPO links to apply to them. What would be the best way to do that?

    a. Set the Enforced flag to No for all GPOs on the Finance parent OU.

    b. Set Block Inheritance on the FinanceIT OU.

    c. Set Block Inheritance on the Finance parent OU.

    d. Use security filtering.

3. Within the FinanceUsers OU there are two different types of users, separated by their membership in security groups but otherwise located in the same place in the directory. You need to apply different GPOs to each set of users. What would be the best way to do that?

    a. Use security filtering on the GPO links to specify which users a given GPO applies to.

    b. Use WMI filtering to query the user object and apply the correct GPO.

    c. Further divide the users into separate child OUs and apply different GPOs to each OU.

    d. Use local Group Policy Objects on the machines those users work on.

This chapter covers the following topics:

- **Configuring Software Installation**: This section describes how Group Policy can be used to push software installation to client computers on the network.

- **Configuring Folder Redirection**: This section describes how Group Policy can be used to change the location of a user's profile folder to a network location.

- **Configuring Scripts**: This section describes how to configure Group Policy to automatically execute scripts during specified startup, logon, shutdown, and logoff events.

- **Configuring Administrative Templates**: This section describes how to import classic Administrative Template files into a Group Policy Object.

CHAPTER 10

Configuring Group Policy Settings

The primary goal of Group Policy is to apply configuration settings on the client machines in an enterprise. This is used to create a consistent and seamless experience for users across the domain regardless of where they physically sit or which specific computer they might be logging on to. This also creates a secure environment where IT staff can be confident that users do not have access to features and functions that could compromise enterprise security efforts.

These settings are used to control what software is installed, where folders are located on the network, what the startup and shutdown experiences are, and of course control access and rights to various Windows features. This chapter covers how to configure commonly used Group Policy settings for these tasks.

"Do I Know This Already?" Quiz

The "Do I Know This Already?" quiz allows you to assess whether you should read this entire chapter thoroughly or jump to the "Exam Preparation Tasks" section. If you are in doubt about your answers to these questions or your own assessment of your knowledge of the topics, read the entire chapter. Table 10-1 lists the major headings in this chapter and their corresponding "Do I Know This Already?" quiz questions. You can find the answers in Appendix A, "Answers to the 'Do I Know This Already?' Quizzes."

Table 10-1 "Do I Know This Already?" Section-to-Question Mapping

Foundation Topics Section	Questions
Configuring Software Installation	1
Configuring Folder Redirection	2
Configuring Scripts	3
Configuring Administrative Templates	4

CAUTION   The goal of self-assessment is to gauge your mastery of the topics in this chapter. If you do not know the answer to a question or are only partially sure of the answer, you should mark that question as wrong for purposes of the self-assessment. Giving yourself credit for an answer you correctly guess skews your self-assessment results and might provide you with a false sense of security.

1. Which type of software package can be deployed via GPO Software Installation?

    a. .EXE

    b. .MSI

    c. .ISO

    d. .BAT

2. Which of the following are targetable locations for folder redirection? (Choose three.)

    a. Root of local C: drive

    b. User's home folder location

    c. Central network storage location

    d. Local user profile location

3. Which of the follow options can be used to execute a script on user logon? (Choose two.)

    a. Store the script in the NETLOGON share found in the SYSVOL

    b. The Logoff policy setting in a GPO

    c. The Logon policy setting in a GPO

    d. Create a script object in the directory

4. Classic Administrative Templates can be imported from which type of file?

    a. .ADMX

    b. .MSI

    c. .XML

    d. .ADM

Foundation Topics

Configuring Software Installation

One of the easier to use and most powerful features of Group Policy is the ability to deploy software installations to remote machines in the network. Traditionally, installing software involved administrative staff physically sitting down at each machine or connecting via Remote Desktop and manually running installation packages. Group Policy allows the deployment of software to be managed and run from a central location and can dynamically handle new users and computers as they join the domain.

There are two different ways to use Group Policy to distribute software:

- **Assign a software package**: When you assign a software package, the software is automatically installed on the client machine. If it is assigned to a user object, it installs when the user logs on to the client, and if assigned to a computer object it installs when the computer starts. Installation is completed the first time a user runs the program.

- **Publish a software package**: When you publish a software package, the software is not automatically installed; rather, it is displayed in the Add or Remove programs dialog box, and users can choose to install it from there.

In both cases, the software package being deployed must be a Microsoft Installer package (.msi). Executable installations that use an .exe file cannot be directly deployed with this method but can be installed instead via startup scripts. The installer file must be copied to a shared folder on the network, known as a distribution point, and computers trying to install the package must have access to that location.

To deploy software via Group Policy:

Step 1.   Log on to a writeable domain controller.

Step 2.   Create a new folder and set the appropriate permissions. Make note of the full UNC for the folder.

Step 3.   Copy the installation package to the folder.

Step 4.   Click **Tools** > **Group Policy Management**.

Step 5.   In the left-hand navigation pane, expand the **Domains** node and then the node for your domain.

Step 6.   In the left-hand navigation pane, right-click the **Group Policy Objects** node and select **New**.

Step 7.   Type a descriptive name for the GPO. Leave the Starter GPO blank. Click **OK**.

Step 8.   If desired, add a security filter at this point to ensure the package is not accidentally deployed outside its intended targets when linked.

Step 9.   Right-click the new policy and select **Edit**.

Step 10.   The GPME launches. In the left-hand navigation pane expand the **User Configuration > Policies > Software Settings** node.

Step 11.   Right-click the **Software Installation** node and select **New > Package**.

Step 12.   Browse to the folder created in Step 2 and select the .msi file to be deployed. Click **Open**.

Step 13.   Select the deployment method to use and click **OK** (see Figure 10-1).

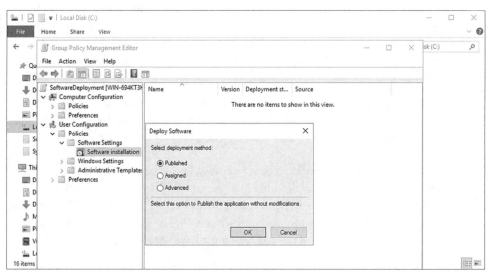

Figure 10-1   Selecting a Deployment Method for a GPO-Deployed Software Installation

Step 14.   Close the GPME and use GPMC to link the GPO to the desired node in the directory.

The software package is now installed or published according to the choice made during Step 13.

Configuring Folder Redirection

Windows stores user settings, application settings, and user files such as documents under the local user profile folder. This is usually in the Users folder found on the C:\ drive of the local machine. The settings and files in these local profiles can only be accessed from the current computer, which can be problematic for users who work on different machines and want to synchronize their data between multiple computers.

While roaming profiles can be used to copy a user's profile data to each computer the user logs on to, this process can cause logon times to slow down and inefficiently copies data around the network. With folder redirection, elements of the user profile can be pointed to a shared network location, and users can work with their documents on a server as if they are on the local drive.

NOTE In the question of roaming profiles versus folder redirection, the answer is often to use both. There are portions of the user profile that shouldn't or cannot be redirected to a network location. Combining both features provides the flexibility to create an efficient and adaptable user experience.

Folder redirection is limited to the profile folders listed in the GPO (see Figure 10-2). To set up folder redirection:

Step 1. Log on to a writeable domain controller.

Step 2. Click **Tools > Group Policy Management**.

Step 3. In the left-hand navigation pane, expand the **Domains** node and then the node for your domain.

Step 4. Create a new GPO or select an existing one.

Step 5. Right-click the GPO and select **Edit**.

Step 6. The GPME launches. In the left-hand navigation pane, expand the **User Configuration > Policies > Windows Settings > Folder Redirection** node.

Step 7. In the right-hand pane, right-click the folder you want to redirect and select **Properties**.

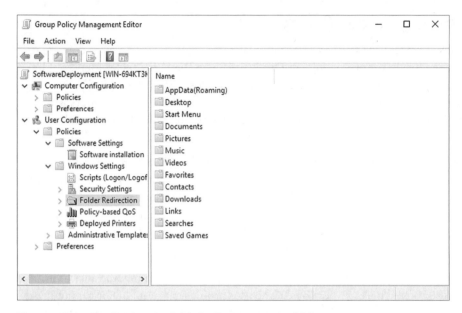

Figure 10-2   The Folders Available for Redirection via GPO

Step 8.   In the **Setting** drop-down list there are two options:

- **Basic**: With basic configuration, you choose a single location where every user (who has the GPO applied) will have the folder redirected to.

- **Advanced**: With advanced configuration, you can choose a different basic configuration for every chosen security group. Users who are not in a defined security group will not have redirection applied.

Step 9.   When choosing a redirect location, whether it's in basic mode for all users or for a specific security group, the **Target folder location** drop-down list has the following options (see Figure 10-3):

- **Redirect to the user's home directory**: This option causes the folder to redirect to the user's home directory. This directory can be overridden on a user-by-user basis in Active Directory and stored either locally or on the network. See Chapter 3, "Creating and Managing Active Directory Users and Computers," for more information.

- **Create a folder for each user under the root path**: This option allows you to define a path to a shared folder. Every user receives her own folder in that location when the GPO is applied. The redirected folder will be a subfolder of that user folder.

- **Redirect to the following location**: This option allows you to define a specific location on the network to redirect the user profile folder to.

- **Redirect to the local userprofile location**: This causes the folder to redirect to the local folder location on the computer. This option is used when you want to turn off and undo folder redirection. Simply removing the GPO does not stop any existing redirection; the user must receive a GPO refresh with this option first.

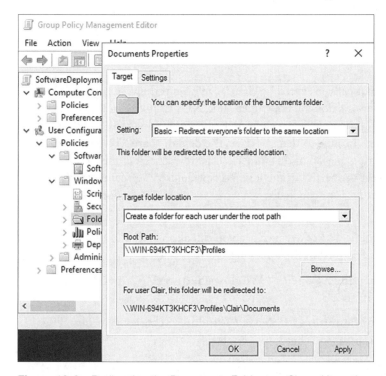

Figure 10-3   Redirecting the Documents Folder to a Shared Location on a Server

Step 10.   Click **OK**.

The chosen redirection will now be applied to the users the GPO applies to during the next refresh.

Configuring Scripts

Another commonly used feature of Group Policy is script execution. By taking advantage of this feature, administrators can ensure various scripts are executed uniformly across domain connected machines. These scripts can be used to copy files, install software, or even generate notifications. Any task that can be scripted with a Windows Script Host (WSH) language is supported, but most frequently scripts are written in Windows PowerShell.

Group Policy and GPOs can execute scripts on client machines during the following events:

- Computer startup
- Computer shutdown
- User logon
- User logoff

Scripts can be automatically executed by client machines if they are copied to the NETLOGON folder of a domain controller. The NETLOGON folder is located in the SYSVOL of the Active Directory, by default C:\Windows\SYSVOL\domain\scripts. You can browse to this folder via the default share \\server name\ netlogon as well. Scripts placed in this folder can be referenced in the Active Directory User object properties in the logon script field. When set up this way, the user copies and executes the specified script when logging on to a domain joined computer.

For more control and flexibility over scripts, you can also use GPOs to define script execution. Scripts are defined in the following GPO locations:

- **User Configuration / Policies / Windows Settings / Scripts**: Use for user logon and logoff scripts.

- **Computer Configuration / Policies / Windows Settings / Scripts**: Used for computer startup and shutdown scripts.

It's important to note that scripts must be copied to a specific location in the SYSVOL folder. This folder is located in

SYSVOL\domain\Policies\{GUID}\User\Scripts\

Where {GUID} is the GUID for the GPO that is publishing the script. Computer scripts are located in a similar folder:

SYSVOL\domain\Policies\{GUID}\Machine\Scripts\

The GPME makes it easy to browse to that location, however, so you do not need to memorize it or copy your script prior to editing the GPO.

To define a script via GPO:

Step 1.   Log on to a writeable domain controller.

Step 2.   Create a new script.

Step 3.   Copy the script file to the clipboard. (We paste it in Step 12.)

Step 4.   Click **Tools** > **Group Policy Management**.

Step 5.   In the left-hand navigation pane, expand the **Domains** node and then the node for your domain.

Step 6.   Create a new GPO or select an existing one.

Step 7.   Right-click the GPO and select **Edit**.

Step 8.   In the left-hand navigation pane, browse to the correct node for the type of script you want to define.

Step 9.   In the right-hand pane, right-click the script type you want to define (Startup, Shutdown, Logon, or Logoff depending on which node you've selected) and select **Properties**.

Step 10.   The script Properties dialog displays two tabs. Choose the appropriate tab for the script you created:

- **Scripts**: This tab is used to define WSH scripts that you want to run during the chosen event.

- **PowerShell Scripts**: This tab is used to define Windows PowerShell scripts to run during the chosen event.

Step 11.   Click the **Show files** button.

Step 12.   Paste the copied script file into the location shown in the new Explorer window that has opened. Close Explorer.

Step 13.   Click **Add**.

Step 14.   Type the name of the script file, with no path information, into the **Script Name** box.

Step 15.   If the script requires any parameters passed in during execution, type them in the **Script Parameters** box (see Figure 10-4).

Step 16.   Click **OK**.

The GPO now executes the script after the next Group Policy refresh and when the chosen event occurs.

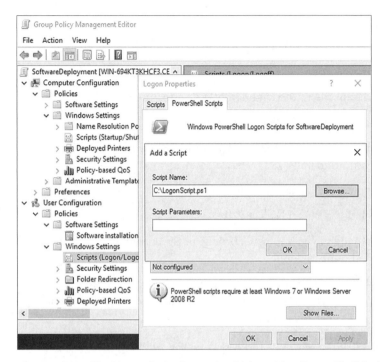

Figure 10-4   The Logon Script Properties Dialog with a PowerShell Script Selected

Configuring Administrative Templates

Within the policies subsection of both the Computer Configuration and User Configuration sections of a GPO are three subcategories: Software Settings, Windows Settings, and Administrative Templates. The options in the first two are defined by Active Directory and Group Policy and cannot be changed. The third category, Administrative Templates, has the capability to be added to and customized by users and software.

Administrative Templates are used to edit registry settings for users and computers in the local registry. Administrative Templates are typically available in what is known as the *local store*. This local store is loaded into the GPME when a GPO is being edited, but it is not persisted or replicated outside the machine on which it is located. This creates a potential problem when there are different versions of Windows on the network or different computers have different templates available. An administrator trying to build a GPO on one machine may not see the same options as an administrator building a GPO on a different machine.

As covered in Chapter 8, "Creating and Managing Group Policy Objects (GPOs)," you can create a central store in the SYSVOL of the domain. Administrative Template settings files copied to this location are replicated to each DC that contains a copy of the SYSVOL and are loaded into all GPME clients running from domain connected machines. This central store allows a consistent view of Administrative Templates regardless of where the GPO is being edited from.

Importing a Custom Administrative Template File

Administrative Templates are defined via XML files with an .ADMX extension. These files define both the registry setting to be configured as well as the UI presentation of the setting in the GPME. ADMX files have only been in use since Windows Server 2008 and Windows Vista. Prior to that, a proprietary format was used with an .ADM extension. ADM files cannot be loaded via the central store. If you want to add ADM file templates, sometimes called Classic Administrative Templates, you must import them into the GPO.

To import an Administrative Template (.ADM) file into a GPO:

Step 1.   Log on to a writeable domain controller.

Step 2.   Click **Tools** > **Group Policy Management**.

Step 3.   In the left-hand navigation pane, expand the **Domains** node and then the node for your domain.

Step 4.   Create a new GPO or select an existing one.

Step 5.   Right-click the GPO and select **Edit**.

Step 6.   In the left-hand navigation pane, navigate to either Administrative Templates section (either under **User Configuration** > **Policies** or **Computer Configuration** > **Policies**).

Step 7.   Right-click the Administrative Templates node and select **Add/Remove Templates**.

Step 8.   The dialog displays any template file currently loaded aside from Local or Central Store templates. Click **Add**.

Step 9.   Browse to the ADM file location, highlight it, and click **Open**.

Step 10.   Click **Close**.

The settings now are available as a child node of the Administrative Templates settings folder. They are added to the proper section, either User Configuration or Computer Configuration, regardless of where you ran the import from, so be sure to check the correct node if you do not see them right away (see Figure 10-5).

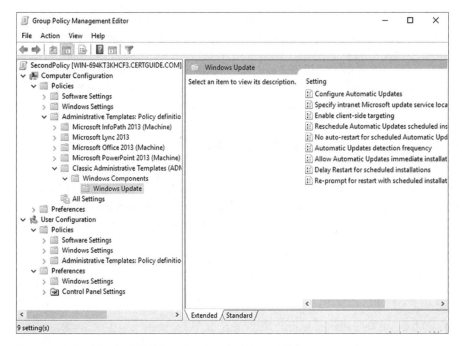

Figure 10-5   Classic ADM Template Loaded into a GPO

> **NOTE**   Classic ADM files for Windows Server 2003, Windows 2000, and Windows XP can be downloaded from Microsoft here: https://www.microsoft.com/en-us/download/details.aspx?id=18664.

Configuring Property Filters for Administrative Templates

There are dozens of different categories of Administrative Templates, with hundreds of different settings among them. This is before any additional templates have been added, such as those for Microsoft Office. Finding and working with the correct settings can be difficult. The GPME has a built-in filtering feature for working with Administrative Templates that allows you to filter the view of settings to make this work easier.

There are five categories of filters you can enable:

- **Managed**: This filter hides or shows managed Administrative Template settings. Managed settings are governed by the Group Policy service and can be removed when a policy setting is no longer within the scope of a user or computer.

- **Configured**: This filter hides or shows policy settings that are configured. A setting can be in one of three states: Enabled, Disabled, or Not Configured. Both Enabled and Disabled are considered to be configured.

- **Commented**: This filter hides or shows policy settings that have a comment associated with them.

- **Keyword filters**: Keyword filters allow you to type a word or words and filter for policy settings that contain that word in either the setting title, the help text, or the comments.

- **Requirements**: Requirements filters allow you to limit the settings to one or more platforms required for the setting to work. The list of platforms is fixed.

To enable Administrative Template filters:

Step 1.   Log on to a writeable domain controller.

Step 2.   Click **Tools > Group Policy Management**.

Step 3.   In the left-hand navigation pane, expand the **Domains** node and then the node for your domain.

Step 4.   Create a new GPO or select an existing one.

Step 5.   Right-click the GPO and select **Edit**.

Step 6.   In the left-hand navigation pane, navigate to either Administrative Templates section (either under **User Configuration > Policies** or **Computer Configuration > Policies**).

Step 7.   Right-click the **Administrative Templates** node and select **Filter Options**.

Step 8.   The Filter Options dialog displays. Any of the choices from the list of five categories of filters can be chosen (see Figure 10-6). Click **OK**.

Step 9.   The Administrative Templates node displays a small filter icon in the navigation tree indicating that filtering is on.

To turn filtering off, just right-click the Administrative Templates node again and select **Filter On**. This deselects that option, and the filter icon disappears from the GPME navigation tree.

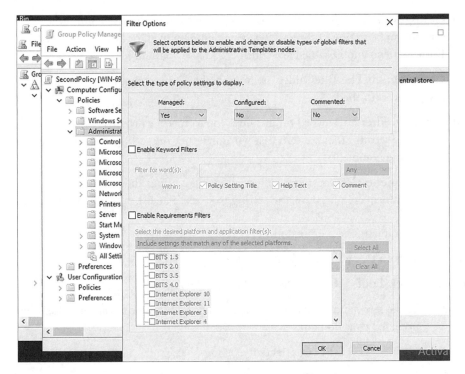

Figure 10-6   The Filter Options Dialog for Administrative Templates

Exam Preparation Tasks

As mentioned in the section "Book Features" in the Introduction, you have a few choices for exam preparation: the exercises here; Chapter 17, "Final Preparation"; and the exam simulation questions in the Pearson Test Prep Software Online.

Review All Key Topics

Review the most important topics in this chapter, noted with the Key Topics icon in the outer margin of the page. Table 10-2 lists a reference of these key topics and the page number on which each is found.

Table 10-2   Key Topics for Chapter 10

Key Topic Element	Description	Page Number
List	Deployment options for distributing software via Group Policy	277
Figure 10-1	Selecting a deployment method for a GPO-deployed software installation	278
Paragraph	Comparing folder redirection to roaming profiles	279
List	Options for redirecting a folder	280
List	Events that can be used to trigger script execution via Group Policy	282
Paragraph	Purpose of the central store for Administrative Templates	285
Paragraph	ADMX versus ADM files	285
List	Categories of filters for Administrative Templates	286

Complete Tables and Lists from Memory

There are no memory tables in this chapter.

Define Key Terms

Define the following key terms from this chapter and check your answers in the glossary:

assigning software, publishing software, folder redirection, security templates, property filters, Custom Administrative Template file

End-of-Chapter Review Questions

The answers to these questions appear in Appendix A. For more practice with exam format questions, use the Pearson Test Prep Software Online.

1. The Finance department recently purchased a new software package that everyone in the department will need the ability to install, although not everyone will. What would be the best way to facilitate that via Group Policy?

    a. Create and distribute installation media such as a DVD or USB drive with the installation package.

    b. Configure a GPO with the installation package and choose to publish the software to all applicable users.

    c. Configure a GPO with the installation package and choose to assign the software to all applicable users.

    d. Deploy the software to the NETLOGON share in SYSVOL.

2. In Active Directory, each Finance user's home folder has been set up on a network share and mapped to the S: drive on their local machine. You are now tasked with deploying their Documents and Media folders to the same location. What would be the best method for accomplishing this?

    a. Deploy a logon script to create a symbolic link for the user directory to the network share.

    b. Set up folder redirection for each folder in a GPO linked to the Finance OU. Configure redirection to the user's home directory.

    c. Set up folder redirection for each folder in a GPO linked to the Finance OU. Configure redirection to the user's userprofile location.

    d. Manually configure the computers in the Finance department.

3. You have downloaded a series of .ADMX files for Microsoft Office and deployed them to the local store on one of your domain controllers. Your remote administrators, who often work from different domain controllers in disparate physical locations, will need to configure those settings on the GPOs they work with. What would be the best way to distribute those settings?

    a. Create a central store in the SYSVOL and copy the .ADMX files to that location.

    b. Distribute physical media with the .ADMX installer to the desired locations.

    c. Share the download link for the .ADMX files with each remote administrator.

    d. Configure a GPO deployment for Administrative Templates.

This chapter covers the following topics:

- **Configuring Control Panel Settings**: This section describes how to use Group Policy to set Windows Control Panel settings on client computers.

- **Configuring Windows Settings**: This section describes how to use Group Policy to set Windows environment configuration options on client computers.

CHAPTER 11

Configuring Group Policy Preferences

Group Policy Preferences, found under both the Computer Configuration and the User Configuration sections of a GPO, are used to set up the initial state of a variety of system preferences. Unlike policies, these preferences are generally editable by the end user after Group Policy has configured them so they provide a consistent starting point for all users even if they later diverge.

Each category of preference in the GPO is represented by its own client-side extension (CSE). There are numerous CSEs for client preferences; this chapter considers the following settings: Printers, Network Drives, Power, Registry, Internet Explorer, Files and Folders, and Shortcuts. These settings are divided into two broader categories: Windows Settings and Control Panel settings.

"Do I Know This Already?" Quiz

The "Do I Know This Already?" quiz allows you to assess whether you should read this entire chapter thoroughly or jump to the "Exam Preparation Tasks" section. If you are in doubt about your answers to these questions or your own assessment of your knowledge of the topics, read the entire chapter. Table 11-1 lists the major headings in this chapter and their corresponding "Do I Know This Already?" quiz questions. You can find the answers in Appendix A, "Answers to the 'Do I Know This Already?' Quizzes."

Table 11-1 "Do I Know This Already?" Section-to-Question Mapping

Foundation Topics Section	Questions
Configuring Control Panel Settings	1-2
Configuring Windows Settings	3-4

CAUTION   The goal of self-assessment is to gauge your mastery of the topics in this chapter. If you do not know the answer to a question or are only partially sure of the answer, you should mark that question as wrong for purposes of the self-assessment. Giving yourself credit for an answer you correctly guess skews your self-assessment results and might provide you with a false sense of security.

1. Which of the following Control Panel settings available in the User Configuration section of a GPO are *not* available in the Computer Configuration section?

   a. Internet Settings

   b. Services preferences

   c. Regional Options

   d. Start Menu preferences

2. One difference between item-level targeting and security filtering is

   a. Item-level targeting can be performed by regular domain users, while security filtering requires elevated privileges.

   b. Item-level targeting is only applied by a single setting in the GPO, while security filtering applies to the entire GPO.

   c. Item-level targeting is limited to filtering for client computer properties, while security filtering can rely on a user object's location in the directory.

   d. There are no notable differences.

3. Which of the following are preferences that can be configured as Windows Settings? (Choose two.)

   a. Registry settings

   b. Power Options

   c. Internet Explorer settings

   d. Ini Files

4. When deploying a registry preference item with the Replace action for an existing registry key, what happens to any existing subkeys of that key?

   a. They are included underneath the new key.

   b. They prevent their parent key from being replaced.

   c. They are deleted before the new key is created.

   d. No changes are made.

Configuring Control Panel Settings

Like the name implies, Control Panel settings are GPO policies that a local user can configure on a machine via the built-in Windows Control Panel. Figure 11-1 illustrates the full list of potential categories, while the exam and this book focus on the following: Printers, Power Options, and Internet Settings.

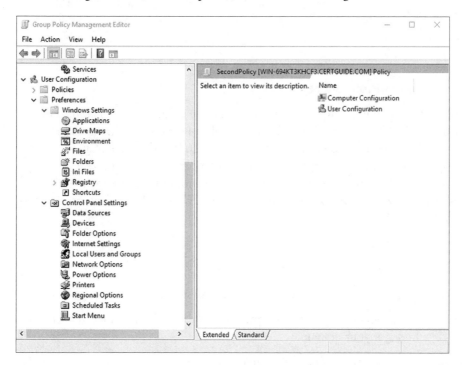

Figure 11-1   The Control Panel Settings Available Under the User Configuration Section of a GPO

The full list of Control Panel settings in a GPO:

- Data Sources (ODBC)

- Devices

- Folder Options

- Internet Settings

- Local Users and Groups

- Network Options

- Power Options

- Printers

- Regional Options

- Scheduled Tasks

- Services

- Start Menu

Configuring Printer Preferences

With the Group Policy Printers extension, you can configure local, shared, and network (TCP/IP) printers without having to rely on scripts or manual administration. The Printers extension can be used to create, update, or delete printers. The extension can also install the appropriate printer drivers under the correct security context. This eases printer setup for enterprise organizations where many PCs are accessing the same printer, particularly when the local users do not have administrative rights to install drivers.

To configure printers:

Step 1.   Log on to a writeable domain controller.

Step 2.   Click **Tools** > **Group Policy Management**.

Step 3.   In the left-hand navigation pane, expand the **Domains** node and then the node for your domain.

Step 4.   Create a new GPO or select an existing one.

Step 5.   Right-click the GPO and select **Edit**.

Step 6.   In the left-hand navigation pane, browse to **User Configuration > Preferences > Control Panel Settings** or **Computer Configuration > Preferences > Control Panel Settings**.

Step 7.   Right-click the **Printers** node and select **New > Local Printer**.

Step 8.   From the **Action** drop-down list select one of the following options:

- **Create**: Creates a new local printer. If a local printer with the same name already exists, no changes are made.

- **Delete**: Removes a local printer from the Printers dialog if it exists. Printer drivers remain installed; only the printer object is removed.

- **Replace**: Creates a printer, deleting any existing printer with the same name beforehand.

- **Update**: Changes the settings for an existing printer if it exists. If it doesn't exist, the printer is created.

Step 9.   Fill in the required settings in the dialog based on the action being performed (see Figure 11-2).

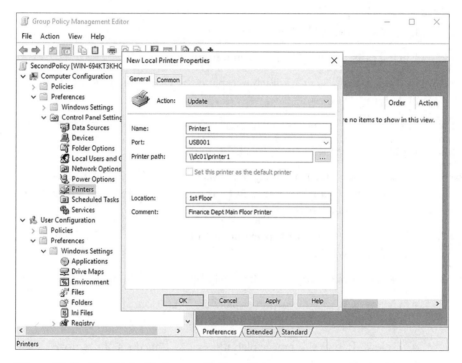

Figure 11-2   The Printer Preference Options Dialog

- **Name**: The name of the printer object to be created/updated/removed.

- **Port**: The local port that the printer is attached to.

- **Printer path**: Type in or search for the shared path of the printer in the directory. This is used to install the correct drivers.

- **Location**: A freeform text field to indicate where the printer is physically located.

- **Comment**: A freeform text field to add any additional comments.

Step 10.   Click **OK**.

The Printers preference item is now listed in the GPME.

Configuring Power Options

The Power Options extension can be used to set up power plans on client machines on the network. This is useful for a fleet that consists of laptops that employees pick up and use in a variety of locations, both docked and undocked. Forcing Power Plan settings can ensure that users are getting the most out of their machines when connected to a power source and the most out of their battery when unplugged.

To configure Power Options:

Step 1.   Log on to a writeable domain controller.

Step 2.   Click **Tools** > **Group Policy Management**.

Step 3.   In the left-hand navigation pane, expand the **Domains** node and then the node for your domain.

Step 4.   Create a new GPO or select an existing one.

Step 5.   Right-click the GPO and select **Edit**.

Step 6.   In the left-hand navigation pane, browse to **User Configuration > Preferences > Control Panel Settings** or **Computer Configuration > Preferences > Control Panel Settings**.

Step 7.   Right-click the **Power Options** node and select **New Power Plan (At least Windows 7)**.

Step 8.   From the **Action** drop-down list select one of the following options:

- **Create**: Creates a new power plan configuration. If a power plan with the same name already exists no changes are made.

- **Delete**: Removes a power plan if it exists. This does not remove built-in power plans.

- **Replace**: Creates a power plan, deleting any existing plan with the same name beforehand.

- **Update**: Changes the settings for an existing power plan if it exists. If the plan doesn't exist, it is created.

Step 9.   Check the **Set as the active power plan** box if you want the plan to be updated as the active plan on the machine.

Step 10.   Navigate the options and select the desired choices for the plan (see Figure 11-3).

Step 11.   Click **OK**.

The Power Options preference item is now listed in the GPME.

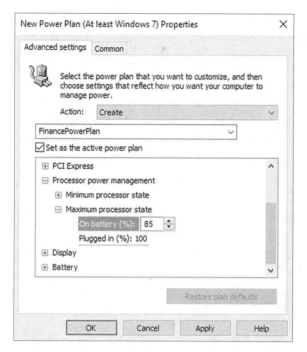

Figure 11-3 The Power Plan Preferences Item Dialog

Configuring Internet Explorer Settings

The Internet Settings extension allows Group Policy to set up much of a user's experience in Internet Explorer, from the default home page and tabs to open on start to advanced security settings. These settings can be pushed to any version of Internet Explorer from 5 through 11, although additional settings objects may need to be created for different versions. Internet settings are only available via the User Configuration section of the GPO; there are no Computer-wide Internet Explorer settings.

To configure Internet Explorer Settings:

Step 1.   Log on to a writeable domain controller.

Step 2.   Click **Tools** > **Group Policy Management**.

Step 3.   In the left-hand navigation pane, expand the **Domains** node and then the node for your domain.

Step 4.   Create a new GPO or select an existing one.

Step 5.   Right-click the GPO and select **Edit**.

Step 6.   In the left-hand navigation pane, browse to **User Configuration > Preferences > Control Panel Settings**.

Step 7.   Right-click the **Internet Settings** node and select the version of Internet Explorer you want to configure. The selection for Internet Explorer 10 applies to both version 10 and 11.

Step 8.   The Properties dialog that appears mirrors the settings dialog found in Internet Explorer itself (see Figure 11-4).

Figure 11-4   The Internet Explorer 10 and 11 Properties Dialog

Step 9.   Modify the desired properties and click **OK**.

The Internet Settings preference item is now listed in the GPME.

Configuring Item-Level Targeting

Item-level targeting is a way to filter or narrow the scope of the preferences contained in a setting to a select group of computers or users in the domain. Similar to security filtering and WMI filtering covered in Chapter 9, "Configuring Group Policy Processing," item-level targeting allows you to further define who should receive which settings. Unlike those filtering options, though, item-level targeting applies to only one configuration item at a time. A GPO may apply to a wide group of individuals or machines, while each preference setting may be limited in its application.

Item-level targeting can filter on any of the items shown in Figure 11-5. Items like Security Group or Site allow for filtering based on the object's place and configuration in the directory. IP Address Range and MAC Address Range allow targeting based on position or place in the network, such as internal versus VPN. Targeting can even be performed on a WMI query, mimicking the WMI filtering for a GPO but at the preference setting level instead.

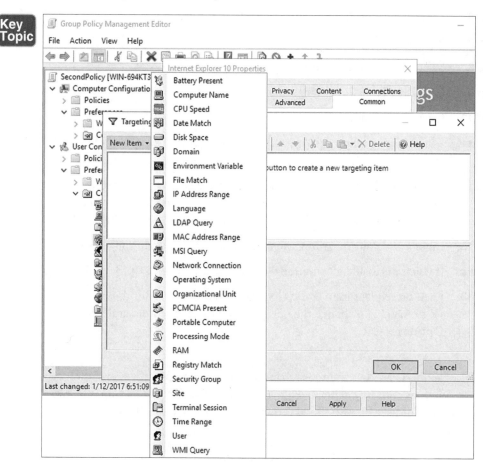

Figure 11-5   Item-Level Targeting Filter Options

Multiple targets can be set up for a single preference setting. Each targeting item results in either a true or a false result, and you can select logical operators (i.e., AND or OR) to combine each item with the previous item in the list. If the entire list evaluates to false, the settings are not applied to the object. Targeting collections allow for the ability to create parenthetical expressions.

To target a setting:

Step 1. Log on to a writeable domain controller.

Step 2. Click **Tools > Group Policy Management**.

Step 3. In the left-hand navigation pane, expand the **Domains** node and then the node for your domain.

Step 4. Create a new GPO or select an existing one.

Step 5. Right-click the GPO and select **Edit**.

Step 6. Create a new preference setting or select an existing one.

Step 7. Right-click the setting and select **Properties**.

Step 8. Select the **Common** tab.

Step 9. Check the **Item-level targeting** box.

Step 10. Click **Targeting**.

Step 11. The targeting editor displays. Click **New Item** and select an item to filter on.

Step 12. A short description of the item displays in the box. On the bottom half of the editor, you can input details for the chosen item. A verbose description of how the item works also is displayed in that box (see Figure 11-6).

Step 13. Input any details regarding the target you want to create and click **OK**.

Step 14. If you want to add an additional target, repeat Steps 11 to 13.

Step 15. Each subsequent item lists its logical operator. By default the operator is set to **AND**. To change the operator, right-click the item and select **Item Options > OR**.

NOTE Most settings can have their test changed from an inclusion to an exclusion via the Item Options context menu as well. For example, the Security Group item target can either test for users in a specified group or users not in a specified group.

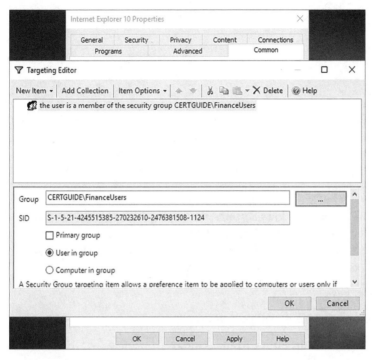

Figure 11-6   The Item-Level Targeting Editor Configuring a Security Group Filter

Step 16.   When complete, click **OK**.

Step 17.   Click **OK**.

The preference now uses the target filter when deciding whether to apply to the object.

Configuring Windows Settings

The Windows Settings node of the GPO Preferences contains environment, drive, and file system configurations used by client machines. The full list of available categories follows, but the exam focuses on the following: Registry, Drive Maps, Files, Folders, and Shortcuts.

The full list of Windows Settings in a GPO:

- Applications

- Drive Maps

- Environment

- Files

- Folders

- Ini Files

- Registry

- Network Shares

- Shortcuts

Configuring Custom Registry Settings

The registry category under Windows Settings allows you to customize the client machine's registry for both users and computers. You can create, update, replace, and delete both keys and values. Registry key name, type, and data are all change-able via Group Policy.

To configure registry keys:

Step 1.   Log on to a writeable domain controller.

Step 2.   Click **Tools** > **Group Policy Management**.

Step 3.   In the left-hand navigation pane, expand the **Domains** node and then the node for your domain.

Step 4.   Create a new GPO or select an existing one.

Step 5.   Right-click the GPO and select **Edit**.

Step 6.   In the left-hand navigation pane, browse to **User Configuration > Preferences > Windows Settings** or **Computer Configuration > Preferences > Windows Settings**.

Step 7.   Right-click the **Registry** node and select **New Registry Item**.

Step 8.   From the **Action** drop-down list, select one of the following options:

- **Create**: Creates a new registry value or key. If a registry entry with the same name already exists, no changes are made.

- **Delete**: Removes a registry value or a key and all its values and subkeys.

- **Replace**: Creates a registry value or key, deleting any existing entry with the same name beforehand. If the target is a registry value, all settings associated with the value are replaced. If the target is a registry key, all values and subkeys are deleted, leaving a default value name with no data.

- **Update**: Changes the settings for an existing value or key if it exists. If the value or key doesn't exist, it is created. This is different from Replace in that it only updates the settings defined within the preference item.

Step 9.   Select a root-level registry node from the **Hive** drop-down list.

Step 10.   Type a new key path in the **Key Path** text box or select the ellipses to browse to an existing key path in the local computer's registry.

Step 11.   To change the default value, check the **Default** box; otherwise, type a value name in the text box next to that.

Step 12.   Select a key value type from the **Value Type** drop-down list.

Step 13.   Type an appropriate value based on the selected value type in the **Value Data** box.

Step 14.   If any additional options are presented, select the appropriate choice. For example, a REG_DWORD can be either Hexadecimal or Decimal (see Figure 11-7).

Figure 11-7   The Registry Key Properties Dialog with a DWORD Value Type Chosen

Step 15.   Click **OK**.

The new Registry preference setting is now listed in the GPME.

Defining Network Drive Mappings

In a shared enterprise environment, you often want users to share access to a folder on a file server. Network paths and UNCs for those folders can be long and difficult to remember, so mapping those shared folders to a letter on the local file system is a popular way to make things easier for your users. Mapped drives can also be moved to new locations on the network transparently and without breaking users' shortcuts or references that rely on the map. Drive maps are only available in the User Configuration section of a GPO.

To configure a network drive map:

Step 1.   Log on to a writeable domain controller.

Step 2.   Click **Tools** > **Group Policy Management**.

Step 3.   In the left-hand navigation pane, expand the **Domains** node and then the node for your domain.

Step 4.   Create a new GPO or select an existing one.

Step 5.   Right-click the GPO and select **Edit**.

Step 6.   In the left-hand navigation pane, browse to **User Configuration > Preferences > Windows Settings**.

Step 7.   Right-click the **Drive Maps** node and select **New > Mapped Drive**.

Step 8.   From the **Action** drop-down list, select one of the following options:

- **Create**: Creates a new mapped drive for users. If the letter is already in use, it is changed and mapped to the defined location.

- **Delete**: Removes a mapped drive for a user.

- **Replace**: Creates a mapped drive for a user, deleting an existing map if it exists.

- **Update**: Changes the settings for an existing map if it exists. If the map doesn't exist, it is created. This is different from Replace in that it only updates the settings defined within the preference item.

Step 9.   In the **Location** box, type or select the network share to map to using its full UNC.

Step 10.   If you want to reconnect the map on each subsequent user logon, check the **Connect** box.

Step 11.   Type a descriptive label in the **Label as** text box.

Step 12. For the drive letter, you can either choose a specific letter from the drop-down list or select to use the first available on the client machine (see Figure 11-8).

Figure 11-8   The Drive Map Preference Item Dialog Box Mapping the S: Drive

Step 13. The **Connect as (optional)** section allows you to specify alternate user-name and password credentials to connect to the shared folder with.

NOTE   **Connect as** should be used sparingly as it can represent a security flaw. Credentials are stored in the GPO in SYSVOL and can be discovered although they are obscured. You should never store administrative credentials in this manner.

Step 14. The **Hide/Show** options can be used to hide the drive in the client machine and override any local settings if needed.

Step 15. Click **OK**.

The drive map is now listed in the GPME.

Configuring File and Folder Deployment

With the File preference extension in Windows Settings, you can copy files to and from network visible locations. While copying, you can also modify the file system attributes. While the preference does have a create action, that only initiates a copy—it cannot create a new file. The Folder extension allows for similar behavior with folders but does allow for creation of new folders. These preferences often are used together to first create a new folder on the network and then copy a file to it.

NOTE   As covered in Chapter 9, the extension runs on the client machine. That means that if you reference a file or folder by its local drive letter, such as C:, when authoring the GPO on a domain controller, that object needs to exist in the same location on the local client machine. You should use UNC paths to shared network folders whenever possible to avoid confusion.

To configure a new file operation:

Step 1.   Log on to a writeable domain controller.

Step 2.   Click **Tools** > **Group Policy Management**.

Step 3.   In the left-hand navigation pane, expand the **Domains** node and then the node for your domain.

Step 4.   Create a new GPO or select an existing one.

Step 5.   Right-click the GPO and select **Edit**.

Step 6.   In the left-hand navigation pane, browse to **User Configuration > Preferences > Windows Settings** or **Computer Configuration > Preferences > Windows Settings**.

Step 7.   Right-click the **Files** node and select **New > File**.

Step 8.   From the **Action** drop-down list, select one of the following options:

- **Create**: Copies a file from the source to the destination. If the file already exists in the destination, no changes are made.

- **Delete**: Deletes a file or files from the targeted location.

- **Replace**: Copies a file from the source to the destination, deleting it from the destination if it already exists.

- **Update**: Changes the settings for a file in the destination location.

Step 9.   In the **Source file(s)** box, type or browse to the location of the file you want to copy.

Step 10.   In the **Destination File** box, type or browse to the location where the file should be copied to.

Step 11.   Select **Suppress errors on individual file actions** to ignore errors that occur in the middle of a copy operation. This can allow a multiple file operation to continue and complete even if one or more files fails to copy properly.

Step 12.   Use the **Attributes** section to set one or more file system attributes for all the files in the destination (see Figure 11-9).

Figure 11-9   The New File Properties Dialog Box

Step 13.   Click **OK**.

The File preference item is now listed in the GPME.

To configure a new folder operation:

Step 1.   Log on to a writeable domain controller.

Step 2.   Click **Tools > Group Policy Management**.

Step 3.   In the left-hand navigation pane, expand the **Domains** node and then the node for your domain.

Step 4.   Create a new GPO or select an existing one.

Step 5.   Right-click the GPO and select **Edit**.

Step 6.   In the left-hand navigation pane, browse to **User Configuration > Preferences > Windows Settings** or **Computer Configuration > Preferences > Windows Settings**.

Step 7.   Right-click the **Folders** node and select **New > Folder**.

Step 8.   From the **Action** drop-down list, select one of the following options:

- **Create**: Creates a new folder

- **Delete**: Deletes a folder and any files or subfolders in it

- **Replace**: Creates a new folder, deleting any folder that exists in the same location with the same name first

- **Update**: Modifies an existing folder

Step 9.   Type the full name of the folder to create in the **Path** box.

Step 10. Use the **Attributes** section to set one or more file system attributes on the folder.

Step 11. Click **OK**.

The Folder preference item is now listed in the GPME.

Configuring Shortcut Deployment

Shortcuts can be a handy way to provide users with links to commonly accessed files, folders, URLs, or even scripting objects. The Shortcut extension allows you to deploy a shortcut to the client machine so that users do not have to create them on their own.

To deploy a shortcut:

Step 1.   Log on to a writeable domain controller.

Step 2.   Click **Tools > Group Policy Management**.

Step 3.   In the left-hand navigation pane, expand the **Domains** node and then the node for your domain.

Step 4.   Create a new GPO or select an existing one.

Step 5.   Right-click the GPO and select **Edit**.

Step 6.   In the left-hand navigation pane, browse to **User Configuration > Preferences > Windows Settings** or **Computer Configuration > Preferences > Windows Settings**.

Step 7.   Right-click the **Shortcuts** node and select **New > Shortcut**.

Step 8.   From the **Action** drop-down list, select one of the following options:

- **Create**: Creates a new shortcut

- **Delete**: Removes a shortcut

- **Replace**: Creates a new shortcut, first deleting any existing shortcut with the same name in the same location

- **Update**: Modifies the settings of an existing shortcut

Step 9.   Type the name of the shortcut to create or modify in the **Name** box.

Step 10.   Select one of the following options from the **Target type** drop-down list:

- **File System Object**: Points the shortcut toward a file or folder

- **URL**: Points the shortcut toward an Internet URL

- **Shell Object**: Points the shortcut toward an object in the shell, such as a printer, share, or Control Panel item

Step 11.   From the **Location** drop-down list, select one of the preset locations to save the shortcut on the local machine. If you choose **<Specify full path>**, the **Name** box must include that path.

NOTE   You cannot use standard environment variables in the path of the shortcut because they are resolved by the GPO before being sent to the client machine. If you want to deploy to a user-specific location, you need to rely on the preset locations in the **Location** drop-down.

Step 12.   Fill in the **Target Path**, **Target URL**, or **Target Object** depending on which target type you chose (see Figure 11-10).

Step 13.   Specify a working directory in the **Start in** text box if needed.

Step 14.   The **Shortcut key** text box can be used to bind a keystroke to launch the shortcut. Select the text box and press the key to create the binding.

Step 15.   Select a window size to launch the shortcut in with the **Run** drop-down menu.

Figure 11-10   The Shortcut Preference Item Dialog Box

Step 16.   Use the **Comment** text box to type any free-text comments.

Step 17.   The **Icon file path** text box can be used to point toward a custom icon file to display the shortcut in Windows Explorer.

Step 18.   Click **OK**.

The shortcut is now listed in the GPME.

Exam Preparation Tasks

As mentioned in the section "Book Features" in the Introduction, you have a few choices for exam preparation: the exercises here; Chapter 17, "Final Preparation"; and the exam simulation questions in the Pearson Test Prep Software Online.

Review All Key Topics

Review the most important topics in this chapter, noted with the Key Topics icon in the outer margin of the page. Table 11-2 lists a reference of these key topics and the page number on which each is found.

Table 11-2 Key Topics for Chapter 11

Key Topic Element	Description	Page Number
List	The full list of Control Panel settings in a GPO	295
Figure 11-4	The Internet Explorer 10 and 11 properties dialog	300
Paragraph	Description of item-level targeting	301
Figure 11-5	Item-level targeting filter options	301
List	The full list of Windows Settings in a GPO	303

Complete Tables and Lists from Memory

There are no memory tables in this chapter.

Define Key Terms

Define the following key terms from this chapter and check your answers in the glossary:

preferences, action

End-of-Chapter Review Questions

The answers to these questions appear in Appendix A. For more practice with exam format questions, use the Pearson Test Prep Software Online.

1. The Finance department relies on a few comprehensive GPOs for their entire branch of the directory. They need to specify individual preferences for different groups of users who all share the same GPOs. What is the best way to implement that?

    a. Provide manual instructions to the users on how to set up their system.

    b. Use startup scripts for their computers to configure the desired preferences.

    c. Create a new OU structure to separate each of the users into an appropriate subbranch in the directory.

    d. Configure item-level targeting for the policy preferences in question to filter them down to the appropriate users.

2. You need to copy an entire directory structure, complete with the files, from a network share to the user's local machine every time the user logs on. What is the best way to implement this?

   a. Deliver physical media, such as a USB drive or DVD with the needed files and folders.

   b. Set up a Folder preference item to create the top-level folder where the files will be stored. Follow that with a File preference item to copy the entire structure from the source directory to a local drive.

   c. Create a startup script in the NETLOGON share to perform the copy operation.

   d. Communicate instructions to the users on how to initiate the copy themselves.

3. Due to vendor constraints, some users are still relying on Internet Explorer 9 while the rest of the office has upgraded to IE 11. You don't have a useful way to distinguish which users are using which version. How can GPO Preferences be used to ensure each user gets the correct version of IE preferences?

   a. Preferences can be set up in a single GPO for multiple versions of IE. The preferences will then apply to all versions found on the target computer.

   b. Survey the users and separate them into security groups based on their responses. Use item-level targeting to apply the correct preferences to the correct security group.

   c. Users will have to depend on their own knowledge of the IE version and apply configuration settings appropriately.

   d. Separate the users into organizational units based on the version of IE they use. Apply different GPOs to the OUs and configure a different version of IE in each GPO.

- **Installing Active Directory Integrated Enterprise Certificate Authority**: This section describes how to install and configure the Windows Server role service for Active Directory Certificate Services.

- **Configuring Certificate Revocation List Distribution Points**: This section describes how to manage certificate revocation lists and deploy them to various distribution points.

- **Configuring CA Backup, Recovery, and Administrative Role Separation**: This section describes how to properly back up and recover Active Directory Certificate Services and how to delegate certificate management tasks.

CHAPTER 12

Installing and Configuring Active Directory Certificate Services

Active Directory Certificate Services (AD CS) has become an important part of most enterprise network infrastructures. As a certificate authority (CA), AD CS allows the server to issue and sign public-key encrypted certificates to security principals. These certificates function as an additional trusted authentication mechanism both on and off the network. Certificates have a role in authentication for many different communication technologies including VPN, Wi-Fi networks, and SSL.

This chapter introduces the various types of CA server that can be set up with AD CS. This includes standard enterprise root CAs as well as subordinate, off-line, and standalone CAs. The chapter also covers the certificate revocation list (CRL) and Online Responder.

"Do I Know This Already?" Quiz

The "Do I Know This Already?" quiz allows you to assess whether you should read this entire chapter thoroughly or jump to the "Exam Preparation Tasks" section. If you are in doubt about your answers to these questions or your own assessment of your knowledge of the topics, read the entire chapter. Table 12-1 lists the major headings in this chapter and their corresponding "Do I Know This Already?" quiz questions. You can find the answers in Appendix A, "Answers to the 'Do I Know This Already?' Quizzes."

Table 12-1 "Do I Know This Already?" Section-to-Question Mapping

Foundation Topics Section	Questions
Installing Active Directory Integrated Enterprise Certificate Authority	1-2
Configuring Certificate Revocation List Distribution Points	3-5
Configuring CA Backup, Recovery, and Administrative Role Separation	6-7

CAUTION   The goal of self-assessment is to gauge your mastery of the topics in this chapter. If you do not know the answer to a question or are only partially sure of the answer, you should mark that question as wrong for purposes of the self-assessment. Giving yourself credit for an answer you correctly guess skews your self-assessment results and might provide you with a false sense of security.

1. When installing a subordinate CA, where does the signing certificate come from?

   a. A subordinate CA can self-sign its own signing certificate.

   b. A subordinate CA must receive a signing certificate from an enterprise root CA.

   c. A subordinate CA can receive a signing certificate from any other CA including root or subordinate and enterprise or standalone.

   d. A subordinate CA can receive a signing certificate from a root CA that is either enterprise or standalone.

2. How does an offline CA issue certificates?

   a. To physical media such as a USB drive.

   b. By being temporarily brought online.

   c. Offline CAs cannot issue certificates.

   d. Through a reverse proxy server request.

3. Which of the following would NOT be a reason to revoke a certificate?

   a. The certificate's private key became compromised.

   b. The issuing CA became compromised.

   c. The issuing CA was migrated to a new server.

   d. The certificate was obtained fraudulently.

4. Which of the following are valid CDP location types? (Choose three.)

   a. Ftp://

   b. Http://

   c. File://

   d. Ldap://

5. Which additional role service is required for Online Responders to function correctly?

   a. Active Directory Domain Services (AD DS)

   b. Internet Information Services (IIS)

   c. Domain Name System (DNS)

   d. Online Responders do not require any other services aside from Active Directory Certificate Services (AD CS).

6. Which of the following can be used to back up a CA server? (Choose two.)

   a. Windows Server Backup

   b. Temporary transfer to a subordinate CA

   c. An offline root CA

   d. The CA console backup wizard

7. What would be the best way to delegate certificate managing permissions to junior IT staff?

   a. Add the user accounts to either the Domain Admins or Enterprise Admins group.

   b. Create a new security group, grant that group permissions to manage certificates in the CA console, and add the user accounts to the new security group.

   c. Share the local administrator credentials for the CA server with the users.

   d. Configure the Enterprise CA in the directory under OUs that those users have administrative control over.

Foundation Topics

Installing Active Directory Integrated Enterprise Certificate Authority

Active Directory Certificate Services (AD CS) enterprise certificate authorities (CAs) are used to create and sign public key certificates for security principals on the Active Directory domain. Enterprise CAs must be installed on a member Windows Server in the AD domain. All computers that are members of the same forest as the enterprise CA automatically trust certificates issued by the CA.

Enterprise CAs come in two different configurations:

- **Root CAs**: Both sign and issue their own certificates.

- **Subordinate CAs**: Issue a certificate but rely on a root CA for their signing certificate.

With these two configurations, CAs can be deployed in a hierarchical fashion with one or more subordinates relying on a single root to make a two-tiered structure. In more complex deployments with three or more tiers, a subordinate CA can receive signing certificates from other subordinate CAs or root CAs.

Recommended practice dictates that you use an online enterprise root CA for your certificates only in smaller organizations. For security purposes, Microsoft recommends an offline standalone root CA with enterprise subordinate CAs in most deployments. This arrangement allows the signing CA (the root) to remain offline most of the time and limit its exposure to potential security issues. Enterprise root CAs are also expected to be unique in a forest, meaning that it is not recommended to have more than one. This means your certificate signatures are reliant on a single potential point of failure.

Installing AD CS on a Server

AD CS certificate authorities are installed with an installation wizard on Desktop Experience versions of Windows Server. AD DS can also be configured on Server Core installations using Windows PowerShell.

For those who are familiar with installing AD CS on Windows Server 2008 or 2012, very little has changed. The process should be familiar. If you are new to Windows Server, the installation wizard is an ideal place to start, as it walks you through all the options and key decisions during installation.

To install online root and subordinate enterprise CAs:

Step 1. Log on to a member server of the AD domain.

Step 2. Start Server Manager from either the Start Menu or the Taskbar.

Step 3. From the Dashboard Quickstart pane, click **Add Roles and Features**.

Step 4. The Add Roles and Features Wizard starts. Click **Next** on the **Before You Begin** page, and then ensure **Role-based or feature based installation** is selected on the **Installation Type** page. Click **Next**.

Step 5. On the **Server Selection** page, ensure that the **Select a server from the server pool** option is chosen, and then click to highlight the current server from the list. Click **Next**.

Step 6. On the **Server Roles** page, check the **Active Directory Certificate Services** box. If prompted to **Add Features that are required...** review the role services that must be installed for AD DS to work and ensure **Include management tools** is checked. Click **Add Features** to return to the Server Roles page.

Step 7. Click **Next**.

Step 8. Review the features that have been selected for you on the Features page. You can check any additional features you want to install at this time. Click **Next**.

Step 9. Review the information on the AD CS page. Click **Next**.

Step 10. Select the **Certification Authority** check box to install a CA (see Figure 12-1). Click **Next**.

Step 11. Review the confirmation page for all the services and features you chose to install. Do not check the **Restart the destination server automatically** box if any other users are currently relying on the server. Click **Install**.

Step 12. The server displays an installation progress page. Note the option at the bottom of the page to **Export configuration settings**, which generates an XML file you can use with PowerShell to install the exact same roles and features on another server.

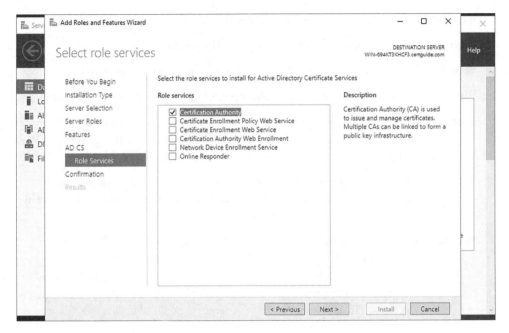

Figure 12-1 Installing the Certification Authority Role Service

Configuring AD CS on a Server

Installing AD CS is only the first step. Once the server successfully runs the Add Roles and Features Wizard, you are prompted with a link to **Configure Active Directory Certificate Services on the destination server**. If you want to perform the configuration at a later point, click **Close**.

Step 1. Click the link to **Configure Active Directory Certificate Services on the destination server**. This launches the Active Directory Certificate Services Configuration Wizard.

Step 2. Review the information provided. If you are not signed in as a member of the Enterprise Admins group, click **Change** and provide credentials for a valid user.

Step 3. Click **Next**.

Step 4. Review the available role services. Select the **Certification Authority** box. Note that if no other CAs exist in the forest, other options may not be available. Click **Next**.

Step 5. Select **Enterprise CA** and click **Next** (see Figure 12-2).

Step 6. Select **Root CA** and click **Next** (see Figure 12-3).

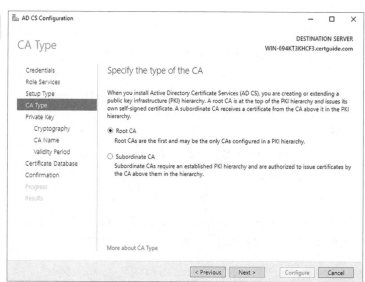

Figure 12-2   Choosing Between an Enterprise CA or a Standalone CA

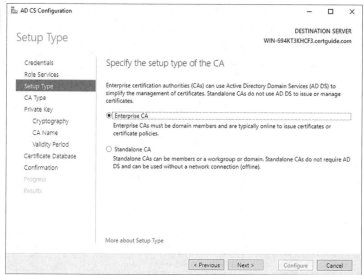

Figure 12-3   Choosing Between a Root CA or a Subordinate CA

Step 7.   Review the options (see Figure 12-4) and click **Next**:

  ▪ **Create a new private key**: This is the choice you will usually want. It generates a new, random, private key for the CA to use when signing certificates.

■ **Use existing private key**: This option can be used when reinstalling or recovering a CA from a previous installation. Also, if you want to transfer CA duties to a new computer, this allows you to export the key from the old CA and import it onto this one.

Figure 12-4   Selecting the Type of Private Key During the AD CS Configuration Wizard

Step 8.   The Cryptography page allows you to select various configuration options for the generated key (see Figure 12-5); leave the default choices and click **Next**.

■ **Select a cryptographic provider**: This allows for the use of a customized software package to generate the key.

■ **Key length**: Enter the number of bits to use in the key.

■ **Select the hash algorithm for signing certificates used by this CA**: Select the desired hashing algorithm for signing certificates.

NOTE   The cryptographic options here can have significant downstream implications both on the security of your AD CS deployment and its certificates as well as compatibility with trusting software. Be sure you understand the full ramifications of any changes to the defaults you want to make to these values.

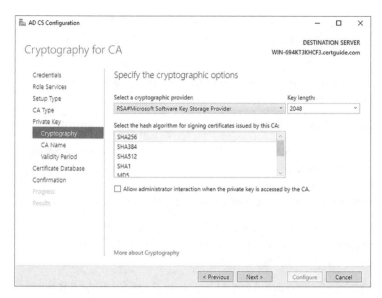

Figure 12-5   Selecting Advanced Cryptography Options During the AD CS Configuration Wizard. As a Best Practice, the Defaults Should Be Used Here Unless You Have a Specific Reason to Change Them.

Step 9.   Specify the common name and name suffix for the CA. As you type, the **Preview of distinguished name** box updates to display the full distinguished name (see Figure 12-6). Click **Next**.

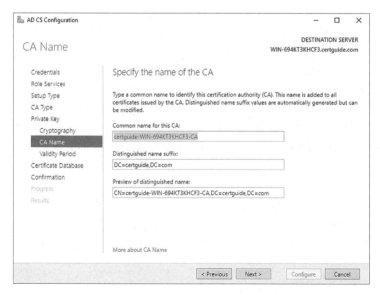

Figure 12-6   Establishing the Common Name and Distinguished Name for the CA in the AD CS Configuration Wizard

Step 10. Choose a period of time for certificates issued by the CA to remain valid. Once a certificate passes its expiration date, it must be reissued. Click **Next**.

Step 11. Specify the locations on the file system to store the certificate database and the database log. Click **Next**.

Step 12. Review your options on the confirmation page and click **Configure**.

Step 13. Upon completion, the results page displays a **Configuration succeeded** message. Click **Close**.

The CA is now up and running and prepared to issue certificates upon request.

A subordinate enterprise CA can be installed on the same forest as the root CA but must be on a different server. Follow the preceding steps to install the AD CS role and then begin configuration:

Step 1. Click the link to **Configure Active Directory Certificate Services on the destination server**. This launches the Active Directory Certificate Services Configuration Wizard.

Step 2. Review the information provided. If you are not signed in as a member of the Enterprise Admins group, click **Change** and provide credentials for a valid user.

Step 3. Click **Next**.

Step 4. Review the available role services. Select the **Certification Authority** box. Note that if no other CAs exist in the forest, other options may not be available. Click **Next**.

Step 5. Select **Enterprise CA** and click **Next**.

Step 6. Select **Subordinate CA** and click **Next**.

Step 7. Review the options, and click **Next**:

- **Create a new private key**: This is the choice you will usually want. It generates a new, random, private key for the CA to use when signing certificates.

- **Use existing private key**: This option can be used when reinstalling or recovering a CA from a previous installation. Also, if you want to transfer CA duties to a new computer, this allows you to export the key from the old CA and import it onto this one.

Step 8. The Cryptography page allows you to select various configuration options for the generated key; leave the default choices and click **Next**:

- **Select a cryptographic provider**: This allows for the use of a customized software package to generate the key.

- **Key length**: Enter the number of bits to use in the key.

- **Select the hash algorithm for signing certificates used by this CA**: Select the desired hashing algorithm for signing certificates.

Step 9. Specify the common name and name suffix for the CA. As you type, the **Preview of distinguished name** box updates to display the full distinguished name. Click **Next**.

Step 10. Select how you want to receive a certificate from a parent CA. Fill in the appropriate text box. Click **Next**.

- **Send a certificate request to a parent CA**: If you have the parent CA available on the network, you can directly send the request by using the CA name (chosen during CA configuration) or the computer name. If the parent CA is online, click **Select** and find the CA in the provided list (see Figure 12-7).

- **Save a certificate request to file on the target machine**: This option allows you to create the request and store it in a file. This file then can be submitted to the parent CA, which in turn generates a file you can later import into this CA. This process is required for an offline parent CA.

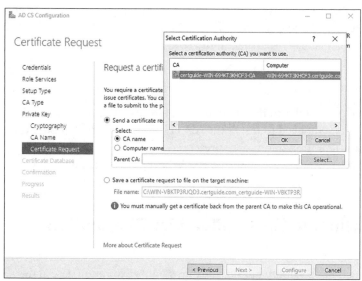

Figure 12-7 Selecting a CA to Issue a Signing Certificate to the Root CA. This Effectively Makes the Signing CA the Parent to the CA Being Configured.

Step 11.   Specify the locations on the file system to store the certificate database and the database log. Click **Next**.

Step 12.   Review your options on the confirmation page and click **Configure**.

Step 13.   Upon completion, the results page displays a **Configuration succeeded** message. Click **Close**.

The CA is now up and running and prepared to issue certificates upon request.

Installing Offline Root and Subordinate CAs

A root CA is at the top of the certificate infrastructure and generates a self-signed certificate. All other CAs are subordinate and rely on and trust that root CA. The certificate that subordinate CAs receive from the root allows them to issue certificates that are validated by the root CA, creating the CA hierarchy or trust path.

If the root CA were to have its security compromised in some fashion, any certificates issued by that root and its subordinates are effectively compromised as well. Certificates are used generally as an additional layer of security and protection for authorization and identification. Because the enterprise relies on this infrastructure, any compromise to its validity threatens large portions of the enterprise network.

To increase the security of the root CA, organizations often install the root as an offline CA. An offline CA is disconnected physically from the network at all times. By isolating the CA in this fashion, the risk of the private keys being compromised is reduced. Signing certificate requests consequently cannot be directly sent to an offline CA. Those requests are written to a file and copied to physical storage, which is manually carried to the offline CA. The offline CA writes its certificate to physical storage as well, which is manually returned to the requesting CA.

Because offline CAs are never attached to the network, there is no need to join them to the Active Directory domain.

Installing an offline CA is similar to the previous steps for installing an online root or subordinate CA. First you need to install the AD CS role and then configure the AD CS server. All configuration options are presented as described previously. For an offline CA, choose to install it as a standalone CA during Step 5 from the preceding list.

Configuring Certificate Revocation List Distribution Points

Every certificate issued has a validity period. It expires on its expiration date and time and is no longer trusted after that point. If a certificate needs to be forcefully expired before its expiration date, it can be revoked by the issuing CA. Certificates may need to be revoked for any of the following reasons:

- The certificate's private key has become compromised.

- The CA's private key has become compromised.

- The certificate was obtained fraudulently.

- The certificate subject (owner of the private key) is no longer trusted or has changed its name.

It won't always be possible to contact the issuing CA for direct confirmation of a certificate's validity. To enable alternate methods for a client to check the status of a certificate, AD CS supports publication of a certificate revocation list (CRL) and delta CRLs. These CRLs can be made available to clients from a wide range of different locations including Active Directory Domain Services (AD DS), web servers, and file system shares.

A CRL is a digitally signed complete list of all revoked certificates published on a regular basis. By default, AD CS publishes an updated CRL every seven days to all defined CRL distribution points (CDPs). CDPs are configured in the Certificate Authority snap-in and can target any of the previously mentioned locations. The full list of CDPs is included with each certificate when it is issued. This means that the certificate contains the information it needs to verify its revocation status, but it also means that changes to a CDP do not retroactively apply to previously issued certificates.

Over time, a CRL grows larger and becomes more unwieldly for a client to download in its entirety. To help reduce this workload, AD CS can also publish smaller CRLs called delta CRLs. A delta CRL contains only the revocations issued since the last regular CRL was published. These delta CRLs can be retrieved by the client and used to more quickly build a complete list of revoked certificates in the local environment. Delta CRLs can be published more frequently than regular CRLs since they are generally smaller and do not have as big an impact on the network.

Creating New CRL Distribution Points (CDPs)

To configure CRL distribution points:

Step 1.   Log on to a Windows Server Certificate Authority.

Step 2.   Start Server Manager from either the Start Menu or the Taskbar.

Step 3.   Select **Tools > Certification Authority**.

Step 4.   Right-click the node for the current CA and select **Properties**.

Step 5.   Select the **Extensions** tab.

Step 6.   From the **Select extension** drop-down list, choose **CRL Distribution Point (CDP)**.

Step 7.   The list is prepopulated with the default CDPs as well as any CDPs you have already added. Click **Add**.

Step 8.   In the **Location** text box, type one of the following types of location URLs (see Figure 12-8):

- **HTTP**: An endpoint on a CA Web Enrollment web server

- **LDAP**: A valid LDAP address in a directory

- **File**: A file path using the file:// protocol

- **UNC**: A network share

- **Local**: A local file path using the local drive letter

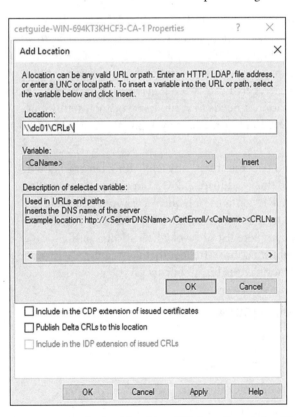

Figure 12-8   Setting Up a New CRL Location on the File System with the UNC Network Share Format

Step 9. From the **Variable** drop-down list, select **<CaName>** and click **Insert**.

Step 10. From the **Variable** drop-down list, select **<CRLNameSuffix>** and click **Insert**.

Step 11. The Location is now populated with the hardcoded portion of the URL you keyed plus additional fields used to uniquely identify the CDP. Click **OK**.

Step 12. With the new URL highlighted, check the boxes labeled **Publish CRLs to this location**, **Publish Delta CRLs to this location**, **Include in CRLs. Clients use this to find Delta CRL locations**, and **Include in the CDP extension of issued certificates**.

NOTE Some of the CDP configuration options are unavailable depending on the type of CDP URL typed in. For example, only LDAP URLs can choose **Include in all CRLs. Specifies where to publish in the Active Directory when publishing manually**.

Step 13. Click **OK**.

The CA now uses the additional CDP for publishing CRLs.

Installing and Configuring Online Responders

Traditional CRLs are consumed by the client in their entirety. When the client needs to check for revocation, it downloads the entire CRL (or the latest delta CRLs) and checks the certificate against the list. Since Windows Server 2008 and Windows Vista, AD CS has offered the ability to query an Online Responder with the certificate identifier to determine whether it is valid. An Online Responder is served as an HTTP service, hosted by IIS, and returns an up-to-date revocation status for a given certificate.

Using an Online Responder reduces the overall amount of network traffic, particularly as a CRL grows in size. The workload for the CDPs is also reduced; in a large enterprise environment with many certificates issued, these performance gains can be substantial.

An Online Responder can be installed on an existing CA or a server that does not yet have AD CS installed. Online Responders require Internet Information Services (IIS) to be installed, and you are prompted to configure that service when adding the Online Responder role service to AD CS.

To set up an Online Responder:

Step 1.   Log on to a Windows server.

Step 2.   Start Server Manager from either the Start Menu or the Taskbar.

Step 3.   Click **Manage > Add Roles and Features**.

Step 4.   Click **Next**.

Step 5.   Select **Role-based or feature-based installation** and click **Next**.

Step 6.   On the Server Selection page, ensure that the **Select a server from the server pool** option is chosen, and then click to highlight the current server from the list. Click **Next**.

Step 7.   If the server is already a CA, expand the AD CS node and select **Online Responder**; then click **Next** (see Figure 12-9).

Step 8.   If the server is not already a CA, check **Active Directory Certificate Services**.

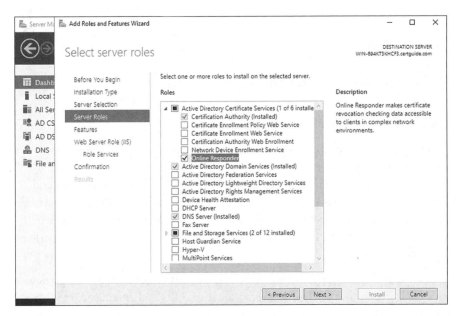

Figure 12-9   Selecting to Install the Online Responder Role in the AD CS Portion of the Server Roles

Step 9.   If prompted to **Add Features that are required...**, review the role services that must be installed for AD DS to work and ensure **Include management tools** is checked. Click **Add Features** to return to the Server Roles page and click **Next**.

Step 10.   Click **Next**.

Step 11.   Review the information on the AD CS page. Click **Next**.

If the server is not already a CA, the Role Services tab displays. Check the **Online Responder** box. If prompted to **Add Features that are required…**, review the role services that must be installed for AD DS to work and ensure **Include management tools** is checked. Click **Add Features** to return to the Role Services page and click **Next**.

Step 12.   The **Web Server Role (IIS)** page displays. Click **Next**.

Step 13.   Review the selected default Role Services for IIS. Click **Next** (see Figure 12-10).

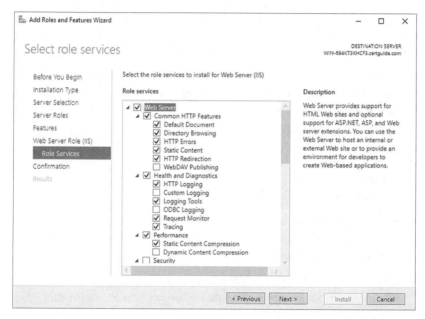

Figure 12-10   The IIS Configuration Page When Installing the Online Responder Role

Step 14.   Review the confirmation page for all the services and features you chose to install. Do not check the **Restart the destination server automatically** box if any other users are currently relying on the server. Click **Install**.

Step 15.   The server displays an installation progress page. Note the option at the bottom of the page to **Export configuration settings**, which generates an XML file you can use with PowerShell to install the exact same roles and features on another server.

Once an Online Responder has been installed, you must create a revocation configuration. A new configuration must be created for each certificate being revoked. The Revocation Configuration Wizard allows you to easily create the configuration, which includes the certificate that it reports the status for, as well as a CRL location where it can determine the current status. A revocation configuration also needs its own signing certificate so that the client can validate the authority of the Online Responder. Perform the following steps to create a revocation configuration:

Step 1. Log on to a Windows Server with the Online Responder service installed.

Step 2. Start Server Manager from either the Start Menu or the Taskbar.

Step 3. Click **Tools > Online Responder Management**.

Step 4. In the left-hand navigation pane, right-click **Revocation Configuration** and select **Add Revocation Configuration**.

Step 5. The Add Revocation Configuration Wizard launches. Click **Next**.

Step 6. Type a short descriptive name for the configuration. It is recommended to include the name of the CA in the configuration name to help identify it. Click **Next**.

Step 7. Choose the appropriate option for the certificate being revoked:

- **Select a certificate for an Existing enterprise CA**: If the signing CA is an enterprise CA on the domain, choose this option to find the certificate from the CA.

- **Select a certificate from the Local certificate store**: If the certificate is available in the Local certificate store on the server being configured, select this option.

- **Import certificate from a File**: If the certificate has been saved to file, such as from an offline CA, choose this option to import the certificate from that file.

Step 8. Depending on the choice from Step 7, one of three different certificate browsing dialogs displays. Select the certificate to revoke and click **Next**:

- **Existing enterprise CA**: You can choose to browse Active Directory for a certificate published in the directory, or choose to browse for a CA by the computer name (see Figure 12-11).

- **Local certificate store**: You can select a revocable certificate from the local store.

- **Import certificate**: You can browse the file system for the certificate file.

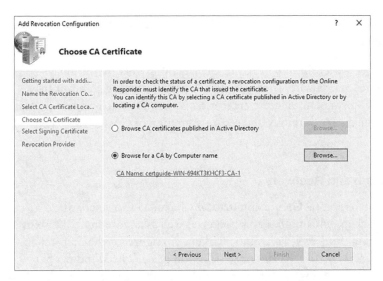

Figure 12-11   Configuring a Revocation, Selecting the Issuing CA by Computer Name for an Enterprise CA

Step 9.   Choose one of the following options for the revocation signing certificate:

- **Automatically select a signing certificate**: The Online Responder selects a signing certificate based on the issuer of the certificate being revoked.

- **Manually select a signing certificate**: The Online Responder does not assign any signing certificate, and the user manually selects a signing certificate.

- **Use the CA certificate for the revocation configured**: This can be selected if the Online Responder is installed on the same computer as the CA.

Step 10.   Click **Provider**.

Step 11.   Select a valid CRL from the list provided. The provider uses this CRL to determine the status of the certificate.

Step 12.   Click **OK**.

Step 13.   Click **Finish**.

The revocation configuration is now listed in the right-hand pane of the Online Responder utility.

Configuring CA Backup, Recovery, and Administrative Role Separation

Certificate authorities are a critical part of the security infrastructure for the network. A loss in service, particularly from issuing CAs, represents a significant risk. As with other critical technologies in the enterprise, a sound backup and recovery plan allows for business continuity and secure migration of CA services when needed.

Configuring CA Backup and Recovery

The settings and database for a CA are automatically included in a standard Windows Server Backup, both a full server backup as well as a more limited system state backup. Ensuring the server has routine backups configured is the first step in ensuring a sound disaster recovery plan for the CA is in place. The Windows Server Backup does not fit all scenarios, however. If the CA shares the server with other roles, rolling the server back wholesale may be too broad and interfere with other operations on the server. Windows Server Backup also cannot be used to migrate the CA to a new server if the need arises.

The Certificate Authority console has built-in backup and recovery features that can be used alongside standard Windows Server Backup. The user must have been assigned Manage CA permissions to perform this operation. The two options for backing up from the CA console are

- **Private Key and CA certificate**: This backs up the CA's public and private keys and the self-signed certificate used when the CA was installed. This can be used to restore the CA on a new computer if the current host fails.

- **Certificate database and certificate database log**: The database allows you to back up and restore certificates that have been issued by the CA.

To back up the CA:

Step 1.   Log on to a Windows CA server.

Step 2.   Start Server Manager from either the Start Menu or the Taskbar.

Step 3.   Click **Tools > Certification Authority**.

Step 4.   In the left-hand navigation pane, right-click the server to back up and select **All Tasks > Back up CA**.

Step 5.   Click **Next**.

Step 6.   On the Items to Back Up page, select one or both of the options as described previously. Checking the **Perform incremental backup** box only backs up changes in the database since the previous backup was performed. If this is the first backup, the option will be grayed out (see Figure 12-12).

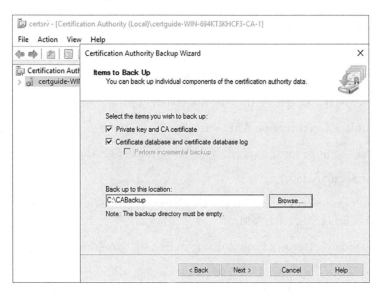

Figure 12-12 Selecting Which Items to Back Up in the CA Backup Wizard

Step 7. Type a location on the file system to save the backup files to, or click **Browse** to navigate to it.

Step 8. Click **Next**.

Step 9. Type a password to encrypt the exported certificate file. This password is needed to restore the file either on this server or on a new server. Click **Next**.

Step 10. Review the details and click **Finish**.

The file location chosen in Step 7 now has the backup. A restore can be performed from the same context menu.

Administrative Role Separation

By default, members of the following built-in Active Directory Domain Services groups can manage a CA:

- Domain Admins
- Enterprise Admins
- Local Administrators

One of the first tasks you should perform is to establish additional security groups for the management of the CA. Once that is complete you can delegate different CA management tasks to those groups, and by extension members of those groups, instead of having to add users to the powerful groups from the preceding list.

To delegate permissions:

Step 1.   Log on to a Windows Server Certificate Authority.

Step 2.   Start Server Manager from either the Start Menu or the Taskbar.

Step 3.   Select **Tools > Certification Authority**.

Step 4.   Right-click the node for the current CA and select **Properties**.

Step 5.   Select the **Security** tab.

Step 6.   The default groups are listed. To add an additional group (it must already exist in the directory), click **Add**.

Step 7.   Use the standard directory browse dialog to find the group to add.

Step 8.   In the box shown in Figure 12-13, select the permissions for the group as described in the following list.

Figure 12-13   Available Permissions for Users and Groups in the CA Console Security Tab

- **Read**: Users with this permission can launch the CA console and view the details but not perform any tasks.

- **Issue and Manage Certificates**: Users with this permission can issue new certificates and revoke existing certificates.

- **Manage CA**: Users with this permission can perform full CA management, including backup and recovery.

- **Request Certificates**: Users with this permission can request a certificate from the CA. By default all authenticated users have this permission.

Step 9.   Click **OK**.

Exam Preparation Tasks

As mentioned in the section "Book Features" in the Introduction, you have a few choices for exam preparation: the exercises here; Chapter 17, "Final Preparation"; and the exam simulation questions in the Pearson Test Prep Software Online.

Review All Key Topics

Review the most important topics in this chapter, noted with the Key Topics icon in the outer margin of the page. Table 12-2 lists a reference of these key topics and the page number on which each is found.

Table 12-2   Key Topics for Chapter 12

Key Topic Element	Description	Page Number
Paragraph	Description of CA hierarchy in Windows	320
Figure 12-2	Choosing between an enterprise CA or a standalone CA	323
Figure 12-3	Choosing between a root CA or a subordinate CA	323
Figure 12-7	Selecting a CA to issue a signing certificate to the root CA	327
Paragraph	Description of offline CA	328
Paragraph	Description of a CRL	329
List	The types of CRL distribution points that can be configured	330
Paragraph	Description of an Online Responder	331
Paragraph	Description of a revocation configuration	334
List	Configuring backup from the CA console	336
List	The permissions available for users and groups in the CA console	339

Complete Tables and Lists from Memory

There are no memory tables in this chapter.

Define Key Terms

Define the following key terms from this chapter and check your answers in the glossary:

certificate, certificate authority (CA), enterprise CA, standalone CA, root CA, subordinate CA, offline CA, certificate revocation list (CRL), CRL distribution point (CDP), Online Responder, revocation configuration

End-of-Chapter Review Questions

The answers to these questions appear in Appendix A. For more practice with exam format questions, use the Pearson Test Prep Software Online.

1. The IT Risk department is concerned about the enterprise root CA being domain joined and connected to the network. They would prefer to have a disconnected CA stored in a secured location without network access. What would be the best way to satisfy this requirement?

   a. Convince the risk department that the security features on the network offer as robust security as possible and there is no need to disconnect the server.

   b. Start up a new offline root CA and new subordinate CAs. Revoke all existing certificates and issue new certificates from the new servers.

   c. Start up a new offline root CA. Migrate the current root CA to that new server via physical media. Uninstall the CA role on the old enterprise root CA.

   d. Configure item-level targeting for the policy preferences in question to filter them down to the appropriate users.

2. The remote office needs its own issuing CA for times when its connectivity to the main office is interrupted. What would be the best way to accommodate this request?

   a. Install a subordinate CA at the remote location, and issue a signing certificate from the root CA at the main office.

   b. Install a root CA at the remote location, and allow them to manage their own certificate chain.

   c. Provide redundant network connectivity to reduce the incidence of network interruption.

   d. Adopt business practices that can deal with intermittent connectivity to an issuing CA.

3. IT staff at the remote location need permissions to manage the on-site subordinate CA, including issuing certificates and backing up the certificate database. How would you grant the necessary rights?

   a. Install a new root CA at the remote location, and allow the remote staff to manage their own certificate chain.

   b. Add the remote IT staff to the Domain Admins or Enterprise Admin security groups on the domain.

   c. Add the remote IT staff to the security groups currently delegated with permissions to the root CA.

   d. Create new security groups for managing the subordinate CA and assign the remote staff to those groups. Delegate permissions on the remote CA to those security groups.

- **Managing Certificate Templates**: This section explains the role that certificate templates play in issuing certificates and how to enable and create templates.

- **Managing Certificate Deployment, Validation, Revocation, and Renewal**: This section describes how to deploy certificates, renew them after expiration, validate certificates, and manually revoke them prior to expiration.

- **Managing Certificate Autoenrollment Using Group Policies**: This section describes how to use Group Policy Objects to automatically enroll and issue certificates to users and computers.

- **Configuring Key Archival and Recovery**: This section describes how to save and archive certificate keys so that a certificate can be re-created and recovered in the event it is lost or corrupted.

CHAPTER 13

Managing Certificates

Once Active Directory Certificate Services (AD CS) has been installed and properly configured, you need to establish a strategy for issuing and revoking certificates. An advantage that AD CS has over third-party CA software is that it is tightly coupled with Active Directory Domain Services (AD DS), allowing not only security to be managed through AD DS but also automation of certificate management.

In this chapter you learn how to use certificate templates to control the properties of issued certificates and how to automate certificate deployment, renewal, and revocation. Using Group Policy for certificate management is also covered.

"Do I Know This Already?" Quiz

The "Do I Know This Already?" quiz allows you to assess whether you should read this entire chapter thoroughly or jump to the "Exam Preparation Tasks" section. If you are in doubt about your answers to these questions or your own assessment of your knowledge of the topics, read the entire chapter. Table 13-1 lists the major headings in this chapter and their corresponding "Do I Know This Already?" quiz questions. You can find the answers in Appendix A, "Answers to the 'Do I Know This Already?' Quizzes."

Table 13-1 "Do I Know This Already?" Section-to-Question Mapping

Foundation Topics Section	Questions
Managing Certificate Templates	1-2
Managing Certificate Deployment, Validation, Revocation, and Renewal	3-4
Managing Certificate Autoenrollment Using Group Policies	5-6
Configuring Key Archival and Recovery	7

CAUTION   The goal of self-assessment is to gauge your mastery of the topics in this chapter. If you do not know the answer to a question or are only partially sure of the answer, you should mark that question as wrong for purposes of the self-assessment. Giving yourself credit for an answer you correctly guess skews your self-assessment results and might provide you with a false sense of security.

1. Which tool is used to view and modify existing certificate templates?

    a. Certificate Template console

    b. Certification Authority console

    c. Server Manager

    d. Certificates MMC snap-in

2. Which step must first be performed when deploying the default certificate templates in Active Directory?

    a. Delegate permissions to the templates.

    b. Enable the templates.

    c. Archive the certificate keys.

    d. Create the templates.

3. Requesting a certificate via the CA Web Enrollment interface is a form of which type of enrollment?

    a. Group Policy enrollment

    b. Autoenrollment

    c. Manual enrollment

    d. Certificate Enrollment Web Service

4. Which step should you perform if you suspect the security of a certificate has been compromised?

    a. Migrate the issuing CA to a new server.

    b. Revoke the certificate.

    c. Reinstall the issuing CA with a new private key.

    d. Renew the certificate.

5. Which Active Directory service implements autoenrollment?

    a. Internet Information Services

    b. Rights Management Services

    c. Directory Services

    d. Group Policy

6. Which directory objects can take advantage of autoenrollment?

    a. Users

    b. Computers

    c. Both

    d. Neither

7. Which additional certificate type is needed to enable key archival?

    a. Key Recovery Agent Certificate

    b. Computer Certificate

    c. OCSP Certificate

    d. User Certificate

Foundation Topics

Managing Certificate Templates

Certificate templates represent a preset collection of properties that a certificate based on that template uses. Enterprise root and subordinate CAs can issue certificates based on a template to requesting entities. You can edit the properties of a template at any time, which affects the properties of certificates based on that template going forward but does not impact previously issued certificates.

> **NOTE**   Certificate templates are only available on enterprise CAs. Standalone CAs cannot use templates as they are stored in the AD DS directory.

Enabling Certificate Templates

A new CA comes installed with a small number of templates installed by default. Active Directory has a larger number of templates that are accessible only after they have been enabled for a given CA. Enabling a template for one CA does not enable it on other CAs in the domain. Once a template has been enabled for a CA, it can be used when issuing new certificates.

To enable a template for a CA:

Step 1.   Log on to a Windows server certificate authority.

Step 2.   Start Server Manager from either the Start Menu or the Taskbar.

Step 3.   Select **Tools > Certification Authority**.

Step 4.   In the left-hand navigation pane, expand the node for the CA you want to manage.

Step 5.   In the left-hand navigation pane, select the **Certificate Templates** node.

Step 6.   The currently enabled templates are listed on the right-hand side of the console (see Figure 13-1).

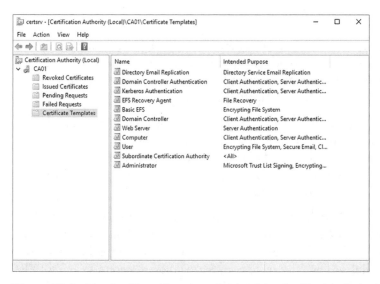

Figure 13-1   The Certificate Templates Node of the Certification Authority, Listing All the Default Templates Available for Enrollment

Step 7.   Right-click the **Certificate Templates** node and select **New > Certificate Template to Issue**.

Step 8.   The Enable Certificate Templates dialog displays with the available templates listed. Select the template to add to the CA and click **OK** (see Figure 13-2).

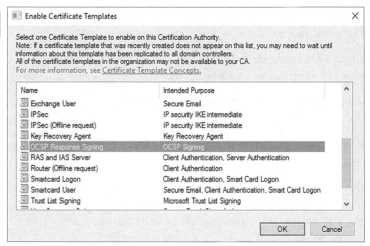

Figure 13-2   Selecting a New Certificate Template to Be Available for Issue by a CA

The template is now available for use from the CA.

Creating New Templates

If you want to create a new certificate template, you must duplicate one of the existing templates. This is done using the Certificates Template console. When creating a new template, you must ensure the compatibility settings are appropriate for your enterprise infrastructure. The two compatibility settings are

- **Certification Authority**: This setting represents the minimum required Windows Server version of a CA that will potentially issue certificates based on this template. If you have earlier versions of Windows running as enterprise CAs, this setting must match or precede those versions. Windows Server 2003 is the oldest supported version.

- **Certificate Recipient**: This setting represents the minimum required Windows Server or Desktop version of the receiving machine for certificates based on this template. If you have servers or clients running earlier versions of Windows, this setting must match or precede those versions. Windows XP/ Server 2003 is the oldest supported version.

To create a new template:

Step 1.   Log on to a Windows server certificate authority.

Step 2.   Start Server Manager from either the Start Menu or the Taskbar.

Step 3.   Select **Tools > Certification Authority**.

Step 4.   In the left-hand navigation pane, expand the node for the CA you want to manage.

Step 5.   In the left-hand navigation pane, right-click the **Certificate Templates** node and select **Manage**.

Step 6.   The Certificate Template console launches. Right-click a template to duplicate and select **Duplicate Template**.

Step 7.   The New Template properties dialog opens. Select the **Compatibility** tab.

Step 8.   Select the minimum CA compatibility from the **Certification Authority** drop-down list (see Figure 13-3).

Step 9.   If you choose a higher level than the source template, you may be prompted with new template options that become available. Similarly, if you lower the minimum, you may be prompted with template options that are being removed.

Step 10.   Select the minimum client compatibility from the **Certificate recipient** drop-down list (see Figure 13-3).

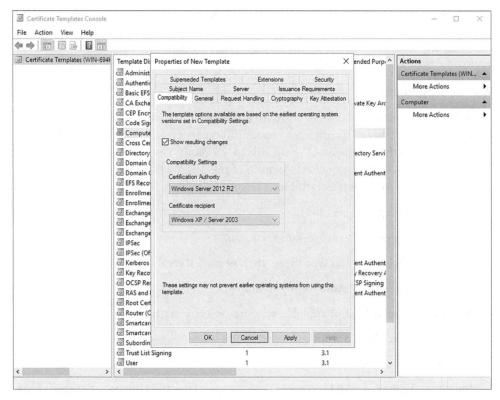

Figure 13-3   The Compatibility Tab of the Certificate Template Properties Dialog When Duplicating a Template

Step 11.   Select the **General** tab.

Step 12.   Type a display name for the template in the **Template display name** box. The **Template name** automatically fills in.

Step 13.   Make any additional property changes you want to make.

Step 14.   Click **OK**.

The new template is now available in the console and can be added to the CA using the preceding steps.

Managing Certificate Deployment, Validation, Revocation, and Renewal

The majority of work done by AD CS is certificate management. You want to configure your CA infrastructure to deploy or issue certificates to requesting entities as needed in a controlled and automated fashion. AD CS allows for both manual certificate deployment as well as automated deployment through something known as *autoenrollment*.

Manual Enrollment

When the requesting device or software does not support autoenrollment, you can manually generate a certificate request. Requests are generated on the client machine, and the enterprise CA responds to the request by issuing a certificate to the client. You use the Certificate snap-in of the Microsoft Management Console (MMC) client to request a certificate.

To manually request a certificate:

Step 1.   Log on to a domain-joined computer.

Step 2.   Click **Start** and type **mmc**; then press **Enter**.

Step 3.   Click **File > Add/Remove Snap-in**.

Step 4.   From the list of available snap-ins, select **Certificates** and click **Add**.

Step 5.   Select **My user account** and click **Finish**.

Step 6.   Click **OK**.

Step 7.   In the left-hand navigation pane, expand the **Certificate – Current User** node.

Step 8.   Right-click the **Personal** node and select **All Tasks > Request New Certificate**.

Step 9.   Click **Next**.

Step 10. Ensure **Active Directory Enrollment Policy** is highlighted, and click **Next**.

Step 11. A list of available source templates for the policy is displayed (see Figure 13-4). Check the **User** box and click **Enroll**.

Step 12. When the certificate has finished installing, click **Finish**.

The certificate has been manually requested and issued. You can verify it is in the local certificate store from the Certificates snap-in in MMC. Expand the **Certificates – Current User / Personal / Certificates** node. The issued certificate is listed with an Issued By the name of the CA.

You can also view the issued certificate in the Certificate Authority console **Issued Certificates** node.

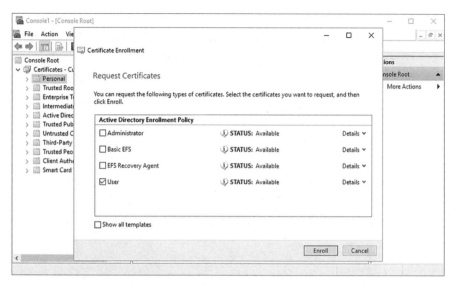

Figure 13-4   Selecting a Certificate Template for a Certificate Request. If the Template Does Not Require Manual Validation, It Will Be Automatically Issued After the User Clicks **Enroll**.

CA Web Enrollment

As an alternative to manual enrollment via the certificates snap-in for MMC, AD CS supports web enrollment. This role service provides a set of web pages that allow a user to interact with and request a certificate from a CA. To use CA web enrollment, you must install the role service with the Add Roles and Services Wizard. Once that's done, the CA server is available at the URL http://<servername>/certsrv.

To install the role service:

Step 1.   Log on to a Windows server.

Step 2.   Start Server Manager from either the Start Menu or the Taskbar.

Step 3.   Click **Manage > Add Roles and Features**.

Step 4.   Click **Next**.

Step 5.   Select **Role-based or feature-based installation** and click **Next**.

Step 6.   On the Server Selection page, ensure that the **Select a server from the server pool** option is chosen, and then click to highlight the current server from the list. Click **Next**.

Step 7.   If the server is already a CA, expand the AD CS node and select **Online Responder**; then click **Next**.

Step 8. If the server is not already a CA, check **Active Directory Certificate Services**; otherwise, expand **Active Directory Certificate Services** and check the **Certification Authority Web Enrollment** box (see Figure 13-5).

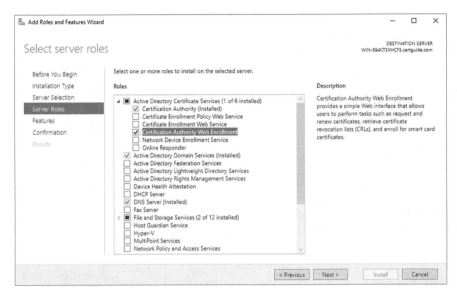

Figure 13-5 Selecting the Certification Authority Web Enrollment Role Service in the Add Roles and Features Wizard

Step 9. If prompted to **Add Features that are required…**, review the role services that must be installed for AD DS to work and ensure **Include management tools** is checked. Click **Add Features** to return to the Server Roles page and click **Next**.

Step 10. Click **Next**.

Step 11. Review the information on the AD CS page. Click **Next**.

If the server is not already a CA, the Role Services tab displays. Check the **Certificate Authority Web Enrollment** box. If prompted to **Add Features that are required…**, review the role services that must be installed for AD DS to work and ensure **Include management tools** is checked. Click **Add Features** to return to the Role Services page and click **Next**.

Step 12. If IIS was not previously installed (for instance, from the Online Responder role), the **Web Server Role (IIS)** page displays. Click **Next**.

Step 13. Review the selected default role services for IIS. Click **Next**.

Step 14. Review the confirmation page for all the services and features you chose to install. Do not check the **Restart the destination server automatically** box if any other users are currently relying on the server. Click **Install**.

Step 15. The server displays an installation progress page. Note the option at the bottom of the page to **Export configuration settings,** which generates an XML file you can use with PowerShell to install the exact same roles and features on another server.

Installing CA web enrollment is only the first step. Once the server successfully runs the Add Roles and Features Wizard, you are prompted with a link to **Configure Active Directory Certificate Services on the destination server**. If you want to perform the configuration at a later point, click **Close**. The following list outlines the steps to configure AD CS.

Step 1. Click the link to **Configure Active Directory Certificate Services on the destination server**. This launches the Active Directory Certificate Services Configuration Wizard.

Step 2. Review the information provided. If you are not signed in as a member of the Enterprise Admins group, click **Change** and provide credentials for a valid user.

Step 3. Click **Next**.

Step 4. Review the available role services. Select the **Certification Authority Web Enrollment** box. Note that if there exists no other CAs in the forest, other options may not be available. Click **Next**.

Step 5. Click **Configure**.

Step 6. When the configuration is complete, click **Close**.

To request a certificate from the CA web enrollment server:

Step 1. Log on to a domain-joined computer.

Step 2. Launch a web browser and navigate to http://*<servername>*/certsrv, where *<servername>* is the name of the server where the CA Web Enrollment Role Service was installed (see Figure 13-6).

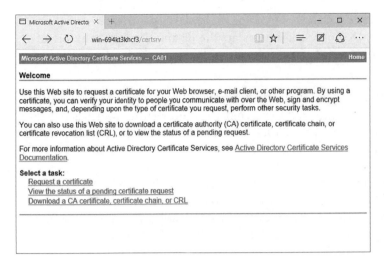

Figure 13-6   The CA Web Enrollment Main Page

Step 3.   Click **Request a certificate**.

Step 4.   Click **User Certificate**.

Step 5.   Click **Submit**.

Step 6.   When the certificate-issued page displays, click **Install this certificate**.

Revoking Certificates

When you revoke a certificate, you are effectively declaring it no longer trustworthy. There are various reasons you might want to revoke a certificate. The CA console allows you to choose from a fixed list of reasons when you revoke.

To revoke a certificate:

Step 1.   Log on to a Windows server certificate authority.

Step 2.   Start Server Manager from either the Start Menu or the Taskbar.

Step 3.   Select **Tools > Certification Authority**.

Step 4.   In the left-hand navigation pane, expand the node for the CA.

Step 5.   Select the **Issued Certificates** node.

Step 6.   In the details pane, right-click a certificate and choose **All Tasks > Revoke Certificate**.

Step 7. In the revocation dialog, choose a reason from the **Reason code** drop-down list (see Figure 13-7).

Step 8. The Date and Time stamp defaults to the current date and time. You can choose a future date and time if you want to delay the revocation.

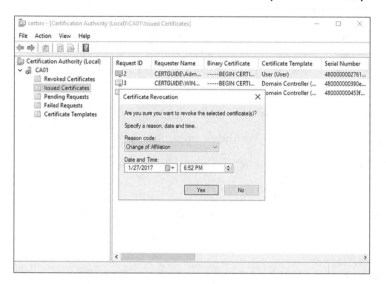

Figure 13-7 Specifying the Reason and Date and Time for a Certificate Revocation

Step 9. Click **Yes**.

The certificate is no longer listed in the **Issued Certificates** node and instead can be found in the **Revoked Certificates** node.

The certificate is not immediately visible in the certificate revocation list (CRL) or delta CRL. The CRL is only updated once every seven days by default, and the delta CRL once every 24 hours. If you want to have the CRL updated sooner, right-click the **Revoked Certificates** node and select **All Tasks > Publish**. From there, you can choose to publish a new CRL in its entirety or just a delta CRL.

Managing Certificate Autoenrollment Using Group Policies

Manual enrollment allows individuals to request and receive certificates from a CA on a one-by-one basis. There are a variety of use cases where manual enrollment is not feasible. Users may not be technically trained enough to work through the process, or there may be a need to issue certificates to computers. In the case of many thousands of certificates that need to be issued, manual enrollment will be time consuming and error prone.

The AD CS feature autoenrollment allows for Group Policy to issue certificates to users and computers without any interaction required. Once configured, certificates are issued to users or computers during the following Group Policy update.

Configuring autoenrollment is a two-step process. First you create a new certificate template and enable autoenrollment on the certificate for the appropriate domain security groups. Once that is complete, you create a GPO to autoenroll domain users or computers.

To create an autoenrollment certificate:

Step 1. Log on to a Windows server certificate authority.

Step 2. Start Server Manager from either the Start Menu or the Taskbar.

Step 3. Select **Tools > Certification Authority**.

Step 4. In the left-hand navigation pane, expand the node for the CA.

Step 5. In the left-hand navigation pane, right-click **Certificate Templates** and choose **Manage**.

Step 6. In the Certificate Templates Console details pane, right-click the **Computer** certificate template and select **Duplicate Template**.

> **NOTE** The prebuilt templates do not have the autoenroll security option available. You must create a new template to create an autoenrollment certificate.

Step 7. Select the **Security** tab.

Step 8. Highlight the **Domain Computers** group in the **Group or user names** box.

Step 9. In the **Permissions** view, ensure the boxes are checked for **Read**, **Enroll**, and **Autoenroll** (see Figure 13-8).

Step 10. Select the **General** tab.

Step 11. Type a description display name in the **Template display name** box.

Step 12. Adjust any other properties as needed and click **OK**.

Step 13. Close the Certificate Templates console.

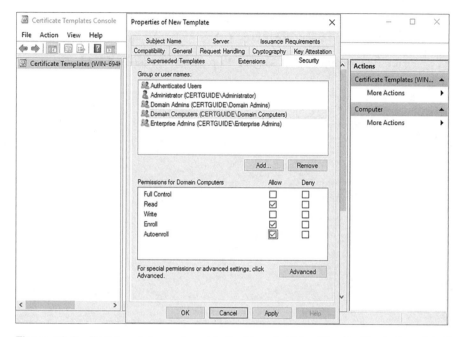

Figure 13-8 Enabling Autoenrollment in the Security Tab of the Certificate Template Properties Dialog When Duplicating a Template

Step 14. In the CA console, right-click **Certificate Templates** and select **New > Certificate Template to Issue**.

Step 15. Select the certificate you just created and click **OK**.

To configure a Group Policy Object to issue the autoenrollment certificate:

Step 1. Log on to a writeable domain controller.

Step 2. Launch Server Manager.

Step 3. Click **Tools** > **Group Policy Management**.

Step 4. In the left-hand navigation pane, expand the **Domains** node and then the node for your domain.

Step 5. Create a new GPO or select an existing one.

Step 6. Right-click the GPO and select **Edit**.

Step 7. In the left-hand navigation pane, browse to **Computer Configuration > Policies > Windows Settings > Security Settings > Public Key Policies**.

Step 8.   In the details pane, right-click **Certificate Services Client – Auto-Enrollment** and select **Properties**.

Step 9.   From the **Configuration Model** drop-down list, select **Enabled** (see Figure 13-9).

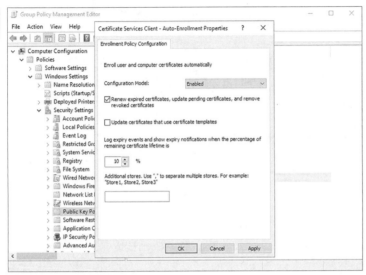

Figure 13-9   The Auto-Enrollment Properties Feature of a Group Policy Object

Step 10.   Check the box labeled **Renew expired certificates, update pending certificates, and remove revoked certificates**. This ensures that updates and changes to the certificate including renewals and revocation are deployed automatically as well.

Step 11.   Click **OK**.

Step 12.   Close the Group Policy Management Editor.

Any object that is included in a link for that GPO and is in the security group enabled for autoenroll on the certificate template now receives the certificate during its next Group Policy update.

Configuring Key Archival and Recovery

The backup and recovery options covered in Chapter 12, "Installing and Configuring Active Directory Certificate Services," help with recovering a CA when it fails or needs to be migrated in some fashion. Certificates themselves can be archived for recovery. In the case of a lost or corrupted certificate, you may not want to reissue a new certificate based on the same template but rather recover or reissue the same certificate.

Key archival allows for this. Key archival is configured at the CA level, both on the CA itself as well as in the certificate template. Once archival has been set up, the CA manages and maintains an archive of keys for the templates that engage in archival. In the event a certificate is lost, a Key Recovery Agent (KRA) can use the archived key to reissue the certificate.

Setting up key archival is a three-step process. First, you must create a KRA certificate and enroll a user or users. Second, you must turn on key archival for a CA. Finally, you configure a new certificate template with key archival.

To create a KRA certificate:

Step 1.   Log on to a Windows server certificate authority.

Step 2.   Start Server Manager from either the Start Menu or the Taskbar.

Step 3.   Select **Tools > Certification Authority**.

Step 4.   In the left-hand navigation pane, expand the node for the CA.

Step 5.   In the left-hand navigation pane, right-click **Certificate Templates** and choose **Manage**.

Step 6.   In the Certificate Templates console details pane, right-click the **Key Recovery Agent** certificate template and select **Duplicate Template**.

Step 7.   Select the **General** tab (see Figure 13-10).

Step 8.   Type a descriptive display name in the **Template display name** box.

Step 9.   Select the **Security** tab.

Step 10.   Click **Add** and find any security groups you want to have KRA capabilities.

Step 11.   Select each of those added users or groups and check the **Read**, **Write**, and **Enroll** boxes (see Figure 13-11).

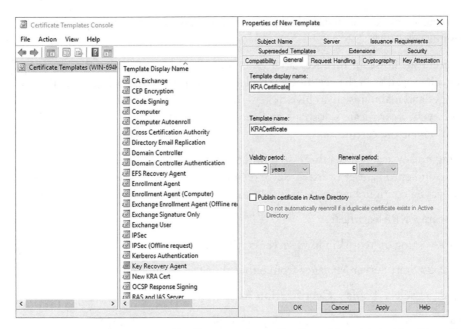

Figure 13-10   Duplicating the Key Recovery Agent Certificate Template to Use When Setting Up a KRA for Key Archival

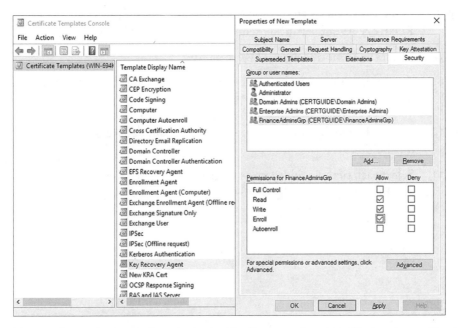

Figure 13-11   Setting Up Security for the Key Recovery Agent Certificate. Groups Granted Enroll Permission Are Allowed to Operate as KRAs.

NOTE It is recommended that you do not use autoenrollment for KRA certificates to increase the security and control over key recovery.

Step 12. Adjust any other properties as needed and click **OK**.

Step 13. Close the Certificate Templates Console.

Step 14. In the CA console right-click **Certificate Templates** and select **New > Certificate Template to Issue**.

Step 15. Select the certificate you just created and click **OK**.

Log on to a domain-joined computer with one of the users added in Step 10 and manually request and install the new certificate. The next step to enable key archival for a CA cannot be completed until an agent has received the certificate.

NOTE The KRA certificate template has the **CA certificate manager approval** options selected by default in the **Issuance Requirements** tab. If you did not uncheck that option when duplicating the template, any requests for the KRA certificate you create need to be manually approved in the CA console under the **Pending Certificates** node.

To enable key archival for a CA:

Step 1. Log on to a Windows server certificate authority.

Step 2. Start Server Manager from either the Start Menu or the Taskbar.

Step 3. Select **Tools > Certification Authority**.

Step 4. In the left-hand navigation pane, right-click the name of the CA and select **Properties**.

Step 5. Select the **Recovery Agents** tab.

Step 6. In the **Number of recovery agents to use** box, select the number of KRAs used to archive and potentially recover the key. This cannot be higher than the number of KRA certificates that have been issued.

Step 7. Click **Add**.

Step 8. Select the certificate(s) issued for the KRAs (see Figure 13-12).

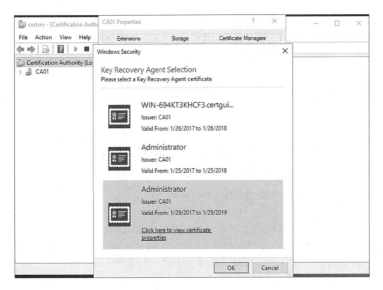

Figure 13-12 Selecting a Certificate for a KRA to Use When Archiving Keys

Step 9. Click **OK** to close the KRA certificate selection window.

Step 10. Click **OK** to close the CA properties dialog.

Step 11. You are prompted to restart AD CS. Click **Yes**.

Step 12. The status of the certificates selected for KRA should now be Valid (see Figure 13-13).

The final step is to enable key archival for a certificate. This is done in the certificate template when duplicating a template. Under the **Request Handling** tab, check the **Archive subject's encryption private key** box. This causes the CA to archive the key, encrypted by the KRAs chosen previously. Those agents can now recover any certificates issued from this template. Keys are not retroactively archived; only new certificates issued from this point forward will be archived.

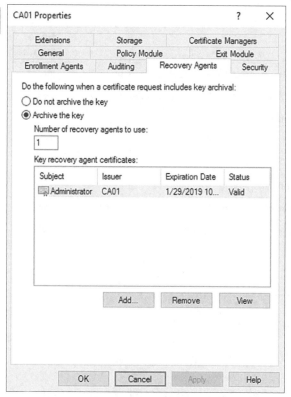

Figure 13-13   The Recovery Agents Tab of the CA Properties Dialog. This Page Shows One KRA Selected with a Valid Certificate.

Exam Preparation Tasks

As mentioned in the section "Book Features" in the Introduction, you have a few choices for exam preparation: the exercises here; Chapter 17, "Final Preparation"; and the exam simulation questions in the Pearson Test Prep Software Online.

Review All Key Topics

Review the most important topics in this chapter, noted with the Key Topics icon in the outer margin of the page. Table 13-2 lists a reference of these key topics and the page number on which each is found.

Table 13-2 Key Topics for Chapter 13

Key Topic Element	Description	Page Number
Figure 13-2	Selecting a new certificate template to be available for issue by a CA	347
List	Options for compatibility settings for certificate templates	348
Paragraph	Manual certificate enrollment	350
Paragraph	CA web enrollment	351
Steps	Revoking a certificate	354
Steps	Creating an autoenrollment certificate	356
Figure 13-9	The Auto-Enrollment properties feature of a Group Policy Object	358
Figure 13-13	The Recovery Agents tab of the CA properties dialog	363

Complete Tables and Lists from Memory

There are no memory tables in this chapter.

Define Key Terms

Define the following key terms from this chapter and check your answers in the glossary:

certificate template, enrollment, manual enrollment, autoenrollment, certificate revocation, key archival

End-of-Chapter Review Questions

The answers to these questions appear in Appendix A. For more practice with exam format questions, use the Pearson Test Prep Software Online.

1. You have been tasked with pushing out a new certificate for user identification to all users of the current VPN solution. How do you begin creating the certificate template?

   a. Creating certificate requests for each of the identified users

   b. Launching the Certificate Template console and duplicating the appropriate certificate template

   c. Modifying the user objects in Active Directory to include the certificate request

   d. Adding the users to the certificate authority for the requested template

2. Which local service would you instruct the users to use to manually request their new certificates?

3. Rather than have all the users manually request certificates, you decide it best to autoenroll the users. Which steps are necessary to implement this? (Choose three.)

    a. Add the users to a security group and give that group autoenrollment permissions on the Security tab of the Properties dialog for the certificate template.

    b. Create a GPO and enable the autoenrollment feature in the User Configuration section.

    c. Edit the user objects in the directory to associate them with the certificate template.

    d. Link the GPO to ensure it is applied to the appropriate users.

4. You enable key archival for the certificate template, but it does not appear that the keys are actually being archived. Which steps might you have missed? (Choose two.)

    a. Enabling archival for the template in the AD DS directory.

    b. Duplicating the original template and creating a new certificate template.

    c. Create a Key Recovery Agent (KRA) certificate and issue that to a recovery user.

    d. Configure the archival properties of the CA to use the issued KRA certificate.

- **Implementing Claims-Based Authentication**: This section describes how to install and configure Active Directory Federation Services (AD FS) to enable claims-based authentication.

- **Configuring Authentication**: This section describes how to enable and configure authentication policies on the AD FS server, including multifactor authentication.

- **Implementing and Configuring Device Registration**: This section describes how to allow domain users to register their own devices, such as tablets and smartphones, for use with AD FS.

- **Integrating AD FS with Microsoft Passport**: This section describes how to set up Microsoft Passport for domain users with Group Policy Objects.

- **Configuring AD FS to Enable Authentication of Users Stored in LDAP Directories**: This section describes how to configure AD FS to connect to and authenticate users stored in third-party LDAP directories other than Active Directory.

CHAPTER 14

Installing and Configuring Active Directory Federation Services

It has become more and more common in recent years to see corporate services expand well beyond the traditional borders of the network. The heavy reliance on third-party cloud-based software, such as Office 365, and an increasingly mobile workforce means IT engineers need a way to expand authentication services beyond the network as well. Active Directory Federation Services (AD FS) is the service that does exactly that. AD FS is used to enable remote services to authenticate users without needing to maintain their own user account database. Instead, authentication requests are forwarded to the AD FS server, which in turn uses your organization's existing Active Directory Domain Services directory for authentication.

This chapter focuses on installing and configuring AD FS for authentication with third-party services such as Office 365. It covers the installation process for AD FS via Server Manager and shows how to configure basic authentication policies and enable multi-factor authentication (MFA) and Microsoft Passport.

"Do I Know This Already?" Quiz

The "Do I Know This Already?" quiz allows you to assess whether you should read this entire chapter thoroughly or jump to the "Exam Preparation Tasks" section. If you are in doubt about your answers to these questions or your own assessment of your knowledge of the topics, read the entire chapter. Table 14-1 lists the major headings in this chapter and their corresponding "Do I Know This Already?" quiz questions. You can find the answers in Appendix A, "Answers to the 'Do I Know This Already?' Quizzes."

Table 14-1   "Do I Know This Already?" Section-to-Question Mapping

Foundation Topics Section	Questions
Implementing Claims-Based Authentication	1-2
Configuring Authentication	3-4
Implementing and Configuring Device Registration	5
Integrating AD FS with Microsoft Passport	6
Configuring AD FS to Enable Authentication of Users Stored in LDAP Directories	7

CAUTION   The goal of self-assessment is to gauge your mastery of the topics in this chapter. If you do not know the answer to a question or are only partially sure of the answer, you should mark that question as wrong for purposes of the self-assessment. Giving yourself credit for an answer you correctly guess skews your self-assessment results and might provide you with a false sense of security.

1. What is the generic term for the role Active Directory Federation Services plays in a claims-based authentication scheme?

    a. Identity provider

    b. Relying party

    c. Service provider

    d. Client

2. Which database is recommended for a multiserver AD FS server farm?

    a. Windows Internal Database

    b. SQL Server

    c. Active Directory

    d. Microsoft Access

3. Which clients can use Windows authentication with AD FS?

    a. Intranet and extranet clients

    b. Extranet clients only

    c. Microsoft Passport clients only

    d. Intranet clients only

4. Which of the following are examples of multi-factor authentication? (Choose two.)

    a. Prompting the user for a password provided via SMS message along with a username and password.

    b. Prompting the user for a password provided via SMS message instead of a password

    c. Requiring the user to have been issued a digital certificate by a trusted party

    d. Requiring the user to possess a digitally signed smart card device along with a username and password

5. Which of the following OSes support Workplace Join for Active Directory? (Choose three.)

    a. Windows 8.1

    b. Windows 10

    c. Android 5.0

    d. Red Hat Enterprise Linux

6. How is Workplace Join enabled for computers on the network?

    a. With a logon script

    b. Using Administrative Templates in a GPO

    c. Manually on a case-by-case basis

    d. By pushing a download from the AD FS logon page

7. What is the PowerShell cmdlet to add a new LDAP server connection to AD FS?

    a. Add-ServerConnect

    b. Add-ADFS

    c. New-ServerConnection

    d. New-AdfsLdapServerConnection

Foundation Topics

Implementing Claims-Based Authentication

AD FS uses a methodology called claims-based authentication. In a claims-based system, there are three entities:

- The user or device trying to access a secure system

- The identity provider, which provides authentication services upon request

- The system that secures the system or data, known as the relying party because it relies upon, or trusts, the identity provider

Claims-based authentication gets its name from the digital tokens that the identity provider supplies. These tokens contain assertions about the user known as *claims*. A claim might be an email address or a list of security groups and is used by the relying party to authorize the user. For instance, a web-based accounting system may contain a list of security groups allowed to access the system. When a user attempts to access the service, which is the relying party in this example, it acquires a claim from the identity provider that includes a list of the security groups the user belongs to. As long as the user belongs to a security group that the relying party authorizes, the user will be granted access to the service.

Important in this methodology is that separation exists for authentication and authorization. To get a claim from the identity provider, the user must authenticate against the identity provider. Authorization to access the data, however, is controlled by the relying party, which can choose whether to trust the claim and whether the claim asserts the user has appropriate access.

Installing a Standalone AD FS Server

Claims-based authentication can span domains and forests, enabling a secure and scalable method for expanding authentication services beyond traditional network boundaries. In its simplest form, a standalone AD FS server acts as the provider for clients by communicating directly with the AD DS domain controller. This setup facilitates third-party software that is installed on your organization's network but either does not support direct AD DS authentication or is otherwise isolated from the domain and cannot directly authenticate.

AD FS can be installed on a domain controller, but it is recommended for security and reliability purposes that the AD FS role be isolated on its own server. The only requirement is the capability for AD FS to have HTTPS communication with a domain controller.

To install AD FS:

Step 1. Log on to a Windows server.

Step 2. Start Server Manager from either the Start Menu or the Taskbar.

Step 3. Click **Manage > Add Roles and Features**.

Step 4. Click **Next**.

Step 5. Select **Role-based or feature-based installation** and click **Next**.

Step 6. On the **Server Selection** page ensure that the **Select a server from the server pool** option is chosen, and then click to highlight the current server from the list. Click **Next**.

Step 7. Check the **Active Directory Federation Services** box and click **Next** (see Figure 14-1).

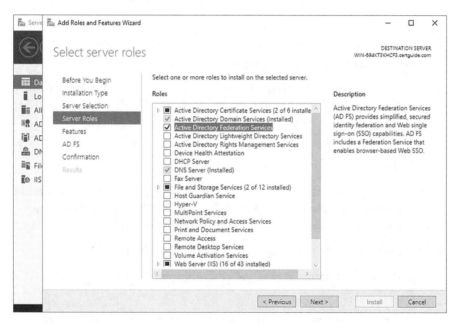

Figure 14-1 Installing the AD FS Server Role with the Add Roles and Features Wizard

Step 8. Click **Next**.

Step 9. Review the AD FS Role Service details page and click **Next**.

Step 10. Review the confirmation page and click **Install**.

The AD FS server must be configured after the role has been installed. Before you can configure AD FS, you need a managed service account for the AD FS service.

You also need a digital SSL certificate, which can be issued from a public provider or from your enterprise AD CS certification authority (CA). The SSL certificate must be exported to a Personal Information Exchange (.pfx) file and is then imported during AD FS configuration.

To obtain the SSL certificate:

Step 1.   Follow the steps outlined in the "Managing Certificate Templates" section in Chapter 13, "Managing Certificates," to duplicate the **Web Server** certificate template.

Step 2.   During duplication, select the **Request Handling** tab and check the **Allow private key to be exported** box.

Step 3.   Grant domain computers the permission to read and enroll this template. If you are on a domain controller, grant that permission to the computer explicitly. (Domain controllers are not in the domain computers security group.)

Step 4.   Follow the steps outlined in the "Managing Certificate Templates" section in Chapter 13 to assign the template to a CA.

Step 5.   Follow the steps outlined in the "Managing Certificate Deployment, Validation, Revocation, and Renewal" section in Chapter 13 to manually request a certificate from MMC. Use the options specified in the following Steps 6 through 17 when requesting the certificate.

Step 6.   Add the snap-in for the local computer account.

Step 7.   Find and request the certificate just created. Click the **More information is required to enroll for this certificate. Click here to configure settings** link immediately below the certificate (see Figure 14-2).

Step 8.   On the certificate properties dialog, select the **Subject** tab.

Step 9.   In the **Subject name** section, select **Common Name** from the **Type** drop-down list.

Step 10.   In the same section, type a name for the service in the **Value** text box. The service name is important when configuring AD FS and should be a DNS-safe value based on the domain name, for example, **fs.certguide. com**.

Step 11.   In the same section, click **Add**.

Step 12.   Repeat Steps 9 through 11 in the **Alternative name** section but for the **Type** select **DNS** (see Figure 14-3).

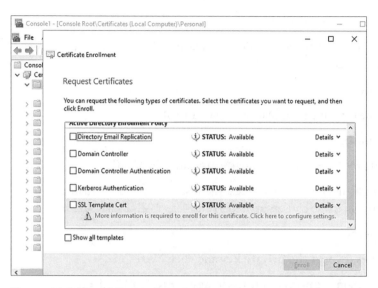

Figure 14-2 The SSL Template Certificate Requesting Additional Configuration Before Enrollment

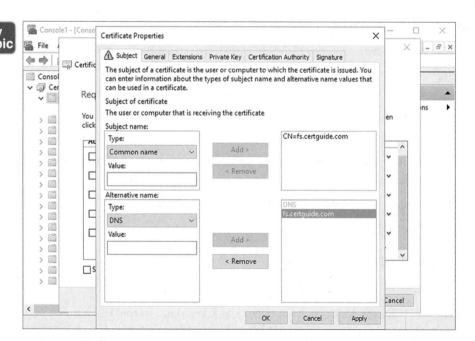

Figure 14-3 The SSL Template Certificate Subject Customized for Use with AD FS

Step 13.   Select the **Private Key** tab.

Step 14.   Expand the **Key Options** section and ensure **Make private key exportable** is selected.

Step 15.   Click **OK**.

Step 16.   Select the certificate template and click **Enroll**.

Step 17.   Click **Finish**.

Step 18.   Navigate to the **Personal / Certificates** node in MMC.

Step 19.   In the right-hand pane, right-click the installed certificate (named after the common name chosen in Step 9) and select **All Tasks > Export**.

Step 20.   Click **Next**.

Step 21.   Select **Yes, export the private key** and click **Next**.

Step 22.   Select **Personal Information Exchange – PKCS #12 (.PFX)**.

Step 23.   Check the **Include all certificates in the certification path if possible** box.

Step 24.   Check the **Export all extended properties** box.

Step 25.   Click **Next**.

Step 26.   Select **Password** and type and confirm a password to encrypt the .pfx file. Be sure to note the password; it is required to import the certificate into the AD FS server.

Step 27.   Click **Next**.

Step 28.   Type a path and filename to save the certificate to. It needs to be accessible to the AD FS server in the next section. Click **Next**.

Step 29.   Review the details and click **Finish**.

Step 30.   Click **OK**.

To configure AD FS:

Step 1.   Log on to the server where AD FS was installed.

Step 2.   Start Server Manager from either the Start Menu or the Taskbar.

Step 3.   Select the notifications from the top menu and click **Configure the federation service on this server**.

Step 4.   Review the details and click **Next**.

Step 5. Review the information provided. If you are not signed in as a member of the Domain Admins group, click **Change** and provide credentials for a valid user.

Step 6. Click **Next**.

Step 7. If this is a different computer than the SSL certificate was issued to, click **Import**. Browse to the .pfx file that was exported and click **Open**.

Step 8. If this computer already has the certificate installed, select it from the **SSL Certificate** drop-down box (see Figure 14-4).

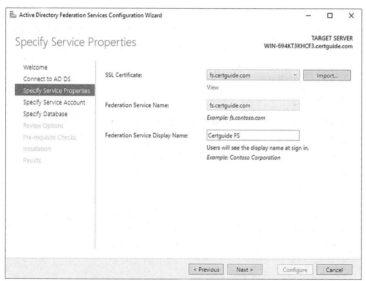

Figure 14-4 Configuring AD FS with an SSL Certificate

Step 9. The **Federation Service Name** populates automatically based on the certificate chosen. It cannot be changed for security purposes.

Step 10. In the **Federation Service Display Name** box, type a friendly display name that will appear on a login page.

Step 11. Click **Next**.

Step 12. Select **Create a Group Managed Service Account** and type a valid name for the account in the **Account Name** text box. Alternatively, you can use a preexisting account that has already been created.

Step 13. Click **Next**.

Step 14. Select one of the following two options and click **Next**.

- **Create a database on this server using Windows Internal Database**: This option creates a local database on the current server. It is an ideal solution for test environments and small implementations. If you have additional servers in the farm, they receive a read-only replica of this database and are required to submit any writes back to the original server.

- **Specify the location of a SQL Server database**: This option stores all AD FS configuration in an SQL Server database that is run and maintained elsewhere on the network. This option allows you to have multiple AD FS servers in a farm share a single data store. This option is ideal for most enterprise-level fault-tolerant implementations.

Step 15. Review your choices and click **Next**.

Step 16. Click **Configure**.

Step 17. When the configuration finishes, click **Close** to close the wizard. AD FS is now installed on the server.

Installing an AD FS Server Farm

In most enterprise deployments, a single standalone AD FS server is not adequate for either disaster recovery resiliency or high-load purposes. AD FS makes it easy to configure a group of AD FS servers on the network that share duties. This group is known as an AD FS server farm.

You can set up an AD FS server by first following the steps previously outlined in this chapter for installing and configuring AD FS on the first server. During the configuration of AD FS, select **Create the first federation server in a federation server farm**. Ensure the SSL certificate is available to be installed on each other server in the farm. Finally, create a group Managed Service Account for the FS service account. The remaining features on the server are configured in the same way as a standalone server. Once the first server in the farm has been configured, you can follow these steps to configure additional servers:

Step 1. Log on to a member server of the domain.

Step 2. Install the AD FS role as described previously.

Step 3. Launch the AD FS configuration wizard.

Step 4. Select **Add a federation server to a federation server farm** and click **Next** (see Figure 14-5).

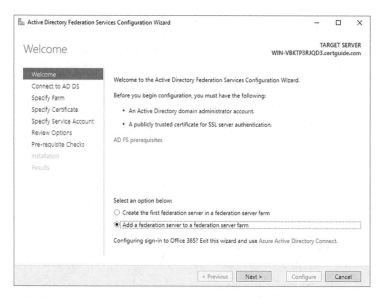

Figure 14-5   Configuring an Additional AD FS Server for an AD FS Farm

Step 5.   Review the information provided. If you are not signed in as a member of the Domain Admins group, click **Change** and provide credentials for a valid user.

Step 6.   Click **Next**.

Step 7.   Select to either find the farm by entering the domain name of the primary server in the farm or connecting to a shared SQL database. You can only choose the SQL database option if you chose an SQL database when setting up the first server in the farm. Click **Next**.

Step 8.   Import the same SSL certificate used when configuring the first server in the farm. Click **Next**.

Step 9.   Click **Select** and use the default directory search tool to find the group managed service account set up for the first server in the farm. Click **Next**.

Step 10.   Review your choices and click **Next**.

Step 11.   Click **Configure**.

Your server farm is now installed and configured.

Configuring Authentication

Once AD FS is installed and configured, you can manage discrete policies for authentication. Global authentication policies allow you to specify which forms of authentication are available for both intranet as well as extranet users. Multi-factor authentication allows you to define an additional method of authentication on top of a username and password such as a digital certificate or mobile app.

Configuring Authentication Policies

Global Authentication Policy is defined through the AD FS Management Console. The console is launched from the Server Manager. You can configure five methods of authentication in the policy:

- **Forms Authentication**: This method allows users to enter their credentials on a web page form to authenticate against the AD FS server. It is available for both intranet and extranet users.

- **Certificate Authentication**: With certificate authentication, the user must already have been issued a digital certificate that it presents when authenticating to the AD FS server. This method is available for both intranet and extranet users.

- **Windows Authentication**: Windows authentication allows credentials to be passed directly to the AD FS server from Internet Explorer. If the user is already logged in to the domain that AD FS is authenticating against, then IE uses the current Kerberos token to perform the login. Otherwise, IE presents a username and password dialog box and passes those credentials to AD FS. This method is only available for intranet users.

- **Device Authentication**: This method allows for hardware devices, such as mobile phones or tablets or even Internet-of-Things (IoT) devices, to authenticate against the AD FS server. This method is available for both intranet and extranet users.

- **Microsoft Passport Authentication**: Microsoft Passport allows users to maintain a single identity and sign-on for various web services and local applications. This authentication method allows users to use their Passport identity to authenticate to AD FS. This method is available for both intranet and extranet users.

To configure authentication policies:

Step 1.   Log on to the AD FS server.

Step 2.   Start Server Manager from either the Start Menu or the Taskbar.

Step 3.   Click **Tools > AD FS Management**.

Step 4.   The AD FS Management Console launches.

Step 5.   In the left-hand pane, navigate to **Service / Authentication Methods**.

Step 6.   Right-click **Authentication Methods** and select **Edit Primary Authentication Methods**.

Step 7.   Select the **Primary** tab.

Step 8.   The Edit Authentication Methods dialog presents two checklists. Enable and disable methods for intranet and extranet users by selecting the desired boxes in each list (see Figure 14-6).

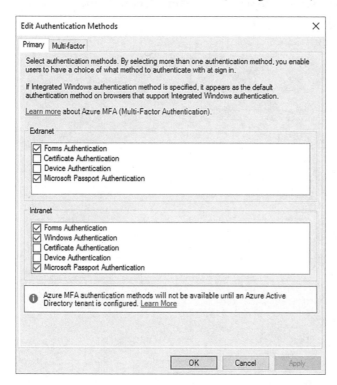

Figure 14-6   Primary Authentication Methods for Intranet and Extranet Users

Step 9.   Click **OK**.

Configuring Multi-Factor Authentication

Multi-factor authentication (MFA) is an authentication method that relies on two or more authentication methods to further validate a logon attempt. A common MFA method is to distribute an app to a user's mobile device. Not only is a username and password required when the user logs on (the first factor), but the user is also sent a one-time password to the mobile app that must be keyed in as well (the second factor). MFA is more secure because it is more difficult for multiple factors to become compromised in the event of a security breach.

MFA is configured in the same dialog as authentication policies. Launch the AD FS Management Console from Server Manager, expand the **Services** node, and right-click **Authentication Methods** to select **Edit Multi-factor Authentication Methods** (see Figure 14-7).

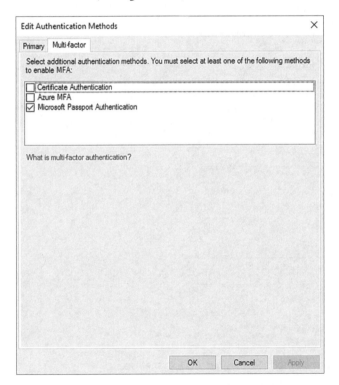

Figure 14-7   Multi-factor Authentication Types Available in AD FS

You can enable three types of MFA authentication:

- **Certificate Authentication**: This MFA requires the user to have an encrypted digitally signed PKI certificate in order to authenticate. Unlike primary certificate authentication, this type of authentication is used in conjunction with the primary authentication, not as a replacement.

- **Azure MFA**: This enables a variety of MFA options available in the Microsoft Azure cloud platform, including mobile app and SMS messaging.

- **Microsoft Passport Authentication**: This MFA allows for users to use their MS Passport accounts as a second factor when authenticating. Again, unlike primary Passport authentication, this is used with the primary method, not in place of it.

Implementing and Configuring Device Registration

Device Registration Service (DRS) allows users to register their devices with Active Directory. Typically, users join their personal mobile devices with the network to enable multi-factor authentication and Single-Sign On (SSO) to secured resources and services. When a device is registered with DRS, it is issued a digital certificate for authentication purposes. This is known as Workplace Join and is available for devices running Windows 8.1+, iOS 6.0+, and Android 4.0+.

DRS is available in two configurations; one for on-premises deployments and a second for MS Azure deployments. With standard on-premises registration, your devices are registered on the local directory and only "recognized" on the network. With Azure, a hybrid scenario is created. Azure handles registration and issuance of certificates and then syncs devices back to the on-premises directory with Azure AD Connect.

You cannot use both in a single AD FS deployment, so you must choose when implementing device registration which method you want to enable.

To implement device registration:

Step 1.   Log on to the AD FS server.

Step 2.   Start Server Manager from either the Start Menu or the Taskbar.

Step 3.   Click **Tools > AD FS Management**.

Step 4.   The AD FS Management Console launches.

Step 5.   In the left-hand pane, navigate to **Service / Device Registration**.

Step 6.   If AD is not already configured for device registration, click **Configure Active Directory** in the right-hand pane and wait for configuration to complete (see Figure 14-8).

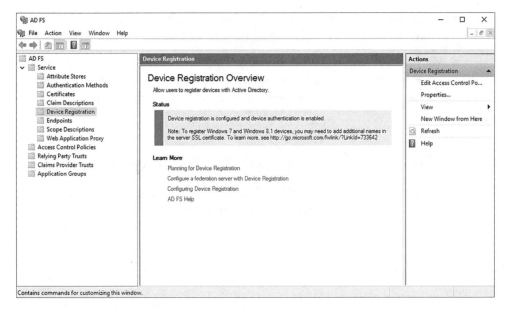

Figure 14-8   Device Registration Successfully Configured and Enabled in the AD FS Management Console

Once implemented, device registration can be restricted using Access Control Policies. Access Control Policies are a set of one or more rules that define who can and cannot access the DRS. The rules are ordered for priority, with the lower numbered rules taking priority over the higher numbered rules. If no rules are listed, all users are denied access by default.

To manage Access Control Policies for DRS:

Step 1.   Log on to the AD FS server.

Step 2.   Start Server Manager from either the Start Menu or the Taskbar.

Step 3.   Click **Tools > AD FS Management**.

Step 4.   The AD FS Management Console launches.

Step 5.   In the left-hand pane, navigate to **Service / Device Registration**.

Step 6.   Right-click **Device Registration** and select **Edit Access Control Policy**.

Step 7.   The current rules are listed. To add a new rule, click **Add Rule** (see Figure 14-9).

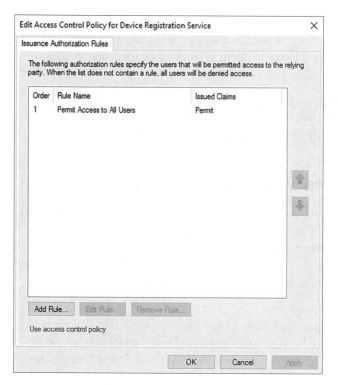

Figure 14-9   The Access Control Policy Rules for Device Registration

Step 8.   Choose a type of rule to add from the **Claim rule template** drop-down box. Each template has a brief description displayed when it is selected.

Step 9.   Click **Next**.

Step 10.   Configure the rule. Options vary based on the rule template chosen in Step 8. For example, you can choose the **Send Group Membership as a Claim** template and then choose which group to include as well as the claim type and value to announce for users who belong to that group.

Step 11.   Click **Finish**.

Step 12.   Use the up and down arrows on the right-hand side of the dialog to adjust the order of the specified rules.

DRS also has some basic properties that can be edited by selecting **Properties** from the context menu of the **Device Registration** node in AD FS Management Console. The properties that can be edited are

- **Maximum number of joined devices per user**: This limits how many devices each individual user can join to the directory.

- **Automatically remove unused devices**: Enabling this setting causes AD FS to automatically clear devices from the directory that have not been used for a specified period of time. This can help to keep the directory cleaner as well as prevent a user from running into their device limit.

- **Number of days before an unused device is removed**: If the preceding setting is enabled, this defines the length of time before a device is flagged as unused and consequently removed from the directory.

Integrating AD FS with Microsoft Passport

With Microsoft Passport, users can begin eliminating the need to maintain multiple passwords to multiple different services. Passport allows users to sign in once, and then have that authenticated identity used to gain access to software and services both on premise as well as on the Internet. Microsoft Passport is available for Windows 10 clients and requires a Windows Server 2016 forest and domain to be integrated with AD FS.

To integrate Microsoft Passport, you must enable and configure DRS as instructed earlier in this chapter. Once DRS is up and running, you can enable automatic registration for domain-joined devices and Microsoft Passport for Work via a Group Policy Object (GPO).

To enable automatic registration and Microsoft Passport for Work:

Step 1. Log on to a writeable domain controller.

Step 2. Launch Server Manager.

Step 3. Click **Tools** > **Group Policy Management**.

Step 4. In the left-hand navigation pane, expand the **Domains** node and then the node for your domain.

Step 5. Create a new GPO or select an existing one.

Step 6. Right-click the GPO and select **Edit**.

Step 7. In the left-hand navigation pane, browse to **Computer Configuration** > **Policies** > **Administrative Templates** > **Windows Components** > **Device Registration**.

Step 8. Right-click **Register domain joined computers as devices** and select **Edit**.

Step 9. Select **Enabled** and click **OK**.

Step 10. Navigate to **Computer Configuration > Policies > Administrative Templates > Windows Components > Microsoft Passport for Work**.

Step 11. Right-click **Use Microsoft Passport for Work** and select **Edit**.

Step 12. Select **Enabled** and click **OK**.

Step 13. Link the GPO at the desired level for your domain.

The final step is to enroll a KDC root certificate on each domain controller. This certificate allows the domain controllers to issue authenticating credentials to Windows 10 clients that join the domain and are affected by the above GPO.

You can request the certificate using the manual enrollment operation described in Chapter 13. Add the snap-in for the local computer account and enroll the Kerberos Authentication certificate (see Figure 14-10).

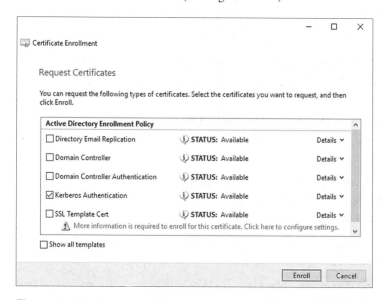

Figure 14-10   The Kerberos Authentication Certificate Required for the Domain Controller to Register Devices with Microsoft Passport

Configuring AD FS to Enable Authentication of Users Stored in LDAP Directories

AD FS has the capability to authenticate users stored not only in AD DS directories but in other third-party directories that implement the Lightweight Directory Access Protocol (LDAP) standard as well. LDAP is a popular standard particularly for Linux, and AD FS can be used to provide a single point of authentication against multiple directories besides AD DS.

For AD FS to recognize the third-party directory, you must create a claims provider trust on the AD FS server. A claims provider trust is a trust relationship that tells AD FS to trust the third-party provider. A single AD FS farm can have multiple claims provider trusts set up with different sources to enable multiple different claims providers. Even a remote AD DS forest can be set up as a claims provider.

To set up a claims provider trust:

Step 1. Log on to the AD FS server.

Step 2. Start Server Manager from either the Start Menu or the Taskbar.

Step 3. Click **Tools > AD FS Management**.

Step 4. Right-click **Claims Provider Trusts** and select **Add Claims Provider Trust**.

Step 5. Click **Start**.

Step 6. Select one of the following options and click **Next** (see Figure 14-11).

- **Import data about the claims provider...**: Select this option if your LDAP application publishes its metadata on an HTTP endpoint. Type that endpoint address into the provided text box.

- **Import data about the claims provider from a file**: If the LDAP application exported its metadata to a file, you can import that information by browsing to the file.

- **Enter claims provider trust data manually**: You can type the LDAP connection information in by hand if you have access to it. You enter that data during the next steps.

Step 7. (If entering data manually): Type a display name for the provider and click **Next**.

Step 8. (If entering data manually): Type the WS-Federation URL for the LDAP application and click **Next**.

Step 9. (If entering data manually): Type the claims provider identifier and click **Next**.

Step 10. (If entering data manually): Click **Add** and browse to the token signing certificate used by the third-party provider (see Figure 14-12).

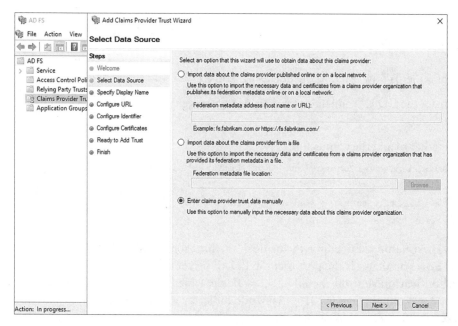

Figure 14-11   Selecting a Data Source for a New Claims Provider Trust in the AD FS Management Console

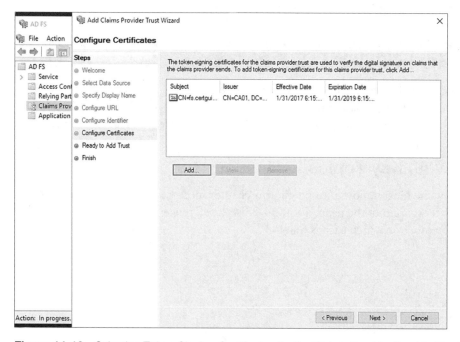

Figure 14-12   Selecting Token Signing Certificates for the Claims Provider Trust to Use When Manually Entering Data Source Information for a New Claims Provider Trust

Step 11.   Click **Next**.

Step 12.   Click **Close**.

The provider is now listed in the details pane in AD FS Management Console.

To create the LDAP connection to your AD FS server, you need to use Windows PowerShell.

The cmdlet to add the connection is

```
New-AdfsLdapServerConnection [-HostName] <String> '
[-Port <Int32> ] '
[-AuthenticationMethod { Basic }> ] '
[-SslMode {None | Ssl | Tls} ]
```

The **-HostName** parameter is the name of the host for the LDAP server. The **-Port** parameter is the port that the LDAP server is listening on. **-AuthenticationMethod** should be set to **Basic**, which is the only method supported by Windows Server 2016. **-SslMode** indicates whether SSL or TLS should be used for connecting to the server.

To create a new LDAP server connection, use the following PowerShell cmdlet:

```
New-AdfsLdapServerConnection -HostName ldapserver -Port 5100 -
AuthenticationMethod Basic -SslMode None
```

Exam Preparation Tasks

As mentioned in the section "Book Features" in the Introduction, you have a few choices for exam preparation: the exercises here; Chapter 17, "Final Preparation"; and the exam simulation questions in the Pearson Test Prep Software Online.

Review All Key Topics

Review the most important topics in this chapter, noted with the Key Topics icon in the outer margin of the page. Table 14-2 lists a reference of these key topics and the page number on which each is found.

Table 14-2   Key Topics for Chapter 14

Key Topic Element	Description	Page Number
Paragraph	Description of claims-based authentication	370
Figure 14-3	Configuring the token signing certification with a subject name for the AD FS server	373
Figure 14-4	Importing and using the token signing certificate for the AD FS server	375
Paragraph	Adding additional AD FS servers to a federation farm	376
List	Available primary authentication methods for AD FS	378
List	Three types of MFA authentication	380
Paragraph	Description of Device Registration Service (DRS)	381
Command	The PowerShell cmdlet to add a new LDAP server connection to AD FS	388

Complete Tables and Lists from Memory

There are no memory tables in this chapter.

Define Key Terms

Define the following key terms from this chapter and check your answers in the glossary:

claim, AD FS farm, multi-factor authentication, forms authentication, Windows authentication, Microsoft Passport authentication

End-of-Chapter Review Questions

The answers to these questions appear in Appendix A. For more practice with exam format questions, use the Pearson Test Prep Software Online.

1. As the organization has grown, you have begun to rely more on cloud-based services, particularly Office 365. Users are complaining about time wasted logging in to various services and a growing number of usernames and passwords they need to remember for those services. Which solution should you research?

   a. Implement a Password locker system where users can store their passwords once and recover as needed.

   b. Cache credentials for third-party sites in the AD DS directory for your users.

   c. Bring services into the internal network so they can authenticate directly against the domain controller.

   d. Implement AD FS as a federated authentication provider to enable Single-Sign On where available.

2. A partner organization has a handful of contractors that will need access to some of the applications and services your team relies on. You have issued certificates to those users with expiration times that will keep them from maintaining access past the date of the engagement. Unfortunately, they are unable to use those certificates when authenticating to your AD FS server. Which troubleshooting step would you take first?

   a. Reboot the relevant AD FS servers and force a Group Policy update.

   b. Ensure certificate authentication is enabled for the AD FS server.

   c. Reboot the client machines and force a Group Policy update.

   d. Configure device registration for the computers that the users are authenticating from.

3. As part of a new initiative, you are going to be allowing users to connect their personal phones and tablets to the network and access some services from those devices. What service in AD FS do you need to configure to enable this?

   a. Microsoft Passport

   b. Third-party LDAP connectivity

   c. Device Registration Service

   d. Microsoft Azure AD Connect

4. You are enabling the Microsoft Passport feature for a number of your users. Which steps must you perform to enable this feature on the desired users in the domain? (Choose all that apply.)

   a. Enable the Group Policy Device Registration in a GPO.

   b. Enable the Group Policy Microsoft Passport for Work in a GPO.

   b. Link the GPO to the domain partitions that contain the users you want to enable.

   d. Upgrade the forest functional level to Windows Server 2016.

5. You are enabling a third-party LDAP directory as a claims provider for your AD FS farm. You have created the Claims Provider Trust object in the AD FS Management Console and now need to establish a connection from the AD FS server to the provider. The provider is hosted at contoso.ldap.local on port 5199 and requires TLS security. What is the correct PowerShell command to create this connection?

- **Installing and Configuring Web Application Proxy**: This section describes how to install and configure the Windows Server 2016 role service for Web Application Proxy.

- **Implementing WAP as AD FS Proxy**: This section describes how to configure the Web Application Proxy service to use a domain-joined AD FS server for authentication services.

With Windows Server 2012 R2, Microsoft introduced a new Remote Access role called Web Application Proxy (WAP). WAP provides reverse proxy functionality for web applications located on your internal corporate network. When users outside the network want to access those applications, WAP provides a secure entry point into the network allowing external access without exposing the web applications themselves. Notably, WAP is closely integrated with Active Directory Federation Services (AD FS) to enable authentication for external users without exposing the AD FS servers.

This chapter introduces WAP and includes how to install and implement typical enterprise deployments. How to integrate a WAP server with an existing AD FS implementation is covered, as well as how to publish various internal web applications.

CHAPTER 15

Implementing Web Application Proxy

"Do I Know This Already?" Quiz

The "Do I Know This Already?" quiz allows you to assess whether you should read this entire chapter thoroughly or jump to the "Exam Preparation Tasks" section. If you are in doubt about your answers to these questions or your own assessment of your knowledge of the topics, read the entire chapter. Table 15-1 lists the major headings in this chapter and their corresponding "Do I Know This Already?" quiz questions. You can find the answers in Appendix A, "Answers to the 'Do I Know This Already?' Quizzes."

Table 15-1 "Do I Know This Already?" Section-to-Question Mapping

Foundation Topics Section	Questions
Installing and Configuring Web Application Proxy	1-2
Implementing WAP as AD FS proxy	3-4

CAUTION The goal of self-assessment is to gauge your mastery of the topics in this chapter. If you do not know the answer to a question or are only partially sure of the answer, you should mark that question as wrong for purposes of the self-assessment. Giving yourself credit for an answer you correctly guess skews your self-assessment results and might provide you with a false sense of security.

1. Where should the WAP role service be installed to minimize network latency and still meet security best practices?

   a. On an isolated server in a perimeter network

   b. On the same server as the AD FS role service

   c. On a writeable domain controller

   d. On any member server in the domain

2. What type of app should you publish if the source application has no ability to natively integrate with AD FS for authentication?

   a. AD FS proxy authentication

   b. Pass-through authentication

   c. Microsoft Azure authentication

   d. Multi-factor authentication

3. You are publishing an app in Web Application Proxy that will use AD FS pre-authentication. Which configuration change is required before you can publish to WAP?

   a. A claims provider trust must be created on the AD FS server for the source application.

   b. The source application must be configured with SSL and a digital certificate.

   c. An AD FS server farm must be installed on the WAP server.

   d. A relying party trust must be created on the AD FS server for the source application.

4. If you are publishing a web application in WAP but it uses an invalid public FQDN, such as app.certguide.internal, which settings do you need to configure to provide public access via WAP?

   a. AD FS preauthentication

   b. External and backend server URLs

   c. Pass-through authentication

   d. OAuth2

Foundation Topics

Installing and Configuring Web Application Proxy

The Web Application Proxy role can be installed on any server on the network that does not have the AD FS role installed. You should also avoid installing the service on a domain controller or other servers with critical security infrastructure.

It is highly recommended that WAP be installed on an isolated machine in a perimeter network location, such as the DMZ. A typical robust installation includes a frontend firewall to separate it from the Internet and a backend firewall to separate it from the corporate network. This topology allows WAP to function as a protection layer against malicious activity from the Internet.

Installing Web Application Proxy

There are two steps to installing and configuring WAP. First, the Remote Access role must be added to the Windows Server. Once that's complete, the Web Application Proxy must be configured.

To install the Remote Access role:

Step 1. Log on to a member server in the domain.

Step 2. Start Server Manager from either the Start Menu or the Taskbar.

Step 3. Click **Manage > Add Roles and Features**.

Step 4. Click **Next**.

Step 5. Select **Role-based or feature-based installation** and click **Next**.

Step 6. On the Server Selection page ensure that the **Select a server from the server pool** option is chosen, and then click to highlight the current server from the list. Click **Next**.

Step 7. Check the **Remote Access** box and click **Next** (see Figure 15-1).

Step 8. Click **Next**.

Step 9. Review the details and click **Next**.

Step 10. Check the **Web Application Proxy** box and click **Next**. If prompted to **Add Features that are required...** review the role services that must be installed for WAP to work and ensure **Include management tools** is checked. Click **Add Features** to return to the Server Roles page.

Step 11. Review the confirmation page and click **Install**.

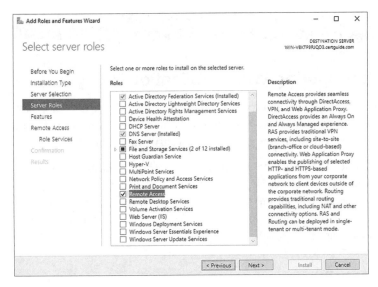

Figure 15-1 Installing the Remote Access Server Role in the Add Roles and Features Wizard

When the installation is complete, you can click the displayed link to **Open the Web Application Proxy Wizard.**

To configure the WAP server:

Step 1.   Click the link to **Open the Web Application Proxy Wizard**. If you closed the Add Roles and Features Wizard, the link can be found in Server Manager by selecting the **Remote Access** role on the left-hand navigation pane and clicking the alert found at the top of the details panel.

Step 2.   Read the welcome text and click **Next.**

Step 3.   Type the AD FS federation service name in the **Federation service name** text box. Be aware that this is not the name of the machine on which the AD FS role is installed but the actual name of the service originally used in the digital certificate subject name and imported during AD FS configuration (i.e., fs.certguide.com—see Figure 15-2).

Step 4.   Type credentials for a domain administrator account and click **Next.**

Step 5.   From the drop-down, select the certificate used to configure the AD FS service (named the same as the AD FS service you typed in Step 3). Click **Next.**

Step 6.   Review the confirmation page, which displays the PowerShell command that executes the configuration. Click **Configure.**

Step 7.   Click **Close.**

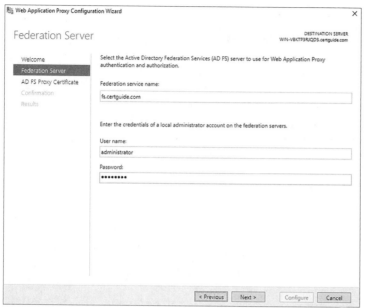

Figure 15-2   Configuring Web Application Proxy (WAP) with the Backend AD FS Service Information

Web Application Proxy is now installed and configured on the server. The Remote Access Management Console launches. You can also launch this console from the Server Manager Tools menu.

Implementing WAP in Pass-Through Mode

Once WAP is up and running, you need to publish each internal web application that WAP will serve. While this book covers preauthentication and integration with AD FS later in this chapter, you can also simply forward appropriate incoming connections to the backend web application and let that application handle any authentication that needs to be performed. This is called pass-through mode.

To publish a pass-through web application:

Step 1.   Log on to the WAP server.

Step 2.   From Server Manager, launch the Remote Access Management Console.

Step 3.   In the left-hand navigation pane, underneath the **Configuration** node, select **Web Application Proxy**.

Step 4.   In the Tasks pane click **Publish**.

Step 5.   The Publish New Application Wizard launches. Click **Next**.

Step 6.   Select **Pass-through** and click **Next** (see Figure 15-3).

Figure 15-3   Configuring a Pass-Through Application in Web Application Proxy

Step 7.   Fill in the following details and click **Next**.

- **Name**: A descriptive name for the app to display in the Remote Access Management Console.

- **External URL**: The front-facing URL that external users will use to access the application. WAP "listens" to this URL and forwards requests that it receives to the backend server URL. It is recommended you use HTTPS for all external-facing URLs.

- **External certificate**: The digital certificate used to enable encrypted HTTPS communication on that URL.

- **Enable HTTP to HTTPS redirection**: This forces HTTP connections to be redirected to HTTPS for added security and easing the user experience.

- **Backend server URL**: This is the web address that the application is reached at internally. WAP forwards all requests that it receives for the external URL to this URL.

Step 8. Review the confirmation page, which displays the PowerShell command that executes the configuration. Click **Publish**.

Step 9. Click **Close**.

The application is now listed in the Remote Access Management Console under published web applications.

Implementing WAP as AD FS Proxy

A big advantage of WAP, and a popular use case, is to preauthenticate incoming requests for internal web applications against your AD FS server. With preauthentication, WAP can handle all the authentication communication with the AD FS server, which limits the exposure that your AD FS server has to the broader Internet.

To implement WAP as an AD FS proxy, you must first create a relying party trust in your AD FS deployment. A relying party trust tells AD FS about an application or service that relies upon AD FS for authentication. With this trust in place, AD FS recognizes incoming requests for the app and redirects the user back to the app appropriately.

To create a new relying party trust in AD FS:

Step 1. Log on to an AD FS server.

Step 2. From the Server Manager, launch the AD FS Console.

Step 3. In the left-hand navigation pane, right-click **Relying Party Trusts** and select **Add Relying Party Trust**.

Step 4. Select either **Claims aware** or **Non claims aware** depending on the support offered in the application you are publishing. Click **Start**.

Step 5. Select one of the following options and click **Next**:

   a. **Import data about the relying party**: Select this option if your application publishes its metadata on an HTTP endpoint. Type that endpoint address into the provided text box.

   b. **Import data about the claims provider from a file**: If the application exported its metadata to a file, you can import that information by browsing to the file.

   c. **Enter claims provider trust data manually**: You can type the connection information by hand if you have access to it. You enter that data during Steps 6 through 9.

Step 6.   (If entering data manually) Type a display name for the provider and click **Next**.

Step 7.   (If entering data manually) If you want to encrypt the digital claims sent to this relying party, import a certificate file using the **Browse** option. The relying party has to be configured with the private key for the certificate to decrypt the claims as it receives them. Click **Next**.

Step 8.   (If entering data manually) If the application supports WS-Federation, SAML 2.0, or both, check the boxes on this screen and type the endpoints for those protocols.

Step 9.   (If entering data manually) Type a unique identifier for the relying party, typically a URL endpoint, and click **Add**. This identifier is used by AD FS to recognize a claims request and in turn is supplied by AD FS in the claim so the relying party knows the claims are targeted for it. You can have as many identifiers as needed to support your application, but AD FS requires at least one (see Figure 15-4).

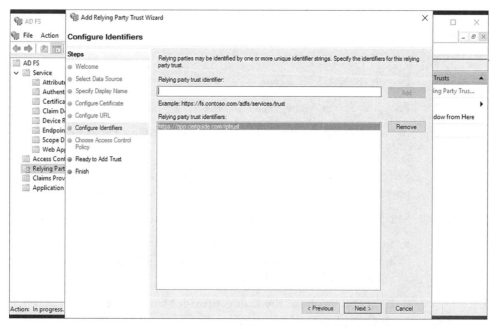

Figure 15-4   Adding Relying Party Trust Identifiers in the Add Relying Party Trust Wizard

Step 10.   Click **Next**.

Step 11.   Select a base Access Control Policy to limit which users can authenticate for this relying party. Click **Next**.

Step 12.   Review the configuration settings and click **Next**.

The application is now listed in the Relying Party Trusts panel. Take note of the Display Name chosen for this application.

To publish a new web application in WAP that uses AD FS for authentication:

Step 1.   Log on to the WAP server.

Step 2.   From the Server Manager launch the Remote Access Management Console.

Step 3.   In the left-hand navigation pane, underneath the **Configuration** node, select **Web Application Proxy**.

Step 4.   In the Tasks pane, click **Publish**.

Step 5.   The Publish New Application Wizard launches. Click **Next**.

Step 6.   Select **Active Directory Federation Service (AD FS)** and click **Next**.

Step 7.   Select one of the following preauthentication methods for the app you are publishing and click **Next**:

- **Web and MSOFBA**: If the client is a web browser, this method allows for HTTP redirects to perform the authentication. Rich clients such as MS Office use the MSOFBA protocol as well.

- **HTTP Basic**: For client applications that are not web browsers and do not support HTTP redirection, this performs authentication with basic HTTP calls.

- **OAuth2**: This is for clients that are preconfigured to use the OAuth2 authentication workflow.

Step 8.   From the list of relying parties, select the relying party trust you created in the previous list (see Figure 15-5).

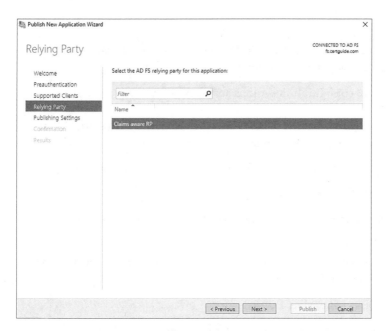

Figure 15-5   Selecting the Relying Party Trust That Represents the Web App Being Published in WAP

Step 9.   Click **Next**.

Step 10.   Fill in the following details (see Figure 15-6) and click **Next**:

- **Name**: A descriptive name for the app to display in the Remote Access Management Console.

- **External URL**: The fully qualified domain name (FQDN) for the front-facing URL that external users will use to access the application. WAP "listens" to this URL and forwards requests that it receives to the backend server URL. It is recommended you use HTTPS for all external-facing URLs.

- **External certificate**: The digital certificate used to enable encrypted HTTPS communication on that URL.

- **Enable HTTP to HTTPS redirection**: This forces HTTP connections to be redirected to HTTPS for added security and easing the user experience.

- **Backend server URL**: The FQDN for the internal web address that WAP uses to communicate with the application. WAP forwards all requests that it receives for the external URL to this URL.

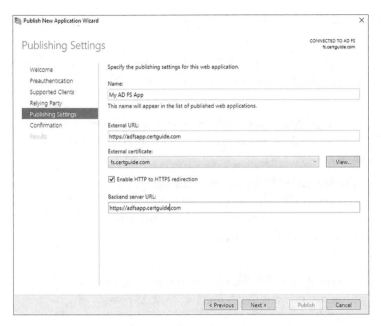

Figure 15-6 The Publishing Settings Page of the Publish New Application Wizard. Note the External URL and Backend Server URL Can Be Different from One Another.

Step 11. Review the confirmation page, which displays the PowerShell command that executes the configuration. Click **Publish**.

Step 12. Click **Close**.

The application is now listed in the Remote Access Management Console under published web applications. As seen in Figure 15-6, each application has both an external URL and a backend server URL, also known as the *internal URL*. Both URLs must contain the FQDN required for communication with the application. The external URL is used by clients trying to reach the application, while the internal URL is the URL that WAP forwards all communication to. Often these URLs are the same, but they can be different. WAP handles all address translation transparently; the client never needs to know the internal URL.

WAP can also use AD FS preauthentication for Remote Desktop Gateway (RDG). RDG is a role service that allows Windows to tunnel a remote desktop session in Transport Layer Security (TLS). This improves security and isolation of remote desktop connections and allows Internet Explorer to be used as the remote desktop client.

You can publish RDG as a WAP app using AD FS preauthentication with the following options:

- If Remote Desktop Web Access and RDG are hosted on the same server, you can publish the root domain name as the backend server URL, for example, https://rdg.certguide.com.

- If Remote Desktop Web Access and RDG are on separate servers, you must publish each RDG virtual directory as separate applications in WAP. They can still share the same external URL.

- Configure RDG to require AD FS preauthentication. See more details here for configuring RDG: https://technet.microsoft.com/en-us/windows-server-docs/identity/web-application-proxy/publishing-applications-with-sharepoint,-exchange-and-rdg

---

NOTE   You can find additional details and documentation for Remote Desktop Gateway here: https://technet.microsoft.com/en-us/library/cc731150(v=ws.11).aspx.

Exam Preparation Tasks

As mentioned in the section "Book Features" in the Introduction, you have a few choices for exam preparation: the exercises here; Chapter 17, "Final Preparation"; and the exam simulation questions in the Pearson Test Prep Software Online.

Review All Key Topics

Review the most important topics in this chapter, noted with the Key Topics icon in the outer margin of the page. Table 15-2 lists a reference of these key topics and the page number on which each is found.

Table 15-2   Key Topics for Chapter 15

Key Topic Element	Description	Page Number
Paragraph	Recommended topology for a secure WAP deployment	395
Figure 15-2	Configuring Web Application Proxy (WAP) with the backend AD FS service information	397
Figure 15-3	Configuring a pass-through application in Web Application Proxy	398
Paragraph	Adding a relying party trust for AD FS proxy through WAP	399

Complete Tables and Lists from Memory

There are no memory tables in this chapter.

Define Key Terms

Define the following key terms from this chapter and check your answers in the glossary:

reverse proxy, Web Application Proxy (WAP), published app, pass-through authentication, AD FS proxy authentication, relying party trust, Remote Desktop Gateway (RDG), HTTP to HTTPS redirects

End-of-Chapter Review Questions

The answers to these questions appear in Appendix A. For more practice with exam format questions, use the Pearson Test Prep Software Online.

1. After installing the Web Application Proxy server, your initial tests reveal that it is not responding to requests that originate from outside your network. Which troubleshooting steps should you attempt? (Choose two.)

    a. Ensure that the front-facing firewall for the WAP server is allowing traffic on TCP ports 80 and 443.

    b. Validate the external URLs for published applications are correct.

    c. Test the AD FS internal logon page.

    d. Discard and reinstall the WAP servers.

2. You have an app published on the WAP server that performs AD FS Proxy authentication. Users are continually reporting connection problems, which turn out to be mistaken connections to the app with HTTP instead of HTTPS. Which method would you use to correct this recurring problem?

    a. Ensure that the front-facing firewall for the WAP server is allowing traffic on TCP ports 80 and 443.

    b. Modify the AD FS relying party trust to allow HTTP connections to authenticate.

    c. Modify the app in WAP to enable HTTP to HTTPS redirection.

    d. Distribute updated instructions to all users of the app emphasizing the HTTPS requirement.

3. You have a remote desktop gateway deployed for your users. The Web Access service is hosted on one server at https://rdweb.certguide.com/rdweb. The gateway is hosted on a different server at https://rdg.certguide.com/rpc. You want to use AD FS to authenticate users accessing the RDG service. How would you configure WAP to support this?

   a. Publish a single app in WAP. Configure the backend server URL for the app to point toward the gateway FQDN. Configure the external URL for the app to point toward the web access FQDN.

   b. Publish two applications in WAP. Configure the backend server URL for both apps to point toward the gateway FQDN. Configure the external URL for one app with the web access FQDN. Configure the external URL for the second app with the gateway URL.

   c. Do not use WAP and configure the RDG authentication directly in AD FS.

   d. Publish two applications in WAP. Configure the backend server URL for one app to point toward the web access FQDN, and the other app to point toward the gateway FQDN. Configure both apps with the same external URL.

- **Installing an Active Directory Rights Management Services Server**: This section describes how to install and configure the Active Directory Rights Management Services role service.

- **Managing AD RMS Templates and Exclusion Policies**: This section describes how to create and manage security templates that users can apply to their documents and how to preemptively exclude specific entities from accessing any documents.

- **Backing Up and Restoring AD RMS**: This section describes the proper methods for backing up and restoring Active Directory Rights Management Services for disaster recovery planning.

Active Directory Rights Management Services (AD RMS) allows users to encrypt common document formats such as emails or Microsoft Word files and leverage Active Directory Domain Services to define who can and cannot decrypt and read those documents. Instead of storing documents in secure file servers, where the protections are lost once the document leaves the confines of the system, AD RMS protections travel with the document itself even if it leaves the network. AD RMS can be used to control which users can read, edit, print, and even copy data to the clipboard.

CHAPTER 16

Installing and Configuring Active Directory Rights Management Services

This chapter covers how to install and set up the AD RMS server, known as a cluster, which can then be leveraged by users to protect their documents. This includes installation of the RMS role, defining the service connection point, managing policy templates that users can use, and backing up and restoring RMS.

"Do I Know This Already?" Quiz

The "Do I Know This Already?" quiz allows you to assess whether you should read this entire chapter thoroughly or jump to the "Exam Preparation Tasks" section. If you are in doubt about your answers to these questions or your own assessment of your knowledge of the topics, read the entire chapter. Table 16-1 lists the major headings in this chapter and their corresponding "Do I Know This Already?" quiz questions. You can find the answers in Appendix A, "Answers to the 'Do I Know This Already?' Quizzes."

Table 16-1 "Do I Know This Already?" Section-to-Question Mapping

Foundation Topics Section	Questions
Installing an Active Directory Rights Management Services Server	1-2
Managing AD RMS Templates and Exclusion Policies	3-4
Backing Up and Restoring AD RMS	5

CAUTION The goal of self-assessment is to gauge your mastery of the topics in this chapter. If you do not know the answer to a question or are only partially sure of the answer, you should mark that question as wrong for purposes of the self-assessment. Giving yourself credit for an answer you correctly guess skews your self-assessment results and might provide you with a false sense of security.

1. Which term is used by AD RMS to refer to a server with AD RMS installed that provides digital rights management services?

    a. Farm

    b. Bank

    c. Cluster

    d. Host

2. Which of the following can be used as the backend database for an AD RMS installation? (Choose two.)

    a. Windows Internal Database

    b. MySQL

    c. SQL Server

    d. XML-based file system

3. Which of the following is true if an AD RMS policy template is updated after some documents have already been authored with the previous version of the template?

    a. All previously authored documents will receive the updated template from the AD RMS server.

    b. All previously authored documents will retain the version of the template that was originally applied.

    c. Document authors will have the option to update previously authored documents with the new template.

    b. Document consumers will have the option to update previously authored documents with the new template.

4. Which of the following are types of exclusion policies? (Choose three.)

    a. Computer

    b. User

    c. Lockbox

    d. Application

5. Which of the following is true when recovering a failed AD RMS cluster on a new server installation?

    a. A new cluster key must be generated and all existing AD RMS protected documents must be updated with a new publishing license.

    b. The cluster key must be manually typed in to the configuration file for the new AD RMS cluster.

    c. Due to the security restrictions on the cluster key, a failed AD RMS cluster cannot be recovered and an entirely new AD RMS cluster must be deployed.

    d. The cluster key must be retrieved from storage and used to install the replacement cluster servers.

Foundation Topics

Installing an Active Directory Rights Management Services Server

Active Directory Rights Management Services (AD RMS) is installed on one or more Windows Servers and is collectively known as a cluster. A cluster of AD RMS servers does not imply a failover or load balancing scenario because even a single AD RMS server is known as a cluster.

The first AD RMS server installed in an Active Directory Domain Services (AD DS) forest becomes the root cluster. Additional AD RMS servers can be added to this cluster, and in certain complex enterprise environments separate clusters called licensing-only clusters can be added to the forest as well. In general, a single root cluster with two or more AD RMS servers for fault tolerance and load balancing is sufficient.

Installing AD RMS

AD RMS requires a service account during configuration. This account must be a regular domain user account and have its password set to never expire. If AD RMS is being installed on a domain controller, this account must be a member of the Enterprise Admins group as well. Before continuing, create this account and note its username and password.

While AD RMS can be installed on any member server in the domain, it runs Internet Information Services and must necessarily be exposed to the Internet to grant licenses to documents outside the network. For this reason it is recommended you install the role on an isolated server not used for any other network services.

To install an AD RMS cluster:

Step 1.   Log on to a member server in the domain.

Step 2.   Start Server Manager from either the Start Menu or the Taskbar.

Step 3.   Click **Manage > Add Roles and Features**.

Step 4.   Click **Next**.

Step 5.   Select **Role-based or feature-based installation** and click **Next**.

Step 6.   On the Server Selection page ensure that the **Select a server from the server pool** option is chosen, and then click to highlight the current server from the list. Click **Next**.

Step 7.   Check the **Active Directory Rights Management Services** box and click **Next** (see Figure 16-1). If prompted to **Add Features that are required...** review the role services that must be installed for AD RMS to work and ensure **Include management tools** is checked. Click **Add Features** to return to the Role Services page and click **Next**.

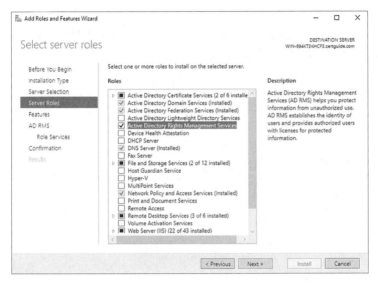

Figure 16-1   Installing the AD RMS Server Role in the Add Roles and Features Wizard

Step 8.   Click **Next**.

Step 9.   Review the AD RMS details and click **Next**.

Step 10.   Ensure the **Active Directory Rights Management Server** box is checked and click **Next**.

Step 11.   Review the confirmation page for all the services and features you chose to install. Do not check the **Restart the destination server automatically** box if any other users are currently relying on the server. Click **Install**.

Step 12.   The server displays an installation progress page. Note the option at the bottom of the page to **Export configuration settings**, which generates an XML file you can use with PowerShell to install the same roles and features on another server.

Configuring AD RMS

After the AD RMS role has been installed, you need to configure AD RMS:

Step 1.   Click the **Perform additional configuration** link.

Step 2.   The AD RMS Configuration Wizard launches. Review the details and click **Next**.

Step 3.   For the first server in the cluster, select **Create a new AD RMS root cluster** and click **Next** (see Figure 16-2).

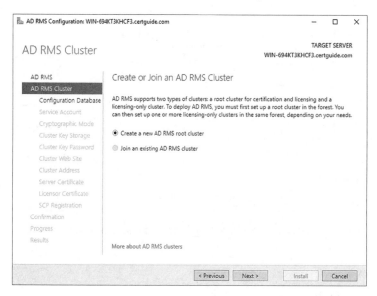

Figure 16-2   Creating the First AD RMS Server in a Cluster with the AD RMS Configuration Wizard

Step 4.   Select one of the following two options and click **Next**:

- **Specify a database server and a database instance**: Select an SQL Server database server and instance to store AD RMS configuration data in. This is the recommended choice for most enterprise installations because multiple servers in the cluster can read and write to this database and share configuration information.

- **Use Windows Internal Database on this server**: This uses a local database on the current server. This option is acceptable for test environments and small implementations, but additional servers in the cluster have read-only copies of the database that are replicated from the original server.

Step 5.   Click **Specify** and type the credentials for the service account you created before starting the installation.

Step 6.   Select a Cryptographic mode and click **Next**. Mode 1 should only be used when you know older AD RMS clients are being used by your users and need to be supported. Mode 2 is more secure and recommended.

Step 7.   Select one of the following options and click **Next** (see Figure 16-3):

- **Use AD RMS centrally managed key storage**: This option stores the key used by AD RMS to sign and encrypt documents in a store managed by AD RMS. All servers in the cluster can share this storage.

- **Use CSP key storage**: If you have a third-party cryptographic service provider (CSP) and want to store the key there, you can choose this option. Note this entails additional work sharing the key with other servers in the cluster.

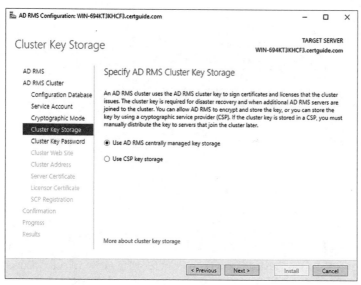

Figure 16-3   Selecting a Key Storage Location for the AD RMS Cluster Key. This Key Is Required by Every Server in the Cluster.

Step 8.   Type and confirm a password to encrypt the cluster key. Retain this password in a safe place since it is not recoverable if lost. Click **Next**.

Step 9.   Select a website from IIS to host the AD RMS virtual directory. This site is used by AD RMS clients to communicate with the AD RMS server. Click **Next**.

Step 10.   Type a fully qualified domain name for the website hosting the cluster. Click **Next**.

Step 11. Select a certificate for secure communications with the AD RMS cluster. This certificate is not used to encrypt documents protected with RMS. Your server may already have an SSL binding certificate, in which case you do not have to specify anything. Click **Next**.

Step 12. Type a name for the server licensor certificate that AD RMS creates. This certificate is used to encrypt documents protected by AD RMS and should have a brief but descriptive name. Click **Next**.

Step 13. You can choose to have the service connection point (SCP) registered now if you are running the configuration as a member of the Enterprise Admins group. If you choose to specify the SCP later, you must perform that operation before AD RMS clients can access the cluster. Click **Next** (see Figure 16-4).

Figure 16-4 Choosing to Register the Service Connection Point (SCP) in Active Directory During Cluster Creation

Step 14. Review the confirmation page and click **Install**.

Step 15. Once AD RMS has finished configuration, click **Close**.

Managing AD RMS Service Connection Point

The service connection point (SCP) for AD RMS identifies the URL that AD RMS clients use to communicate with the cluster. This information is stored in the AD

DS directory so domain-joined computers can look up the SCP and autodiscover connection information for AD RMS to request use and publishing licenses.

The AD RMS Configuration Wizard offers to register the SCP in the directory during installation as shown previously. If the user running the installation is a member of the Enterprise Admins security group, this registration will succeed. If not, or if you choose to skip that step during installation, the SCP can be registered at a later point using the AD RMS Management Console.

To maintain the SCP:

Step 1. Log on to the AD RMS server. You must be logged on as a member of the Enterprise Admins group to perform this operation.

Step 2. Start Server Manager from either the Start Menu or the Taskbar.

Step 3. Click **Tools > Active Directory Rights Management Services**.

Step 4. The AD RMS Management Console launches. In the left-hand navigation pane right-click the cluster node and select **Properties**.

Step 5. Select the **SCP** tab (see Figure 16-5).

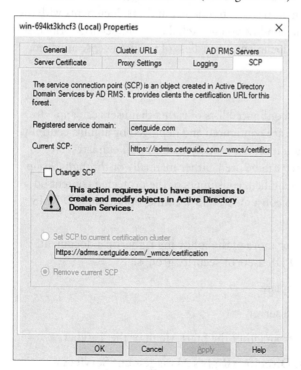

Figure 16-5   The SCP Tab of an AD RMS Server Properties Dialog. Here the Current SCP Is Displayed Where It Can Be Registered, Changed, or Deleted as Necessary.

Step 6.   Select the **Change SCP** check box.

Step 7.   Select **Set SCP to current certificate cluster** to update the SCP to the correct value. Alternatively, you can select **Remove current SCP**, but this operation is only recommended for advanced users in certain circumstances.

Step 8.   Click **OK**.

Step 9.   Click **Yes** to confirm the change.

Managing AD RMS Templates and Exclusion Policies

There are few central management tasks for an AD RMS server. Once it's up and running, it is a service largely used by document authors to protect documents and document consumers to gain access to protected materials. Two useful management tasks, however, are the creation of policy templates and exclusion policies.

Policy templates are used to save document authors time by providing a preconfig-ured selection of security restrictions that can be applied wholesale to a document. These are useful when a department or team frequently authors documents with the same restrictions. Exclusion policies allow you to exclude specific security principals from being granted access to any document, regardless of the use license attached.

AD RMS Policy Templates

AD RMS policy templates are preconfigured lists of rights that users can apply to their documents. These templates are configured and deployed by admins centrally and reduce the amount of configuration required by end users. Templates have to be deployed to a client before they can be used, either manually or through Group Policy. Once a template has been applied, consumers of the protected content do not need a copy of the template to consume it; only a connection to the AD RMS server is required.

A policy template can define one or more of the following rights on a document. Each right can be assigned to AD DS users or security groups.

To create an AD RMS policy template:

Step 1.   Log on to the AD RMS server.

Step 2.   Start Server Manager from either the Start Menu or the Taskbar.

Step 3.   Click **Tools > Active Directory Rights Management Services**.

Step 4.   In the left-hand navigation pane, expand the node for the cluster.

Step 5.   In the left-hand navigation pane, select **Rights Policy Templates**.

Step 6.   In the Actions pane, click **Create Distributed Rights Policy Template**.

Step 7.   Click **Add**.

Step 8.   Fill in the following details and click **Add**:

- **Language**: Select the language to add the identifier for. Multiple identifiers can be created for every language you intend to support.

- **Name**: Enter a short descriptive name for the template so that users will recognize it.

- **Description**: Provide a more in-depth description of the template indicating what rights it declares.

Step 9.   Repeat Steps 7 and 8 for each language you need the template to support (see Figure 16-6). Click **Next**.

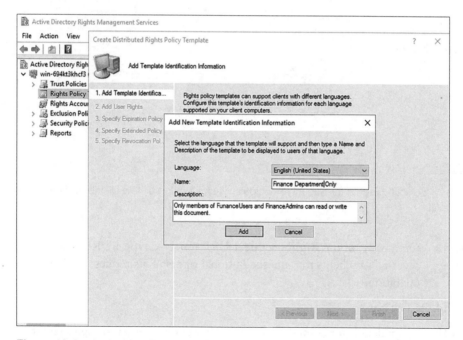

Figure 16-6   Add a New Template Identifier for the English Language. Multiple Identifiers Can Be Added for Additional Languages.

Step 10.   Click **Add**.

Step 11.   Type the email address for a user or group you want to define policy rights for. The security principal must have an email address in the AD DS directory before it can be used in a policy template. Click **OK**.

Step 12.   Ensure the group you want to define rights for is selected in the **Users and rights** list box; then select the desired rights in the **Rights...** list box. Any right that is not explicitly defined will be denied (see Figure 16-7).

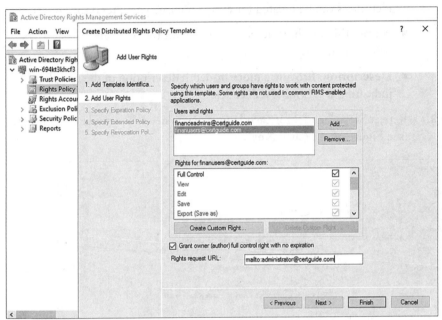

Figure 16-7   Selecting Rights for Security Principals When Creating a New Distributed Rights Policy Template

Step 13.   Optionally, in the **Rights request** URL text box, type a URL that can be accessed for clients to request additional rights. This request is a manual operation.

Step 14.   Click **Next**.

Step 15.   Select details for content expiration. Content can be set to expire either on a specific day and time or after a specified amount of time from when it is authored.

Step 16.   Optionally set a use license expiration. Regardless of content expiration, when a consumer use license expires, the user must connect to AD RMS to receive a new use license (see Figure 16-8).

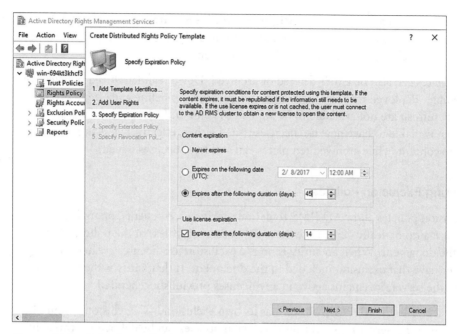

Figure 16-8   Selecting an Expiration Policy for Both the Content Protection License as Well as Any Use Licenses Issued by the AD RMS Server

Step 17.   Click **Next**.

Step 18.   Select any of the following optional policies and click **Next**:

- **Enable users to view protected content using a browser add-on**: Check this box to allow the content to be accessed with the AD RMS Client add-on for Internet Explorer.

- **Require a new use license every time**…: Check this box to force the user to contact the AD RMS server for a new use license every time the document is opened or accessed. This overrides any expiration settings chosen earlier.

- **Name-value pairs**: This list box can be populated with a list of key-value pairs of information embedded with any document protected with this template. Client software can read and display this data or be programmed to perform additional tasks based on the values.

Step 19.   If you want the rights policies to have the capability to be revoked, check the **Require revocation** box. Then supply the identifying information for the certificate revocation list (CRL) where the revocation can be found.

Step 20.   Click **Finish**.

The template is now listed in the **Rights Policy Templates** node of the AD RMS Management Console. Existing templates can be updated by selecting them in the console and clicking **Properties** in the Actions pane.

Templates can also be either deleted or archived. Deleted and archived policies are no longer deployed through the template deployment pipeline and after a group policy refresh are not available to be applied to content. Deleted templates are no longer available to have new use licenses issued either, effectively locking users out of the content, while archived templates can still have licenses issued.

Configuring Exclusion Policies

Exclusion policies allow AD RMS to define specific users, clients, or applications that are automatically denied use license requests regardless of the policies defined on the document. When an entity is on the exclusion list, licenses created by the server have that exclusion included in the document. If that entity is then removed from the server, it remains active in any licenses previously generated.

Each server in the AD RMS cluster has its own exclusion list. Exclusions should be added to every server in the cluster. Exclusion policies can be defined for three different types of entities listed in Table 16-2.

Table 16-2   Types of Exclusions in AD RMS

Exclusion Type	Description
User	AD DS directory security principals defined by their email address.
Lockbox	AD RMS clients defined by their lockbox version. Specify a minimum version required to exclude older AD RMS clients.
Application	AD RMS-enabled applications defined by their executable filename and version. Specify a minimum version to exclude older applications.

To add an exclusion policy for users:

Step 1.   Log on to the AD RMS server.

Step 2.   Start Server Manager from either the Start Menu or the Taskbar.

Step 3.   Click **Tools > Active Directory Rights Management Services**.

Step 4.   In the left-hand navigation pane expand the node for the cluster.

Step 5.   In the left-hand navigation pane select **Exclusion Policies**.

Step 6.   Click **Manage AD RMS user exclusion list**.

Step 7. In the actions pane click **Enable User Exclusion**.

Step 8. In the actions pane click **Exclude RAC**.

Step 9. Type the email address of the security principal to exclude and click **Finish** (see Figure 16-9).

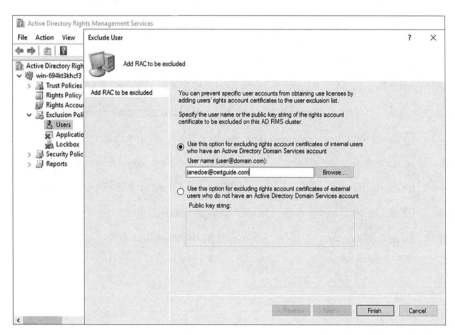

Figure 16-9 Identifying a Rights Account Certificate (RAC) to Add to the Exclusion List for an AD RMS Server

Applications and lockboxes are excluded by following the same steps with different details required during Step 9.

Backing Up and Restoring AD RMS

Backing up AD RMS is more complex than other Windows Server services. This is due to the secure nature of the operations that AD RMS is asked to perform. There are three steps to performing a complete AD RMS backup:

Step 1. **Know the cluster key password**: This password was defined when the cluster was first installed. If you do not have the cluster key password any longer, use the steps in the list that follows to generate a new password.

Step 2. **Export the trust publishing domain**: This process, detailed later in the chapter, saves the trust domain in an XML file, which can then be archived and backed up with the regular file system backups.

Step 3.   **Back up the AD RMS database**: If SQL Server is used for the backend database for AD RMS, then the regular SQL backup process is sufficient to back up the databases. If the server uses Windows Internal Database, then the databases are either backed up using standing Windows Server Backup or with a third-party backup utility that can connect to Windows Internal Database (such as SQL Server Management Studio).

To generate a new cluster key password:

Step 1.   Log on to the AD RMS server.

Step 2.   Start Server Manager from either the Start Menu or the Taskbar.

Step 3.   Click **Tools > Active Directory Rights Management Services**.

Step 4.   In the left-hand navigation pane expand the node for the cluster.

Step 5.   In the left-hand navigation pane expand the **Security Policies** node.

Step 6.   In the left-hand navigation pane select the **Cluster Key Password** node.

Step 7.   Click the link to **Change cluster key password**.

Step 8.   Type and confirm the new password in the supplied dialog. Click **OK** (see Figure 16-10).

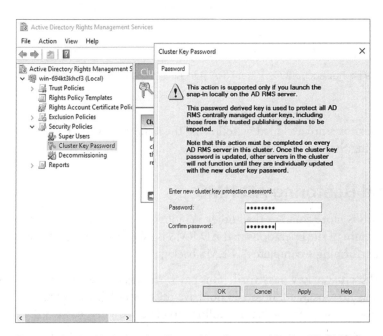

Figure 16-10   Updating the Cluster Key Password for an AD RMS Server. This Is Necessary Only When the Existing Cluster Key Has Been Lost or Forgotten.

Note this operation must be repeated on every server in the cluster. As the dialog describes, each server in the cluster will not function until it has been updated with the new cluster key password.

To export the trusted publishing domains:

Step 1. Log on to the AD RMS server.

Step 2. Start Server Manager from either the Start Menu or the Taskbar.

Step 3. Click **Tools > Active Directory Rights Management Services**.

Step 4. In the left-hand navigation pane expand the node for the cluster.

Step 5. In the left-hand navigation pane expand the **Trust Policies** node.

Step 6. Select the **Trusted Publishing Domains** node.

Step 7. In the actions pane, click **Export Trusted Publishing Domains**.

Step 8. Click **Save As** and browse to a location and type a filename to save the file as. The information is saved in that location as an .xml file (see Figure 16-11).

Step 9. Type and confirm a password to encrypt the .xml file. This password will be needed if and when the file is imported into a new or rebuilt cluster (see Figure 16-11).

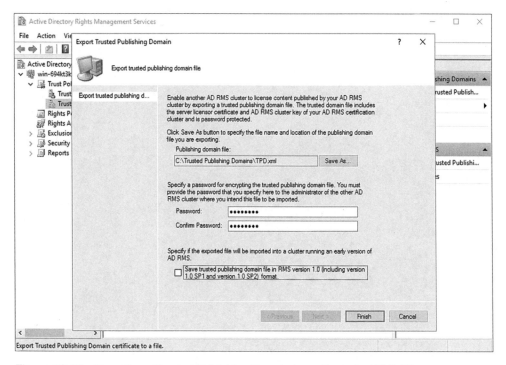

Figure 16-11 Exporting a Trusted Publishing Domain to an Encrypted XML File

Step 10.   Check the **Save trusted publishing domain file in RMS version 1.0...** box if you expect to import the file into an older version of RMS.

Step 11.   Click **Finish**.

The encrypted domain file is written to the specified location.

In the event that your AD RMS cluster is destroyed, corrupted, or otherwise rendered unusable, you can recover the cluster by reinstalling AD RMS on new servers. Follow these steps to recover AD RMS:

Step 1.   Restore the backed up database.

Step 2.   Install and configure the AD RMS role. During this operation, choose to join an existing cluster. When you are prompted for the database, provide the location of the restored database. You also need the cluster key password so the new installation can reuse the same private key as the lost or corrupted AD RMS cluster. If the key was stored in a CSP, you need to be able to access that key and manually add it to the new server.

Step 3.   Import the trusted publishing domain file. You need the password used to encrypt the file to complete this operation.

Exam Preparation Tasks

As mentioned in the section "Book Features" in the Introduction, you have a few choices for exam preparation: the exercises here; Chapter 17, "Final Preparation"; and the exam simulation questions in the Pearson Test Prep Software Online.

Review All Key Topics

Review the most important topics in this chapter, noted with the Key Topics icon in the outer margin of the page. Table 16-3 lists a reference of these key topics and the page number on which each is found.

Table 16-3 Key Topics for Chapter 16

Key Topic Element	Description	Page Number
Paragraph	Description of an AD RMS cluster	412
List	Database choice for AD RMS, which impacts the backup and recovery process	414
Figure 16-3	Private cluster key storage selection, which impacts the backup and recovery process	415
Paragraph	Description of a service connection point (SCP)	416
Figure 16-7	Selecting the rights to apply to a security principal in a rights policy template	420
Table 16-2	Types of exclusions in AD RMS	422
Steps	Required steps for proper AD RMS backup	423
Steps	Steps to perform a successful AD RMS cluster recovery	426

Complete Tables and Lists from Memory

Print a copy of Appendix B, "Memory Tables" (found on the book website), or at least the section for this chapter, and complete the tables and lists from memory. Appendix C, "Memory Tables Answer Key," also on the website, includes completed tables and lists to check your work.

Define Key Terms

Define the following key terms from this chapter and check your answers in the glossary:

AD RMS cluster, AD RMS root cluster, cluster key, service connection point (SCP), rights policy template, use license, exclusion policy

End-of-Chapter Review Questions

The answers to these questions appear in Appendix A. For more practice with exam format questions, use the Pearson Test Prep Software Online.

1. You are deploying AD RMS at your organization. You have been instructed to ensure that there is appropriate fault tolerance for the servers so that content access is not interrupted. Your organization has access to high-availability SQL Server, Oracle, and MySQL farms. Which of the following options would be most appropriate for the AD RMS backend databases?

   a. Utilize the built-in Windows Internal Database on the AD RMS server to keep everything contained locally.

   b. Store the backend databases on the SQL Server farm so they are included in regular backups and available to every server in the cluster.

   c. Store the backend databases on the MySQL farm so they are included in regular backups and available to every server in the cluster.

   d. Deploy a new SQL Server installation on the AD RMS server for back-end database storage to keep everything contained locally.

2. The Finance department is regularly using AD RMS to protect sensitive documents in their department. The process of applying policies to a document to ensure all required entities can access it without unnecessarily exposing it is becoming repetitive and prone to user error. You build and deploy a collection of policy templates that they can use for their most common policy needs. What steps would you take for users who need to protect a document in a unique way not covered by one of the policies?

   a. Either provide training to the user on how to properly build a protection policy in the AD RMS client they are using, or gather the necessary details and publish a new template.

   b. Grant the users in question rights to create and maintain policies on the AD RMS server.

   c. Nothing. The templates can be adjusted on the fly when they are being applied to the documents.

   d. Adjust the templates on an as-needed basis on request from the users.

3. Your manager wants to make sure the AD RMS cluster is being properly backed up in case of a disaster. You know that the SQL database where the backend is being stored is being backed up by the database team. What other steps must you take to ensure there are proper backups in place? (Choose two.)

   a. Nothing. As long as the AD RMS databases are properly backed up, the cluster can be recovered.

   b. Export the trusted publishing domains to a file location where the exported file will be backed up by routine file system backups.

   c. Copy the cluster key to an encrypted file and save that file to a location where it will be backed up by routing file system backups.

   d. Ensure you know the location and any security credentials for the cluster key. If the key is managed by AD RMS, be sure you have the cluster key password documented.

CHAPTER 17

Final Preparation

The first 16 chapters of this book cover the technologies, protocols, design concepts, and considerations required to be prepared to pass the Microsoft Certified Solutions Associate (MCSA) Identity with Windows Server 2016 70-742 exam. While these chapters supply the detailed information, most people need more preparation than just reading the first 16 chapters of this book. This chapter details a set of tools and a study plan to help you complete your preparation for the exams.

This short chapter has two main sections. The first section lists the exam preparation tools useful at this point in the study process. The second section lists a suggested study plan now that you have completed all the earlier chapters in this book.

NOTE Appendix B, "Memory Tables," and Appendix C, "Memory Tables Answer Key," are available on the website for this book, which you can access by going to www.pearsonITcertification.com/register, registering your book, and entering this book's ISBN: 9780789757036.

Tools for Final Preparation

This section lists some information about the available exam prep tools and how to access them.

Pearson Cert Practice Test Engine and Questions on the Website

Register this book to get access to the Pearson IT Certification test engine (software that displays and grades a set of exam-realistic, multiple-choice questions). Using the Pearson Cert Practice Test Engine, you can either study by going through the questions in Study Mode or take a simulated (timed) 70-742 exam.

The Pearson Test Prep practice test software comes with two full practice exams. These practice tests are available to you either online or as an offline Windows application. To access the practice exams developed with this book, see the instructions on the card inserted in the sleeve in the back of the book. This card includes a unique access code that enables you to activate your exams in the Pearson Test Prep software.

Accessing the Pearson Test Prep Software Online

The online version of this software can be used on any device with a browser and connectivity to the Internet, including desktop machines, tablets, and smartphones. To start using your practice exams online, simply follow these steps:

Step 1. Go to: http://www.PearsonTestPrep.com.

Step 2. Select **Pearson IT Certification** as your product group.

Step 3. Enter your email and password for your account. If you don't have an account on PearsonITCertification.com or CiscoPress.com, you need to establish one by going to PearsonITCertification.com/join.

Step 4. In the **My Products** tab, click the **Activate New Product** button.

Step 5. Enter the access code printed on the insert card in the back of your book to activate your product.

Step 6. The product now is listed in your My Products page. Click the **Exams** button to launch the exam settings screen and start your exam.

Accessing the Pearson Test Prep Software Offline

If you want to study offline, you can download and install the Windows version of the Pearson Test Prep software. There is a download link for this software on the book's companion website, or you can just enter this link in your browser:

  http://www.pearsonitcertification.com/content/downloads/pcpt/engine.zip.

To access the book's companion website and the software, simply follow these steps:

Step 1. Register your book by going to PearsonITCertification.com/register and entering the ISBN: 9780789757036.

Step 2. Respond to the challenge questions.

Step 3. Go to your account page and select the **Registered Products** tab.

Step 4. Click on the **Access Bonus Content** link under the product listing.

Step 5.   Click the **Install Pearson Test Prep Desktop Version** link under the Practice Exams section of the page to download the software.

Step 6.   Once the software finishes downloading, unzip all the files on your computer.

Step 7.   Double-click the application file to start the installation, and follow the onscreen instructions to complete the registration.

Step 8.   Once the installation is complete, launch the application and click the **Activate Exam** button on the My Products tab.

Step 9.   Click the **Activate a Product** button in the Activate Product Wizard.

Step 10.   Enter the unique access code found on the card in the sleeve in the back of your book and click the **Activate** button.

Step 11.   Click **Next** and then click the **Finish** button to download the exam data to your application.

Step 12.   You can now start using the practice exams by selecting the product and clicking the **Open Exam** button to open the exam settings screen.

Note that the offline and online versions sync together, so saved exams and grade results recorded on one version are available to you on the other as well.

Customizing Your Exams

Once you are in the exam settings screen, you can choose to take exams in one of three modes:

- Study Mode
- Practice Exam Mode
- Flash Card Mode

Study Mode allows you to fully customize your exams and review answers as you are taking the exam. This is typically the mode you would use first to assess your knowledge and identify information gaps. **Practice Exam Mode** locks certain customization options, as it is presenting a realistic exam experience. Use this mode when you are preparing to test your exam readiness. **Flash Card Mode** strips out the answers and presents you with only the question stem. This mode is great for late-stage preparation when you really want to challenge yourself to provide answers without the benefit of seeing multiple choice options. This mode does not provide the detailed score reports that the other two modes do, so it should not be used if you are trying to identify knowledge gaps.

In addition to these three modes, you can select the source of your questions. You can choose to take exams that cover all the chapters, or you can narrow your selection to just a single chapter or the chapters that make up specific parts in the book. All chapters are selected by default. If you want to narrow your focus to individual chapters, simply deselect all the chapters and then select only those on which you want to focus in the Objectives area.

You can also select the exam banks on which to focus. Each exam bank comes complete with a full exam of questions that cover topics in every chapter. The two exams printed in the book are available to you as well as two additional exams of unique questions. You can have the test engine serve up exams from all four banks or just from one individual bank by selecting the desired banks in the exam bank area.

You can make several other customizations to your exam from the exam settings screen, such as the time of the exam, the number of questions served up, whether to randomize questions and answers, whether to show the number of correct answers for multiple answer questions, or whether to serve up only specific types of questions. You can also create custom test banks by selecting only questions that you have marked or questions on which you have added notes.

Updating Your Exams

If you are using the online version of the Pearson Test Prep software, you should always have access to the latest version of the software as well as the exam data. If you are using the Windows desktop version, every time you launch the software, it checks to see whether there are any updates to your exam data and automatically downloads any changes made since the last time you used the software. This requires you to be connected to the Internet at the time you launch the software.

Sometimes, due to many factors, the exam data may not fully download when you activate your exam. If you find that figures or exhibits are missing, you may need to manually update your exams.

To update a particular exam you have already activated and downloaded, simply select the **Tools** tab and select the **Update Products** button. Again, this is only an issue with the desktop Windows application.

If you want to check for updates to the Pearson Test Prep exam engine software, Windows desktop version, simply select the **Tools** tab and select the **Update Application** button. This ensures you are running the latest version of the software engine.

Premium Edition

In addition to the free practice exam provided on the website, you can purchase additional exams with expanded functionality directly from Pearson IT Certification. The Premium Edition of this title contains an additional two full practice exams and an eBook (in both PDF and ePub format). In addition, the Premium Edition title also has remediation for each question to the specific part of the eBook that relates to that question.

Because you have purchased the print version of this title, you can purchase the Premium Edition at a deep discount. There is a coupon code in the book sleeve that contains a one-time-use code and instructions for where you can purchase the Premium Edition.

To view the Premium Edition product page, go to www.informit.com/title/ 9780789757036.

Memory Tables

Like most *Cert Guides* from Pearson, this book purposely organizes information into tables and lists for easier study and review. Rereading these tables can be useful before the exam. However, it is easy to skim over the tables without paying attention to every detail, especially when you remember having seen the table's contents when reading the chapter.

Instead of just reading the tables in the various chapters, this book's Appendixes B and C give you another review tool. Appendix B lists partially completed versions of many of the tables from the book. You can open Appendix B (a PDF available on the book website after registering) and print it. For review, you can attempt to complete the tables. This exercise can help you focus on the review. It also exercises the memory connectors in your brain, plus it makes you think about the information without as much information, which forces a little more contemplation about the facts.

Appendix C, also a PDF located on the book website, lists the completed tables to check yourself. You can also just refer to the tables as printed in the book.

Chapter-Ending Review Tools

Chapters 1 through 16 each have several features in the "Exam Preparation Tasks" section at the end of the chapter. You might have already worked through these in each chapter. It can also be useful to use these tools again as you make your final preparations for the exam.

Suggested Plan for Final Review/Study

This section lists a suggested study plan from the point at which you finish reading through Chapter 16, until you take the MCSA 70-742 exam. Certainly, you can ignore this plan, use it as is, or just take suggestions from it.

The plan uses four steps:

Step 1.   **Review key topics and "Do I Know This Already?" (DIKTA) quiz questions**: You can use the table that lists the key topics in each chapter, or just flip the pages looking for key topics. Also, reviewing the DIKTA questions from the beginning of the chapter can be helpful for review.

Step 2.   **Complete memory tables**: Open Appendix B from the book website and print the entire thing, or print the tables by major part. Then complete the tables.

Step 3.   **Review "End-of-Chapter Review Questions" sections**: Go through the Q&A questions at the end of each chapter to identify areas in which you need more study.

Step 4.   **Use the Pearson Cert Practice Test engine to practice**: The Pearson Cert Practice Test engine can be used to study using a bank of unique exam-realistic questions available only with this book.

Summary

The tools and suggestions listed in this chapter have been designed with one goal in mind: to help you develop the skills required to pass the MCSA 70-742 exam. This book has been developed from the beginning to not just tell you the facts but help you learn how to apply the facts. No matter what your experience level leading up to when you take the exams, it is our hope that the broad range of preparation tools and even the structure of the book help you pass the exam with ease. We hope you do well on the exam.

Answers to the "Do I Know This Already?" Quizzes and End-of-Chapter Review Questions

Chapter 1

Do I Know This Already? Quiz

1. D. Active Directory is made up of many different services, but the most widely used service is Active Directory Domain Services (AD DS), which contains the directory and all the functionality of the original Active Directory service from Windows 2000 Server.

2. A, B, C, D. AD DS is made up of many different components including schemas, forests, domains, trees, organizational units, objects, attributes, and GPOs.

3. A. After AD DS installation, the server promotion step occurs. At this point the server stops being a member server and becomes a domain controller. It can but does not have to be a global catalog or FSMO server.

4. B. Every forest in AD DS requires a forest root, which has special capabilities for managing the forest. By default, the first server promoted to domain controller is assigned the role of forest root.

5. C. Group Policy is used to configure four settings: Registry settings, Security settings, Group Policy preferences, and software installation.

6. D. AD FS delivers a claims token to the relying party that contains assertions or claims about the user. It is up to the relying party to decide what authorization the user has based on those claims.

7. C. In a federated identity deployment, the identity provider asserts the identity and provides claims to the relying party, which uses the assertion and claims to authorize access.

8. **A.** A certificate authority (CA) creates certificates upon request and validates certificates that are presented to it.

9. **B.** The publishing license (PL) is the license generated by AD RMS to restrict a document. The PL contains all the restrictions chosen by the author when rights management was applied.

10. **A.** A client licensor certificate (CLC) is issued by the AD RMS server and used to encrypt the document. The CLC is also used to sign the publishing license (PL), which describes the permissions and restrictions for the document.

End-of-Chapter Review Questions

1. Active Directory Domain Services (AD DS), Active Directory Federation Services (AD FS), Active Directory Certificate Services (AD CS), Active Directory Rights Management Services (AD RMD), Active Directory Lightweight Directory Services (AD LDS)

2. Active Directory Rights Management Services (AD RMS). AD RMS provides encryption and rights management for Microsoft Office documents shared both within and outside the organization.

3. **D.** Active Directory Certificate Services (AD CS) can produce PKI-encrypted certificates that users can install on their machines and use as further identification when they access the network via VPN. AD DS already provides the primary authentication metric, AD FS only extends existing authentication measures to additional clients, and AD RMS is used to encrypt and protect documents.

4. **A, C.** Define security at the organization, group, or individual level. Apply security systemically without manual intervention. GPOs allow the systematic application of policies to groups of objects in the AD DS directory. The process of organizing users and computers into separate hierarchies is done by AD DS itself. AD FS is the service that provides federation identity authentication.

5. Active Directory Federation Services (AD FS). AD FS allows systems outside your organizational network to authenticate users against your AD DS directory.

Chapter 2

Do I Know This Already? Quiz

1. A. Namespaces for child domains must be contiguous with their parent domain and consequently with each other.

2. D. The Windows Server Desktop Experience relies on the Server Manager utility to install roles and services. PowerShell scripts and command-line tools can be used as well.

3. B. While there are certain circumstances in which AD DS would be installed without then promoting the server to a domain controller, it is unusual. Installing AD DS is almost always followed immediately by promotion.

4. A, B. Functional levels are maintained for the entire domain or forest. New domain controllers do not have an impact on those levels. Every writeable domain controller in the domain has the ability to be a global catalog and DNS server.

5. C. Similar to installing AD DS and following with a promotion, AD DS cannot be uninstalled until the server has first been demoted to a member server.

6. A, D. Windows Server 2012 or 2012 R2 are the only valid OSes that can be upgraded to Server 2016.

7. C. The PowerShell cmdlet Install-WindowsFeature is used to install AD DS as well as any other server roles that can be installed with the Add Roles and Services Wizard.

8. B. The PowerShell cmdlet **Install-ADDSForest** is used to promote a server to a domain controller after the AD DS role service has been installed.

9. D. The **ntdsutil** utility provides many different management services for AD DS from the command line. Much of what it does has been reproduced in PowerShell, but it is still required to create IFM media.

10. A. A staged installation allows you as an administrator to control and limit the exposure of administrative privileges. Users setting up the controller for the second stage do not require that access.

11. C. Due to the risk of directory corruption and USN rollback, a domain controller can be cloned successfully only when it has first been made a member of the Cloneable Domain Controllers group.

12. A, B, D. Active Directory relies on SRV, A, and CNAME records to properly resolve and route network traffic for Active Directory. MX records are mail exchange records and are used by Microsoft Exchange server but not by Active Directory.

13. B. The forest schema contains all the object class definitions for the entire forest. This includes which attributes are included in the global catalog.

14. B. Active Directory Users and Computers can be used to transfer the RID, PDC, and infrastructure master roles.

15. A. Active Directory Domains and Trusts, used to manage various domain-wide properties and settings, is used to transfer the domain naming master role.

End-of-Chapter Review Questions

1. B. Install a single-domain forest and separate objects into OUs based on their physical location in the central or regional office. The physical separation of the offices and the desire for remote administration is not enough to justify anything more than a single-domain installation. OU delegation can ensure the appropriate staff in the appropriate locations have the permissions they need.

2. A, D. Redundancy in the event of a failure of the first DC. Improved performance during periods of high usage.

   Additional DCs are used to provide redundancy for disaster recovery and business continuity purposes and can improve performance by balancing or splitting authentication requests. Remote administration does not require additional DCs, and additional DCs do not improve security in any way.

3. C, D. Transfer the domain naming master to the second DC; install a copy of the Global Catalog on the second DC.

   The domain naming master is an FSMO role and can only be applied to one server at a time; it must be transferred. The global catalog can be replicated across many servers at once.

4. **Install-WindowsFeature -Name AD-Domain-Services -IncludeManagementTools**

   This cmdlet installs the AD DS role on a Windows Server and ensures all prerequisites and management tools are included as well.

5. **Install-ADDSForest -DomainName yourdomainhere.com -InstallDns**

   This cmdlet promotes the server to a domain controller. It will use default values for all the parameters typically chosen during a GUI installation. The **-InstallDns** parameter installs the DNS server during promotion.

6. **ntdsutil**

7. D, B, A, C. The first stage of a staged installation is to pre-create an account for the new domain controller and establish which credentials it will use during promotion. Then the remote server can have AD DS installed, and finally it can be promoted to a domain controller.

8. B. **Get-ADDCCloningExcludedApplicationList** will analyze the system for any potentially problematic software. The cmdlet can be rerun with the **-GenerateXml** switch to add those applications to a "safe list" so that the process can continue.

9. C. Manually add the required records to the DNS host(s). If you choose to use your own DNS hosting service, Microsoft cannot add the required records automatically. You will need to add the appropriate records by whatever method your DNS host requires.

10. A, B, C. SRV, A, and CNAME records are all required in the DNS host. MX records are mail exchange records for email routing and are not used by domain controllers.

Chapter 3

Do I Know This Already? Quiz

1. A, C, D. The legacy Active Directory Users and Computers tool as well as the newer Active Directory Administrative Center are both valid in Server Desktop Experience installations. For Server Core, Windows PowerShell must be used.

2. D. As a safety feature, the only way to remove an account with **Protect from accidental deletion** enabled is to edit the account and remove that flag. Otherwise, all delete operations against it are blocked.

3. B. Template accounts can have most of the configuration work for new users completed. A simple copy operation allows those configurations to be brought into a new user object.

4. A. **New-ADUser**

5. B. **Get-ADUser**

6. **C, D. csvde** is the utility used to extract information from AD DS and place it in a comma separated value (.csv) file. The **ldifde** utility works the same but uses a line-separated file format. **dcpromo** and **djoin** are utilities related to domain controller promotion and domain joining.

7. **A.** Both **csvde** and **ldifde** can be used for import or export, but by default they export data from the directory to the file system.

8. **C.** The Default Domain Policy already exists in Group Policy and is used whenever another Group Policy doesn't already apply.

9. **D. djoin** starts the offline domain join process. **dcpromo** is used to promote a member server to a domain controller, while **csvde** and **ldifde** are used for importing and exporting data from the directory.

10. **C. Set-ADUser**

11. **A. Set-ADAccountPassword**

End-of-Chapter Review Questions

1. **B. Get-ADUser -Filter -SearchBase "OU=East,dc=certguide,dc=com" -SearchScope subtree | Set-ADUser -Replace @{City="Springfield"}**

   The **Get-ADUser** cmdlet can take the **-Filter** property to select a specific group of user objects. The results can then be piped into the **Set-ADUser** cmdlet to run an update against all the resulting objects.

2. **C.** Create and configure a template user; then copy that to create each new user.

   A template user account can be easily and quickly set up and then used as a base for a copy operation for each new user account needed.

3. **User Principal Name (UPN).** The UPN represents one identifier a user can use to authorize against the directory. It follows the format of an email address with a user id, @ symbol, and the domain DNS name.

4. **profile path**

5. **ActiveDirectory, Get-ADUser, Enabled, $usr**

   This script imports the ActiveDirectory library to load the AD DS PowerShell cmdlets. **Get-ADUser** is run to select an identity from the directory and store it in the **$usr** variable. The enabled flag is set to false, and then the **$usr** object is passed to the **Set-ADUser** cmdlet.

6. **csvde -i -f newUsers.csv**

   The **csvde** command works with csv files, and specifying the **-i** parameter indicates import mode.

7. For offline domain join, the **djoin** utility is first run on a DC to create a configuration file. That file is then copied to the target machine where **djoin** is run again referencing that file.

8. **$pw = ConvertTo-SecureString NewPassword1 -AsPlainText -Force**

   **Get-ADUser -Filter -SearchScope subtree -SearchBase
   "OU=East,dc=certguide,dc=com" | Set-ADAccountPassword -Reset
   -NewPassword $pw**

   The **Get-ADUser** cmdlet can pipe user objects into the **Set-ADAccountPassword** cmdlet, which takes a PowerShell secure string as the new password parameter.

Chapter 4

Do I Know This Already? Quiz

1. B. Organizational units (OUs) are used to define the structure of a directory and isolate objects from one another for administrative purposes.

2. A. Groups are used to collect directory objects to be collectively assigned permissions on the network.

3. C. Universal groups are used to assign permissions to related resources in multiple domains. Domain local and global groups can only have members from the domain they are created in.

4. D. The cmdlet for creating a new security or distribution group is **New-ADGroup**.

5. B. The cmdlet for creating a new organizational group is **New-ADOrganizationalUnit**.

6. C. The cmdlet for adding a user, computer, or other object to a group is **Add-ADGroupMember**.

7. B. The IGDLA method uses domain local groups as rule groups that have permissions assigned to them, while global groups operate as role groups that collect the users. The global group is then made a member of the domain local group.

8. A. Delegation allows the assignment of common tasks and permissions to a subset of users for a subset of resources. Password resets are one of the common tasks available.

9. D. The Restricted Groups element of a GPO contains settings that allow you to add a security principal to a local group when the policy is processed.

10. B. The command line utility **redircmp** changes or redirects the default location for new computers that are added to the domain. The location set with **redircmp** only applies when a new computer object is added and no target location is specified.

End-of-Chapter Review Questions

1. D. The purpose of OUs is to separate objects in the directory according to administrative needs. By creating child OUs for each security profile and assigning GPOs to those OUs, you can ensure that policies are effectively applied to the correct users. Applying the GPOs to each individual user is time consuming, error pone, and requires constant attention as staff turnover and changes need to be reflected in the directory.

2. A, C. When OUs mirror organizational structure, permission for the management of those OUs can be delegated along organizational lines. GPOs, which are also likely to describe policies that apply to organizational entities, can also be easily applied to OUs. OUs do not offer additional security benefits or isolation from malware.

3. Security, Distribution. Groups can either be security groups used to assign permissions on the network or distribution groups used to distribute emails to groups of individuals.

4. E, D, A in that order. A global group cannot be directly converted into a domain local group, but it can be first converted to a universal group and then be converted to a domain local group. The first step can only occur if the group is not a member of another group, however.

5. **New-ADGroup FinanceFolderAccess -GroupScope Global -GroupCategory Security**

6. B. The **Add-ADGroupMember** cannot take user objects in the pipeline. You need to use the **Add-ADPrincipalGroupMember** cmdlet to use the pipe from **Get-ADUser**.

7. Two OUs; one for managers and another for regular Finance department us-
    ers. Two Global security groups, one containing all users in both OUs and an-
    other containing only the Manager users. Each security group would be added
    as a member to a different domain local group. Finally, access to the shared
    network folders would be granted to the appropriate domain local group.

8. role group. Role groups are intended to represent a role in the organization,
    such as FinanceManagers. This is distinct from rule groups, which are in-
    tended to represent one or more security rules. Role groups are then granted
    permissions by being made a member of a rule group.

9. A. Granting the password reset permissions on the top-level OU and disal-
    lowing inheritance ensures that only proactively specified users will have this
    control over the FinanceManagers OU.

10. **Redircmp ou=FinanceComputers,ou=Finance,dc=certguide,dc=com**

Chapter 5

Do I Know This Already? Quiz

1. B. The Network Service context straddles the line between the local system
    and local service accounts by authenticating as the machine account but having
    limited local access.

2. A, D. Service accounts are used by automated services and should rarely have
    their passwords changed because of the havoc that could cause on automated
    systems.

3. A. The Local Service account is the least privileged of the three service ac-
    count contexts.

4. C. The cmdlet to create a new Group Managed Service Account is
    New-ADServiceAccount.

5. B. With Kerberos Delegation, the application uses the security context of
    the user using the app. This is sometimes referred to as "pass-through"
    authentication.

6. A. The "constrained" part of the phrase Kerberos Constrained Delegation
    means that delegation is limited to specified services only.

7. D. Unlike other settings in the Default Domain Policy, which follow the
    LSDOU rule for order of precedence, Account Policies are only applied from
    the Default Domain Policy.

8. **B.** The minimum password age prevents a user from quickly cycling through the password count in order to reuse a recently used password.

9. **D.** When determining which PSO to use, PSOs applied directly to a user always take precedence over inherited PSOs.

10. **A.** Unless you delegate permissions explicitly, only members of the Domain Admins group can create and modify PSOs.

End-of-Chapter Review Questions

1. **C.** Group Managed Service Accounts (gMSAs) provide administrators with an easily managed identity that a service can use to authenticate on the domain. Option D is a possibility, but the creation of a gMSA instead of an sMSA allows for more flexibility and easier administration if the HR system moves or grows to multiple machines.

2. **setspn srvFinance -s http/srvFinance.certguide.com**. The **setspn** command adds an SPN to an object. The **-s** switch defines the SPN to add. SPNs are formatted as **<type>/<domain>**. See the section "Managing Service Principal Names" for more details.

3. **B, C.** While it may be tempting to simply add that staff to the Domain Admins group, it is more secure to only grant them administrative capabilities over their own OU. You might also want to provide a PSO for them to apply to their users if they want to override the password settings in the Default Domain Policy.

4. New-ADServiceAccount **-Name srvFinance -DnsHostName srvFinance. certguide.com -PrincipalsAllowedToRetrieveManagedPassword grpFinance**. The **New-ADServiceAccount** cmdlet creates the account. It takes the name of the account in the **-Name** parameter and the name of the managing security group in the **-PrincipalsAllowedToretrieveManagedPassword** parameter. The **-DNSHostName** parameter must be included as well.

Chapter 6

Do I Know This Already? Quiz

1. **B. ntdsutil** contains a snapshot menu that allows both the creation and the mounting of snapshots.

2. **C. dsamain** is used to host an LDAP server connection to the mounted snapshot.

3. **D.** Backing up AD DS is done with the standard Windows Backup Utility installed as part of the Windows Server Backup feature.

4. **C.** A nonauthoritative restore is performed when the restored controller needs to be brought "up to speed" with the directory by receiving replication updates. Alternatively, an authoritative restore replicates the restored data out to the other controllers on the domain.

5. **A, D.** AD DS can be brought offline either by rebooting in DSRM mode or by simply stopping the AD DS service in Windows.

6. **B. ntdsutil** will perform an offline defragmentation of the ntds.dit file. It must be then manually copied over the production copy for AD DS to use the new file.

7. **D.** The Active Directory Users and Computers tool will clean metadata from the directory if you delete a domain controller from the domain controllers container.

8. **B, C.** RODCs accept password changes and logon time stamps as part of their normal operation but need to forward those changes to a writeable domain controller to be replicated to the domain.

9. **D.** Password Replication Policies allow you to specify accounts that have their password cached on an RODC, but by default no accounts are set up with this.

10. **A. repadmin** is the utility that reports on replication status.

End-of-Chapter Review Questions

1. **C.** Snapshots are a point-in-time read-only version of the directory. They can be created quickly and browsed easily using standard AD DS tools like Active Directory Users and Computers.

2. **ntdsutil snapshot list all**

   ntdsutil snapshot delete *<index>*

   The **ntdsutil** command can be used to list the snapshots and their associated index number. That index is then used in the **ntdsutil delete** command. It is important to note that any mounted snapshots must be unmounted before they can be deleted.

3. **A.** With no other services on the server and because the entire directory is stored elsewhere on the domain, it is simplest to start with a fresh install, promote the server to a DC in the existing domain, and allow replication to bring the RODC back up to speed. If network latency is a concern, you can perform an Install From Media (IFM) installation to physically ship an up-to-date copy of the directory to the RODC.

4. C. While it's possible to rebuild the entire server from a fresh installation, the added complication of deploying the web applications and their databases means it's more appropriate to recover the server from a recent backup. After the recovery is complete, a nonauthoritative restore means that other DCs in the domain will replicate any changes needed to bring the directory up to speed.

5. Either perform an authoritative restore for the OU in question, or look to the Active Directory Recycle Bin. There are two valid answers here. The more complex route would be to perform a restore from a recent backup and use **ntdsutil** to designate the OU on the restored directory as authoritative, which would cause it to replicate itself out to the other domain controllers. If the domain has the Recycle Bin enabled, however, it would be much simpler to find the OU in the deleted objects container and restore it from there.

6. Clean the metadata from the directory. If you want to reuse the same server name as the failed server, you will not be able to rejoin the domain until the old computer object has been cleared from the directory. Deleting the object from the Domain Controllers container clears the metadata and allows the new server to successfully join.

Chapter 7

Do I Know This Already? Quiz

1. C, D. Before the forest functional level can be raised to Windows 2016, you must be running Server 2016 on all servers in the forest and have raised the domain functional level for all domains in the forest to Windows 2016.

2. A. The Active Directory Domains and Trusts tool offers options for raising forest and domain functional levels. This feature is not found in Users and Computers, Sites and Services, or the Administrative Center.

3. A, C. In-place upgrades to 2016 can only be performed from Server 2012 or 2012 R2. For older Windows OSes, you must demote and replace with servers running Server 2016.

4. B, C. In a one-way trust relationship between two domains, one is known as the trusting domain and the other the trusting domain. In a two-way trust, both domains are considered trusted and trusting.

5. A. In an incoming trust, security principals in the remote domain are being granted access to local domain objects. This means the local domain is trusting of the remote domain, or put another way the remote domain is trusted.

6. D. External trusts allow for a trust relationship between two domains in different forests. A forest trust would also allow for this but include all the domains in each forest in a transitive trust relationship.

7. B. Sites represent physical locations and can have multiple subnets associated with them so the servers would all be placed in the same site for replication purposes.

8. C. Active Directory Sites and Services offers features for managing sites and their associated subnets. These options are not found in Domains and Trusts, Users and Computers, or the Administrative Center.

9. A. **New-ADReplicationSubnet**

End-of-Chapter Review Questions

1. A. The recommended upgrade path is to demote existing servers and promote new servers whenever you can. If that is not possible in your environment, you can run in-place upgrades from Server 2012 R2 to Server 2016.

2. B. Server OSes earlier than 2012 cannot be upgraded in place and consequently must be replaced with servers running 2016.

3. D. A shortcut trust is used between two domains in the same forest to circumvent the domain tree and allow authentication traffic to communicate directly between the two domains instead of traversing the tree.

4. **New-ADReplicationSite -Name "Berlin"**

   New-ADReplicationSubnet -Name "10.0.0.0/24" -Site Berlin

   Two cmdlets must be used—the first to create the site, and the second to create the subnet.

Chapter 8

Do I Know This Already? Quiz

1. A, B, D. GPOs can be linked to domains, OUs, sites, groups, and individual security principals such as users or computers.

2. C, D. The Group Policy Management Console and Group Policy Management Editor work together to provide administrative access for almost all GPO functionality.

3. B. Starter GPOs are limited to the Administrative Templates section, which is the only section of a GPO that can be customized via ADMX files.

4. **D.** When GPMC backs up a GPO, it creates a folder in the specified location named for the ObjectID of the GPO being backed up.

5. **B.** A migration table is used to create a mapping for domain-specific values when copying a GPO between domains.

6. **C.** In GPMC, the Group Policy Objects node administers delegation rights for the creation of new GPOs.

7. **A, D.** GPO templates are stored in and replicated along with the SYSVOL file folder. The AD DS directory contains the GPO container object.

8. **B.** Microsoft has used the ADMX extension to represent the XML formatted files it uses since they replaced a proprietary format using ADM with the introduction of Windows Server 2008.

End-of-Chapter Review Questions

1. **D.** Just creating a GPO does not apply it to the domain. A GPO must be linked to a domain node before the settings will take effect.

2. **B, D.** For GPOs applied to the same node or OU, the link order can be used to prioritize GPOs and ensure a more important GPO takes precedence. The Enforced link setting will cause the GPO link to override conflicts with GPOs linked to child nodes.

3. **A, C.** The easiest way to restore the default domain GPO is to run the **dcgpofix** utility, which will automatically revert the Default Domain Policy to its original settings. If a backup of the default domain GPO was taken, the GPMC restore option can revert the GPO to that backup as well.

4. **C.** For custom GPOs, the restore utility will revert the settings of a GPO to their values from when the backup was taken.

5. **D.** GPO versioning is contained in the SYSVOL and is replicated to each DC along with the built-in SYSVOL replication process.

Chapter 9

Do I Know This Already? Quiz

1. **D.** GPOs are applied in LSDOU order, which means GPOs on the OU are processed last and overwrite any GPOs processed previously.

2. **B.** When a GPO link has its Enforced flag set to yes, it will apply to all children objects in all child OUs regardless of any GPO settings linked on those OUs. Enforced will also override blocking of inheritance.

3. A. Security filtering allows you to specify security groups that GPOs should apply to. Any objects not members of the specified group will not receive the GPO settings.

4. B. Replace mode causes the Group Policy client to ignore all user object GPOs and only apply GPOs for the computer object.

5. D. Disable Detection of Slow Network Connections will turn off the speed detection feature entirely, regardless of what value is configured in the Configure Group Policy Slow Link Detection setting.

6. A. **Invoke-GPUpdate** is the PowerShell cmdlet that forces a Group Policy update on a remote computer.

End-of-Chapter Review Questions

1. A. GPO links set to be Enforced are automatically given precedence over GPO links on child nodes.

2. B. Block Inheritance is used to block any GPO links from parent nodes down to the current node.

3. A. Security filtering is a fast and easy way to differentiate GPOs between users. Option C is also valid, although it may be too much work to divide and manage users in those two separate OUs.

Chapter 10

Do I Know This Already? Quiz

1. B. GPO Software Installation requires a Microsoft Installer package (.msi) file. Other types of installation packages can be converted to an .msi via third-party software or installed with a script.

2. B, C, D. Folder redirection can only redirect to network locations, the local user profile location, or the home folder location as specified in the directory object's home folder attribute. It cannot target a specified location on a local drive.

3. A, C. Scripts can be executed on user logon via GPO or by using the NETLOGON share found in the SYSVOL.

4. D. Prior to the introduction of XML-based .ADMX files, Group Policy used .ADM files for what are now known as Classic Administrative Templates.

End-of-Chapter Review Questions

1. C. Assigning software makes it available for installation at the user's behest without forcing it to be installed.

2. B. Folder redirection can be configured to the same location as the home folder. The userprofile location is a local folder.

3. A. ADMX files can be distributed around the network by including them in the central store, located in the SYSVOL. The files will be copied along with the regular SYSVOL replication process.

Chapter 11

Do I Know This Already? Quiz

1. B. Internet Settings, Regional Options, and Start Menu preferences are all exclusive to the User Configuration portion of a GPO. Conversely, Services preferences are only available via Computer Configuration.

2. B. Security filtering is configured at the GPO level and consequently applies to the entire GPO. Item-level targeting must be configured for each preference setting individually.

3. A, D. Power Options and Internet Explorer settings are both configured via Control Panel settings, not Windows Settings.

4. C. The Replace action causes any existing values, settings, or keys to be removed before the defined key is created.

End-of-Chapter Review Questions

1. D. Item-level targeting allows for preferences in the same GPO to target and apply to different groups of users, even when the GPO itself targets all of those users.

2. B. Files and Folders can be used in combination to deliver an entire folder structure from one location to another. Using a local drive letter in the destination ensure the copy will place files in the local file system every time the setting is processed on a client machine.

3. A. The Internet Explorer preferences target specific versions. Multiple preference items can be created in a single GPO and will apply as appropriate when the GPO is processed on the client.

Chapter 12

Do I Know This Already? Quiz

1. C. Subordinate CAs must receive a signing certificate from another CA. That "parent" CA can be any type of CA.

2. A. An offline CA is disconnected from the network and consequently must issue certificates to a file, which are then imported manually by the requesting entity.

3. C. The CA that issued the certificate can be securely migrated from one server to another for many reasons. This process does not invalidate the certificates it has issued.

4. B, C, D. CRLs can be hosted via HTTP, FILE, LDAP, UNC network shares, and the local file system. FTP is not a valid CDP location type.

5. B. Online Responders use IIS to host the web service that will respond to validation requests.

6. A, D. CA backups are included in the Windows Server Backup utility under the System State item. The CA itself can be backed up to the file system using the CA console backup wizard as well.

7. B. Permissions for managing the CA and issuing certificates can be granted to domain security groups in the CA console. This alleviates the need to unnecessarily add users to sensitive roles such as Domain Admins.

End-of-Chapter Review Questions

1. C. An offline root CA can be set up with the same public-private key pair used on the old server. It must be backed up to a file and physically transferred to the new server. Once running, the existing enterprise root CA should be shut down and removed from the network.

2. A. A subordinate CA at the remote location can issue certificate requests on behalf of the root CA at the main location. It needs to have a signing certificate from the root CA provided during setup to establish the hierarchy.

3. D. Each CA can have its management delegated to different security groups. Ideally, the remote staff should not have such broad access to the network via the Domain Admins and Enterprise Admins groups, nor should they have managing access to the root CA unless it's otherwise needed.

Chapter 13

Do I Know This Already? Quiz

1. A. Templates are managed in the Certificate Template console, launched from the Certification Authority console.

2. B. Each CA has a few basic templates available for issuance by default, but the majority of the templates in the directory must be enabled by adding them to the CA before they can be used.

3. C. The CA Web Enrollment form requires a user to manually interact and request a certificate.

4. B. If a certificate is no longer secure, you should immediately revoke it and publish the revocation to the CRL and delta CRL.

5. D. Group Policy implements autoenrollment by enabling the feature in GPOs and executing the enrollment during a policy update.

6. C. Group Policy can autoenroll both user and computer objects to a certificate.

7. A. The Key Recovery Agent (KRA) certificate allows the archived key to be encrypted and only holders of the certificate to perform the recovery operation when needed.

End-of-Chapter Review Questions

1. B. New certificates are created by duplicating existing certificates. The properties of the new template can be modified as needed to support their intended use.

2. The Certificates snap-in of Microsoft Management Console (MMC). With this tool, users can create a certificate request and have the certificate issued.

3. A, B, D. Autoenrollment is enabled via both the certificate template as well as Group Policy. It needs to be configured in both places to work properly.

4. C, D. Archival does not function until a KRA certificate has been created, issued to at least one user (the KRA), and then enabled in the properties for the CA.

Chapter 14

Do I Know This Already? Quiz

1. A. AD FS is known as the identity provider because it provides identifying information about the client to the relying party.

2. B. An SQL Server database can be connected and written to by all AD FS servers in the server farm. This provides independence and fault tolerance that the Windows Internal Database does not.

3. D. Windows authentication requires the user to be authenticated against an AD DS domain; due to that requirement, it is only available to intranet users.

4. A, D. Any authentication that requires more than one factor, for instance, password *and* SMS, qualifies as multi-factor authentication. A smart card device and a username and password also qualifies as two factors. Answers b and c only include a single factor and consequently are not multi-factor.

5. A, B, C. Workplace Join is available for devices running Windows 8.1+, iOS 6.0+, and Android 4.0+.

6. B. Workplace Join is configured via the Administrative Templates section of Computer Configuration in a Group Policy Object.

7. D. The PowerShell cmdlet to add a new LDAP server connection to AD FS is **New-AdfsLdapServerConnection**.

End-of-Chapter Review Questions

1. D. The main goal of AD FS is to allow authentication outside the network to third-party services and cloud-based applications.

2. B. If you want to use certificate authentication, either as a primary method or a multi-factor method, it must first be enabled in AD FS.

3. C. Device Registration Service (DRS) allows users to register their own devices on the network in AD DS. These devices can then be used as part of the authentication process for various services.

4. A, B, C. A GPO with two policies enabled, Device Registration and Microsoft Passport for Work, must be applied to all users who want to use Microsoft Passport.

5. New-AdfsLdapServerConnection **-HostName contoso.ldap.local -Port 5199 – AuthenticationMethod Basic -SslMode Tls**. The cmdlet to create the connection is **New-AdfsLdapServerConnection**. The hostname is supplied in the **-HostName** switch; the port is supplied in the **-Port** switch. The -AuthenticationMethod switch can only be set as **Basic**, and **Tls** security is defined in the **-SslMode** switch.

Chapter 15

Do I Know This Already? Quiz

1. A. Because WAP is exposed to the public Internet, by design it should be installed on its own server to minimize the impact in the event it is compromised. WAP should also be installed on a perimeter network, such as a DMZ, to isolate it as much as possible from the enterprise. It cannot be installed on the same server as AD FS.

2. B. With a pass-through application, WAP does not attempt to perform authentication and simply hands the incoming request to the target internal URL. The web app itself is responsible for any required authentication.

3. D. AD FS cannot recognize incoming authentication requests, nor trust the distribution of claims, until it has a trust object created for the relying party.

4. B. WAP allows for distinct external and internal URLs for communication. This means a valid public FQDN can be used for the external URL, while the internal-only FQDN can be used for the internal URL.

End-of-Chapter Review Questions

1. A, B. Web Application Proxy sits in the perimeter network and listens for regular web traffic much like a web server. The firewall between the WAP server and the Internet must allow Port 80 and 443 traffic inbound to the server. WAP also listens for specific URLs that are published as applications. Those URLs must match what users are attempting to access.

2. C. Web Application Proxy can perform HTTP to HTTPS redirection if it is configured in the published app in WAP.

3. D. WAP can be used to preauthenticate Remote Desktop Gateway if the URLs are configured properly. When the gateway and web access roles do not share a server, two WAP apps are required, pointed toward the FQDN of each respective service. Those apps can share a single external URL.

Chapter 16

Do I Know This Already? Quiz

1. C. AD RMS uses the term "cluster" to refer to the AD RMS servers even if there is only a single server.

2. A, C. AD RMS can store its configuration information in either a local Windows Internal Database or a centrally located SQL Server.

3. B. The template policies are attached to the document with the publishing license. Updates to the template only apply to new or reauthored documents that have the changed template applied. Existing documents that are "out in the wild" cannot get a new or updated template attached.

4. B, C, D. AD RMS exclusion policies can be defined for users, lockboxes, or applications.

5. D. The cluster key is the private key used for the licensor certificate granted to the AD RMS server. It should be stored in a secure location so it can be recovered in the event a cluster needs to be rebuilt. If a new key is generated, it is in effect a new cluster and cannot manage licenses issued by the old cluster. To recover a cluster, the key must be recovered from its storage location.

End-of-Chapter Review Questions

1. B. AD RMS can store its databases on an SQL Server to share with all servers in the cluster from a centrally managed high availability location.

2. A. AD RMS templates are useful for common protection needs, but unique or one-off cases need to be either properly built by the user or put into a new template.

3. B, D. An AD RMS cluster requires the cluster key and trusted publishing domains to be fully recovered.

Glossary of Key Terms

Account Policies   The collection of policies in Group Policy that apply to user account passwords, lockout, and Kerberos policy.

action   Create, delete, replace, or update. The four operations that all preference settings can perform.

AD FS farm   A group of AD FS servers that share a configuration. Used to provide fault-tolerance and performance for authentication.

AD FS proxy authentication   Allowing WAP to act as a proxy for AD FS for authentication.

AD RMS cluster   One or more AD RMS servers.

AD RMS root cluster   The primary AD RMS cluster for protecting documents and granting access to documents.

ADAC   Active Directory Administrative Center. A newer tool from Microsoft for managing AD DS.

ADUC   Active Directory Users and Computers. One of the legacy tools for managing AD DS.

assigning software   Configuring GPO to install software when it is applied.

attributes   The key-value pairs that define an object. Each object in the directory has a collection of attributes with varying values.

authentication   The process of validating who the user is.

authoritative restore   A restoration of AD DS in which the restored information is considered authoritative and replicated out to the other domain controllers.

authorization   The process of deciding what an authenticated user can and cannot do in a system.

autoenrollment   Allowing Group Policy to automatically enroll a user or computer in a certificate deployment.

central store   A collection of ADMX files describing Administrative Template options to be used by all computers on the domain.

certificate   A digital credential used to certify the identity of a user, computer, or other system on a network. Certificates are issued by and validated by a certificate authority (CA). Certificates are also used to prove ownership of a public key.

certificate authority (CA)   A server that can issue certificates upon request to authorized requesters. The CA's signature is used to validate a certificate.

certificate revocation   Flagging a certificate as no longer valid for one or more reasons.

certificate revocation list (CRL)   A list of all certificates that a CA has explicitly revoked prior to their expiration time.

certificate template   A base set of properties to be used when issuing a new certificate.

claim   An assertion made by an identity provider about a secured entity such as a user's email address or a computer's FQDN.

client licensor certificate   The certificate issued by an AD RMS server that contains the public key for encrypting the data on the document. Also used to digitally sign the publishing license (PL).

client-side extensions (CSE)   The executable on a Windows machine that applies GPO settings to the computer.

cloning   Creating a copy of a virtual machine. This common practice can cause trouble for the domain if the VM is a domain controller.

cluster key   The private key for the licensor certificate issued to the AD RMS cluster. Required for all servers in the cluster and to recover the cluster if necessary.

comma separated values (CSV)   A text file where each line contains a record, and values for the record are separated by commas.

computer   An object in the directory representing a computer on the network.

containers   Special types of objects in the directory that are used for organization and hierarchy.

CRL distribution point (CDP)   A location on the network where a CRL is stored and accessed by clients who need to validate whether a certificate has been revoked.

custom administrative template file   The file storage used for Classic Administrative Templates.

default containers   The default location that new user and computer objects added to the domain are placed into, when no other location is specified.

default domain GPO   The default GPO included in every domain that applies to all objects in the domain.

defragmentation   Reclaiming unused space in the .dit file from object removal and changes.

delegating   Granting specific GPO creation, linking, or editing permissions to users without granting full domain admin access.

delegation   Granting authority for administrative access over an individual OU to a subset of users.

deleted account   An account that has been removed from AD DS and is no longer available.

demotion   The process of turning a domain controller into a member server.

Desktop Experience   The Windows Server installation that includes a full GUI for administration.

DFSR   Distributed File System Replication. A newer method for replication changes to the SYSVOL file.

disabled account   An account in AD DS that has been disabled and cannot be logged on to.

domain controller   A special server in the domain used for authentication of network users as well as physical storage for the AD DS directory.

domain functional level   The basic feature level available to the domain. Must be as high as or higher than the forest functional level.

domains   The root namespace and top-level container for all the objects in a network. Multiple domains can be grouped into trees with contiguous namespaces or forests with noncontiguous namespaces, or both.

enrollment   Requesting and being issued a new certificate based on a template.

enterprise CA   A CA that is part of an AD DS domain and can store its issued certificates in the directory.

exclusion policy   A list of specific users, applications, and clients that are denied issuance of a use license.

external trust   A trust relationship between domains in different forests that only include the specified forest. Useful for creating a trust with a pre-Windows 2003 domain.

filtering   Limiting the objects that a GPO applies to by filtering for either specific security groups or WMI values.

folder redirection   Redirecting a user's profile folder to a network location so it is accessible from multiple computers.

forest   A collection of domains with noncontiguous namespaces maintained in a single AD DS directory database.

forest functional level   The basic feature level available to the forest.

forest trust   A trust relationship between two forests that allows the forests to share resources with security principals in the other forest.

forms authentication   Authenticating a user with a web page interface to collect the username and password.

FSMO   Flexible Single Master Operations. Specific roles in AD DS that must be on one and only one domain controller.

global catalog   A secondary database that AD DS relies upon to speed up searches and reduce load on domain controllers.

GPO link   A logical reference to a GPO from a domain, OU, group, site, or security principal that tells Group Policy to apply the GPO settings.

group   Special AD DS objects that can have other objects as members. Referenced by software on the network for authorization.

Group Managed Service Account (gMSA)   A service account in AD DS that is associated with a manageable group of computers.

group nesting   The process of making one group the member of another. An important concept for IGDLA.

Group Policy   The AD DS integrated technology that manages the application of security settings across the domain.

Group Policy Management Console (GPMC)   The utility used to create, manage, delegate, and link GPOs.

Group Policy Management Editor (GPME)   The utility used to edit a GPO.

Group Policy Object (GPO)   A collection of security and configuration settings that are managed by Group Policy and systematically applied to a group of users or computers.

group scope   Either universal, global, or domain local. Each group scope defines who can be members and what the group can authorize.

group type   Either security or distribution. Security groups are used to authorize access on the network, and distribution groups are used by Exchange for email distribution lists.

home folder   A location on the network where a user can store and retrieve files from any computer.

hosting a snapshot   Exposes a mounted snapshot on a specified port for LDAP querying.

HTTP to HTTPS redirects   A feature of WAP that allows it to redirect incoming HTTP requests to internal URLs that require HTTPS.

identity federation   The process of exposing authentication systems to outside services so they can rely on existing authentication frameworks instead of creating and maintaining their own.

identity provider   The service in identity federations that provides authentication to the relying party.

IFM   Install from Media. A way to store the directory in a file so it can be loaded onto a new domain controller instead of being replicated over the network.

IGDLA   Identity, global groups, domain local groups, and access. A way to structure group membership and authorization to ease administration.

importing a GPO   Reverting a GPO's settings to the previously taken backup of a different GPO.

inheritance   The application of GPOs to both the node it is linked to as well as any children of that node.

Kerberos Constrained Delegation (KCD)   Allowing a server to delegate authentication to the user using a service with limitations on the services to which a server can delegate.

key archival   Storing a copy of a certificate's private key to be used in the event the certificate must be recovered or re-created.

line-separated values   A text file in which each line contains a value and records are separated by a blank line.

local group   Groups in Microsoft Windows that control permissions on the local computer.

Local Group Policy Object   A GPO that exists only on the computer where it is defined.

locked account   An account in AD DS that has tripped an alert to lock it (such as too many failed logon attempts) and requires unlocking before it can be used.

lockout threshold   The number of failed logon attempts that will trigger an account to become locked out.

loopback processing   Prioritizing computer-specific GPOs over user GPOs when the computer and user objects are located in different directory locations.

manual enrollment   Using a manual process such as the MMC Certificates snap-in or CA Web Enrollment to enroll in a certificate.

metadata   The information stored in AD DS about domain controllers.

Microsoft Passport authentication   Authenticating a user who is domain joined with a registered Windows 10 client machine.

mounting a snapshot   The process of loading a snapshot onto the file system.

multi-domain   A domain configuration with multiple domains to serve different parts of the organization.

multi-factor authentication   Using two or more authentication methods to authenticate a user for additional security.

multi-forest   A domain configuration with multiple noncontiguous domains collected into a forest.

namespace   The text labels that the name of a domain is comprised of, for example, certguide.com. Contiguous namespaces share a root name with each other, such as west.certguide.com and east.certguide.com.

nonauthoritative restore   A restoration of AD DS in which the restored information is updated or overwritten by other domain controllers.

objects   Objects in Active Directory Domain Services represent the physical entities that make up a network. They are a collection of key-value pairs organized into a hierarchal structure in a domain. Everything in the directory, from users and computers to organizational units, are objects.

offline CA   A CA that is disconnected from the enterprise network. This can improve security for the CA, which can be critical for root CAs.

one-way trust   A trust relationship in which one entity is trusted.

online responder   An IIS-based web service that can perform a validation check for a certificate on-demand.

organizational units (OUs)   A structural element of an AD DS directory and the most common and useful type of container. OUs are the level at which GPOs are typically applied.

pass-through authentication   Relying on the source app for authentication instead of AD FS Proxy.

password complexity   Password requirements such as mixed case that force the user to choose more secure passwords.

password history   The number of user passwords retained by AD DS to prevent password reuse.

Password Replication Policy (PRP)   The policies that define which users' passwords can be cached on an RODC.

Password Settings Objects (PSOs)   Fine-grained password policy objects that define separate password policies than the default domain policy.

preferences   GPO settings that can configure the environment on the client computer.

processing order   The order in which GPOs are processed for an object when multiple GPOs apply. First processed GPOs are superseded by subsequently processed GPOs.

profile path   The location on the network to store the user's profile such as My Documents, Desktop, and so on.

promotion   The process of turning a member server into a domain controller.

property filters   Criteria for displaying Administrative Template policy settings to reduce screen clutter with unused policies.

PSO precedence   The process by which AD DS determines which PSO applies to an object when more than one PSO applies.

published app   A mapping in Web Application Proxy of an external URL to an internal URL.

publishing license   The list of permissions and restrictions for the protected content of a document. Digitally signed by the client licensor certificate (CLC) to prevent tampering.

publishing software   Configuring GPO to add software to the Add/Remove programs list so the user can install.

realm trust   A trust relationship between a domain and a non-Windows Kerberos realm.

relying party   The service in identity federation that relies upon the identity provider for authentication services.

relying party trust   A trust object in AD FS that defines an app that relies on AD FS for authentication.

Remote Desktop Gateway (RDG)   A remote access service in Microsoft Windows that allows remote desktop connections via a TLS tunnel.

restoring a GPO   Reverting a GPO's settings to a previously taken backup.

reverse proxy   A proxy server that receives incoming public network requests and directs them to the appropriate server on the internal network.

revocation configuration   A configuration item in an Online Responder that represents a certificate to be validated as well as the source CRL to perform the validation against.

rights policy template   A preconfigured list of policy rights and denials published centrally and deployed to users for protecting documents in an easy and consistent fashion.

RODC   Read-Only Domain Controller. A type of domain controller with limited permissions and data.

root CA   The CA at the top of the CA hierarchy, responsible for self-signing its own signing certificate.

security identifier (SID)   A unique ID for a security principal in the AD DS directory that is used to assign permission in domains.

security templates   Administrative Template settings from versions of Windows prior to Server 2008 and Vista.

Server Core   The lightweight Windows Server installation that does not include a GUI interface and requires administration tasks to be performed via command line or PowerShell.

Server Manager   The GUI utility installed on Server 2016 Desktop Experience that is used for most server administration tasks.

service accounts   Security authentication context used by background services in Windows.

service connection point (SCP)   An entry in the AD DS directory that tells clients what the endpoint is for communicating with the cluster. Allows autodiscovery for domain joined clients.

service principal names (SPNs)   Unique identifiers for a service instance used by Kerberos authentication.

shortcut trust   A trust relationship between two domains that is direct and allows authentication traffic to skip traversing the entire tree.

single domain   A domain configuration with only one domain, suitable for smaller or centrally located organizations.

site   A logical grouping of zero or more domain controllers in Active Directory usually used to represent a physical location.

site link   A description of the speed and reliability of the network connection between two sites. Used to determine efficient replication paths and ensure site coverage.

slow-link processing   Group Policy's recognition of a slow or intermittent network connection when applying GPOs.

snapshot   A point-in-time copy of the AD DS directory.

staged installation   A method of installing an RODC where an on-site administrator prepares the domain for the RODC so that off-site personnel don't require administrative credentials to promote the server.

standalone CA   A CA that is not joined to a domain and manages its certificate databases exclusively.

Standard Managed Service Account (sMSA)   A service account in AD DS that is associated with a single computer.

starter GPO   A collection of Administrative Template settings that can be used to seed a new GPO with predetermined values.

subnet   A contiguous range of IP addresses associated with a site.

subordinate CA   A CA that does not self-sign its own signing certificate but rather acquires that from another CA, forming a CA hierarchy.

system state   The collection of system state resources that includes most of the AD DS objects needed for a successful backup.

template account   A nonactive account used as a basis for creating new accounts.

tree   A collection of domains with contiguous namespaces and a single shared parent. The domains certguide.com, west.certguide.com, and east.certguide.com make up a domain tree.

trust   A relationship between two domains, trees, or forests that allows them to share resources and authentication.

two-way trust   A trust relationship in which both entities are trusted.

UPN   User Principal Name. A user identifier that uses an email-address style @ symbol followed by the domain name.

use license   The digital certificate granted to a user for consuming an AD RMS protected document.

user   An object in the directory representing a user on the network.

User Principal Name (UPN)   An identifier for a user object that includes both the account name and the domain name in the format of an email address, for example, ben@certguide.com.

virtual service account   A local service account specific to a service that authenticates to the domain as a machine account.

Web Application Proxy (WAP)   Microsoft Windows' built-in reverse proxy server. Can handle both AD FS authentication as well as pass-through authentication.

Windows authentication   Authenticating a user by validating the user's AD DS provided Kerberos token.

Index